REBEL
IMAGINARIES

REBEL IMAGINARIES

DUKE UNIVERSITY PRESS *Durham and London* 2021

Labor, Culture, and Politics in Depression-Era California

ELIZABETH E. SINE

Designed by Courtney Leigh Richardson
Typeset in Minion Pro and Century Gothic by Westchester Publishing Services

Library of Congress Cataloging-in-Publication Data
Names: Sine, Elizabeth E., [date] author.
Title: Rebel imaginaries : labor, culture, and politics in depression-era
California / Elizabeth E. Sine.
Description: Durham : Duke University Press, 2021. | Includes
bibliographical references and index.
Identifiers: LCCN 2020019352 (print) | LCCN 2020019353 (ebook)
ISBN 9781478010326 (hardcover)
ISBN 9781478011378 (paperback)
ISBN 9781478012900 (ebook)
Subjects: LCSH: Working class—Political activity—California—
History—20th century. | Working class—California—Economic
conditions—History—20th century. | Labor movement—California—
History—20th century. | Labor market—California—History—20th century. |
California—Economic conditions—20th century.
Classification: LCC HD8083.C2 S564 2020 (print) | LCC HD8083.C2 (ebook) |
DDC 322/.20979409043—dc23
LC record available at https://lccn.loc.gov/2020019352
LC ebook record available at https://lccn.loc.gov/2020019353

Cover art: Detail of Coit Tower, San Francisco, California, USA. John Langley Howard. Courtesy of Wikimedia Commons.

For Nicholas, Raymond, and Leah

PROLOGUE. Capitalism and Crisis in Global California

During the first week of January 1933, thousands of people from throughout California marched to the state capitol in Sacramento. The first to set out was a contingent of local residents, farmworkers, and activists who departed from El Centro and Brawley, just north of the U.S.-Mexico border, on January 2. As these determined travelers made their way through San Diego and toward Los Angeles over the next three days, additional marchers took to the roads, embarking from Ventura and from Eureka in the northern reaches of the state. By January 7, three more groups left from San Francisco, Oakland, and Redding. The ranks of the marchers swelled as they passed through cities, towns, and the countryside, as hundreds and sometimes thousands of people joined in for part or all of the remaining distance.[1]

The routes they traveled were well trodden. They trekked along major arteries that every day carried goods from farms, factories, and ships to markets near and far; the same roads were used by itinerant workers and their families to follow shifting and seasonal labor demands. Yet the aims of the marchers who headed to Sacramento in early 1933 were markedly different from those of the others who routinely passed down these same roads.[2] The marchers were a motley bunch—multiethnic, interracial women, men, and children—who survived on wages from a range of different jobs. They included ethnic Mexican, Japanese, Chinese, Filipinx, African American, and European American textile workers, lumber workers, teamsters, small farmers, agricultural workers, longshore workers, and domestic workers, as well as many who were jobless. Despite their differences, their march was an act of common struggle forged from the political and economic challenges they shared amid the Great Depression. It was a March against Hunger, under-scoring how basic human needs could provide a powerful basis for solidar-ity. Yet the march also reflected participants' awareness of the ways in which struggles against starvation were linked with struggles against other indig-nities. The marchers carried signs that read "WE WANT BREAD! NO MORE PROMISES—WE REFUSE TO STARVE!" "We demand UNEMPLOYMENT INSURANCE!" "Repeal the criminal syndicalist law!" "FARM RELIEF!" "Free Tom Mooney!" "Free the Scottsboro boys!" "Stop the Deportation of Un-employed Aliens!"[3] More than an appeal for reforms and relief from the government, the march was an assertion of political power by people who refused the forms of subordination that California's economy and the poli-tics of the Depression had imposed on them. At the same time that they called attention to prevailing injustices and pressed for concessions from the region's political establishment, the marchers also gestured toward a broader reimagining of life in Depression-era California.

The march represented a convergence of struggles that reverberated throughout the state and around the globe in early 1933. The market economy's bleakest days were accompanied by the uprising of aggrieved populations worldwide, who faced similarly devastating conditions and a common sense of their own precarity. Hundreds of thousands of people participated in hunger marches throughout the western United States during the first week of January, on the heels of a nationwide hunger march to Washington, DC, in December 1932. In Alabama, Black and White sharecroppers battled for the right to organize. In Barcelona, Spanish workers clashed with police and called for a general strike, while residents of the Xauen region of Morocco revolted against Spanish imperialism. London railroad workers prepared to strike in the face of impending wage cuts, while peasants in India revolted against British colonial soldiers and refused to pay taxes to landlords. In Tokyo, thousands of working-class people faced mass arrests for their at-tempts to organize. In Managua, rebel peasants and workers clashed with U.S. Marines.[4]

Back in California, authorities had their hands full. Recognizing the state as a key site in the global crisis because of its economic wealth and historic role in global economic development, politicians, business leaders, and so-cial scientists desperately sought to restore "a desirable balance" in industrial and social relations. According to their assessment, such a step was critical to addressing the broader problem of "world unrest."[5] In the months that preceded the statewide hunger march, the most esteemed intellectuals from California's leading universities met to tackle what they saw as the pressing question of "the nature and controllability" of the state's social forces and to figure out how to quell the "acute dissatisfaction" and "social distress" that exacerbated the "existing breakdown of economic machinery in the present world-wide depression."[6] In the months after the march, U.S. politician and presidential advisor Bernard Baruch expressed the fears of many political and economic leaders when he noted, "Maybe the country doesn't know it yet, but I think we may find we've been in a revolution more drastic than the French Revolution. The crowd has seized the seat of government and is trying to seize the wealth. Respect for law and order is gone."[7]

Throughout the country and across the world, the Great Depression generated innumerable attempts to secure a sense of order and shape the future of the global economy. In California such efforts carried particular urgency, precisely because so much was at stake. By the time of the Great Crash in 1929, California stood as a critical node for a world being stitched together by industrial capitalism. Not only was the state a leading global producer of gold, silver, mercury, and several other minerals, but it was also the number-one producer of oil in the world. It brought more agricultural goods to market than any other region of the United States. It was the nation's leading commercial fishery and one of its largest producers of timber and lumber.[8] It had also developed a substantial manufacturing base, with Los Angeles rivaling Flint and Detroit in the production of automobiles and leading the nation in the production of aircraft.[9] It was a major center of national and global finance, with San Francisco serving as home to the "Wall Street of the West." Booms in California real estate, tourism, advertising, and motion picture production further made the state a key shaper of mass culture and consumer desire. As a center of global artistic production, California increasingly helped to define the very notions of capitalist modernity and progress that it came to emblematize.[10] In economic as well as cultural terms, California's development facilitated the broader transformation of the United States from a debtor nation to the world's largest exporter and international creditor by the end of World War I. It would subsequently accelerate the country's emergence as a global superpower by the end of World War II.[11]

While the concerns of authorities revolved around safeguarding regional development for the future, they also recognized the vital role that California had historically played in shaping the national and global economy. The roots of California's economic power can be traced backward over a half century before the crash, to developments that simultaneously accelerated California's incorporation into the United States and its integration into the globalizing capitalist economy. Following the gold discoveries of 1848, the world rushed in, seeking the wealth California had to offer. At the same time, Californians looked increasingly outward, pursuing new markets, transportation routes, and labor pools from across the Pacific and throughout Latin America. California rapidly became an intersection for hemispheric and transpacific circuits of capital and labor and a key engine of U.S. empire and the global economy. By the end of the nineteenth century, the influence and investments of the state's industrial leadership helped draw regions of China, Japan, Hawai'i, the Philippines, Mexico, Central America, and the Caribbean into California's imperial orbit. These developments caught the attention of Karl Marx, who wrote from London to German-born labor organizer and New Jersey resident Friedrich Sorge in 1880, asking Sorge to gather what information he could on conditions in California. "California is very important for me," Marx explained, "because nowhere else has the upheaval most shamelessly caused by capitalist centralization taken place with such speed."[12]

What political geographer Edward W. Soja has described as the "Californianization of capitalism"—that is, a tilting of the global spatial economy of capitalism toward California—was not strictly a consequence of the region's abundant natural resources, though these did provide the latent potential for such a transformation.[13] At least as important were the social arrangements that took shape within the state, along with its patterns of resource and social management, which enabled the extraction and development of its resources at a pace and scale that stretched the imaginations of the world's most ambitious entrepreneurs.[14] In sync with the broader history of U.S. western expansion, the advancement of industry, infrastructure, and prosperity in California relied on conquest and unequal arrangements of race and labor. These arrangements in turn subjected the region's diverse Indigenous and immigrant populations to sharp asymmetries of wealth and power and the self-justifying logic of White supremacy.[15] California's early settlement entailed the brutal displacement and decimation of Indigenous people, through practices that ranged from land confiscation and segregation to state-sanctioned genocide. Not coincidentally, the nation's Indian wars reached their peak of violence in the very regions of California that generated the most wealth in gold during the late nineteenth century.[16] The completion of huge infrastructure projects and the extraction of wealth through mining and industrial agriculture were made possible by the concurrent importation, exploitation, and social and cultural exclusion of an increasingly transnational and multiethnic workforce, which included workers with ethnic ties to China, Japan, India, the Philippines, Mexico, Armenia, Italy, Alaska, Hawai'i, and African American populations in the Deep South.[17]

The state's economy continued to expand and diversify during the first three decades of the twentieth century, especially through the growth of manufacturers based in Los Angeles and Southern California. The rise of California's manufacturing sector further concentrated wealth in the hands of industrial elites and tightened the interdependency between the state's economic and political leadership. By the 1920s, industrialists had secured extraordinary sway over local- and state-level policy making, occupying public offices and wielding their organizational power through employers' associations. Virtually without interference from government, and often with the government's outright support, business leaders fixed labor policies within the state and compelled smaller businesses to conform to policies that served the interests of larger ones.[18] The level of political control that California's industrial leaders enjoyed so struck investigators with the La Follette Civil Liberties Committee that they concluded in 1942, after a five-year study of labor-employer relations across the country, that "to a greater degree than this Committee has found elsewhere, associations of employers in California . . . have been able to impose their influence upon the social and economic structure of the state."[19] Concentrated wealth and political power, in other words, had become some of the California economy's most distinguishing characteristics.

As industry grew and diversified, so did the state's labor base. The economy drew large numbers of workers from across the continent and overseas with the promise of comparatively higher wages and better working conditions. At the same time, industrial leaders refined their tactics for cultivating a workforce that was not only large and cheap, especially when compared to the profits it produced, but also fluid, flexible, and docile—characteristics they deemed critical for meeting the needs of a quickly growing and changing economic terrain. Racially targeted hiring, wage differentials, and other discriminatory practices gave rise to a complex, locally varied system of racialized labor segmentation as well as a massive and racially heterogeneous working-class population.[20] By 1930 California was among the most diverse states in the nation. Its African American population remained relatively small, especially compared to most southern states, though it did have more African American residents than any other state in the U.S. West. It also contained more non-White people of "other races" than any other state in the union. Although the state as a whole accounted for less than 5 percent of the total U.S. population, it contained roughly 26 percent of the nation's ethnic Mexican inhabitants, 67 percent of its Filipinx, half of its Chinese, and over 70 percent of its Japanese inhabitants.[21] The state's White population was also ethnically heterogeneous. Roughly half of its White population comprised first- and second-generation immigrants during the first two decades of the twentieth century, though by the 1920s these populations were becoming outpaced by an influx of U.S.-born whites, especially from the Midwest.[22]

Those who came to California during the early twentieth century included large numbers of women, who were drawn to the state by the prospect of jobs and wages, and also the need to perform nonwaged domestic labor to support their husbands and families. From the days of the gold rush and for much of the late nineteenth century, migration to California was overwhelmingly male dominated. Correspondingly, the state's political and cultural institutions were most directly and thoroughly defined by men. Combined, these features led journalist Carey McWilliams to describe California at the turn of the century as "essentially a man's state."[23] By the 1910s and 1920s, the expansion of industry created a new demand for female labor, especially in low-wage and low-skilled positions, and growing numbers of primarily women of color came to fill them. White women increasingly took on this work as well, though the bulk of their labor remained based within their own households.[24] As the ratio of male to female California residents approached equilibrium leading into the 1930s, racialized inequality among women and the political dominance of White men continued to permeate gender politics within the state.

What emerged in the region as a result was a patriarchal and multiracist pattern of capitalist modernization that reinforced the boundaries of the national body politic at the same time that it fueled global economic advancement both within and well beyond California's borders. As historians David R. Roediger and Elizabeth D. Esch have shown, California was at the "leading edge" in pioneering a distinctly multiracial brand of White supremacy, in which racial differences and divisions among working people served as crucial instruments of population management.[25] The "common sense" of race that took hold in California promoted intergroup competition and conflict, which, by inhibiting unity among workers, contributed to the ascendance and durability of regional hierarchies. Racial and gender divisions among working people were a driving force behind Indian removal, Asian exclusion, the quota system inaugurated by the 1924 Johnson-Reed Act, policies prohibiting miscegenation and interracial marriage, and those authorizing Mexican and Filipinx repatriation. All of these projects, in turn, were foundational to California's annexation, incorporation, and maintenance as part of the American nation-state.[26]

As California emerged as an important site in wider circulations of labor and capital between the 1880s and 1920s, it also became a locus of major fault lines on which the global market system would quake during the 1930s. With a bounty of natural resources and among the world's most rapidly developing sectors for finance, commerce, and agricultural production, California served as a beacon for early twentieth-century capitalist fantasies of boundless growth and prosperity. Yet its patterns of growth were far more volatile, and its social and political institutions far more unstable, than its boosters, investors, and observers liked to admit. Underlying its image as a model of modern capitalism's promise were vast inequality and constant contestation—indeed, sometimes violent confrontation—between capitalist brokers who sought to subordinate California's human and natural resources to the dictates of profit and power on the one hand and the people and land who proved insubordinate to those imperatives on the other.[27] In the words of McWilliams, California's history was marked by a "notorious lack of social and political equilibrium. . . . The state is always off balance, stretching itself precariously, seeking to run the rapids of periodic tidal waves of migration" to fill its insatiable demand for labor while striving to maintain its status quo and regarding "each wave of migration . . . with fear and trembling."[28] These antagonisms and imbalances, which accompanied and threatened California's development throughout the early twentieth century, were put in stark relief amid the crisis of the 1930s. The Great Depression accentuated the deep-rooted tensions and disequilibrium of California society, proving regional patterns of economic expansion to be unsustainable. In his analysis of the devastated global economy at the onset of World War II, with particular attention to the role of the United States' western frontier in the making of the crisis, Austrian political economist Karl Polanyi wrote in 1944, "As the lower ranges of labor could not any more be freely replaced from an inexhaustible reservoir of immigrants, while its higher ranges were unable to settle freely on the land; as soil and natural resources became scarce and had to be husbanded," the same region that had "been adduced by economic liberals as conclusive proof of the ability of a market economy to function" was torn at the seams by the "cumulative strains" endemic to its own system of social relations.[29]

California experienced some of the earliest signs and some of the most intense symptoms of the crisis that struck the world in the 1930s. The state's agricultural sector was in recession through most of the 1920s. Its construction and real estate markets, which drove regional development during the first decades of the twentieth century, began to decline by 1926. Financial markets began contracting around the same time, and stock prices in California's major banks fell sharply during the summer of 1928. Employers sought to minimize the impact of the stagnating economy on profits by passing costs on to workers, which meant wage cuts, reductions in consumer spending, and unemployment were all on the rise well before the 1929 stock market crash.[30]

After the 1929 crash, as a spiral of financial panic and protectionist policies expanded the crisis to global proportions, the fallout in California was especially severe. Just as California's reliance on speculative industries made the state a source of crisis for the national and global economy, it also made it one of the sites where the Depression's devastating consequences were most acutely felt. Unemployment within the state climbed as high as 28 percent, exceeding the historic peak of nationwide unemployment, which reached 25 percent in 1933.[31] Its social and economic problems were only exacerbated by the dislocations of populations that occurred in this period, especially as California became the prime recipient of interstate migrants from the southern Great Plains following the drought and dust storms that began there in 1933. In all, an estimated 300,000–400,000 Dust Bowl refugees came to California during this period, more than to any other single state.[32] In part because of the severity of its internal economic and social tensions, California's political scene was also more polarized than in other parts of the country. The same years that saw California's Democratic Party nominate a lifelong socialist for governor also experienced fierce resistance to reform by reactionaries within the state's right wing. In fact, as historians of the era have noted, conservative opposition to New Deal policies in California appears to have been stronger than in almost any other state.[33]

By 1933–34, according to historian Richard Lowitt, California decidedly stood out as "the most chaotic and tumultuous state in the Union."[34] Established authorities were eager to defend their positions and investments, but their legitimacy and their idealized notions of California as a place of inimitable and inevitable prosperity were becoming unglued. For those who had long suffered from inequality and exploitation in California, the Depression signaled the continuation of preexisting struggles, along with the extension of hardships that were already quite familiar. For those who had previously enjoyed moderate levels of financial security and social mobility, the Depression brought new troubles, new suffering, disappointed hopes, and escalated levels of uncertainty. Long-standing social divisions among working people persisted. The outcomes were entirely unforeseeable.

ACKNOWLEDGMENTS

Rebel Imaginaries draws on the support, encouragement, and input of many people. During my time as a graduate student at the University of California, San Diego (UCSD) and beyond, it is difficult to overstate the impact that Luis Alvarez and Danny Widener have had on my work, or the inspiration they have lent to it. In addition to his brilliant guidance and challenging questions, I thank Luis for his reminders along the way that academic work is as much about listening as it is about asserting, that the process is as important as the product, and that the richest modes of learning are those anchored in community. To Danny, thanks for encouraging me to see history simultaneously as a tool kit and as art, and for pressing me to ask the urgent questions about the past that can help us to find where openings exist in the present. Both of them have modeled for me what it means to treat academic work as an avenue for social justice. For both of them, I hold profound gratitude and utmost respect. Other faculty members at UCSD have also influenced the project from its formative stages. Dave Gutiérrez provided support for and feedback on the project from the very beginning, always urging me to keep in view the vital question of why my research matters in the first place. Sara Clarke Kaplan, Nancy Kwak, and Dayo Gore also offered crucial guidance to the project as mentors. I am fortunate to count all of them among my teachers.

Beyond UCSD, this book has benefited from mentorship, advice, and feedback from many people in many places. I thank George Lipsitz for his generosity of time and spirit, his support of this project from early on, and his feedback on the manuscript, which has strengthened this book and me as a scholar. George also welcomed me into the School of Unlimited Learning (SOUL) at the University of California, Santa Barbara, which has been a lifeline for my work while on California's Central Coast. In addition to workshopping part of my manuscript, the SOUL community has lent vital energy to my research and writing, and I express my appreciation to all involved. David Roediger also read the manuscript in its entirety. His work and vision have impacted my research in profound ways, and his input and revision suggestions have helped tremendously to shape this into a better book.

This book bears the imprint of an academic community that reaches far and wide. I am particularly indebted to my very good friends, colleagues, and comrades Cutler Edwards and Maki Smith, who have read and discussed so many versions of so many sections of this manuscript that it is virtually impossible to imagine having completed it without them. I hope that each of them can see their ideas at work here. From conference panels to workshop sessions to more casual conversations, many others have contributed to this project in many forms along the way. Thanks to Kevan Antonio Aguilar, Mayra Avitia, Dawson Barrett, Anita Casavantes Bradford, Rachel Ida Buff, Amy Campos, Graham Cassano, Ernie Chávez, Susan Chen, Wendy Cheng, Jason Derby, Kevin Fellezs, Kate Flach, Jonathan Gómez, Laura Gutiérrez, Romeo Guzmán, Christina Heatherton, Gaye Theresa Johnson, Gloria Kim, Mary Klann, Jorge Leal, Kevin Leonard, Lisa Lowe, William McGovern, Alina Méndez, Liz Mikos, Natalia Molina, Tejasvi Nagaraja, Mychal Odom, Yesika Ordaz, Israel Pastrana, Jimmy Patiño, Marla Ramírez, Jorge Ramírez, Alicia Ratteree, Ryan Reft, Stevie Ruiz, Nayan Shah, James Shrader, Megan Strom, Kim Warren, and Howard Winant. Early on in this book's formulation, I had the opportunity to share a portion of the project at a workshop organized by the Western History Association. The feedback I gathered there from Bill Deverell, Stephen Aron, Jon Christensen, Virginia Scharff, Richard White, Linda Nash, and John Mack Faragher helped me to refine and develop my arguments and analysis. Benny Andrés Jr. and James Gregory read key chapters at crucial junctures in the book's development, sharing comments that have significantly strengthened those chapters and the project as a whole. Steven Isoardi graciously permitted me to use an image of the Al Adams Band from his collection in chapter 5 of this book. Jeff Zalar encouraged me to pursue an academic career in the first place. At California Polytechnic State University (Cal Poly), I have been welcomed by a supportive campus community, which has helped nurture the project to its completion. I am particularly grateful to all members of Cal Poly's History Department for helping me feel at home here.

Profound thanks and immense admiration to my San Luis Obispo–based activist family, some of my greatest teachers of all. In this I include those who remain anchored here and those I have met here who have since moved elsewhere. I thank especially Preston Allen, Stephanie Allen, Natalie Bowers, Leola Dublin Macmillan, Julie Fallon, Katie Grainger, Courtney Haile, Julie Lynem, and Gina Whitaker, who exemplify every day the very best of the ideas and practices that I explore in this book. Their brilliance and dedication to a better world never cease to inspire me. Additional gratitude goes to Natalie, whose courageous heart and sharp political mind are accompanied by a keen editorial eye, which she lent to this project in key moments.

This book would not exist without the help of the archivists, librarians, and library staff on whom this research depends. In particular, I appreciate the assistance and support of Josh Bennett and Rachel Borum at Round Valley Public Library; Robin Walker at the International Longshoremen's and Warehousemen's Union Archives; Conor Casey at the University of Washington Libraries' Special Collections; Peter Filardo at Tamiment Library and Wagner Labor Archives at New York University; David Kessler at the Bancroft Library at the University of California, Berkeley; Catherine Powell at the Labor Archives and Research Center at San Francisco State University; and Michele Welsing at the Southern California Library for Social Sciences and Research. Thanks also to the staffs at the Brawley Public Library; California State Archives; Corona Public Library; El Centro Public Library; Hoover Institution; Huntington Library; Mendocino County Historical Society; Franklin D. Roosevelt Presidential Library; San Francisco Public Library; Stanford Special Collections, University of California, Los Angeles, Special Collections; University of California, Santa Barbara, Special Collections; and Willits Library.

Gisela Fosado has ushered this manuscript through the publication process with all the graciousness and expertise that any author would hope to have in an editor. I thank her along with Alejandra Mejia, Annie Lubinsky, and all at Duke University Press for helping bring this project to life.

Financial support from the Fund for Labor Culture and History, University of California Center for New Racial Studies, Roosevelt Institute, Bancroft Library, Center for Global California Studies, University of California Humanities Research Institute, Latino Studies Research Institute, University of California Office of the President, UCSD Department of History, and Cal Poly College of Liberal Arts made this research possible.

Last, and especially, I thank my friends and family who have supported me throughout this journey. David Malcolm, Liz Hauser, Heather Malcolm,

Meredith Wheless, Jon Wheless, Stacia Law, and Eric Law uplift and sustain me in more ways than I can name, across time and distance. Asher and Conner bring joy and levity to it all. Emma Capri casts a bright light on the future. Jean and Tom Sine have shared in all the joys and challenges that writing this book has entailed, providing encouragement every step of the way. I will never be able to express adequately in words my gratitude to my mother, Shelley Malcolm, for all she has done for me, all she has taught me, and all that she is.

For Nick, my anchor, my buoy, my cocaptain and companion: immeasurable gratitude and love. For Raymond and Leah, who make life ever sweeter, ever brighter, and ever more magical: I love you more than all the books ever written could ever capture. May you know and feel that love in all that you do. This book—and my heart—are for you.

Introduction

The Politics and Poetics
of Rebellion

The language and thought of revolution cannot be a prose which sees volcanoes as mountains: it is necessarily a poetry which understands mountains as volcanoes, an imagination which reaches out towards unseen passions, unseen capacities, unseen knowledges and power-to-do, unseen dignities.—JOHN HOLLOWAY, *Crack Capitalism*

These are upheavals like earthquakes. The revolution, the upheaval of the masses of the population, is a tremendous event that people cannot control. —C. L. R. JAMES, "Walter Rodney and the Question of Power"

This book investigates the crisis of capitalism in California during the Great Depression and corresponding efforts by people from the grassroots to imagine and pursue their liberation on their own terms. From the upsurge of rural agricultural strike activity in 1928 to the acceleration of urban defense mobilization upon U.S. entry into World War II in 1941, the book's narrative charts the deepening instability of California's relationship to the global economy through the everyday self-activity of the region's social majorities. Its protagonists are less the union leaders and politicians who often occupy the spotlight in narratives of the era's social movements. They are more members of families and communities who worked in fields, in factories, on ships, and on docks; they are artists, performers, and grassroots intellectuals; they are Indigenous Californians, as well as immigrants and descendants of immigrants from Mexico, the Philippines, China, Japan, and the formerly slave South. Many of them occupied the margins of mainstream California society. Despite playing a fundamental role in the making of California, many of them remain unknown. Amid the turmoil and unpredictability of the 1930s, these multiethnic working populations advanced visions of themselves and their world that challenged the dominant political discourses and modes of social organization. They constructed political identities less around national, ethnic, or racial affiliations than around a sense of their relationship to broader, global circulations of grassroots struggle. They pursued the dignity, autonomy, and freedom that prevailing institutions denied them and expressed alternative imaginings of what life in and beyond the Great Depression might have been. In an era marked by deep uncertainty and radical possibility, *Rebel Imaginaries* traces how these populations made sense of the conditions they confronted, pursued self-defined needs and aspirations, and changed their surroundings and themselves in the process.

During the Depression era, California's social majorities became the subjects of wide-ranging efforts to determine the contours of a modern political order. As people from all parts of society sought to interpret the unfolding conditions and to find a way out of the economic disaster, numerous business and political leaders, professional intellectuals, middle-class reformers, and leaders of nationwide labor and left organizations sought to fashion the lives of California's populations to suit their own political visions. As widely as their agendas varied and as deeply as their objectives sometimes conflicted, these constituencies agreed that social management was necessary to the future of regional development. Together, they nourished a dominant tendency toward a politics of rationalized governance that sought order through disciplined social organization from the top down.

Dominant though it was, this political impetus was far from totalizing. Many people in California pushed back against the forms of subjection they faced and sought dignity in ways that challenged prevailing governance and development patterns. These Californians were as ideologically diverse as those whose authority they contested. They were linked, however, by shared vulnerabilities and shared desires to determine the directions of their own lives. In their daily struggles, they gave rise to a contrasting, sometimes directly oppositional politics of grassroots autonomy that prioritized community-based social organization, creative and collaborative self-definition, and the integral relationship between imagination and transformation.

As this book examines the contestations between these opposing political currents, it reveals how grassroots movements challenged the racialism, nationalism, and rationalism on which California's modernization relied and posited alternative imaginations of modernity. Against the racial divisions that defined regional capitalist development, the grassroots insurgencies that swept California during the 1930s expressed a multiracialism that embraced the differentiated nature of grassroots struggles. Against the national boundaries of social belonging and political participation, they embodied a spirit of internationalism that underscored the interconnectivity of global emancipatory movements. Against the rationalist notions of progress guiding modern Western thought, they advanced a politics of surrealism that regarded the liberation of desire and imagination as an indispensable political priority. These movements criticized sharply not only the alienating forces of the market and the homogenizing pressures of national culture but also the pressures for uniformity that underpinned some calls for political unity. They worked through established institutions when it served them to do so and abandoned them when it did not. As the Depression deepened and the political future became increasingly unclear—as debates concerning the proper balance between disciplined organization and the creative, spontaneous self-activity of working people pervaded and polarized progressive circles—the movements under investigation here asserted the necessity of imagination to the pursuit of liberation and posited social transformation as an objective without a predetermined end.

Poetry in Times of Crisis

In January 1937, in the midst of an agricultural strike that was holding up the pea harvest across California's Central Coast, Philippine-born writer and labor organizer Carlos Bulosan recalled sitting on the lawn of the San Luis Obispo County jail with his friend José, who had just been released after doing time for his labor organizing activities. Bulosan recounted the words of his comrade that day in his autobiographical account, *America Is in the Heart*. "This is a war between labor and capital," José remarked, acknowledging a perspective on working-class unrest that was held by many. Yet he added, "To our people, however, it is something else. It is an assertion of our right to be humans again."[1] The struggle that José described was not easily encapsulated by protest demands, organizational manifestos, or political platforms. Resisting dehumanization often presumed the necessity of better wages and working conditions. It frequently entailed efforts for fairer access to wage work and equal citizenship rights. Yet it was never reducible to any of these things. The "right to be humans again"—to make life livable and to claim a sense of dignity that was denied by the established order—might be considered an inherently ambiguous objective. The concept undoubtedly held different meanings for different people and sometimes fueled conflicts among those who sought it. Varied as its contents may have been, it constituted a key animating force behind some of the era's most tremendous disturbances to the social order.

Although waged and experienced at the local level, the battle that Bulosan described—a battle for a dignified existence, against dehumanization—had much further-reaching social and political implications. Black newspaper editor and activist Charlotta Bass put it another way. In 1939, as the conflicts of the Depression era accelerated the drive toward war across Europe, Bass addressed Los Angeles radio audiences, noting, "We are living in one of the most significant epochs in all history, an age of stupendous conflict, whether military or intellectual." She explained, "We in America have the sanity to fight our internal battle without recourse to arms. However, in essence, it is the same struggle taking place with bloody horror throughout Europe. It is the same tremendous clash of thought and theory, the same bitter battle of progress and prejudice, hatred of the new and disgust for the old."[2] As Bass emphasized, contemporary battles of arms and of ideas were integrally linked in a worldwide conflict over the future of society. The conflict at hand did not revolve strictly around the direction of policies, the selection of political leaders, or the relationship of workers to their employers, although it encompassed all of these. More fundamentally, this was a contest over the horizons of politics. It brought to the fore questions of what could be created and what should be preserved, what was imaginable and what was possible. It entailed clashes over prospects for addressing the contemporary crisis, for rebuilding society and determining the place of people within it. The conflict linked local and national events to international and global ones. From Bulosan's San Luis Obispo to Bass's Los Angeles, the efforts of marginalized populations to alter their circumstances and better their lives were not disconnected from the unfolding global conflict but can be seen as constitutive fronts within it. Like their contemporaries in eastern China, the Tigray region of Ethiopia, Spain's Catalonia, and Anastasio Somoza García–controlled Nicaragua, they asserted claims to dignity and fought the destructive effects of prevailing modernization patterns. Although observers in their time and since have more commonly treated them as the objects of politics than as the subjects, during the Depression working-class Californians contributed to a broader reshaping of the political terrain within and beyond California.

The perspectives of both Bulosan and Bass urge us to consider how, as much as the Great Depression was marked by soaring inflation, poverty, unemployment, and catastrophic human suffering, it was also an era of intensified conflict between contrasting visions and aspirations for the future. In hindsight, of course, we know a great deal about the era's conflicts and their impacts. Many scholars have chronicled how national efforts to resolve the crisis gave rise to a New Deal order, marked by corporatist expressions of political liberalism and a reconstructed military-industrial economy. They highlight how the New Deal offered unprecedented concessions to working people, from the legalization of collective bargaining rights, to the redistributive effects of a graduated income tax, to a social security system and broader social safety net that encouraged the growth of a sizable middle class leading into the mid-twentieth century. Increasingly in recent decades, researchers have also revealed how these same measures played an important role in resurrecting many of the social divisions that had been destabilized by grassroots movements in the early and mid-1930s. By directing unemployment insurance, federal home-loan assistance, and other workforce protections primarily to White men, and by explicitly excluding agricultural and domestic workers from their benefits, the New Deal reinforced barriers dividing rural from urban, private from public, masculine from feminine, and low-wage and overwhelmingly non-White from higher-wage and largely White sectors of the labor market. In these respects, the New Deal worked to secure capitalism by consolidating racial and gender-based subordination. We know well, then, that the era's movements did not shape the world according to their visions. We know that, for many, the emergent political order, and the war, did more to shore up social boundaries and intensify exclusion and suffering than to alleviate them.

Yet, before the dust settled and dreams were deferred, the uncertainties of the 1930s presented a widened terrain of political possibility. The crisis wrought by the Depression loosened the hold of established norms and hierarchies, making the future perhaps more unpredictable than ever. The moment intensified fears and anxieties for many, to be sure. For some, it bred hopelessness. But it also nourished dreams of a different world. It opened up space for communities with long histories of political struggle to advance their visions and to reinvent their movements and themselves. In the spirit and pace of "revolutionary time," the movements that emerged and converged in this era generated a momentum that helped some to view their circumstances in a different light and to work toward reshaping their future with new vigor.³ Despite the political closures that we now know came later, in the earlier moments of the crisis those developments were neither foreseeable nor fixed. And the dreams that grew amid the rupture of the age—visions of what might have been—merit a fuller investigation.

California is far from the only site where such dreams can be traced. However, it is an especially valuable site for investigating them. California contained many of the features that came to define modern capitalism during the twentieth century, including agribusiness, manufacturing, commerce, finance, real estate, advertising, tourism, motion pictures, and military development, all supported by the labor of a globalized, multiracial workforce. The state thus offers a cross section of the modernizing U.S. economy that can shed light on broader patterns of capitalist development and crisis. Moreover, as a major center of global economic advancement and growth, California was also a place where political stakes were especially high, political attitudes were especially polarized, and political antagonisms grew especially intense, making the contours of political struggles within the state distinctly visible and ripe for investigation. In other words, in addition to serving as a central node of the developing global economy in the early twentieth century, California also puts into relief the ways people have experienced, made sense of, and responded to these same phenomena. Despite the particularities that defined them, the struggles of Californians during the Great Depression had profound resonance with and relevance to popular struggles well beyond their local and regional context.

Amid the chaos of the crisis, many competing forces sought to graft their political visions onto California and the people who inhabited it. Significantly, the different visions of California that crystallized at this time were shaped by divergent interpretations of the crisis itself. For urban and rural industrial elites who controlled the state's resources, markets, and political institutions, the problem of the Depression was in part how to maintain authority and profits in a stagnating economy. As some of the nation's wealthiest and most powerful interests, the state's political and economic leadership had a great deal at stake in the effort to salvage their investments and secure their social positions. Yet inextricable from this imperative was the necessity of responding to the assertion of a new form of social power by the grassroots.⁴ In a general sense, of course, the problem of grassroots insubordination was far from novel. California's elites had proven adept at innovating strategies of social control to contain labor and political disturbances. Yet the grassroots solidarity that elites confronted during the 1930s threatened the stability of the social order in a new and profound way. The popular movements in this period were of a scope and scale that the region had not previously seen; they traversed divisions that had long ordered capitalist society and undermined the narrative logic that had equated California's ascendance with social progress. In the resulting crisis of power, business and political leaders tested old tactics for restoring social order and invented new ones. They combined established methods of repression and terror with new modes of interemployer organization, urban-rural industrial alliance, and campaigns of co-optation.[5] Ultimately, by the 1940s, their experiments gave way to a new corporate liberal order that worked to absorb and appropriate radical elements under the banner of multicultural Americanism.[6]

Of course, California's elites were not wholly responsible for suppressing the region's popular movements. Sometimes inadvertently and at other times with conscious intent, labor leaders employed top-down methods of representation that marginalized the needs and interests of working-class constituents. Liberal advocates for racial justice pursued narrow definitions of civil rights that reinforced the subordination of purportedly un-American populations. Some civic activists strove to reinscribe the racial and gender boundaries of established political institutions. Middle-class property owners frequently sided with industrial and municipal elites in their efforts to rid their neighborhoods and local establishments of populations they regarded as troublesome and transient. Professional journalists and social scientists often denigrated popular protests for failing to conform to prevailing notions of proper political participation. Middle- and working-class people carried out vigilante raids, strikebreaking activities, and acts of racist terror against fellow workers.[7] In these and other ways, people across the social spectrum—many of them self-designated agents of the "public good" and seekers of a well-ordered society—disparaged grassroots struggles and fortified dominant power relations. Along with the region's elites, they struggled to contain the grassroots unrest and rebellion.

Meanwhile, across California's multiracial and multiethnic working populations, diverse and seemingly disparate ethnic Mexican, Filipinx, Asian, African American, Native American, and European American communities offered an alternative account of the crisis. Many working-class Californians experienced the Depression less as a sudden disruption of a longer march of progress and prosperity than as a manifestation of the deeper failings and destructive consequences of a political and economic system whose success had relied on their subordination. For these Californians, the crisis had more to do with laying bare the interconnectivity and interdependence of grassroots struggles against oppression than with threatening reserves of wealth or prospects of social mobility. Just as Bass described the contemporary global conflict, they waged battles for dignity as much through direct-action confrontations as through production of new ideas *about* dignity. They generated a culture of opposition during the 1930s that cut across racial, ethnic, and regional divisions and assumed a wide variety of forms. These included small acts of resistance such as shirking or foot-dragging at the workplace; expressive culture that ranged from music and murals to stage and screen performances; community ties and circuits of communication forged in neighborhoods, migrant camps, pool halls, and breadlines; innovative organizing practices that sought workplace democracy; and coordinated confrontations with urban and rural employers, including major strike actions. The Californians who built the region's culture of opposition during the 1930s rejected the racial capitalist development of preceding decades and expressed social visions that elevated the dignity of ordinary people over the imperatives of building the nation and the market.[8] They exacted important concessions from elites in the age of the New Deal but also had a lasting impact on the political imaginations and social movements that shaped working-class struggles in subsequent generations.

California's grassroots oppositional culture was shaped by the wide range of progressive currents that converged and evolved in the southwestern United States during the late nineteenth and early twentieth centuries. Historical challenges to dominant institutions had made California a laboratory of the political left. California fostered vibrant and variegated traditions of socialism, anarchosyndicalism, and social democratic progressivism. It was home to an influential branch of the Communist Party USA, as well as an assortment of progressive and left-wing party detractors. It provided fertile ground for advocates of a leftward shift in the Democratic Party and the New Deal, independent progressives who supported Upton Sinclair's End Poverty in California campaign, and those who spurned the nation's electoral system altogether. Californians were Trotskyists, Wobblies, Italian anarchists, and Magonistas.[9] They promoted an array of ethnic-oriented agendas against discrimination and segregation. They included advocates of racial internationalisms and diasporic anti-imperialisms.[10] The multifaceted terrain of left politics in California calls into question the tendency of scholarship on interwar social movements to treat the Communist Party as the central pivot of popular efforts for social change.[11] As historian Robin D. G. Kelley has underscored in his study of the Communist Party in Alabama, California was a great distance, both physically and psychologically, from party headquarters in New York, not to mention Moscow, and the party-affiliated movements that took hold in the region were fundamentally shaped by local conditions and locally driven concerns.[12] In this respect, the work of party organizers might best be viewed not as an emblematic expression of political radicalism but as part of the "movement of many movements" that constituted California's popular front political milieu.[13]

Proceeding from this broadened framework, this book departs from narrower understandings of the popular front as a highly specific political formation that emerged from the Communist Party in 1934, in which the Comintern abandoned the sectarian tactics of the Third Period for the construction of alliances with liberal and socialist groups in the interest of defeating fascism in Europe.[14] Significantly, even if we were to pursue this more orthodox framework, California's history complicates the traditional, Moscow-centered narrative we inherit. In fact, as historian Robert W. Cherny has revealed, popular front organizing strategies took shape on the ground in California well before they became the official policy of the party, and, moreover, events in California played an important role in informing the party's ultimate transition toward building a People's Front.[15] Building on the insights of Cherny and many others, I use the phrase "popular front" here to reference the broader movement culture that crystallized in California during the Depression era and that gave expression to new political solidarities across racial, ethnic, national, gender, and ideological divisions. Correspondingly, this book seeks a history of the popular front from below that illuminates how people made sense of the multiplicity of ways in which emancipation and liberation were presented to them. It aims to shed light, in other words, on how people sought to define freedom for themselves in a world where freedom held different meanings for different people.

The oppositional culture that crystallized in the 1930s was not monolithic. It was an expression neither of political unity nor of a common identity. Rather, it grew out of the multifaceted, heterogeneous, and sometimes contradictory efforts of aggrieved people and communities to defend their dignity in the face of varied experiences of oppression. It had roots in a wide range of geographic, intellectual, ideological, and cultural traditions. Yet it was also more than the sum of its parts. Working people's culture reflected grassroots efforts to navigate and stand up to the varying forms of dehumanization they faced. It was the channel through which they made sense of the social conditions they confronted, critiqued racial capitalist power, and mobilized against it. While its forms and impact varied across different locations and communities, it was marked by common threads. Three of those threads constitute the focus of this book.

First, California's oppositional culture was animated by a *multiracialist* politics that challenged the racial divisions structuring global capitalist development within the state and the U.S. West more broadly. When a lettuce strike in the Imperial Valley in January 1930 drew together Mexican, Filipinx, African American, and White workers, ushering in a wave of interethnic mobilizations across the state, agribusiness leaders decried what they viewed as a "young Red revolution" that appeared to be unfolding across the industry.[16] When the surge of multiracial strike activity peaked during the summer of 1934, and San Francisco became the epicenter of a three-month coastwise strike that linked workers of all races and trades and overrode employers' strikebreaking efforts, authorities sought to break up grassroots solidarities with tear gas, clubs, and guns. Even beyond the front lines of industrial conflict, in the seemingly more benign contexts of everyday life, interracial socialization and affiliations provoked the shuttering of dance halls, raids on organizational meetings, and the destruction of works of art. As authorities well recognized, such multiracial practices of working-class association complicated the operations of California's economy and broader imperatives for social and political order. Moreover, they underscored how Californians were reimagining political solidarities to embrace and value difference.[17]

Second, this book also illuminates the *internationalism* that informed the era's popular movements, as they contested the border-policing nationalism that drove the search for order and ultimately framed the New Deal. In 1935 W. E. B. Du Bois's ground-shifting *Black Reconstruction in America* emphasized the inadequacy of a national frame for confronting social injustice within the United States. He urged that the struggles of African Americans and other oppressed people in the United States had to reckon with the global realities of empire, to account for the fact that "in Africa, a black back runs red with the blood of the lash; in India, a brown girl is raped; in China, a coolie starves; in Alabama, seven darkies are more than lynched; while in London, the white limbs of a prostitute are hung with jewels and silk. Flames of jealous murder sweep the earth, while brains of little children smear the hills."[18] The connections were not lost on California's working people; many were immigrants whose lives and familial ties reached across national borders and who were acutely aware of the miseries confronting people beyond the United States. Californians—in writing, speech, and art—conveyed that their own struggles were "but a local phase of a world problem."[19] They engaged these ideas in practice as they built international boycotts and solidarity strikes, promoted the rights of trans-national migrants, rallied to support Ethiopia in the face of Italy's invasion, and even took up arms with revolutionary forces in Spain. The international character of California's oppositional struggles generated alternative practices of citizenship and belonging. At the same time, it also contributed to a broader reshaping of established White-dominated and Western-centric traditions of left internationalism, reinterpreting the possibilities of socialism, communism, and anarchism. Californians regarded popular struggles in disparate localities and nations as interconnected, collectively shaped by incursions of empire, race, and capitalism on a global scale. They saw the solutions to local and domestic problems as lying in the remaking of the wider world.[20]

Third, Californians embraced a politics of *surrealism* that challenged the rationalist strictures governing American liberal thought. Although it is often cited as part of a litany of artistic and literary avant-gardes of the early twentieth century—alongside postimpressionism, futurism, cubism, fauvism, and Dadaism, among others—surrealism was a movement not strictly of aesthetics but of culture and politics in a much fuller sense. Regarded by its participants as a fundamentally revolutionary movement, surrealism embodied a quest for emancipation from the world's misery, to create an elevated and more expansive sense of reality.[21] Californians who engaged and embodied this strain of politics recognized how patterns of oppression relied on a restrained imagination. They saw that material redistribution and, ultimately, liberation required cultural transformation. To this end, they combined conventional strategies of boycotts, strikes, and picket lines with a cultural politics driven toward reenvisioning everyday life. In the artwork that accompanied their protests, in the murals they painted with Works Progress Administration commissions, and in the jazz music that filled their homes, neighborhoods, and dance halls, working-class Californians generated new ideas about democracy and freedom. Applying their cultural politics to more traditional channels of political action, they turned labor unions and electoral politics into sites for redefining solidarity, representation, and participation. They challenged narrow conceptions of art as a mere vehicle for propaganda or as something separate from politics altogether. They countered prevailing tendencies to treat freedom as an abstract ideal or a distant goal. Instead, they treated art and freedom as urgent and integral features of the practice and process of emancipatory political struggle.

In a significant way, *Rebel Imaginaries* is an exploration of the relationship between poetry and rebellion. On one level, the book tells of the cultural expressions and political imaginations—the poetry, so to speak—that emerged from the rebellions of the 1930s. "Poetry" here refers not strictly to the literary form but, in the surrealist sense, to the creative and experimental practice of breaking from inherited strictures, of reimagining and reinventing what exists in ways that might lead to alternative ways of knowing and being. For surrealists, poetry was not just a mode of writing but the source from which a new world might emerge. As Mauritian writer and artist Malcolm de Chazal put it, "Poetry has an aim; absolute human freedom."[22] In this spirit, this study examines how insubordinate subjects drew on established ties of community and kinship, how they forged new channels of collectivity and coalition and negotiated commonalities and differences, as they contributed to making a broader oppositional culture.

Yet, even as it examines the poetry that Depression-era Californians generated, on another level this book can also be read as a meditation on rebellion itself *as* a kind of poetry. Struggles for dignity entailed breaking with the structures, rhythms, and patterns that guided and disciplined social life. These battles against subordination also necessarily involved acts of creation, a "moving against the barriers of that which exists," a "subversion and transcendence of definitions," as political theorist John Holloway has described it.[23] They reflected a "negation of humiliation" that was simultaneously a reclamation of dignity. They were acts of innovation that required both imagination and improvisation. Borrowing from Martinican theorist Suzanne Césaire, theirs was a struggle "to finally transcend the sordid antinomies of the present: whites/Blacks, Europeans/Africans, civilized/savages—at last discovering the magic of the mahoulis, drawn directly from living sources."[24] In the end, it was a continuously evolving effort to make freedom reality and to make poetry life.[25]

The story this book tells about poetry and rebellion in 1930s California is necessarily one of contradiction and contestation. Studying the era's culture of opposition from the bottom up reminds us that the making of movements was not, and has never been, an orderly event, carefully planned and thoroughly disciplined. Rather, this process was marked by disorder, chaos, and emotion. People struggling for dignity and autonomy were fueled not purely by public and collective concerns but also at times by individualistic and materialistic motives. They often reinscribed racial, gender, and class divisions even as they strove to move beyond them. Indeed, the coalitions that formed during this period neither transcended nor elided cultural, racial, and ideological differences but, on the contrary, were shaped and often disrupted by them. In attending to these points of contestation, the present study pursues a fuller understanding of the tensions and conflicts that shaped life in California during the Great Depression, and of the political practices that helped sustain grassroots notions that prevailing arrangements of power and domination were not inevitable—that living with pride and dignity, and building a world that facilitated doing so, was worth struggling for.

The Art of Labor, the Labor of Art: Culture and Politics in the 1930s

Working-class culture is widely regarded as a critical axis of the conflicts and crises that punctuated the early New Deal era. Too frequently, however, the study of culture has been constrained by efforts to find internal cohesion and consistency in the objectives of the era's movements. More to the point, scholars have tended to take the social democratic and corporatist agendas advanced by union leaders and politicians as reflecting the aspirations of working people in general. They have focused overwhelmingly on the ways working people became oriented around a left-liberal progressive politics and an inclusionary, multicultural brand of Americanism.[26] One of the most prominent templates we have for examining the culture and politics of working people in the 1930s is Michael Denning's notion of the "cultural front," whose central legacy he defines as a thoroughgoing "laboring of American culture."[27] Denning's work has been seminal in shifting our gaze beyond the activities of formal political organizations and bringing culture into focus as a category of historical analysis. Rejecting a narrow focus either on official channels of the Communist Party or on battles waged strictly at the point of production, Denning argues powerfully that the social movements of the 1930s and 1940s reshaped American culture through a more diffuse and multifaceted range of contestations over meaning and identity. Particularly productively, Denning underscores the significance of ethnicity in the making of the working-class culture he explores. The historical bloc that defines what he calls "the Age of the CIO [Congress of Industrial Organizations]" was largely the product of an immigrant working class. Moreover, he emphasizes, it was first- and second-generation immigrant workers' experiences of ethnic subordination that fueled their engagement with some of the era's most distinctive cultural forms and, ultimately, their contributions to a "pan-ethnic" redefinition of both Americanism and internationalism.[28]

As generative as Denning's work has been for studies of working-class identity, movements, and culture in the 1930s and 1940s, in casting workers' struggles and politics within the frame of American culture's "laboring," his work also confines our understanding of the popular front in significant ways. More specifically, even as he seeks to capture the wide-ranging and multidimensional character of the era's movements, his approach nonetheless eclipses some of those movements' heterogeneity and short-circuits the insurgent character of the imagination that animated them. Most gravely of all, in binding the fate of multiethnic communities to a trajectory of laboring, such an analysis risks reimposing the very structures of oppression from which many in these communities sought liberation. As historian David R. Roediger has urged, while "labor radicalisms are *part*" of what fueled working-class struggles in the 1930s, "they do not exhaust dreams for a new world."[29]

To account more fully for the scope of political possibilities opened up by grassroots struggles in the Depression era, I take cues from contemporary surrealist theorists, who saw in the uprisings of the interwar era not a common political agenda but a common emancipatory impulse. For surrealists, the deepening global crisis of the Great Depression was accompanied by the making of an international revolutionary movement—one anchored in a desire for freedom and oriented toward the freeing of desire from the strictures of rationalism imposed by modern and Western thought.[30] Surrealism provides crucial insight into the historical moment of the Great Depression not simply because this period marked the peak of the endeavors of André Breton, Louis Aragon, and others to elaborate surrealist ideas as part of a self-conscious aesthetic and intellectual enterprise. Rather, it is useful especially because it captures a way of thinking about politics that helps us to move beyond the constraints of worn ideological categories and toward a more open-ended exploration of what moves people. Unlike other early twentieth-century avant-gardes such as postimpressionism, futurism, cubism, and fauvism, surrealism drew momentum from liberatory struggles occurring outside Europe and from a vantage point that was distinctly anti-Eurocentric.[31] Surrealists advanced a critique of capitalism that simultaneously denounced the role of colonialism, imperialism, and White supremacy in shaping the modern world. They exalted the value of imagination, creativity, and improvisation for the pursuit of social transformation and championed efforts to breach the distinction between art and life, dreams and reality, ideas and actions. Perhaps most important, in advancing a vision of revolution without a fixed or predetermined end, surrealism gives us a valuable epistemological frame for investigating—and seeing the potential power of—the practices of self-definition and self-activity engaged by working people as they sought to make life livable on their own terms.[32]

The conceptual tools that surrealism offers prove especially vital when we consider how centering the struggles of working-class communities in a study of Depression-era California requires broadening the way we traditionally think about political activity. Indeed, most of the poor, racialized, and immigrant women and men who constituted California's working-class populations during the 1930s did not have full access to participation in the formal institutions that usually define the edges of what is political. Marginalized by dominant conceptions of national identity and "rational" or "authentic" political subjectivity, they commonly drew on a wider range of social and cultural resources—from music and games to community ties—as they fashioned identities for themselves and evaded, confronted, and challenged the circumstances of their everyday lives. Taking seriously the self-activity of working-class communities thus mandates that we heed Kelley's assertion that "politics is not separate from lived experience or the imagined world of what is possible; to the contrary, politics is about these things."[33]

The point here is not to suggest that all forms of grassroots struggle and resistance can simply be subsumed under the classification of "surrealist." Nor is it to imply that surrealist expressions of politics are somehow better or more important than others.[34] Rather than deploying surrealism either as a unifying, umbrella-like construct or as a marker of political superiority, I draw on it as a resource that bursts open the containers through which we often view different forms of political activity. The insights that surrealism offers might assist us in looking beyond the terms of order we have inherited, to explore the fuller range of inventiveness, creativity, and political possibility generated by people at the grassroots.[35] From this vantage point, surrealism lends us a route to expand and multiply, rather than consolidate or enclose, the kinds of politics that can be imagined, interpreted, and enacted—in the past as well as, perhaps, the present.

Rather than fitting neatly into dominant narratives of an emergent, nationalist political consensus, the movements under examination here—and, I argue, significant currents of working-class movements in 1930s California more broadly—engaged a politics born out of the embattled circumstances of everyday life and driven toward the manifold goal of making life livable. At the heart of their endeavors was a refusal of the conditions and classifications that capitalist modernization imposed on their lives and an impulse to move beyond them. They struggled to define and organize their lives according to their desires, at the same time that they drew on modes of historical memory and social learning that underscored the interdependence of their struggles with those that surrounded them. The identities they forged and the sense of autonomy they sought were anchored—not tidily within the boundaries of national, racial, and industrial categorizations so frequently ascribed to them—but in a sense of the multiplicity, variability, and intersectionality of a wider array of popular struggles against subordination. Theirs was a multiracialist and internationalist politics of working-class autonomy that challenged the social divisions of capital at the local level while contributing to a global circulation of struggles against the subjugating forces of Western imperialism and racial capitalism. At once oppositional and prefigurative, the movements of working-class Californians that are the subject of this study underscored the value of regarding democracy and freedom not strictly as political objectives but as actually lived and embodied elements of the process of political struggle.[36]

Considering the politics of Depression-era social movements through the frame of surrealism reshuffles the ways we understand the key political dilemmas confronting working people in the 1930s. For most, the problem of politics had less to do with deciding how to cast electoral ballots or determining which political organization to join than with developing methods for pursuing broad visions of social transformation without sacrificing the priorities of creative autonomy and democratic participation.[37] For many people at crucial junctures, industrial labor provided a generative site for such pursuits. Mobilizing at the workplace around labor-oriented concerns exerted pressure at one of the most vulnerable sites in capitalism's circuitry, dramatized the power of working people in the economy, and carried the potential to wrest otherwise unimaginable concessions from political and economic elites. All of these factors helped to make labor a central rallying point for nationwide progressive and radical political organizations, which in turn provided crucial resources and comradeship to working people. Certainly, some of the most historic gains made by working people in this era occurred at work sites, in moments and places where popular desires to utilize the resources and political avenues that national progressive organizations made available to them corresponded with the imperatives of those organizations to draw on the energies of mass working populations.

Policy, too, proved an important fulcrum for Depression-era oppositional movements. Efforts to impact policy at local, state, and national levels were critical to grassroots efforts to survive and respond to prevailing injustices and to the incursions of the militarized racial state. In political education drives, ballot-box measures, and electoral campaigns, Californians made claims on legal rights and public goods and redrew the boundaries of the nation itself. Their initiatives reflected more than an attempt to gain inclusion within existing institutions; they advanced a social warrant that mandated a redistribution of resources and transformed the meanings of citizenship, representation, and political participation, with substantive structural consequences for people in and beyond California.[38]

Yet neither workplace- nor policy-centered movements ever encompassed the totality of grassroots political activities or emancipatory hopes. For many aggrieved and working-class communities in the 1930s, life conditions demanded more than access and inclusion within existing institutions or the fulfillment of modernity's promises; they made necessary a reconceptualization and transfiguration of the very terms that organized the modern world. In the words of writer Ralph Ellison, to struggle for freedom in the face of oppression was as much an artistic as a political task, one that required the invention of "new definitions of terms like *primitive* and *modern*, *ethical* and *unethical*, *moral* and *immoral*, *patriotism* and *treason*, *tragedy* and *comedy*, *sanity* and *insanity*."[39] Resisting dehumanization implied cultivating new ideas about labor and leisure, new ways of living and belonging, and new modes of social relations.[40] For innovations of this sort, established discourses, aesthetic conventions, and avenues of political participation were important and strategic but never sufficient modes of expression. For this reason, much of the work of liberatory struggle occurred, as anthropologist and political scientist James C. Scott has put it, "like infrared rays, beyond the visible end of the spectrum," on that wider terrain of politics we call culture.[41] As cultural theorist Paul Gilroy notes, some of the most radical challenges to modernity have not been spoken or written but "played, danced and acted, as well as sung about, because words . . . will never be enough to communicate [their] unsayable claims to truth."[42] Culture provided a repository for social visions that not only "reveal[ed] the internal problems in the concept of modernity" but also "partially transcend[ed] modernity," thus providing a pathway toward "individual self-fashioning and communal liberation."[43]

Framing this inquiry into California's working-class struggles as an examination of the region's culture of opposition is one way to begin to think about the multitude of grassroots movements for dignity and autonomy that emerged there in the 1930s as part of a wider struggle for transformation and hegemony.[44] The point here is not to posit work and art, politics and culture, as distinct, binary realms of activity. Rather, my objective is to explore how, in the context of early twentieth-century capitalism, these categories presented a dialectical contradiction that Californians worked to resolve in a multiplicity of ways. I hope to illuminate how the art of labor protest and the labor of artistic production together provided grounds for reimagining life and producing new, oppositional modes of being and belonging.

Cultural expressions in themselves cannot transform the world. They do not "topple regimes, break chains, or stop bullets."[45] In fact, they often reinforce prevailing structures of power and provide means of accommodating to existing conditions. However, as cultural theorist Stuart Hall insists, they are one of the arenas where the "struggle for and against a culture of the powerful is engaged" and where a newly democratic culture "might be constituted."[46] In the words of cultural critic George Lipsitz, "Politics and culture maintain a paradoxical relationship in which only effective political action can win breathing room for a new culture, but only a revolution in culture can make people capable of political action."[47]

In examining California's Depression-era "revolution in culture" on the terms of the people who created it, this study remaps the way we see 1930s California in both temporal and spatial terms. Early twentieth-century California contained one of the most diverse landscapes of any region of the continent, including natural and cultural resources that varied widely across different localities. It was a driver of the national economy and of U.S. imperialism. It was a global crossroads for capital and labor and a site for the production of the kinds of mutually impacting transnational patterns that Earl Lewis has called "overlapping diasporas."[48] In the midst of the global crisis of the 1930s, California was also a land of many possible futures. Although historians in retrospect have drawn a fairly direct line from California's emergence as ground zero for Anglo-American conquest and capitalist modernization in the mid-nineteenth century to a fully industrialized and multicultural Golden State by the mid-twentieth century, this book urges attention to the fissures and breaks in that narrative that the 1930s represented. This study traces how the global crisis of capitalism in the 1930s was experienced by Californians across a range of different localities and valences—across what Latinx cultural critic Juan Flores has described as the "cross" (as in cross-racially and cross-ethnically), the "intra" (considering intra-ethnic relations of class, gender, sexuality, and citizenship), and the "trans" (highlighting the transnational reach of local grassroots experiences).[49] It tracks how Californians confronted the uncertainties of the era and sought to redefine the contours of their lives in a multitude of ways, with many possible outcomes for the trajectory of California's development. Against dominant inclinations to hunt out traces of historical inevitability, I hope to recapture a sense of the 1930s in California as an era of disruption and unpredictability, a conjuncture where "history's continuum shatter[ed]" and "new horizons shimmer[ed]."[50]

Organization

What follows is an examination of the making of California's grassroots oppositional culture as an interethnic, multiracial, and transregional phenomenon. It moves across rural and urban divisions in California's landscape, to illuminate the expressions of grassroots radicalism that emerged through contestations over labor, policy, and art. It reveals the multiracialist, internationalist, and surrealist politics that animated California's oppositional culture, ultimately showing how everyday Californians challenged racial capitalist development and American imperialism. While each of these political currents receives varying levels of attention within different parts of the chapters that follow, all three elements are present and integrally shape the narrative throughout all parts of the text.

Part I examines radical currents of grassroots politics in sites of industrial labor. It begins in the rural, industrialized agricultural region of the Imperial Valley, where a lettuce strike by Mexican, Filipinx, African American, and White workers in January 1930 marked one of the earliest upsurges of multiracial, industry-wide collective direct action during the Great Depression. Chapter 1 takes the 1930 lettuce strike and subsequent formation of the multiracial Agricultural Workers' Industrial League as a point of departure for examining the crystallization of an oppositional grassroots politics of multiracialism. As multiracial, cross-trade strike activity in agriculture peaked in 1933–34, political tensions in California's commercial capital also reached a boiling point. In the spring of 1934, the major port city of San Francisco became the epicenter of a coastwise waterfront strike and the site of the largest and longest general strike in U.S. history since the general strike of the slaves during the Civil War. Chapter 2 examines how mobilizations for workplace democracy on San Francisco's waterfront in the summer of 1934 became a site on which Black, Asian, Latinx, and White workers linked wide-ranging struggles against racial capitalist development in the city.

Part II examines how established channels of policy making became vehicles for grassroots radicalisms that redefined the role of the state and reimagined the nature of citizenship. Chapter 3 examines grassroots responses to repatriation policies and to the wave of deportations that swept California during the 1930s. From targeted populations' informal social and cultural practices to the immigrants' rights activism of groups like El Congreso de Pueblos de Habla Española (Spanish-Speaking People's Congress) and the Committee for the Protection of Filipino Rights, the chapter investigates how grassroots actions reconceptualized national belonging, political participation, and rights. Chapter 4 explores the shifting coalitional solidarities and tensions that shaped efforts toward a leftward shift in the Democratic Party in California. Taking Upton Sinclair's gubernatorial campaign in 1934 as a point of departure, it examines how efforts to take over California's Democratic Party and to harness it to grassroots needs and interests presented new possibilities and limitations for grassroots movements.

Part III shifts the lens away from sites and moments of direct political confrontation to examine the production and circulation of oppositional culture in wider ambits of grassroots struggle. Chapter 5 examines how art served as a critical battleground for working-class residents of Los Angeles—the culture industry's capital and a nationwide pacesetter for open-shop unionism. The chapter focuses especially on the ways Angelenos utilized public visual art, community theater, and jazz to advance oppositional forms of cultural representation and expressions of belonging and identity. Chapter 6 deepens the investigation of jazz culture's radical potential, to reveal how jazz expanded the range of frequencies through which Native people in and around Northern California's Round Valley Reservation imagined their liberation, challenged the assumed separation of the physical from the spiritual, and redefined relationships across tribal affiliations and ethnic populations.

Examining how Depression-era Californians sought to make their lives livable across each of these sites does not provide us with a comprehensive or conclusive account of the era's social movements. However, it does offer us a new way of looking at them. Considering these sites as a small sampling of the many movements that made up the region's Depression-era political landscape illuminates how grassroots expressions of multiracialism, internationalism, and surrealism energized popular struggles across a wide range of different valences and by a multitude of means. An imaginative and open-ended politics rooted in the everyday lives of aggrieved communities, grassroots radicalisms manifested themselves in the liberatory desires and hopes of people in rural and urban regions, at the workplace and in the neighborhood, in places of labor and of leisure, in political confrontations and artistic expressions, in forms of coalition and community, and even in expressions of identity that reinforced social exclusions and divisions. These radical currents were not confined to a specific location or to a group of people with a specific racial, ethnic, or gender affiliation. They cannot properly be understood as a specific strategy of organizing or protest. They were not ideologies. As the movements that unfolded across California reveal, the political imaginations that crystallized at the grassroots during the 1930s embodied the pervasive contradiction of the age between aspirations for dignity and those for social transformation. In the struggles they animated lie crucial lessons concerning the relationships among struggle, freedom dreams, solidarity, and social change.

Part I.

THE ART OF
LABOR PROTEST

1

Multiracial Rebellion
in California's Fields

On New Year's Day, 1930, at the peak of the Imperial Valley's lettuce harvest, several hundred ethnic Mexican and Filipinx farmworkers in the vicinity of Brawley, California, walked off their jobs, protesting a recent wage cut and deplorable working conditions. Within a few days, the strike expanded across the valley to include an estimated five thousand workers. The mere fact of the strike's occurrence, not to mention its scale, was remarkable, to be sure. In an industry where workers' obedience was mandatory and in a locality where violence was a common instrument of governance, overt direct-action resistance carried the threat of severe and sometimes deadly repercussions. Many of the strikers had learned this lesson firsthand, having participated in the Mexican-led cantaloupe strike in 1928, the largest local strike action before the 1930 lettuce walkout, or in the dozens of smaller work stoppages and wildcat strikes that had occurred across the valley during the preceding decade. These disturbances had provoked scores of arrests, deportations, beatings, and murders by both official and unofficial law enforcers. In this environment, openly confronting employers in any capacity was a gravely serious matter.[1]

Yet what was especially noteworthy about the January 1930 mobilization—and what made it especially troubling to the social order—was the striking coalition's composition and the expression of interracial political solidarity that it set forth. In merging the political efforts of Mexican and Filipinx farmworkers, the action departed from earlier strike actions, which had preserved racial divisions between these groups and reinforced patterns of labor segmentation that growers worked hard to maintain.[2] As events unfolded, the strike expanded to include Chinese, Japanese, Punjabi, African American, and White workers as well. Some of the strikers were Magonistas who had aided the Partido Liberal Mexicano's (Mexican Liberal Party) takeover of northern Baja in 1911. Some of them were veteran labor advocates who helped organize workers in the 1922 revolt by Imperial and Mexicali Valley farmworkers. Others were Wobbly-influenced anarchists and syndicalists, political dissidents of varying stripes, and anticolonial internationalists. The strike also became a locus for political organizing by a handful of Southern Californian Communist Party activists, who arrived from Los Angeles toward the end of the strike's first week and who saw in the uprising the makings of a truly mass movement.[3] According to a report by the *Daily Worker*, the lettuce strike heralded "the beginning of mass rebellion by all the scores of thousands of bitterly exploited Mexican, Filipinx, Hindu, Japanese, and Chinese agricultural laborers, who slave for the big open-shop fruit growers and packers under conditions bordering closely on peonage."[4]

The formation of a broad-based, multiethnic, interracial coalition of farmworkers in the Imperial Valley lettuce strike was not an anomalous or isolated incident. Rather, it was one of the earliest of many such alliances forged in the wave of strikes that swept California agriculture during the 1930s. Strike activities in the Imperial Valley during 1930 gave rise to the Agricultural Workers' Industrial League, an affiliate of the Communist Party's Trade Union Unity League and one of the first agricultural unions in California to include Mexican and Filipinx farmworkers along with smaller numbers of White, Japanese, and Black laborers (see figure 1.1).[5]

The following year saw the organization of the Cannery and Agricultural Workers Industrial Union (CAWIU), which quickly expanded into a statewide network that included tens of thousands of Mexican, Filipinx, Black, Puerto Rican, Japanese, and White members. Local branches of the CAWIU played a central role in at least twenty-four of the thirty-seven strikes documented at the height of statewide agricultural strike activities in 1933, including the largest work stoppage of the era, the San Joaquin Valley cotton strike of October–November of that year, during which eighteen thousand Mexican, Filipinx, Black, and White cotton workers formed a picketing zone that stretched over one hundred miles and spanned four counties.[6] The overlapping efforts of independent ethnic unions, interethnic union

FIGURE 1.1 Members of the Agricultural Workers' Industrial League, arrested and detained for their involvement in labor organizing activities in the Imperial Valley, 1930. Courtesy of Imperial County Historical Society, Pioneers Museum, Imperial, California (H15-02_J2-2).

alliances, and multiethnic unions manifested during the Depression decade in approximately 140 strikes, which involved over 127,000 workers from across California.[7] Many of these strikes resulted in partial wage increases and at least modest improvements in working conditions.[8] Nearly all of them inflamed the fears of agribusiness elites about the "young Red revolution" that seemed to be unfolding across the industry.[9] Perhaps most important, these movements reenvisioned the racial boundaries of labor unionism and gave expression to visions of multiracialism that differed radically from—indeed, posed fundamental challenges to—those that dominated the agricultural labor market and broader patterns of racial capitalist development during the early twentieth century.[10]

As one of the Depression era's earliest eruptions of outright rebellion within an industry that was foundational to California's economy, the multiracial strike actions that occurred in and beyond the Imperial Valley open a window onto the historical roots of radical political currents that crystallized within the state during the 1930s. Looking specifically at the social and cultural practices of Imperial Valley farmworkers during the years that preceded the 1930 lettuce strike not only helps to shed light on how the strike and the subsequent wave of strikes came to be but also deepens understandings of the constructions of unionism and the cross-racial coalition that animated the upheaval. As this chapter will illustrate, the alliances formed by Imperial Valley farmworkers were shaped by the varied traditions of radicalism that overlapped in the Imperial Valley's fields, grassroots knowledge that derived from farmworkers' experiences of racial capitalist development in the region, and the community ties and networks that farmworkers forged in the course of their everyday struggles. By 1930 these developments contributed to the production of an oppositional expression of multiracialism at the grassroots. Against dominant patterns of racial competition and hierarchy that governed the region's political economic development, grassroots expressions of oppositional multiracialism hinged on a sense of mutual interdependence and shared vulnerability that linked the varied struggles of farmworkers with one another. Indicative of neither a unifying political agenda nor a homogenizing "class" or "American" identity, this multiracialist politics treated difference and intersectionality as constitutive features of political solidarity, within a collective struggle against the dehumanizing effects of racial capitalism and American imperialism. It was motivated not primarily by the prospect of wages, work conditions, or resources made available by the state or by national labor unions but rather by more quotidian and locally rooted desires for dignity and autonomy within farm working communities.

Racial Capitalist Development and Oppositional Knowledge Production in the Imperial Valley

Foundational to grassroots articulations of multiracialism in the 1930s Imperial Valley were working populations' experiences of political economic development patterns that had made the Imperial Valley a key engine of the U.S. economy and a major intersection for global circuits of capital and labor during the first three decades of the twentieth century. On the eve of the Depression era, the Imperial Valley was in many ways a microcosm of western American capitalist advancement. The massive water projects that transformed this section of the Colorado River Delta into an irrigated garden valley epitomized imperialist fantasies of humans' mastery over nature and fueled new experiments with large-scale commercial farming.[11] Between 1910 and 1930, the amount of cultivated farmland within the Imperial Valley expanded over fivefold, from roughly 76,000 acres to over 400,000 acres, roughly 6 percent of California's statewide total at the time. During this time, the region became a major supplier of extensive (machine-harvested) crops such as hay, barley, and cotton as well as more labor-intensive crops, ranging from melons to citrus, peas, lettuce, asparagus, tomatoes, sugar beets, and a great many other specialty fruits and vegetables.[12]

Enabled in significant part by technological advances in intensive farming practices and the expansion of southwestern irrigation and rail networks, the valley's agricultural growth also hinged on shifting social arrangements that concentrated political and economic power among agribusiness elites, while deepening inequality and vulnerability for the region's social majorities. The increasing prevalence of absentee landownership and tenancy, the construction of a new class of farm managers, and cooperative partnerships and associations among agribusiness leaders made possible agribusiness productivity on a vast scale. These same patterns encouraged a shift of wealth upward, sharpening inequalities among farmers and facilitating the increasing dominance of the large commercial farms reliant on high-value, labor-intensive crops.[13] Agricultural expansion went hand in hand with the institutionalization of labor contracting and managerial oversight, piece-rate wages that bound workers' income to their ability to produce profits for growers, and temporary, seasonal patterns of work that tied the rhythms of workers' lives to those of the agricultural market.[14] Patterns of labor management were deliberately uneven and differentiated across an ethnically diverse workforce, supporting a system of labor segmentation that pitted groups of workers against each other to keep labor costs low and laboring people divided.[15]

A vast body of scholarship has shown how the racial segmentation of labor in the United States between the late nineteenth and early twentieth centuries contributed to a distinct, multiracist pattern of White supremacy, in which difference and domination often reinforced each other. Building on strategies first developed by southern slaveholders, employers used racially differentiated practices of labor recruitment, hiring, wage scaling, and management to promote intergroup competition and inhibit working-class unity. These same practices supported a wider infrastructure of racial segregation that extended well beyond the workplace, ranging from laws that prohibited miscegenation and intermarriage, to customs of racial propriety and deference, to traditions of exclusion in residential housing and public facilities.[16]

The Imperial Valley proved to be a major engine for the production of multiracial managerial strategies that facilitated national and capitalist development during the early twentieth century.[17] At the same time that it became a pacesetter for global agribusiness development and a driver of U.S.

capitalist expansion, the Imperial Valley also served as a laboratory for the innovation of modern strategies of racialized labor management. Following the early enlistment of local Indigenous Cucapá labor in the late nineteenth century, Imperial Valley employers increasingly recruited other non-White and immigrant workers in their efforts to harness a cheap and flexible labor pool.[18] Global economic dislocations resulting from industrialization generated a ready supply of precisely this sort of labor for agricultural development in the U.S. Southwest, first from China especially, subsequently from Japan, and by the 1910s predominantly from Mexico and the Philippines.[19] These transnational migrants were joined by African Americans from the Deep South during the early twentieth century and by poor Whites who came from the southern and midwestern regions of the country in relatively small numbers during the 1910s and 1920s and en masse during the Dust Bowl migration of the 1930s.[20] Between 1910 and 1920, the valley's population tripled from 13,591 to 43,453 people. This included 6,414 Mexican residents, 2,500 European immigrants, 1,986 Japanese, 1,185 Native Americans (most of whom lived on the Indian reservation in the eastern part of the county), 1,648 Black residents, 88 Chinese, and 381 "Others" (which included Filipinx, South Asians, and Koreans). Combined, the residents of color within the county amounted to approximately one-quarter of the total population.[21]

The overwhelming presence of ethnic Mexican labor in the local workforce by the late 1920s (an estimated 90 percent of laborers in the county, according to one study) led some observers to assume that Imperial Valley farm labor "has come to mean Mexican" labor generally speaking.[22] Yet such a description obscures the extent to which labor management on the region's farms remained a distinctly multiracial enterprise. In fact, Mexican labor was constructed as widely favorable precisely by weighing its advantages against those of differently racialized working populations.[23] For instance, a representative of Fresno Farms Company explained in 1928, "The Filipinos have a higher standard of living and for that reason some farmers prefer them," but at the same time, they also had a reputation for being more militant and tending "to ask for more wages than the Mexicans."[24] Investigators from the California Department of Industrial Relations reported being told that Filipinx workers were "steadier, more tractable, and more willing to put up with longer hours, poorer board, and worse lodging facilities," especially compared to White workers.[25] Some growers thought valley farms could fare best by replicating the racial order of the South, recruiting "the picturesque Negro with his music and drollery," who was "missed by the old-time cotton growers."[26] Others fiercely opposed measures to import Black workers in larger numbers and expressed a preference for other sources of racial labor.[27] Many California farmers and boosters argued that Mexican workers' supposed backwardness and docility suited them ideally for farm labor.[28] Others emphasized the value of what they insisted was the foreign and "impermanent" nature of Mexican migrant labor, which enhanced the migrants' fitness for low-wage labor while limiting the threat they posed to local culture.[29]

While strategies of labor recruitment and management varied somewhat from farm to farm, by the late 1920s a general division of labor had emerged that made competition between Mexican and Filipinx workers a central fixture of work patterns in the valley's fields, with smaller numbers of other workers of color reinforcing this dynamic. Meanwhile, higher-paying packing-shed jobs tended to be held by White workers and to be marked by competitive relations between ethnic immigrant and native-born populations.[30] Collectively, these multiracial labor management practices that took shape in the Imperial Valley undergirded the region's ascendance into an engineering wonder and an economic powerhouse, to which the world's agriculturalists looked as a model of large-scale desert farming.[31]

By the end of the 1920s, the Imperial Valley stood as a model of racial capitalist agricultural development and progress. Local boosters heralded in a promotional brochure, "The world is Imperial Valley's market." As the brochure noted, the global reach of the valley's economy was reflected in its local labor market: "In addition to the usual supply of American farm laborers, Imperial Valley crops utilize negroes and Mexicans for cotton; Mexicans for mil maize cutting; Swiss milkers, Jap-inese for cantaloupe picking; American for general ranch work, together with a scattering of Hindus, Filipinos, and Portuguese, who adapt themselves to whatever work is required." As the narrative ran, this cosmopolitan workforce combined with modern transportation technologies to make the valley a critical node in the world economy, permitting the "shipment of lambs and hogs to Kansas City; cotton goes to Japan and Liverpool; cantaloupes, early table grapes, fruits and vegetables roll by the carload into all the leading markets of the United States."[32]

Despite the grandness of their depictions, the valley's growers and boosters never held a monopoly on the ways in which regional development patterns were understood. Against dominant narratives that portrayed the Imperial Valley as a lodestar for capitalist fantasies of economic growth and prosperity, the early twentieth century also saw the formation of an oppositional body of knowledge about regional development at the grassroots. In some cases, this knowledge took the form of consciously articulated political ideas. In most cases, it was expressed by the myriad ways in which workers confronted, evaded, and challenged the many indignities they experienced as they sought to make their lives livable on their own terms. This body of knowledge did not translate into a common political ideology or agenda. Nor did it reflect a universalizing identity among farmworkers. Rather, it was born out of the varied circumstances that shaped workers' lives, was driven by a sense of the vulnerabilities they shared, and contributed to a sense of the relational and interdependent nature of their struggles against the dehumanizing effects of racial capitalist development.

Farmworkers routinely pushed back against the dehumanizing effects of racial capitalist development in ways both visible and surreptitious.[33] As growers' demands for production efficiency became increasingly constricting throughout the 1920s, workers of all ethnicities engaged in work slowdowns, stole from farmers and their families, and destroyed the property of their employers.[34] Instances abounded of workers quitting or deserting without fulfilling their contracts in response to being affronted on the job. As one grower explained, one of the major obstacles to a regimented work discipline was that workers "can leave readily and are apt to do so. If you wish to correct them they will answer back, and if you stick to your point they may all quit."[35] Efforts to assert fuller control over workers' bodies and the temporal rhythms of the workday challenged the time-work discipline that governed the grower-worker relationship and reflected a fuller drive for autonomy. As one worker named Mr. Martinez explained, "We Mexicans do not mind working hard but we do not like to be driven. We will do much more work if we are allowed to work undisturbed and set our own pace."[36]

At times, workers pushed back directly against the racial managerial practices that growers employed to promote interracial competition among them. For example, Mr. Rowe, of the Los Angeles–based Southern California Employment Agency, explained that one "cannot easily pay Mex[icans] and whites differently on [the] same job as Mex[icans] will quit when they find it out."[37] That workers outwardly rejected the differential wage practices that sustained racial hierarchies in California's fields underscores the tenuousness of labor management in California's fields. It also reveals how efforts for a just wage could be linked to a broader challenge against the racial segmentation of the workforce. In withholding their labor power from offending bosses, deserters provoked adjustments in labor management practices by farmers and farm labor supervisors, who sought to maintain wage discrimination by assigning racial groups who received different rates of pay to distant sections of the fields with the intent of averting communication between them.[38] They also call our attention to grassroots knowledge about wage scaling and labor segmentation as a structural issue that would not be resolved by blaming immigrant populations or other groups engaged in battles over low-paying jobs.

Some workers were keenly aware that although patterns of agricultural labor management were racially differentiated, the extreme imbalance of power in Imperial Valley fields meant that certain vulnerabilities were widely shared among workers. As one farm laborer in Brawley remarked of agri-business employers, "They control everything, such as City Councils, committees, [and] don't care what kind of houses we live in, or if we starve. . . . Unconsciously," he went on, "we [workers] lower the wages, because we go away to look for work, not knowing beforehand if work is to be had. We go from place to place and as we have to eat, we offer our services for less, in order to be able to work. Capital likes to pay us as little as they can."[39] The uneven distribution of suffering among the valley's working-class populations enabled some workers to identify their struggles against economic exploitation as struggles against racial oppression. As one farmer's servant in Hemet noted, "It is the brown arms that have picked the oranges, lemons, cantaloupes, . . . picked the watermelon for year in and year out, and some have nothing left but a broken body."[40]

Many farm laborers became acutely attuned to the patterns of hiring that pitted racialized immigrant populations against each other, driving down wages for all workers and helping to keep working populations divided. For example, Filipinx laborer Manuel Luz characterized patterns of racialized economic competition among workers as expressions of a perpetual "cycle to demoralize the newcomers to this country." Drawing on his observations in the Imperial Valley, San Joaquin Valley, and Santa Barbara County farms during the 1930s, Luz explained that White workers "claimed that we [Filipinx workers] were to blame for lowering the wages. But these people wouldn't work in the fields anyway . . . [and] when we tried to organize ourselves to get higher wages, so we could be equal to them, we didn't get their support. That's the irony of the whole thing."[41]

Luz recognized that the experiences of his community were not exceptional, however. Rather, he described them as reflecting an established custom of race and labor in Southern California's fields. "This boss I had in Fresno," Luz recalled. "He was Armenian. He told me that they experienced the same thing when they first were getting started in this country."[42] Racial tensions resulting from the "cycle of demoralization" that Luz described would only intensify later in the 1930s, when poor White migrants flooded into the state from the southern Great Plains. As Pixley-born farmworker John Sánchez recalled, "White people would come up and tell my dad, 'Why don't you Mexicans stay in Mexico? Why do you have to come over and take our jobs?' . . . And then, it wasn't too long afterwards—several years afterwards that the Okies started coming over and taking our jobs. . . . And so we got to where we hated the Okies that was coming over to take our jobs, you know."[43]

While multiracial patterns of economic competition created serious obstacles to the formation of collectivity among workers, the destructive consequences of racial competition were not lost on the workers themselves. Some workers were aware that their experiences of daily indignities and exploitation had parallels with those of other workers and their communities. Such awareness provided the raw material for the construction of a sense of shared struggle. Sánchez noted of the African American neighbors and friends with whom he worked, attended school, and spent time, "Well they was treated like we were; they was treated pretty bad, you know. . . . They was mistreated by white people just like we were—the Mexican kids, you know."[44] Firsthand knowledge about the role of multiracial management in the valley and about the linkages between the varied struggles of the valley's working communities was not universal and did not guarantee an oppositional politics among farmworkers. It did, however, carry the potential to generate new forms of cross-racial solidarity and to encourage workers to breach the social divisions on which the agricultural market relied.

Overlapping Traditions of Political Struggle

Just as they were rooted in grassroots experiences of multiracial capitalist development in the Imperial Valley, the forms of multiracialism that crystallized among workers in the early Depression era were also shaped by overlapping traditions of political struggle that converged in the valley's fields. The same circuits of labor recruitment and migration that fueled economic development in the Imperial Valley also made the region a site of intercultural crossing and oppositional cultural formation. In this respect, the grassroots communities who contributed to the construction of oppositional multiracial solidarities, which in turn animated the strike waves of the 1930s, drew on a longer history of insurgency, one that stretched across generations as well as national borders.

The historical legacies of multiple revolutionary movements converged in the Imperial Valley's agricultural fields. For Mexican-origin communities in the region, the 1910 overthrow of Porfirio Díaz's dictatorship in Mexico was an active memory, either experienced firsthand or inherited through the stories of a parent generation. A significant number of local *mutualista* (mutual aid society) members were "formerly organized revolutionary activists on this side," as Benito Juárez Mutual Aid Society president Ben Saenz described it.[45] Many of these activists played a formative role in the Imperial Valley Workers' Union and drew on a rich history of organizing experience and anarchosyndicalist political traditions as they contributed to strikes in 1928, 1930, and thereafter.[46] In addition to these individuals with direct connections to the revolution, popular *corridos* (Mexican folk ballads) indicting class inequities and U.S. imperial incursions in Mexico proliferated in the region, reminding listeners about "La causa de la crisis / En la que atravieza nuestra bella nacion" (the cause of the crisis / that is sweeping our beautiful nation) and celebrating the heroism of revolutionary figures like Pancho Villa: "Aunque dicen que in Mexico se matan . . . nuestra bandera en sus manos flameara" (Although they say that he was killed in Mexico, . . . in his hands our flag still waves).[47] Such ballads helped to sustain affective links to the revolutionary struggle north of the border. They also aided the circulation of an oppositional body of grassroots knowledge about the Mexican revolution, U.S. imperialism, and racial capitalism.[48]

Local Filipinx communities had an analogous relationship to the revolutionary victory against Spanish colonialism in the Philippines and subsequent efforts to end U.S. domination on the islands. According to Philippines-born author and labor organizer Carlos Bulosan, "the revolutionary tradition of the Philippines is deeply rooted," such that it coursed through "the bloodstream of the people's cultural heritage."[49] Filipinx Californians sustained and adapted personal ties, kinship networks, and collective memories that stretched across the Pacific, connecting to grassroots struggles in the Philippines in ways that enabled the construction of transnational, anticolonial Filipinx American identities.[50] In addition to their connections to Philippine struggles for independence, Filipinx workers in Southern California also brought to the region the perspectives and organizing experience they had gathered elsewhere in the transpacific migratory circuit. Sociologist Moon-Kie Jung has shown how Filipinx, Japanese, and other racial groups who ultimately formed the International Longshoremen's and Warehousemen's Union in Hawai'i rearticulated racial and class divisions on the islands to build a political community that oriented labor struggles around a distinctive working-class interracialism.[51] Historian Rudy P. Guevarra Jr. has further illuminated how interethnic organizing in Hawaiʻi served as a template for Filipinx engaged in labor struggles in the Imperial Valley and throughout California. As Guevarra reveals, Filipinx migrants who came to California both as voluntary migrants and as exiled "agitators" were at the helm of cross-racial organizing efforts in the 1930s.[52]

Just as Mexican and Filipinx communities in the Imperial Valley had ties to historical revolutionary movements abroad, many African Americans who lived and worked in the area had grandparents who had helped bring an end to slavery and whose battles against Jim Crow in and beyond the Deep South continued into the late nineteenth and twentieth centuries. The historical emancipatory struggles of African Americans framed Black confrontations with racial segregation and violence in the Imperial Valley. Moreover, Black institutions such as churches, businesses, fraternal societies, and political organizations that emerged across Imperial and San Diego Counties during the 1920s—including a regional chapter of the Garveyite Universal Negro Improvement Association—both reflected and nurtured community ties, shared histories, and liberatory visions among them.[53]

For some workers, local traditions of radicalism and multiracial organizing within the Imperial Valley also figured prominently as features of a shared historical memory. As farmworker Frank Maneze recalled, "Before us, . . . the IWW [Industrial Workers of the World] had planted the seed, they did organizing around here. In fact, the IWW is the foundation of most of the organizations around here. It was the necessary forerunner to the CIO [Congress of Industrial Organizations] and started things that didn't necessarily die."[54] The IWW helped mobilize Imperial Valley workers' support for the Magonistas in 1911 as well as their participation in the transborder Mexicali-Imperial Valley agricultural strike in 1922.[55] By 1929, as a result of brutal suppression by agribusiness employers and their allies, according to contemporary writer Carey McWilliams, "the I.W.W. was merely a tradition in the labor movement" in the Imperial Valley and was, "for all practical purposes, defunct."[56] Despite the organization's fragmentation during the 1920s, the Wobblies demonstrated the necessity of multiracial unionism in the face of racial capitalist oppression and contributed to an undercurrent of oppositional multiracialism that continued to animate farmworkers' struggles into the 1930s.

The traditions of radicalism and multiracialism that converged in the Imperial Valley evoked different meanings and memories for everyone who identified with them, to be sure. They did not preordain a progressive or radical politics in the valley. Nor can they be taken to represent fixed or enclosed frameworks of past historical experience. Rather, they produced mutually impacting processes of self-definition and served as historical co-ordinates that located California agriculture's multiracial workforce within a longer genealogy of shared struggle.

Community Making in a Multiracial Landscape

While the forms of multiracialism that took hold in the 1930s Imperial Valley thus had deep historical and transnational roots, they were continually reshaped at the local level by the immediate circumstances of daily life. The everyday practices through which workers redefined community ties reconstituted notions of belonging and opened up new possibilities for the building of political solidarities.

Before the ascendance of a multiracial union movement in the valley and in California more broadly, the primary sites of agricultural working-class political organization were ethnically oriented unions and fraternal societies. In the Imperial Valley, local chapters of the Confederación de Uniones Obreras Mexicanas (Confederation of Mexican Labor Unions), the Mexican Agricultural Workers Union, the American Mexican Union, the Filipino Labor Union, the Filipino Labor Association, and the Filipino Labor Supply Association arose to serve the distinct needs of the ethnic Mexican and Filipinx communities.[57] These institutions emerged largely as a response to the differential nature of racialization and race management in California's fields.[58] They forged new channels of political cooperation between American-born and new immigrant workers, often across lines of skill, trade, language, and citizenship status. They modeled alternative notions of collectivity and social membership to those that dominated the labor market and, in the words of historian David G. Gutiérrez, represented the "manifestations of the first efforts at concerted collective action."[59]

Yet the ethnic orientation of early unions and fraternal organizations also lent itself in significant ways to the reinforcement of prevailing patterns of patriarchal racial competition among agricultural laborers. Most early unions and mutual aid societies reserved leadership positions for men and either explicitly or implicitly restricted membership to persons of a given ethnic ancestry. As El Centro resident and Benito Juárez member Juan Estrada asserted of the Mexican Agricultural Workers Union, which formed in Brawley amid the upsurge of the 1928 cantaloupe strike, "I don't think anybody wants Filipinos in the union."[60] As Estrada suggested, the organizers of the Agricultural Workers Union explicitly excluded Filipinx workers, whom they continued to regard as competitors rather than allies.[61] The organization also did not include Punjabi, Chinese, Japanese, or other non-Latinx workers.[62] These racial exclusions undoubtedly constrained the union's potential as a force for change in the local economy and may have accelerated the end of the cantaloupe strike that the union led in May 1928. Given the departure from established organizing traditions that the 1930 lettuce strike represented, we can reasonably speculate that the shift toward grassroots multiracialism was at least in part strategic, driven by practices of social and organizational learning that underscored the lessons of grassroots actions in 1928.

In addition to lessons learned in the course of earlier mobilizations, the solidarities at the center of the 1930 lettuce strike must also be considered an outgrowth of community-making practices that occurred beyond the front lines of industrial confrontation. Well before they appeared in the formal centers of grassroots organizing campaigns, expressions of interethnic and cross-racial collectivity occurred on the more informal political terrain of everyday cultural and social practice. In and beyond the fields, farmworkers forged networks of communication, kinship, and support that challenged the logic of racial competition and nurtured an ethos of reciprocity and collaboration. For instance, workers' ties across the different localities in which they lived and worked were the basis for a "grape-vine telegraph" that carried information about favorable and unfavorable places to work, as well as information about political efforts to unionize or strike.[63] Information sharing across different work sites facilitated navigation of the migratory circuit by alerting workers to conditions in different farms and towns, including relative degrees of racial hostility, access to public facilities, and proximity to family and kin.[64] Such networks also strengthened social ties between workers who were differently situated within the labor market. They nurtured a sense of mutuality and interdependence among dispersed and seemingly disparate populations and opened up new channels for community formation across spatial boundaries.

Beyond the fields, workers constructed spaces of home and community around social relationships that departed from growers' regulations. Against growers' pressures to settle in camps close to ranches where they could be kept under regular surveillance, some workers moved their settlements some distance away, to enhance their sense of autonomy. As Clovis laborer Mr. Martinez explained, "I prefer living here under the trees here than living out at the camps. We are our own masters here and have our own little things."[65] Despite the masculinist language that he employed, the spaces of home and community that Martinez described drew largely on ties and social networks that were fostered by farm working women. Historian Devra Anne Weber has highlighted the significance of women's informal networks in shaping farm working communities and social worlds. Women forged bonds around common concerns and practices of resource sharing that included not only sisters, mothers, aunts, and cousins but also women they met on different ranches. The forms of mutual support and friendship that they generated not only provided an important foundation for the making of grassroots identities and modes of collectivity but also served as a political resource and an informal organizational basis for mutual aid and labor organizations that ultimately emerged in California agriculture.[66]

Within farm labor camps, the informal networks that farmworkers built around basic elements of survival, such as shelter and food, functioned as spaces of sharing, cultural production, and dialogue. It was not uncommon for these networks to link workers across the lines of race, nationality, and gender that so deeply structured their experiences in the workplace and local society. For example, John Sánchez explained:

> We'd gather at different Mexican families in the evenings to eat. One day, one family would cook a big pot of beans and make a lot of tortillas, and we'd all gather at this one house: three, four, five, six families—and some of the colored families, black families, too, would gather there—and we'd eat all that food. And then, the next day, they have another food gathering at another place and the same thing would be over and over again. You know: making tortillas and beans and stuff like that—and that's the ways we kept from getting hungry.[67]

A sense of shared need and vulnerability functioned in many ways as an adhesive for grassroots communities in these spaces. According to Sánchez:

> Of course we didn't have anything—of course we didn't have doors to lock or anything—we just left our stuff like that opened as it was, you know. And there was many times we'd come back from work and we'd find a note on the stove and whoever it was: "Sorry we had to come into your house, but we was hungry and we just cooked a few little things to eat and we thank you."[68]

Discreet and indirect as they were, basic practices of trust and mutuality such as these countered the norms of race and labor competition that enabled racial capitalist agriculture to function. On the one hand, attention to the multiracial social ties that took shape in farm labor camps reveals that spaces of community were often more loosely guarded by authorities and frequently contained a wider range of possibilities for oppositional cultural formations. On the other hand, the boundaries between sites of work and sites of community—sites of labor and of leisure—were never concrete, and politics engaged within the camps carried the potential to reshape interactions in the fields.[69]

Within the camps, workers also sang, danced, and played music, forging ties out of shared challenges and values while learning about their differences and the particularities of each other's experiences.[70] Through oral traditions, folk tunes, and other modes of cultural production, farmworkers circulated a shared system of knowledge about the depredations and possibilities of life on California's farms. Often, such traditions captured experiences and modes of identification that were familiar and translatable across different immigrant working communities. For example, one corrido that circulated among Mexican-origin populations in the border region during this period sang about the evils of "unkind employers / who don't give their people / enough money to buy trousers." The ballad proceeded:

I'm not criticizing the country;
But I can certainly tell you
That many of the laborers
Are naked up to their navels.

The rich go in automobiles
A good horse and a good saddle
And the poor peones
Go digging wild radishes.

The peon is always stooping
Working at it so hard
That they always expect to see his head
When they look toward his feet.

They treat him like a slave,
Not like a useful helper
Who pours out for the rich
Up to the last drop of sweat.[71]

Songs such as this reflected and nurtured a collective critique of prevailing power arrangements while validating the grievances of many agricultural workers. The experience of exploitation and oppositional sentiment conveyed by the corrido would likely have been recognizable not only to ethnic Mexican workers but also to Filipinx and other non-White workers during the 1920s. Of course, later in the 1930s, when an influx of poor White midwesterners poured into the region in search of work, the songs they brought with them would pick up similar themes. For instance, one sang, "How in the world can a poor man eat? / Flour up high, cotton down low / How in the world can you raise the dough? / Clothes worn out, shoes run down / Old slouch hat with a hole in the crown / Back nearly broken, fingers all worn / Cotton going down to raise no more."[72]

The production and circulation of folk ballads and other cultural forms produced distinct forms of cultural dialogue among workers. The collective nature of folk music, a musical form that was by nature passed on across localities and generations, made it a particularly important transmitter of many of the complexities and nuances of grassroots experiences, anxieties, and aspirations, which were not as readily translatable through traditional modes of discourse or conventional spaces of social interaction.[73] As such ballads traveled with workers throughout the Imperial Valley and the broader Southwest, as they were sung and resung by workers in the fields and beyond them, they carried the potential to affirm the sorts of ethnicity-specific identities and divisions that structured the regional economy. At the same time, these cultural expressions also held out the possibility of nourishing multivalent identities that embraced both ethnic particularity and interethnic affinity.[74]

Beyond the camps and migration circuits, cross-racial affinities and relationships also developed in sections of local towns where farmworkers congregated during their time away from the fields. Often, workers gathered in places that were segregated or deemed peripheral to the town, where they could avoid regulations that aimed to prevent large assemblies of non-White residents. In Imperial Valley towns such as Brawley, Westmoreland, and Calexico, businesses owned by African American or Mexican American proprietors were generally regarded as friendly to working-class people of color. Brawley's G Street in particular had a reputation as a place where Mexican residents enjoyed "more liberties" than in other parts of town. Many people in surrounding White and middle-class neighborhoods condemned the district as a locus of vice, liquor, and "mujeres malas" ("bad women"), a site that nourished offensive behaviors and threatened the propriety of decent and upstanding citizenship. For the people who frequented the restaurants and pool halls that dotted G Street, however, these were vibrant sites of socialization, affiliation, and intimacy.[75]

Considering the wider range of spaces and practices through which Imperial Valley workers constructed notions of collectivity reveals that the emergence of multiracial organizing practices in the 1930s did not represent a sudden development or sharp departure from the longer history of local grassroots struggle. Rather, the forms of grassroots multiracialism that overtly threatened regional hierarchies and modes of production during the 1930s reflected a longer process of community building and rebuilding that characterized working-class life in a rapidly changing multiracial landscape.

Multiracialism and the Culture of Opposition

The wave of strikes that swept the state during the 1930s both embodied and energized grassroots notions of multiracialism that had begun to take hold among significant segments of agricultural workers during the preceding years. Convictions regarding the interdependence of the struggles of differently racialized populations led to transgressive forms of multiracial collaboration, including the construction of solidarities between different ethnic labor organizations and the ascendance of multiracial unionism. "In order to have an equal justice one must have equal power," one Filipinx newspaper proclaimed. "On that same principle, the Filipino workers as well as other workers must understand that the justice of their cause lies in UNITED EFFORT, equally powerful as their highly organized enemies, who, from time immortal, denied them their daily bread."[76] Translating grassroots knowledge about the relational character of grassroots struggles into a political strategy of multiracial direct action, one worker declared amid the Imperial Valley's pea strike in May 1934, "The Filipinos and Mexicans won't scab."[77]

The expressions of political unity and solidarity that animated the Depression-era strike actions should not be taken to represent a common identity or ideology, however. They did not resolve or transcend differences and tensions within the labor movement. Nor did they give rise to anything that resembled cultural uniformity. Rather, these mobilizations underscored the differentiated and interdependent character of grassroots struggles in the face of the dominant development patterns of racial capitalism. They included a broad-based movement of people as diverse as the transnational, multiracial workforce on which California agriculture relied. They also reflected the multiplicity of identities, influences, and agendas that such people maintained. At the center of the agendas advanced by these mobilizations were many traditional concerns that were vital to working people's efforts for increased autonomy, including wages, hours, and working conditions. At the same time, the rhetoric of the strikers often reflected a mixture of strategies and aspirations that combined calls for better wages, sick pay, unemployment insurance, and the abolition of child labor with symbolic references to the inspiration of Mexican and Filipinx revolutionary figures, articulations of demands for civil and human rights, and invocations of American democratic traditions and discourses of fair play.[78] In all cases, they struck at the core of agricultural development patterns that hinged on multiracial labor management, and they advanced understandings of grassroots multiracialism that underscored shared needs and vulnerabilities.

Beyond the Fields

In the spring of 1934, painter John Langley Howard put the finishing touches on a mural that he entitled *California Industrial Scenes*, which included a prominent panel depicting a multiracial mass of striking workers, marching together through an industrial agricultural landscape (figure 1.2). The image is a depiction of militant multiracial solidarity, with what appears to be a Latinx worker, a Black worker, and an Anglo worker at the helm of the march and in the foreground of the fresco. It makes clear reference to the agricultural labor movement that culminated in the months that preceded Howard's completion of the mural. Rather than appearing on the wall of a building in an Imperial Valley or San Joaquin Valley town as one might expect, however, Howard's mural was placed on an interior wall of the newly constructed Coit Tower, overlooking the city and port of San Francisco from the top of Telegraph Hill.[79]

Howard's mural was commissioned by representatives of District 15 of the Public Works of Art Project, a government program to employ artists that would later be succeeded by the Federal Art Project of the Works Progress Administration. Along with twenty-five other local artists and ten assistants in San Francisco, Howard was charged by local authorities with the task of producing a monument to the city's beauty and modernity in a project entitled "Aspects of California Life." For the project's commissioners, plans for the murals carried forth city leaders' attempts to reinscribe a narrative of social cohesion, order, and faith in urban progress in a period of social turmoil and political unrest. Yet, for many of the murals' painters, the project presented an opportunity to convey and support the expressions of political insurgency crystallizing at the grassroots. Rather than the picturesque cityscapes and landscapes that local project coordinators envisioned, they painted scenes that Bernard Zakheim, one of the leading

FIGURE 1.2 John Langley Howard, *California Industrial Scenes*, 1934. Public Works of Art Project fresco in Coit Tower, San Francisco.

artists and spokespersons for the project, described as "not so much historical as actual," inextricably linked with "what is happening right now in the United States."[80]

The painting of the murals had occurred simultaneously not only with California's agricultural strikes but also with mounting unrest among working and unemployed people in the city of San Francisco. The turmoil unfolded with particular intensity on the waterfront, where longshoremen, seamen, teamsters, and municipal workers walked out on their jobs on May 9, beginning a massive and extended strike that paralyzed the port of San Francisco and obliterated the farcical sense of order, stability, and social consensus that city leaders strove to cultivate. The relevance of Howard's rendering of the agricultural labor movement for the contemporary moment in San Francisco is indicative of critical continuities between the oppositional struggles that unfolded across the rural-urban divide.

"A Different Kind of Union"

The Politics of Solidarity
in the Big Strike of 1934

The summer of 1934 was a season of upheaval for San Francisco. As thousands of workers on local docks and ships walked off their jobs beginning on May 9 and vessels throughout the harbor came to a standstill, the Pacific coast's chief entrepôt became the epicenter of a massive coastwise strike that lasted eighty-three days, caused a breakdown in coastal and transoceanic commerce, and culminated in a citywide general strike in July.[1] It also inaugurated a system of worker control in the maritime and longshore industries that would endure for the following quarter century. On one level, the strike was a manifestation of the wider economic and social crisis that marked the contemporary moment. As an open and direct confrontation waged by waterfront workers and their allies against local employers and business leaders, the strike exposed the ruptures of prevailing patterns of economic development and undermined municipal efforts to cast the city as a well-ordered model of cosmopolitan modernity. At the same time, as it drew together overlapping networks of working-class communities, across craft lines as well as racial and ethnic divisions, the mobilization also marked new directions and experiments in the forging of grassroots solidarities.

For everyone involved, these were days of disorder, chaos, and conflict. Yet for the strike's participants and supporters, they also ushered in a palpable sense of political possibility. In the words of sailor and strike documentarian Mike Quin, "an almost carnival spirit" filled the streets of local working-class neighborhoods, where meetings, picket lines, and informal gatherings joined workers who were usually divided, workers who performed different jobs under different conditions and lived in different parts of the city.[2] According to Revels Cayton, an organizer within the segregated local of the Marine Cooks and Stewards Union and seasoned advocate of racial justice and Black equality, "We were a great crowd during [those] days," not only because of the sense of empowerment that accompanied standing up against their employers but also because "the union was afire and alive [with] great feeling[s] of brotherhood and camaraderie."[3]

San Francisco's "Big Strike" of 1934 offers a valuable window onto the ways people navigated and responded to the crisis of the Great Depression. Historical inquiry in recent decades has deepened our understanding of the strike's significance, especially regarding the role of grassroots radicalism in its making, as well as its impact on the trajectory of popular front politics.[4] The strike produced what has been heralded as "one of the most democratic labor unions in the country"—first the Pacific Coast Branch of the International Longshoremen's Association (ILA) and subsequently the International Longshoremen's and Warehousemen's Union. Together, San Francisco's waterfront labor movement and the organizations it generated modeled both rank-and-file empowerment and interracial unionism.[5] These developments have been held up as embodying the racially inclusive, social democratic impulse that dominates narratives of working-class politics in this era.[6]

That San Francisco provided the pulse for such an immense mobilization is no surprise. As a capital of global finance and commercial shipping, San Francisco was a critical juncture, and fault line, in the broader capitalist market economy. The city's development throughout the late nineteenth and early twentieth centuries focused overwhelmingly on facilitating the movement of goods and capital over land and sea, which made the work of moving cargo along the docks an especially crucial site for labor management as well as grassroots resistance.

While the location of the strike's nexus in San Francisco is thus relatively unsurprising, the formation of a broad-based, multiracial front in the city as a key source of the strike's political momentum remains a remarkable development that requires further examination. Of course, San Francisco was the main entry point for international migrants on the West Coast. It was also a highly spatially concentrated city. These factors combined to make the city a site of intercultural crossing for working people from across the

Americas and Pacific world. Yet the political coalescence of diverse Latinx, Filipinx, Black, Asian, and White ethnic populations within the city was far from an inevitable consequence of their coexistence. Indeed, San Francisco employers viewed the political potential of the city's multiracial workforce in quite the opposite light—that is, as a reliable source of working-class social division. Unlike in California's agricultural fields, where structures of domination relied more directly on the threat of physical violence, San Francisco's urban developers prided themselves on their ability to bring diverse cultural elements into the fold of an urban cosmopolitan model of racial capitalist modernity. Put another way, if California farmers pioneered multiracist patterns of labor management in the U.S. West, San Francisco employers and business leaders perfected these strategies and made them a cornerstone of their efforts for economic stability. In fact, the comparatively strong foothold that organized labor had in San Francisco relative to most other U.S. cities in the late nineteenth and early twentieth centuries can be seen, at least in part, as reflecting employers' willingness to grant some concessions to exclusionary White craft unions in order to minimize the potential impact of labor on the urban economy as a whole.

San Francisco's Big Strike of 1934 thus represented an extraordinary shift away from the historical conventions of organized labor and so presents a generative lens for examining the making of popular front solidarities. However, we still have a great deal to learn about why and how the interracial solidarities that distinguished San Francisco's waterfront labor movement were forged and negotiated on the ground, by the individuals and communities who composed the city's multiracial working class. How did San Francisco's aggrieved populations, especially its racially marginalized populations, navigate their relationship to the city's labor movement amid the upheaval of the 1930s? How did the strike figure into their lives and political imaginations? What might attention to the self-activity of these communities tell us about San Francisco's trade union movement, the racial politics of popular front coalitions, and the practice of solidarity more generally? In seeking answers to these questions, this chapter highlights the resonances and tensions that characterized relationships within and among San Francisco's working-class communities. It underscores how the strike was shaped as much by heterogeneity and contestation among workers as it was by collectivity. It illuminates how the strikers challenged normative codes of racial and gender relations at the same time that they advanced essentializing notions of working-class masculinity as a route toward industry-wide organization. Ultimately, this chapter reveals how those involved in San Francisco's Big

Strike constructed a multiracialist vision of political solidarity that linked people across racial, ethnic, national, gender, and craft lines, a vision that revolved less around a common identity or ideology than around a shared sense of vulnerability and shared desires for dignity.

Struggle and Community Formation in Early Twentieth-Century San Francisco

The affinities that animated San Francisco's waterfront trade union movement in the summer of 1934 were not entirely new. Rather, they had roots in a protracted history of struggle and in the dislocation, dispossession, and subordination that marked people's varied experiences of capitalist advancement in the region in the late nineteenth and early twentieth centuries. Deepening our understanding of the political solidarities that took shape on the waterfront and in the city in that moment thus requires that we situate the strike amid patterns of political and economic development and working-class community formation in the city during the years leading up to the strike.

By the early twentieth century, San Francisco had become a "world-class city" and a symbol of urban cultural modernity.[7] Local patterns of urban development had made the city a key nerve center in the global economy and U.S. imperial expansion since the 1870s. As the West Coast's chief port city and a major nexus of commerce, finance, and manufacturing, San Francisco provided an important lifeline for, and profited richly from, economic growth in California and the broader coastal region as well as colonial ventures beyond U.S. borders: from gold mining in the Klondike in the late 1890s, to the acquisition of Hawai'i and the Philippines in 1898–99, and the completion of the Panama Canal in 1914.[8] By 1925 the city itself produced nearly $530 million in manufactured goods per year, ranging from cigars and glass to textiles and ships. Its shipping and rail networks moved goods produced both locally and throughout California to the market, while at the same time giving Californians access to goods from across the hemisphere and the Pacific. In fact, by 1925 the total value of goods that moved through the port annually had grown to exceed $1.8 billion.[9] The city became an important base for multinational corporations like the United Fruit Company, which controlled vast expanses of territory across Latin America and operated its own "banana terminal" along Channel Street. Local financiers and merchants also fought hard to gain control over Central American coffee production. By the 1920s they had helped establish San Francisco as "the premier port of the world for Central American coffees." In turn, they deepened the dependency of Central American coffee growers on San Francisco economic interests.[10]

Visions of modernization that equated urban progress with expanded influence and industrial prosperity guided the main currents of the city's public culture and had visible manifestations in its evolving urban landscape. Along with its docks, factory buildings, and warehouses, the city's new skyscrapers, monuments, museums, and an opera house at the turn of the century dramatized its position on the world stage.[11] As reflected in the words of the locally based Bank of Italy president James Bacigalupi in 1923, the financiers and political architects of San Francisco's development often imagined the city as a "budding empire," a "great economic, social, and cultural area . . . which stretches [beyond the formal municipal boundaries] from the sun-scorched Tehachapi Mountains to the snow-capped peak of Mt. Shasta; from the sentinel Sierras to . . . an awakening Orient." If adequately nourished by a spirit of entrepreneurialism and properly managed to promote growth, Bacigalupi remarked, San Francisco had the potential to become a metropolis "as mighty, if not mightier, than the world has ever known."[12]

The outward thrust of city leaders' imperial ambitions, combined with the labor demands of industrialization within the city, helped to make San Francisco a key intersection for global circuits of working-class migration during the half century before the Great Depression.[13] San Francisco served as a primary point of entry for new immigrants to the United States throughout this era, and first- and second-generation immigrants continuously constituted the majority of its resident population, sometimes reaching as much as 70 percent.[14] The proportion of Chinese- and Japanese-origin residents remained relatively steady after the turn of the century as a result of exclusionary immigration laws that targeted those populations. In 1930 they collectively constituted about 2.6 percent of the city's population, or approximately 16,494 out of 634,394 total residents, according to the federal census.[15] They were joined by ever-growing numbers of newcomers from across the United States, southern and eastern Europe, and various sites throughout the Western Hemisphere and Pacific Rim during the first three decades of the twentieth century. While immigrants from Italy, Russia, Greece, Turkey, and the Balkans made up the bulk of San Francisco's foreign-born population between 1900 and 1920, these groups became the focus of anti-immigrant campaigns that led to the passage of the Johnson-Reed Act in 1924.[16] Around this same time, local employers seeking to fill low-skilled and low-wage positions especially in the city's maritime, service, canning, and fishing industries turned increasingly to African American, ethnic Mexican, and Filipinx workers. Each of these groups remained small in relation to the overall population of the city. However, all of them grew substantially in the years leading up to 1930.[17] For instance, the number of African American San Franciscans grew by 131 percent between 1910 and 1930, reaching 3,803 out of the city's 634,394 total population.[18] The city's Latin American population grew to between fifteen thousand and twenty thousand by the 1920s, with ethnic Mexicans making up the majority.[19] While it is difficult to assess the number of Filipinx in the city because of the character of census categories, the number of Filipinx arriving annually through the port of San Francisco expanded dramatically from less than seven hundred per year between 1920 and 1922 to nearly five thousand per year by the end of the decade.[20]

Because of the centrality of transoceanic trade and travel to the life of the city, jobs related to waterfront transportation constituted one of the most crucial sectors of the local workforce. According to the 1930 census, nearly 12,000 out of the city's workforce of 191,000 worked as longshoremen, sailors, or deckhands or in other trades directly related to water transportation. If teamsters, railroad workers, and other transportation and communication workers on whom seafaring commerce relied are included, the figure is closer to 35,000, nearly one-fifth of the city's workforce.[21] The majority of the waterfront workforce was foreign born. It was also internally racially divided.[22] While the city's non-White immigrants could be found in nearly all lines of waterfront work on the eve of the Great Depression, they were largely excluded from positions of authority and most heavily concentrated in what were deemed menial and service-oriented jobs. For example, while African Americans worked as seamen, longshoremen, and in a range of other positions, most of them served as cooks and stewards on ships. Filipinx workers were concentrated among the ranks of deckhands, while Mexican and other Latinx workers were represented most heavily among ship scalers.[23]

The overall numbers of non-White waterfront workers were relatively small. According to the 1930 census, there were just 28 Black workers and 67 workers of "other [non-White] races" among the 3,098 longshoremen and stevedores in San Francisco. Among the 7,727 sailors and deckhands in the city at the time, 73 were Black, and 1,241 were of "other [non-White] races."[24] Despite their small numbers, Black and other longshoremen of color "had a strong balancing lever on the waterfront," as one scholar put it.[25] Especially because they might serve as strikebreakers, racially marginalized workers could significantly impact the directions and outcomes of waterfront labor actions. Thus, employers sought to utilize these workers as a key arm of racial management, a means of maintaining and exploiting divisions among workers, especially through the use of racially differentiated wage scales.[26]

The selective and racialized hiring practices that characterized waterfront work reinforced a broader infrastructure of power relations that extended well beyond the workplace. At the same time that San Francisco's resident population was becoming increasingly heterogeneous, wealth, political power, and the capacity to speak on behalf of the general welfare of the city at large became increasingly concentrated in the hands of local captains of industry, finance, and commerce. Throughout the late nineteenth and early twentieth centuries, the city's business leaders had played an active role in shaping policy at local, state, and federal levels. They not only occupied public offices but also organized through a range of private and semipublic channels to represent their interests and to enact and oversee urban policy measures. They provided a dominant force in the coordination of activities in the fields of housing, education, and immigration and in the making of major water, power, transportation, and military base projects.[27] As it turned out, according to San Francisco historian William Issel, "the New Deal ... posed less of a threat than it might have [to the political influence of San Francisco business leaders] had business leaders not occupied such a secure place in the policy-making process by the beginning of the 1930s."[28] Viewing their private interests and civic responsibilities as fundamentally interconnected, San Francisco business leaders worked to foster urban-industrial advancement in the name of the public good. Their agenda was fueled in part by competition with rapidly growing cities in the East Bay, especially Oakland, and along the coast, from San Diego and Los Angeles to Seattle.[29] Yet many of them also recognized that San Francisco's potential to outpace its rivals hinged on their ability to maintain some semblance of civic unity and cooperation within a rapidly changing urban community. To this end, they promoted a spirit of civic nationalism that often ran at odds with the realities of the city's growing ethnic and cultural diversity.[30]

As in many cities across the United States during the 1910s and 1920s, the influx of new migrant groups raised anxieties among many San Franciscans regarding the sustainability of urban progress and the preservation of American institutions. The seeming unassimilability of "these chaotic elements," as San Francisco educator John Swett put it, threatened the sense of unity that city leaders strove to cultivate.[31] As the *San Francisco Chronicle* reported, "excessive immigration" of "morally and physically very undesirable persons," "stimulated by foreign steamship companies," was "straining our assimilating powers to a very dangerous degree."[32] At the same time that some waterfront employers feared that immigration restriction would disadvantage San Francisco by strangling commerce and countering the city's role as a port of entry for migrants, workers, and travelers, there was widespread concern that waves of non-White immigration especially from Latin America and across the Pacific would encourage "another race agitation on the pacific coast."[33] In the words of California governor Hiram Johnson in 1912, "If the immigration that is coming to us through the [Panama] Canal is permitted to congest in our cities . . . ultimately the conditions of awful poverty presented by our Eastern Cities will be reproduced in our centers of population in California." In Johnson's assessment, proper measures needed to be taken to determine "the best means for taking care of and distributing the immigration" and to prevent such conditions "from becoming a part of our social structure."[34]

In the city at large, racialized anxieties about the city's demographic changes derived not only from employers and elites who promoted exclusionary visions of urban progress but also from a local tradition of organized labor forged in the crucible of White supremacist and anti-immigrant politics.[35] To borrow historian Alexander Saxton's phrasing, hostility toward new immigrant populations had proven a "powerful organizing tool" for White workers and a "common ground" from which to negotiate with the city's progressive Republican political leadership.[36] The construction of the White workingman as the standard of working-class masculinity, and the White workingmen's brotherhood as the proper vehicle for working-class justice, established a dynamic in which efforts to improve the lot of labor tended to sharpen the exclusion of non-White and nonmale workers.[37] White unions played a decisive role in the making of exclusionary legislation targeting Chinese and subsequently Japanese populations. By the 1910s they had redirected their antagonism against newcomers from southern and eastern Europe and, increasingly during the 1920s, those from Latin America and the U.S. South.[38]

The racist attitudes that imbued the main channels of the local union movement did not reflect the views of all advocates of labor, however. San Francisco was a site of convergence for an array of progressive and radical political traditions during the late nineteenth and early twentieth centuries, from various branches of socialism and anarchism to ethnic-oriented progressivisms and racial internationalisms. Even though they did not dominate the dynamics or directions of working-class organization in the city during its early history, some of these currents presented significant challenges to the racial divisions and craft loyalties promoted by the market and mainstream unions. During the early 1920s, the Industrial Workers of the World, popularly known as the Wobblies, stood as one of the most powerful representatives of a burgeoning syndicalist tradition among workers on the waterfront. While the group fragmented under the pressure of fierce political repression, the Wobblies contributed to an undercurrent of radicalism and inclusionary unionism that was subsequently taken up by a growing local chapter of the Communist Party. As historian Bruce Nelson notes, like the Industrial Workers of the World, by the Depression era the Communist Party stood out as one of the only White-led organizations that exhibited a clear interest in organizing non-White and new immigrant workers.[39] Many former Wobblies found a natural home in the party.[40] Collectively, these overlapping organizational networks helped prepare for the type of insurgency that would crystallize on San Francisco's waterfront in 1934.

The transformation of San Francisco's population, the flowering of radical political currents, and reactions against both of these also reshaped the city's geography during the early twentieth century. Significantly, outside of Chinatown, patterns of residential segregation in San Francisco were looser and less rigid than in other major metropolitan regions in this era. Many of the racially restrictive statutes and housing covenants common in other cities were virtually absent from San Francisco.[41] Still, racial hostility and informal practices of housing discrimination pushed non-White San Franciscans into a disproportionate share of the city's substandard housing and encouraged the formation of ethnic enclaves. Along with racial tensions within the city more generally, patterns of racial concentration became more pronounced as the population became increasingly diverse during the 1920s.[42] During the 1930s, some African Americans could be found within every major residential district, but they overwhelmingly resided in clusters within the Western Addition, especially around the Fillmore district, and South of Market.[43] Latin American San Franciscans, too, lived all over the city, though their largest concentrations were in North Beach, surrounding our Lady of Guadalupe Catholic Church, and along the waterfront, especially in the South of Market area.[44] Japanese residents largely resided in the Western Addition and its Japantown neighborhood but could also be found in other parts of the city. A section of Kearny Street became Manilatown, home to several hundred Filipinx in the 1920s and 1930s, while other Filipinx San Franciscans moved into the Fillmore, Western Addition, and South of Market areas. The scattered ethnic communities reinforced a diversity of racial and cultural identities. Yet these enclaves' proximity to each other also meant these neighborhoods served as sites of interethnic encounter and interaction.[45]

On the one hand, the racial boundaries imposed by discriminatory real estate practices, economic competition, and norms of social propriety and racial deference deepened the marginalization of communities of color. In the words of Lora Toombs Scott, an African American resident of San Francisco's Western Addition during the 1930s, "We lived in a world apart." For Scott and many others, racial divisions were palpable not only in the city's geography but also in the social relationships that formed within it. As she put it, "When we had White friends, . . . they were either neighbors or storekeepers or people with whom we had done business. . . . We were friend-ly, not intimate."[46] As Edward Alley, another Western Addition resident, described it, "They [White San Franciscans] went one way and we went a different way."[47] Chinatown resident Edwin Low affirmed, "You associated with them [White people] but . . . you weren't connected with them." That social distance served as a continual reminder of the racial hierarchy in the city. In his words, "You knew your place . . . you know."[48]

Yet these communities were far from isolated. At times, patterns of racial concentration reinforced antagonisms between and among marginalized communities.[49] At other times, everyday practices of survival, struggle, and community formation brought communities of color into close relations with each other and fostered interdependency and collectivity among them. Non-White communities frequented many of the same restaurants, pool halls, and other establishments and entered into common networks of friendship and affiliation.[50] As African American San Franciscan Earl Watkins described, while most restaurants, hotels, roller-skating rinks, and other businesses in the Western Addition and Chinatown were segregated, "Japanese restaurants were open to you. . . . If you were a person of color, you couldn't rent," but "the Japanese would rent to you, they were our friends, Filipinos too. We would go to their pool halls and shoot pool as teenagers."[51] In some cases, non-White residents also spoke back against the exclusionary boundaries of local society in each other's defense. According to Edward Alley, "We got along great with the Japanese. The Japanese and the Negro got along great. I always had a good relationship. . . . A Japanese, if we were in a restaurant and a White fellow came and said he didn't allow Blacks to come in there and eat, the Japanese would say, 'If you don't like it we will go some place else to eat.'"[52]

Revels Cayton recalled the mutual support and cohabitation that took shape in the home of his friend and fellow labor activist Ben Fee. At a time when Cayton was living with Fee and his wife in their two-room apartment in Chinatown, he remembered that "at dinner time the place filled up with about nine guys, and then after they had dinner they all left. But around 11 o'clock the same nine guys came back and they all went to sleep there." According to Cayton, "This was the way they were getting by . . . you know saving money."[53] Beyond the economic benefits of shared housing, these forms of mutual reliance reflected ties of kinship and friendship, ties that had the capacity to become politicized. Cayton noted that following a later strike on the waterfront in 1936–37, Fee helped him craft a proposal to the Marine Cooks and Stewards Union challenging anti-Black discrimination in hiring by guaranteeing there would always be at least one Black patrolman in San Francisco and at least one in Seattle.[54]

As small or mundane as they may seem at a glance, the incipient forms of interracial collaboration that Watkins, Alley, and Cayton described signified a deeper dialectical process at work, resulting from the development patterns that had solidified San Francisco's position as an imperial metropolis by the late 1920s. The same shifting patterns of labor recruitment and employment that helped to produce a cheap, flexible, and divided workforce, and the same institutions of racial and class segregation that helped to preserve the city as a stronghold of White supremacy, generated new and otherwise unimaginable relations between people from across the globe—people who had roots in widely different geographies, nations, ethnicities, and cultural, intellectual, and political traditions. Although they were as likely to reinforce as to challenge the existing power relations, the intercolonial crossings that occurred in the city carried the potential to facilitate forms of transnational, multiracial political solidarity and resistance that linked opposition to local indignities with global experiences of displacement, dislocation, and dehumanization. By the eve of the Great Depression, the overlapping diasporas that helped to make San Francisco a key nerve center of the American imperium and the global market economy also made the city a critical node in global circulations of grassroots struggle.[55]

The Evolution of Intercommunity Relations in the Early Years of the Depression

The Great Depression deepened deprivation and poverty among all working-class San Franciscans, though its impact was neither homogeneous nor evenly distributed. The Depression fell hardest on populations who had long been marginalized from access to public resources and institutions.

Non-White San Franciscans were disproportionately represented among the ranks of the unemployed and the poor, and many confronted the additional threat of the era's repatriation drives.[56] At the same time, conditions that had previously been restricted to non-White and new immigrant groups were in part generalized onto wider circles of White San Franciscans. This relative democratization of suffering made possible a new sense of the relationships among workers and working-class communities and, for some, put into relief the striking parallels between their struggles. Within this context, and amid the broader political polarization that marked the early 1930s, working-class communities carved out new spaces in city streets, relief shelters, breadlines, and meeting halls, as well as local taverns and nightclubs, where they built dialogues about the travails of daily life and forged new interdependencies out of shared vulnerabilities.

San Franciscans' sense of their own local circumstances was informed by struggles that were occurring beyond the Bay Area. Many local working people had personal connections or familial ties to communities on strike in the agricultural fields and auto and textile plants, or to people engaged in battles across the continent and the globe. A significant proportion of the city's residents performed seasonal work in the fields and fisheries or had themselves been directly involved in contemporary struggles outside the city. They brought their experiences and stories with them as they engaged with local working people in a wide range of venues. Community newspapers regularly published articles about labor conflicts and movements occurring throughout California and across the country. Articles about California's agricultural strikes in particular were regular features in the local community press, as was the threat of repatriation drives.[57]

San Franciscans' sense of the interconnectivity between their various struggles took fuller shape as they established new social ties and engaged in new forms of dialogue. The trials of everyday life amid the Depression often drew people into contact with one another in new ways and within new social spaces. From breadlines and soup kitchens to homeless encampments, places for seeking relief, shelter, or work became sites of convergence, conversation, and new forms of social articulation.[58] Radical and left-leaning organizations, including activists with the local Communist Party, played no small part in creating such spaces and cultivating such convergences. For example, on November 6 and 7, 1931, San Francisco's local Unemployed Councils, affiliated with the Communist Party's Trade Union Unity League, held hearings in and around the city. While one purpose was to gather information about people's ground-level experiences to inform party strategy, the hearings created a unique space for political dialogue about the varied struggles of San Francisco residents. The discussions within them undoubtedly heightened attendees' awareness of their shared challenges and vulnerabilities, as well as the many differences among them. While personal experiences and testimonies varied with differences in age, gender, race and ethnicity, citizenship status, marital and familial status, educational background, work experience, and place of residence, sharing and hearing each other's experiences provided an opportunity to see how their stories fit together and to identify commonalities between their struggles.

Joblessness, hunger, undernourishment, and illness were common concerns and sources of misery among those who shared their testimonies before the Unemployed Councils.[59] Many who fell behind on bills and rent lost electric power or their homes altogether and experienced displacement and dislocation.[60] Poverty and transiency, in turn, made many into targets of police harassment and both legal and extralegal violence.[61] Discussions about these challenges affirmed people's awareness that their experiences were not anomalous or isolated. As Floyd Torrence noted about his experience as a husband and father of three who had been unemployed for six months and had seen his children go "without food for 18 hours straight," "We know there are lots of families in the same condition."[62]

At the same time that dialogues like those organized by the Unemployed Councils underscored certain similarities in the challenges people faced, they also urged an appreciation for the specific vulnerabilities of certain segments of the working-class population—especially those who could be categorized as non-White or noncitizen, as well as the very young and the very old. Non-White, immigrant, and elderly workers were often the first to lose their jobs and had the hardest time acquiring relief, owing in large part to discriminatory methods of relief distribution and, for some, the physical challenges of standing in line, whether for soup or a job, for lengthy periods of time.[63] In addition to the material deprivation caused by poverty, unemployment, and homelessness, nonnormative gender roles and behaviors, non-Whiteness, and noncitizenship subjected people to added social challenges. For example, a man noted as "P. Pauv," a Fillmore resident and janitor who had been unemployed for eight months, described himself as "among those men who have committed the crime to stay single" and, additionally, of being "foreign born." Pauv noted, "They let me into this country when they wanted people to work here. At the present time there is not work. . . . You have to work five or six days to get one day's work. And those one day jobs are getting scarcer and scarcer. The only solution for me this winter will be the slop line."[64] A Japanese worker who had been out of work for six months asserted that he was "living on what support friends are giving me. Can't get a job because I am a foreigner, and there is no place to get relief for workers like me either."[65] W. Williams, an African American worker who had been unemployed for eighteen months, explained that he had "worked for the city three weeks out of about 4 months on the bond issue. Been jobbing around and since house work is running out, selling soap. But everybody else is doing the same. . . . Now, I am not even existing—I am just here, getting by."[66] Joe Comme, a Filipino Western Addition resident who made batteries for a living and who had been unemployed for seven months, explained that he was "getting along on my savings, and taking a few chances on gambling."[67] Another man explained, "The only way I am getting by is my wife working. I am doing nothing."[68] Running throughout these participants' testimonies was a thread that linked their common deprivation with a shared sense of the tenuousness of their claims to normative concepts of masculinity. A level of economic stability was crucial not only to survival but also to the construction of an identity as a self-possessing masculine subject, and the desire to obtain this carried the potential to catalyze activism among male workers across racial and ethnic divisions.

Many of the hearings' participants complained about the limitations of existing unions and charitable organizations, pointing out that these groups were often insufficient to meet the grassroots needs they proposed to serve and sometimes reinforced existing inequalities by serving a few at the expense of the many.[69] Some men noted how unions, rather than assisting them in times of struggle, readily suspended their members when they could not afford to pay dues. Moreover, with respect to the conditions and suffering that rank-and-file workers experienced, "the AFL [American Federation of Labor] did nothing."[70] One worker, John Bonavito, who came to San Francisco from Pennsylvania's coal camps, recalled how the AFL leadership "tells us to go on strike—and after the strike they tell us to go on down and work under the same conditions as we had been striking 3–4 months to get away from."[71]

Recognizing commonalities between many of their struggles and the problems with existing institutions and organizations, some pressed the value of organizing collectively. Louis Truich, an ex-serviceman who knew he would not receive his bonus for several years, asserted, "Fellow workers I have come to the conclusion there is no chance for us any more except we got to organize—put our shoulder by the wheel and roll them out." As he explained, "We have everything in this world—lots of wealth, lots of food to eat—and we are all born into this world with a right to it—and we have got to fight for this right and get it into our own hands."[72] J. M. Hafner, a married man with one child, added, "One thing I cannot agree on, comrades—that there is no more work to do. I can not agree with that. I think the world never started yet. I think the work never really started. Our work is just beginning to start. We got to work damn hard to get started, but we will."[73]

The discussions and social networks that people were building throughout the city developed with particular intensity along the city's waterfront, the crux of the local economy and the site of some of the city's most miserable and dehumanizing patterns of labor. Seafaring and waterfront workers had been subject to historically brutal working and living conditions in and beyond San Francisco. Popular opinion of them as "misfits," "failures," and part of a "semi-underworld element" only reinforced their subordination to the rest of society.[74] The casualization of labor along the San Francisco waterfront worsened especially after the crushing of local strike actions in 1916 and 1919. During the 1920s, with the establishment of a company-controlled union, the Blue Book Union, employers acquired a whole new scale of power over workers. A shape-up system of hiring—a haphazard and unregulated system that required men to line up by the dozens in the hope of getting selected for an open position—deepened the insecurity of waterfront workers and encouraged ferocious competition. At the same time, speedups enhanced the demands placed on those who acquired work while enabling employers to avoid paying overtime. As a publication by the San Francisco local of the ILA later recounted, during the 1920s a system developed in which "a small minority of men were privileged to work themselves to death while a majority were reduced to the level of casual labor."[75]

The same kinds of conversations that took place in the Unemployed Councils' hearings occurred on ships and docks throughout the early 1930s. In 1932 a small mimeographed publication, *Waterfront Worker*, began circulating among longshore workers and provided a new channel for sharing ideas and visions of alternatives to the Blue Book union.[76] While the paper's origins are not entirely clear, most historians agree that it was started by a group of activists who were members of the Communist-affiliated Marine Workers Industrial Union (MWIU). Although the national Communist Party leadership claimed ownership and responsibility for the paper, it provided a platform for discussion about a host of issues confronting longshore workers and seamen and energized forms of activism that departed strikingly from the party line. For instance, at a time when national party leadership was encouraging longshore workers to join the MWIU, *Waterfront*

Worker endorsed a more open-ended struggle to crush the Blue Book union and create a "real union" from the ground up, one directly responsive to the needs and interests of workers themselves. "Such a union," the paper's editors stressed, "cannot be built from the outside. It must be built by us, the stevedores, right here on the docks."[77]

By the middle of 1933, longshore workers began to form a local chapter of the ILA, an AFL-affiliated union. At roughly the same time, the National Industrial Recovery Act's Section 7a went into effect, affirming workers' right to join any organization of their choosing and to bargain collectively with employers. The contemporaneity of these events has led some historians to treat the National Industrial Recovery Act as a cause or stimulant of working-class mobilization. However, Mike Quin, a participant in the 1934 strike, offers a more accurate analysis. As Quin explains, "Both the NRA and the organizational revolt of the longshoremen sprang from the same social causes, occurred simultaneously, and influenced each other."[78]

Waterfront employers responded to the formation of a local chapter of the ILA through a mixture of refusing to hire ILA members and subjecting them to targeted harassment and threats, which proved effective in preventing longshore workers from joining the union in large numbers early on. While a September 1933 ruling by the Regional Labor Board affirmed workers' right to join any organization of their choosing and opened the doors to expanding and strengthening the union movement, it did little to make employers amenable to these developments. Employers persisted in refusing to recognize or negotiate with the new union.

Meanwhile, tensions also escalated between the ILA's conservative district leadership and a local contingent of militants that had emerged as rank-and-file leaders among San Francisco's longshoremen. At the center of the group was the Australian-born longshoreman and organizer Harry Bridges, who would become the most recognized and celebrated figure in the 1934 strike. Bridges along with several others rejected the prevailing ILA leadership's accommodationist approach to bargaining with employers as well as the top-down manner in which the ILA made and implemented decisions without worker input. These militants, along with the writers behind *Waterfront Worker*, played a critical role in articulating an alternative vision of unionism and encouraging the wider pool of workers on the waterfront to remake the ILA according to their own needs and interests.[79]

In February 1934 longshore workers along the Pacific Coast held a coastwise rank-and-file convention to draft demands for a uniform West Coast agreement to present to employers. The convention took place in San Francisco with elected delegates representing fourteen thousand longshore workers in various ports along the coast. They demanded an hourly wage of one dollar, a thirty-hour workweek, a six-hour day, and a union-controlled hiring hall. The hiring hall, they acknowledged, was the crux without which the other demands were meaningless. As Regional Labor Board director George Creel, President Franklin Delano Roosevelt and a mediation board that he appointed, and also ILA leaders Joseph Ryan and William J. Lewis attempted to reach an agreement that would settle the conflict, frustrations mounted among the rank and file, as did their collective refusal to negotiate away their demands. When employers failed to accede to the demands of the rank and file by a May 7 deadline, longshore workers collectively called a strike that began on May 9.

Forging a Coalition and (Re)Defining Solidarity

While historical undercurrents of political radicalism, daily struggles and modes of survival, and early Depression-era crossings and convergences had helped to prepare fertile ground for new forms of solidarity, the formation of a broad, cross-craft, interethnic, multiracial popular front alliance among waterfront working communities in this period was not a given. Among a working population whose struggles were historically shaped by racial divisions and exclusionary notions of *herrenvolk* republicanism, the very meaning of collective struggle was deeply fraught.[80] The ILA itself was split on whether to include workers of color, and although some rank-and-file militants actively sought to recruit them, few non-White longshoremen joined the union before the walkout began.[81] Indeed, in the mobilization's early stages, there was little reason to expect that employers' classical tactic of exploiting racial tensions by hiring non-White strikebreakers would not succeed in keeping the workforce divided and promptly restoring productivity along the waterfront.[82] In the early hours of May 9, the same morning that longshore workers along the coast walked off their jobs and initiated the strike, a gang of Black and Filipinx longshore workers stationed on San Francisco's Pier 35 attempted to unload cargo from the ship the *Diana Dollar*. White strikers were quick to meet them on the scene, and a conflict erupted that quickly broke into violence. Not long after the clash was suppressed by police, another broke out on Main Street, where non-White workers were lining up to register as strikebreakers.[83] While the imperative to crush any obstacle to the strike's success provided the outward rationale for unionists' violence against the strikebreakers, these events also registered deep and persistent currents of racism and racial violence within the local labor movement. As these events illustrated to union organizers how racial antagonisms played into the hands of employers, they also provided what Communist Party California chair Sam Darcy cited as one of the early "lessons" of the strike movement.[84]

Following this initial series of confrontations with strikebreakers, ILA organizers attempted to win the support particularly of Black longshore workers and their communities, in a campaign that elicited a mixture of responses from those communities. While at least one gang of sixteen Black strikebreakers readily joined the strike, walking off the job with White long-shoremen on the spot, others in the community exhibited deeper reservations about doing so. For instance, as the local Black newspaper, the *Spokesman*, reported on the second day of the strike, when two representatives of the ILA approached a group of Black workers with a formal appeal to "refrain from seeking work" for the duration of the strike, their audience responded by "interrogat[ing]" the organizers, pressing them especially on the question of Black workers' position within the union in the aftermath of the strike. Seeking to ease the obvious skepticism of the crowd, the ILA representatives replied that those "who threw in [their] lot with the union would be recognized," and an "open policy" with respect to non-White workers would be adhered to.[85]

Whether they recognized that their position as a strategically important part of the union's political base gave them a degree of leverage in their relations with the ILA, or whether they simply wished to distance themselves from the antagonism with which the union had historically confronted them, Black longshore workers' initial reluctance or refusal to support the strike should not be viewed as strictly a product of employers' manipulation but as a politicized response to the long-standing hostility of organized labor toward their communities. Moreover, their actions affected the course of the movement and the meanings attached to its notions of collective struggle and workplace democracy. Ultimately, their actions urge us to view the ILA's adoption of a policy of racial inclusion not strictly as a measure handed down from union leadership but as one that was forged by pressure from the bottom up.[86]

As African American longshoremen pressed for a more inclusionary expression of unionism, ILA organizers redoubled their outreach to San Francisco's Black community. By May 16 the ILA began circulating a series of memoranda "TO ALL THE NEGRO PEOPLES OF THE BAY AREA REGION." Seeking to dispel the "rumors" that "Negro longshoremen are not allowed to join the International Longshoremen's Association," the notices insisted that "the ILA does accept Negroes as members . . . [and] is for the workers 100% regardless of race, creed, or color or nationality."[87] If such a declaration was not enough, the ILA sought to provide additional evidence of the union's commitment to racial justice. The group highlighted that, under pressure from San Francisco's rank-and-file militants, the twenty-seventh Annual ILA Convention had "adopted a resolution of protest against the frame-up of the 9 innocent Scottsboro Boys." Moreover, they emphasized, "5 colored brothers are members of the central strike committee [and] Negro longshoremen speak at all strike meetings."[88] As events unfolded, the ILA's outreach extended beyond letters and declarations toward more direct engagement and door-to-door recruitment. In fact, according to journalist Thomas C. Fleming, who wrote for the *Spokesman* at the time of the strike, Harry Bridges himself played a leading role in such efforts. According to Fleming, "Bridges went to black churches on both sides of San Francisco Bay and asked the ministers: could he say a few words during the Sunday services? He begged the congregation to join the strikers on the picket line, and promised that when the strike ended, blacks would work on every dock on the West Coast."[89] As ILA organizers' stated commitment to a policy of racial inclusion became a more central component of the union platform, the participation of local communities of color in strikebreaking activities declined significantly. At least one Black longshoreman actively helped to form antiscab committees. Very few San Francisco residents were reported to have taken work as strikebreakers after the strike's earliest days.[90]

While local longshoremen, strikebreakers, and potential strikebreakers redefined the contours of solidarity within the ILA, other waterfront workers, especially among the lower-skilled and racially marginalized ranks of seamen, seized the opportunity to advance their own struggles in the wake of the walkout. Within hours of the longshoremen's initiation of the strike on May 9, seamen "of all ratings" walked off the ships to join the picket lines.[91] They included a large proportion of ethnic Mexican, Latinx, Filipinx, Chinese, and Black deckhands, scalers, cooks, and stewards. Many among this diverse contingent were traditionally excluded from the AFL-affiliated International Seamen's Union (ISU) and had been a critical source of political energy within the local chapter of the Communist MWIU in the years before the strike. Significantly, the striking seamen were driven not only by their support for the longshoremen's battle but also by their recognition that the mobilization presented a "golden opportunity for seamen" to "strike for our own demands."[92] By the end of the strike's first day, the seamen set about

FIGURE 2.1 African American longshore worker under arrest during the waterfront strike in San Francisco, 1934. Courtesy of International Longshoremen's and Warehousemen's Union Archives.

organizing a mass strike conference for the evening of May 10. The meeting resulted in the formation of a United Front Strike Committee, a channel through which strikers aimed to build "ONE rank and file controlled UNION" for "all seamen"—"employed or unemployed," "on a ship or on the beach," "organized or unorganized, regardless of affiliation," and across lines of "race, political opinion, religion, or anything else."[93] Meeting participants also drafted their shared demands for a wage increase based on the 1929 scale, an increase in the number of watches on duty (to a total of three), the formation of a seamen-run shipping bureau, and use of a rotary system of hiring.[94]

In fusing their efforts for improved wages and work conditions with demands for rank-and-file control and inclusionary popular front unionism, San Francisco's striking seamen not only pushed back against the dehumanizing pressures of the commercial and labor market but also departed from the MWIU national leadership's policy of dual unionism and defied the limits of the ISU's organizational identity as a "White workingmen's brotherhood."[95] Through their efforts to build a trade union that joined the forces of "every seaman," the strikers claimed space for themselves in the central currents of the local labor movement.[96] In the process, they actively challenged the racial and gendered constraints that had historically anchored and nurtured that movement. Their actions offended the political and racial sensibilities of ISU organizers, who derided the MWIU activists as adherents of a "communist organization whose membership [is] largely Mexican and Filipino" and overwhelmingly made up of "SCALERS," not "bona fide seamen."[97]

Conservative unionists were not the only ones discontented by the actions of the multiracial rank and file. Some middle-class activists within communities of color saw little to be optimistic about in the mobilization unfolding on the waterfront. In view of the local labor movement's long history of racism, San Francisco journalist and *Spokesman* editor John Pittman observed that "the kind of labor represented by the striking longshoremen—union labor—never seems to need the loyalty of Aframerican workers until it calls a strike." He explained that, on the one hand, "the employers use him for a cat's paw, discarding him no sooner than he has done the dirty work of breaking the strike," and, on the other hand, "the unionists use him for a 'good thing,' c[h]asing him out of jobs which he has helped them win." Thus, Pittman believed that "union labor has kept as ruthless a heel on the Negro worker's throat as has the exploiting employer. And there is only a small sign that it is changing its tactics."[98]

While Pittman saw in the embedded racism of organized labor grounds for distrusting the current mobilization as fueled by forces "as ruthless" as waterfront employers, many of the people working on the waterfront took a different perspective. In fact, the relative genuineness of White workers' commitment to racial equality seems to have been less significant to working people of color than the perceived possibility for advancing their own struggles and enhancing their autonomy through their own self-activity. As Kenneth Finis explained, "This is one of the things that divide . . . the Black bourgeoisie from the labor movement, is that the people who have never held a union card are very quick to denounce the labor movement as racist."[99] While the solidarities that workers forged around the agenda of unionization neither transcended nor elided the internal racial contradictions of the labor movement, in identifying the movement as one that belonged to them, non-White workers helped to redefine its composition and political directions. Notably, Pittman himself would shift away from his misgivings about the ILA. By the end of the strike, Pittman not only supported it but also turned the *Spokesman* into an organ for the strikers' cause and lent its printing presses to the Communist paper *Western Worker*. Pittman himself would eventually join the party and serve as editor of *Western Worker* and its successor, *People's World*.[100]

Rather than accept the trade union movement as the exclusive domain of White men, as many union leaders had historically insisted, movement participants recognized it as a vehicle for their own needs and desires and claimed it as their own. The Filipinx section of the MWIU, which organized to address the particular concerns of Filipino seamen within the broader movement, asserted in a flyer the importance of Filipinx support for the longshore strike (see figure 2.2). As the group explained, "Any working-class Filipino, may he be seaman or stevedore, . . . whether belonging to the Union or not," should recognize that the strike was not only for the betterment of White workers; "it is also for our own good. . . . THEIR WELFARE IS OUR WELFARE!!! UNITE & FIGHT."[101]

The predominantly Mexican scalers' section of the MWIU also drew up its own demands—from a minimum wage, to overtime and holiday pay, to employer recognition of a democratically elected scalers' gang committee—to pursue alongside those of the broader seamen's and longshoremen's movements.[102] The sense of solidarity articulated through these assertions hinged less on a unified set of objectives than on a sense of shared vulnerability and mutual interdependence. As an African American representative of the East Bay chapter of the International Labor Defense (ILD) observed,

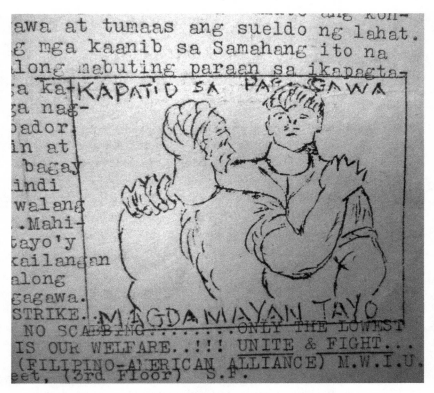

FIGURE 2.2 "Lahat Ng Marino Filipino"/"Brothers in Labor—Let's Support One Another." From a flyer for the Filipino-American Alliance, a subcommittee of the Marine Workers Industrial Union in San Francisco, 1934. San Francisco Waterfront Strikes Scrapbooks, 1934–1948, BANC MSS 2004/187 c, Bancroft Library, University of California, Berkeley.

"Many Negro workers are beginning to realize . . . that they can not better their conditions at the expense of the white workers, no more than the white workers can better their conditions at the expense of the Negroes."[103] All this contributed to a sense that, as an editor of the *Waterfront Worker* put it, "this is not a white man's strike, but a strike of all workers, regardless of race, color, creed, or nationality."[104]

These expressions of solidarity spread beyond the ranks of longshore workers and seamen, to workers throughout virtually all industries related to the waterfront. By May 13 San Francisco Teamsters joined the longshore workers and MWIU seamen on strike. The following day, Oakland Teamsters did the same, along with the Boilermakers and Machinists Union, who declared a boycott against all ships worked by scabs. Between May 15 and

May 16, strikes were declared by the Sailors' Union; the Marine Firemen, Oilers, Watertenders and Wipers; and the Marine Cooks and Stewards, all of which were affiliates of the ISU. At this point, the conservative ISU leadership had little choice but to declare a strike as well. The Ferryboatmen's Union; the Masters, Mates and Pilots; and the Marine Engineers Beneficial Association also began demanding pay increases and improvements without declaring a strike. Thus, by the middle of May, the vast majority of workers on the waterfront and related trades were on strike, advocating their own lists of demands as well as those of the longshore workers, and practically the entire port of San Francisco was tied up.

As the established AFL union leadership, employers, and government officials sought to settle the strike in its early stages by purporting to represent the best interests of the public—declaring that a speedy end to the strike was "in public interest" and vital to the maintenance of "industrial peace"— the strikers solidified and articulated their own vision of the political process.[105] As the ILA's Strike Bulletin put it, "Governor Merriam in his statement in the Sunday papers takes the position that 'THE STRIKE SHOULD BE SETTLED IN THE INTERESTS OF THE PEOPLE—and in the interests of the State of California.' This has always been the stand of the International Longshoremen's Association. . . . THE LONGSHOREMEN ARE THE PEOPLE. We certainly should be the ones to be considered."[106]

On May 19, in response to the latest effort by assistant secretary of labor Edward McGrady to achieve a settlement with employers without consulting the striking rank and file, the longshore workers passed what Mike Quin described as "the most important resolution of the strike" by a unanimous vote.[107] Specifically, they ruled that, first of all, any negotiation related to the strike must be referred back to the rank and file for approval and, second, that the longshoremen would not return to work until the seamen also achieved some settlement of their grievances. This resolution formalized longshore workers' shared vision for a political protest that was anchored in the priorities of rank-and-file power, democratic and inclusionary participation, and political solidarity across racial and craft lines.

As working-class San Franciscans redefined the bases of political solidarity on the waterfront, they challenged some of the basic structures of regional capitalist development and contributed to the formation of a wider culture of opposition. The waterfront strikers and their allies not only rendered inept the efforts of union leadership, employers, and government officials to represent the needs and interests of the working public but also confronted and challenged some of the cornerstones of established systems of rule, experimenting with alternatives to these. At perhaps the most foundational level, the assertions of power by waterfront workers eroded the legitimacy of prevailing channels of authority and representative leadership. When Joseph Ryan, the national leader of the ILA, arrived in San Francisco to try to negotiate a settlement with shipowners and employers, he, like McGrady and others, claimed to represent the longshoremen while dismissing their key demands for a union-controlled hiring hall and expressing apathy about a policy of closed-shop unionism. Rank-and-file workers were quick to speak for themselves and denounce Ryan as their supposed spokesperson. They not only printed articles in their papers about his efforts to sell them out but also held a mass meeting on the night of June 19 to address their problems with him and the question of how to proceed politically.[108]

As the fraudulent nature of those who attempted to represent the interests of the strikers became increasingly obvious, the established authorities' crisis of power intensified. Indeed, one measure of the waterfront mobilization's threat to the local power structure was the increasing reliance of city and business leadership on force and coercion to subdue it. On Memorial Day, in the wake of Ryan's failed attempt to end the strike, San Francisco's police department began to enforce a long-standing antipicketing law. Violence ensued as the police unleashed full force against a youth antifascist demonstration (a transgressive spin on the festivities that the city had planned for the day), injuring dozens of young protestors as well as innocent bystanders. The Memorial Day assault galvanized the public and intensified political divisions throughout the city. The day's events contributed to a fuller sense that, as 1934 strike veteran Blackie Soromengo described this historical moment, "no matter what direction you looked, there was a failure of leadership of all the nation's institutions. That went for the people who headed our unions as well as those in political parties and the government." There was an urgent need to build "a different kind of union" and to reenvision social and power relations more broadly.[109]

The failure of leadership that Soromengo described opened up space for grassroots communities throughout the city to define and pursue their own needs and desires. To this extent, the strike became a locus for conversations about the possibilities of social change and the future of social relations. By the time of the Memorial Day assault, the strike was occupying the headlines of all major newspapers and was a centerpiece of popular discussions across the Bay Area. According to Quin, "San Francisco was living and breathing strike. Everyone was discussing it. Everyone was trying to understand it. Everyone had something to say about it and something to ask about it. Homes, restaurants, and public places became virtual open forums, and people were rapidly taking sides. Bitter disagreements were splitting homes and friendships; at the same time new bonds of sympathy and common viewpoint were being forged—bringing people together, creating new ties."[110]

Working-class San Franciscans created the "new ties" and affinities that Quin described in part by refusing the categorizations ascribed to their communities, and the divisions promoted among their communities, by the nation's political institutions and labor market. Displacing the established imagery of the European American workingman as the embodiment of working-class dignity and rational political subjecthood, the articulations of solidarity that emanated from the waterfront strike cast the trade union movement as a people's movement in a much broader sense. The *Western Worker* lauded that "greetings of solidarity were given by Levino of the striking cooks, Ben Fee of the Chinese seamen, Paul Valdez of the Filipino Seamens Club, Fritz Deuer of the Typographical Union, and Elaine Black of the International labor defense." The same article announced, "Negro strikers were fighting side by side with the whites," and despite "the efforts of the capitalist press to split the workers on color lines . . . all colors are represented among them."[111] Similar declarations appeared throughout ILA and MWIU publications and urged, "Let's stick together. Black and White—Unite and fight. Nothing can defeat us."[112] These messages intended as much to reflect as to foster a sense of shared struggle across racial, ethnic, and craft lines and to encourage the idea that, as one writer for the ILA's Publicity Committee put it, "All nationalities were represented [in the strike], but this mixture of races had no effect on the solidarity of the strike," a fact that "surely explodes the old theory that the workers must be of one nationality to present a united front."[113]

As the strike carried on into early July, the city leaders and the Industrial Association grew more impatient. As they continued to blame the strike on "communist infiltration" of the workforce, they set about coordinating a campaign to open up the port by force. The Industrial Association sent a telegram to President Roosevelt warning that if a settlement did not bring an end to the strike in the next few days, "efforts will be made to start movement of cargoes to and from docks and it appears inevitable that an industrial conflict of character too serious to contemplate will be the outcome."[114]

On July 5 the Industrial Association began its campaign to open the port. As the onslaught unfolded, the police opened fire into a crowd of protestors, injuring many and killing two men, Nicholas Bordoi and Howard Sperry, in an event that became known as Bloody Thursday. In the aftermath of Bloody Thursday, thousands of people filed down Market Street in a funeral march commemorating the slain strikers and demonstrating their solidarity. Public support for the strike and opposition to the civic and industrial leadership culminated in a general strike that shut down the city for three days, from July 16 to 19.

"A Strike Is a Small Revolution"

In an oral history interview, Harry Bridges described what he saw as the revolutionary implications of the 1934 strike: "You see," Bridges explained, "in a small way, temporarily a strike is a small revolution." As Bridges put it, "A strike is a very serious thing. . . . It simply means a form of revolution because you take over an industry or a plant owned by the capitalists and temporarily you seize it. Temporarily you take it away. . . . That's another way of saying to an employer or an industry—in this case, we said it to the shipowners of the whole world—You might be worth millions or billions—we don't say you own this until we tell you to operate."[115] The strike, in other words, was a performance of working-class power that dramatized the vulnerability of reigning employers and city leaders as well as their dependence on working people. It was a reclamation of working-class dignity in the face of the dehumanizing forces that structured their lives. At the same time, as a performance of new kinds of solidarities and social relations, the strike also prefigured radical alternatives to prevailing social norms and hierarchies.

By the time the Longshoremen's Board handed down its arbitration award on October 12, granting longshore workers a six-hour day, ninety-five cents per hour, overtime pay, and a jointly run union hiring hall, the strikers and their allies had achieved most of the demands they had been striking for. The structural changes that the strike produced transformed patterns of work along the waterfront and gave rise to a rotation, or "low-man-out," system of hiring that displaced the notorious shape-up and helped equalize work opportunities in the years to come.[116] Beyond these important gains, the workers made what labor organizer and organic intellectual Stan Weir has described as "a successful bid for dignity."[117] In connecting their immediate grievances with management to a broader struggle for working-class autonomy and more participatory and democratic social relations, participants in San Francisco's waterfront union movement challenged conventional notions of working-class solidarity, which had tended to hinge on claims to Whiteness and masculine self-possession. Instead, they advanced an alternative expression of masculinity grounded in mutual interdependence and vulnerability. The strikers' construction of working-class manhood provided a basis for political collectivity among diverse working communities, even as it reinforced patriarchal gender politics and marginalized those who did not or could not fit within its bounds.

The increasing inclusiveness of labor politics amid the strike did not by any means resolve or transcend differences and tensions within the movement. The grounds of masculinity and productive labor on which the movement evolved carried their own inherent contradictions and exclusions, and the struggle against racist and anti-immigrant forces among workers was necessarily ongoing. Nor did the victories of the local confrontation suggest that similar achievements were imminent elsewhere. In fact, in many places, the strikes that erupted in agriculture and on the waterfront intensified concerns about the threat posed by grassroots insurgencies, accelerated efforts at political repression by authorities, and sharpened hostilities toward racial inclusion.

Beyond the workplace, efforts to subdue popular unrest increasingly recruited local, state, and federal arms of governance, including channels for making and enforcing policy. Across and beyond the state, officials leveraged policy to consolidate the boundaries of the national membership in California, to delimit the distribution of public resources and relief, and to restore the sorts of social divisions that workers were undermining. Such policies served as mechanisms of social management, especially by setting the terms of citizenship and the relationship of the government to the people. Yet the terms of order were neither firm nor fixed. These became key battlegrounds on which grassroots Californians waged their struggles for dignity. Shifting our gaze to examine working-class contestations over policy amid the Depression reminds us that the making of the region's oppositional culture was not just a story of industrial confrontation; it was also a battle over the nature and function of state power, over the relationship of the state to working people, and over the capacity of insubordinate communities to define their own terms of being and belonging.

Part II.

POLICY MAKING
FOR THE PEOPLE

3

Reimagining Citizenship in the Age of Expulsion

Growers and cotton pickers entered into a standoff at the camp that the strikers had built just outside of Corcoran in Kings County, California. The valley-wide work stoppage that began on October 4, 1933, had already halted the cotton harvest for several days, and the growers, ginners, financiers, and allied politicians who formed the upper echelons of California's agricultural power structure raced to restore production before the crop rotted in the fields. Within the camp, the workers held strong. They had set up their tent city on a four-acre plot that a local small farmer had opened up to them. At first, the camp served as a refuge for workers who had been driven out of company housing by growers and who had nowhere else to turn. Within a week, 3,500 workers resided within its barbed-wire perimeter, and they turned the parcel into an organizing base for fellow strikers and their allies in the Cannery and Agricultural Workers Industrial Union (CAWIU).[1] Reflecting organizing patterns that had become increasingly common across California since 1930, the residents of the camp were as diverse as the workforce from which they came. They were a cross-generational cohort. The vast majority were of Mexican descent, though a small remainder likely included Filipinx, African American, and Anglo-American workers, many of whom had migrated from the Midwest in the wake of the drought and Dust Bowl. Many were U.S. citizens. Many were not. Most of them performed migratory work, traveling to different parts of the state to labor on different farms and sometimes in factories, following seasonal demands. Together, the Corcoran encampment residents represented the multiracial, transnational, transitory, low-wage labor force that simultaneously formed the basis of California's industrial economy and the margins of American national identity.[2]

The agribusiness leaders struggling to contain the strike made the camp a target of their efforts. Recognizing Corcoran not only as a key focal point of the cotton industry but also as a critical nerve center for the labor movement, they saw dismantling the camp as a necessary step toward restoring their own authority across the valley. Forced evictions had driven defiant workers from growers' property, but now those workers had regrouped in larger numbers. Threats and sporadic violence contributed to a broader climate of intimidation but so far had not broken the strikers' resolve. Local forces of law and order determined that more "drastic action" was needed.[3] Farmers armed themselves. The sheriff deputized hundreds of local residents. As their various attempts to pressure the strikers back to their jobs failed, growers ramped up their campaign, requesting government assistance in driving them out of the country altogether. Cotton farmers wired the U.S. immigration commissioner in Washington to help break up the movement by "deport[ing] all those aliens" on the pickets and in the camps, targeting Mexicans especially as "public charges" and "menace[s] to peace and health."[4] Imagining that the threat of deportation might be enough to encourage workers back to their jobs, state labor commissioner Frank C. McDonald warned the Corcoran camp residents: "I will warrant that there is not one of you who wants to go back to Mexico!" he is reported to have hollered. The Mexican occupants of the camp retorted, however, "No, no, we all want to go back!" They informed the commissioner that a segment of those on strike had already telegraphed Mexican president Plutarco Elías Calles with a request for repatriation and were awaiting his reply.[5]

The workers' response likely confounded McDonald, who had intended his invocation of returning workers to Mexico as a threat rather than an offer. Indeed, McDonald's assertion reflected a broader set of exceptionalist assumptions that privileged American nationhood as superior and desirable vis-à-vis the rest of the Western Hemisphere, assumptions that not only reflected dominant attitudes in the United States at the time but also have continued to pervade popular discussions about immigrants and their histories since. The exchange also problematizes the narratives we have inherited about labor politics and culture during the 1930s more generally, which have largely revolved around tracing the emergence of a nationally oriented brand of working-class Americanism.[6] The political identities and aspirations of this particular group of workers do not fit neatly within such a paradigm. For them, leaving the United States for Mexico appears to have seemed less a fate to be dreaded than a viable and preferable alternative to life in California. The revelation of their exchange with McDonald thus raises critical questions about belonging and social membership among California's multiracial and international workforce during the age of immigrant expulsion. How are we to make sense of the Corcoran strikers' request for repatriation, and what does it mean for broader understandings of working-class politics in 1930s California? Can their response be understood thoroughly within a nationalist frame, either as a rejection of American patriotic sentiments or as an affirmation of Mexican ones, or did it reflect something else altogether? How did the experiences of these Mexican strikers relate to those of other ethnic Mexicans and the other marginalized working-class populations alongside whom they lived and labored? How did ethnically marginalized and immigrant working communities view their place in society at a time when the dominant political forces regarded them as alien, as threatening to the national polity, and even, in some cases, as expendable? What did social belonging and citizenship mean for them?

Beyond its implications for the cotton strike in 1933, the standoff between McDonald and the camp residents can be seen as a flash point within a larger battle over the contours and meanings of citizenship amid the Great Depression. Deepening economic devastation, intensified competition over resources, and the heightened political assertiveness of workers nationwide troubled many Americans' hopes of fostering stability and cultural cohesion within the nation. As in other industrial nations across the globe, these developments roused chauvinistic nationalist sentiments in the United States and fueled tendencies to blame the nation's troubles on immigrant and purportedly un-American populations.[7] In this context, the legal boundaries of American citizenship, the geopolitical borders of the nation-state, and policies governing migration and deportation became crucial political weapons for those seeking to address the broader crisis by managing the nation's political culture and composition. The preceding half century had invested the federal government with unprecedented authority over matters of immigration and citizenship and produced historic legislation for immigration restriction and border enforcement.[8] Depression-era efforts to shore up the country's borders even further brought the ascendant power of the federal government to bear along with that of state and local institutions, resulting in a sweeping campaign of immigrant expulsion. Enacted through both overtly coercive practices of deportation and purportedly voluntary repatriation projects, this campaign drove the removal of possibly millions of people from the United States to Mexico, the Philippines, and dozens of other countries during the 1930s.

The drives for immigrant removal contributed to a historic reversal in overall migration flows during the 1930s, when rates of out-migration from the United States exceeded immigration rates for the first time. Thousands of individuals were deported from the United States in this era, on charges ranging from unlawfully entering the United States to becoming a public charge, advocating the overthrow of government, carrying a contagious disease, or being a person of poor moral character.[9] Yet repatriation served as an even more common method of expulsion. Officially understood to indicate the voluntary departure of immigrant populations to their country of origin, repatriation entailed concerted drives to encourage, intimidate, and coerce hundreds of thousands of people to leave the United States during the 1930s. The bulk of these, perhaps around one million, were ethnic Mexicans, and most of them, approximately 60 percent, were in fact not immigrants but U.S. citizens. Over two thousand of those repatriated were Filipinx.[10]

California became a major theater of the Depression era's expulsion drives and a key site for contemporary contestations over the boundaries and contents of the nation. The state's role as a driver of international labor recruitment during the late nineteenth and early twentieth centuries had helped make it one of the most ethnically diverse states in the union and home to one of the largest concentrations of non-White and new immigrant populations. These same processes in turn made it an important testing ground for deportation and repatriation policies and a major locus for elaborating a multifaceted expulsion regime. At the same time, it was also one of the places where grassroots responses to Depression-era expulsions, and corresponding imaginings of citizenship and belonging, came most fully into view.

This chapter examines how racially marginalized, working-class Californians responded to the Depression era's deportation and repatriation campaigns in order to illuminate how these populations constructed notions of belonging and social membership for themselves amid the age of immigrant expulsion. It departs from the group-specific framework that has guided much of the literature on repatriation, which has tended to focus on ethnic Mexicans in relative isolation from other groups. Instead, this chapter assumes an analytic that is relational and multiracial, reflecting the social landscape in which repatriations were carried out and in which targeted populations lived and sought to procure their livelihoods. Correspondingly, this work situates repatriation's main targets—ethnic Mexicans and Filipinx—in relation to each other and in relation to other populations also impacted by the era's expulsion policies, albeit in ways that were often less obvious or less direct. As I consider the particularities and differences that distinguished these populations' repatriation-era experiences, I argue that they collectively contributed to a broader, multifaceted effort to reimagine social membership and belonging from the ground up. Marginalized Californians advanced expressions of belonging that were based more in local and transnational community networks than in the nation. They continued Reconstruction-era traditions of struggle for a fuller democratization of citizenship and for the expansion and enrichment of civil rights. Yet they combined these imperatives with transfigurative and transnational conceptualizations of social membership and justice. Their social visions embraced difference over conformity and relied on bottom-up political participation more than top-down administration. In the end, grassroots notions of transnational belonging underscored the primacy of dignity and autonomy, over and above national inclusion or any identitarian classification, within struggles against subordination.

Never the Citizen

In the midst of the cotton strike in October 1933, the threat of expulsion emerged as an expedient measure to counter workers' intransigency and pressure them back to the fields. Yet practices and policies that combined imperatives for political repression with ethnocentric aggression against purportedly un-American populations had a much longer history in the United States generally and in California specifically.[11] Anxieties about the presence of foreign nationals were integral to California's history as a global-economic engine and had accompanied immigrant labor recruitment in the state since at least the 1850s. Anti-immigrant movements in California played a vital role in the enactment of an array of racially restrictive policies within the state as well as landmark immigration restriction legislation at the federal level.[12] The consolidation of federal authority over immigration and citizenship during the late nineteenth century armed government officials with new legal tools for controlling the nation's borders and its composition, which included plenary power to exclude and expel unwanted populations. Throughout the early twentieth century, authorities experimented with these new powers, reaching beyond immigration restriction per se to elaborate restrictions on naturalization, denaturalize some U.S.-born citizens, and implement a variety of removal practices.[13] Following the end of World War I, Californians witnessed the increasing use of deportation as an instrument of criminal justice. They also experienced a campaign for Mexican repatriation during a brief but severe recession in 1920–21.[14] By the 1930s, such strategies had shifted from the margins to the mainstream of law enforcement, providing a means to systematically disrupt burgeoning social movements and to manage the size and composition of the state's labor base, unemployed populations, and relief recipients. Immigrant expulsion thus emerged as a mechanism for responding to the crisis of the Depression and shoring up the nation's boundaries by rooting out unwanted immigrant populations.

As California's unemployment rate skyrocketed to exceed that of the nation, and as the state became a hotbed of labor protest, the very populations that employers had recruited to fill low-wage industrial jobs throughout the early twentieth century became the subjects of emergent efforts at ethnic removal. As the largest source of recent population growth and the most readily deportable population owing to California's proximity to the U.S.-Mexico border, Mexican-origin populations became a major target of anti-immigrant hostilities and of the Depression-era expulsion campaign. Not just in California but nationwide, efforts to drive out Mexicans through raids, intimidation, and systematic deprivation became standard practice among both formal and informal channels of law enforcement. While it is impossible to know for certain, estimates suggest that Mexican-origin populations constituted 46.3 percent of those deported from the United States during the Depression despite being less than 1 percent of the nation's population.[15] The campaign had particularly devastating consequences for ethnic Mexicans in Los Angeles, home to the largest Mexican population outside of Mexico.[16] There, deportation raids "assumed the logistics of full-scale paramilitary operations" and resulted in the removal of up to one-third of the city's Mexican-origin residents.[17]

Although a focal point, Mexican-origin populations were not the only ones affected. Filipinx populations, who were a small proportion of the nation's population, had a visible-enough presence in California (over thirty thousand of the forty-five thousand Filipinx U.S. residents lived in California) to provoke widespread backlash and a concerted effort to secure their removal.[18] Attempts to halt the flow of immigrants from the Philippines and to deport or repatriate those residing in the United States intensified throughout the early 1930s. Yet the position of the Philippines as an unincorporated

U.S. territory and the status of Filipinx as U.S. nationals complicated these endeavors. Eventually, advocates of Filipinx exclusion began to see Philippine independence as a route toward reducing the presence of Filipinx within U.S. borders. In 1934 the exclusionary movement culminated in the passage of the Tydings-McDuffie Act, which promised eventual independence to the Philippines, reclassified Filipinx as aliens rather than U.S. nationals, established new immigration restrictions for Filipinx, and paved the way for the implementation of a Filipinx repatriation program the following year.[19]

The expulsion drives fused racist and nativist impulses with efforts to repress political subversion wherever it was believed to exist. Their contours and effects thus varied across different localities, depending on the nature of the perceived threats, revealing how expulsion functioned as a malleable instrument of social control with potentially devastating consequences for all who occupied precarious positions in U.S. society. As historian Kunal Parker underscores, the expulsion drives constructed as foreign not only immigrants "from elsewhere" but also marginalized groups within the United States, including those with access to formal citizenship.[20] In addition to Mexican and Filipinx populations, in different locales and moments, expulsion efforts also targeted Asians and Asian Americans, Latinx from across the Western Hemisphere, Russians, Germans, Italians, Spanish, and others deemed to threaten the security and stability of the U.S. polity and economy.[21] There is some indication that expulsion drives in some cities also targeted African Americans and diasporic Black populations. According to a report by the New York–based Labor Research Association, under the pretext of "investigating gambling and bootleg joints," in numerous cities outside the South "Negro men and women are herded into the police stations" by local police and immigration officials, much as other non-White communities were. "The illiterate ones are declared foreigners, and are held for deportation to the West Indies, Africa, or Latin America," the Labor Research Association observed. "Those who are unemployed are deported to the south, only to be declared 'vagrants' there and subsequently sentenced and hired out as convict labor."[22] While it is difficult to know how widespread the practice of expelling African Americans to the South and beyond actually was, the report makes clear that the precarity of African Americans' citizenship figured into the wider political thinking and discussions about the expulsion regime in this period.[23]

The expulsion campaign was multifaceted, not monolithic. It involved a diverse array of social actors, including not only immigration officials but also representatives at all levels of government, including sheriffs, deputies, and police, as well as private individuals, conservative labor unions, nativist groups, patriotic organizations, welfare agencies, and employers. Deportation served as one of its key methods of implementation. Yet the tedious and time-consuming legal protocols that formal deportation entailed made it far too inefficient to meet the ambitions and sense of urgency of expulsion advocates. For this reason, deportation became just one component of a wide-ranging effort to target unruly and undesirable populations, restrict their mobility, and promote their departure from the United States. This campaign ultimately relied not just on deportation but on a range of banishment and exile procedures, intimidation tactics, propaganda, restriction of welfare and relief, exclusionary practices, a broader climate of political and racial terror, and a far-reaching campaign of repatriation.[24]

For the populations subjected to these campaigns, the distinction between overtly coercive deportation and formally voluntary measures of removal could be significant: it could be a matter of life and death depending on the charges and the destination in a given case. The difference mattered greatly, for instance, to Greek laborer Peter Panagopolous and Japanese worker Taira Renji, both of whom faced deportation sentences in 1933 after being arrested for their involvement in labor organizing activities. As Panagopolous, Renji, and the International Labor Defense (ILD), which led the effort to defend them, recognized, being classified as politically subversive and deported to the authoritarian states of Greece and Japan, respectively, would likely result in their condemnation to lengthy prison sentences, if not death sentences, in their countries of origin. When the ILD proved unable to reverse the charges completely, the group focused on commuting their sentences from deportation to voluntary departure, allowing the defendants to leave the United States as migrants rather than as prisoners. This line of action continued to guide the work of ILD activists and others defending foreign-born, left-leaning, and labor-oriented political activists throughout the 1930s.[25]

At the level of formal policy, repatriation fell within the broader rubric of voluntary removal. Its officially voluntary character enabled authorities to skirt the time- and resource-consuming legal protocols that deportations required. Generally speaking, this made repatriation especially efficient for removing large numbers of people from the country. The particular contours of repatriation in practice shifted over the course of the Depression decade, however. Between 1929 and mid-1933, the Hoover administration sponsored a Mexican repatriation program that was unprecedented in scale at the time. Yet, as historian Marla Andrea Ramírez highlights, it was after that program came to an end under the Roosevelt administration in late

1933 that the campaign reached its most extensive and tragic proportions.[26] Municipal and state-level authorities continued efforts to expel populations they deemed troublesome however they saw fit, subjecting targeted populations to new levels of intimidation, harassment, and coercion. At the same time, repatriation programs frequently were cast as benevolent policies that benefited repatriated populations and generally had the support of the governments of receiving countries. In the case of Mexican repatriation, Mexican state officials advocated the value of returnees as potential contributors to the cultivation of the country's peripheral territories, which they argued might help to facilitate Mexican economic development while simultaneously securing Mexican control over regions coveted by U.S. corporations.[27] In the Philippines, the nationalist leadership supported the exclusionary policies aimed at Filipinx Americans, at least tacitly if not overtly, as part of the Faustian bargain of Philippine independence, even though some leaders would express concern about the aggressive way these policies were carried out.[28]

Despite the formal definitions and procedures that distinguished repatriation, deportation, and other policies of immigrant expulsion, for many of those targeted for removal from the United States, the commonalities were as significant as the differences. Observers and presses within California's ethnic communities frequently used the terms "deportation" and "repatriation" interchangeably.[29] Some even suggested that repatriation be considered "a new form of deportation."[30] From the vantage point of ethnic workers in California, the intricacies that differentiated repatriation from deportation in law often broke down in the on-the-ground application of these policies and in grassroots experiences of them. Analyzing the situation of ethnic Mexicans in the 1930s Southwest, Puerto Rican–born civil rights activist Isabel González challenged the mythology that all repatriations were voluntary. González charged that in practice "the term ['repatriation'] cover[ed] everything from voluntary departure to nocturnal kidnapping by immigration authorities."[31] In the context of the Depression, she highlighted, many of those "encouraged" to "repatriate" were given little to no choice in the matter. Local agencies often denied immigrants welfare relief, restricting the life chances of immigrant populations in the United States and pressuring them to leave the country. González highlighted that in California and elsewhere, "Mexican families on relief had no choice; either they agreed to repatriation, or were cut off the relief rolls" and left with few alternative means of survival.[32] Such practices were by no means applied to Mexicans alone. As Mexican repatriation entered its most expansive stage and initiatives to repatriate Filipinx gained momentum, the parallels caught the attention of some within Los Angeles's African American community. As the Los Angeles–based Black newspaper *California Eagle* charged in July 1933, American nativists were hard at work attempting "to do with the Filipinx just what they are doing with the Mexicans." For both groups, an *Eagle* editor wrote, repatriation proved to be "voluntary only up to a point" and was frequently "used as a club over their heads."[33]

Analyses that compared or conflated repatriation with deportation turned not only on the coercive dimensions of both policies in practice but also on the common purpose that appeared to lie behind them. It was clear to many in California that expulsion policies, however voluntary or coercive, were part of a coordinated government effort to address the present crisis through the management of troublesome populations and, by extension, the removal of expendable ones. According to the Los Angeles–based Spanish-language daily *La Opinión*, "The cause of voluntary repatriation and the cause of forced repatriation (deportation) is at bottom the same." In *La Opinión*'s analysis, "the scarcity of work in the United States" had raised anti-immigrant attitudes and bolstered efforts to "reduce to a minimum the possible number of immigrants" while "expel[ling] the greatest number of them." The subjects of these efforts, *La Opinión*'s writers emphasized, included not only those "who went on settling here illegally" or were charged with a particular crime but also those "who for other reasons" were simply "not welcome."[34] The "other reasons" for being unwelcome ranged widely. They encompassed a full spectrum of activities, behaviors, and characteristics that were deemed destructive or threatening. They sometimes had less to do with anything deportees and repatriates had done than with who they were or what they represented. As one writer for the *California Eagle* contended, such policies enforced "the point . . . that these people are inferiors and undesirables."[35] In other words, both deportation and repatriation constructed targeted populations as foreigners who existed outside dominant notions of American identity and were therefore marginal or expendable for the nation.[36] The policies functioned collectively as part of a broader strategy of social management, in what Carey McWilliams described as a larger "transition from sporadic vigilantism to controlled fascism, from the clumsy violence of drunken farmers to the calculated maneuvers of an economic-militaristic machine."[37]

As part of a broader campaign of political repression, the expulsion drives functioned to disrupt strike activities not only by detaining and removing strike organizers and activists but also by provoking divisions among working-class populations. Referencing the racial and national division that had historically riddled labor politics in California, the Committee for the Protection of Filipino Rights observed that the same policies that made Filipinx vulnerable to expulsion during the 1930s were "frequently used by anti-labor interests to drive a strike-breaking wedge into the ranks of unionism."[38] To be sure, explicit efforts by employers to hire immigrant workers as strikebreakers were just one way in which racial and national divisions were deployed to undermine the era's social movements. Historian David G. Gutiérrez has shown how the sharpening of anti-immigrant attitudes in the Depression era deepened divisions in ethnic Mexican communities, particularly over how to relate to new immigrant populations. As in the case of the influential civil rights organization the League of United Latin American Citizens, Gutiérrez highlights how pressures for cultural assimilation and immigrant exclusion, and the redoubling of efforts to block claims to U.S. citizenship, contributed to fracturing subordinated populations, helping to keep them divided and vulnerable.[39]

As powerful as the pressures of immigrant removal were in 1930s California, the threat of expulsion was sometimes as significant as the act of expulsion itself. Industrial leaders disagreed about how far the expulsions could go before hurting the regional economy. In fact, large-scale industrial employers spoke strongly in favor of limiting the use of deportation and repatriation, in order to maintain the cheap immigrant labor base on which they relied. Yet, even in places where employers fought to restrict the removal of Mexican and Filipinx workers, the broader climate created by the expulsion regime had important effects on workers and work conditions. After all, as Isabel González argued, "the real purpose of the deportation and 'repatriation'" was actually "not to fit the labor supply to the number of jobs, but to further intimidate, oppress and force the Mexican workers to accept an even lower standard of living and to be used in a competitive sense against the other workers in the area."[40] By deepening the vulnerability of ethnic Mexicans, Filipinx, and other racialized working populations, the Depression era's campaigns for immigrant removal helped to maintain their subordination, continue their exploitation, and ensure that they would be, to borrow the phrase of historian Mark Reisler, "always the laborer, never the citizen."[41]

Against Marginalization, toward Self-Definition

Just as the expulsion drives of the 1930s grew out of a wide-ranging effort to achieve social stability by managing the boundaries of citizenship and social membership, the targeted populations' responses to expulsion policies reflected their multifaceted attempts to secure a dignified sense of social belonging in the face of political and social institutions that marginalized them. Far from embodying a unified identity or agenda, the responses of working-class Californians to the expulsion drives of the 1930s were as varied as working-class Californians themselves. Some resented and resisted pressures to depart the country. Others—like the strikers featured at the opening of this chapter—welcomed repatriation as a means of escaping present strife and seeking a better life elsewhere. For many, including both those who departed and those who remained in the United States, the expulsions of the 1930s served as only the most recent reminder that a sense of belonging and dignity would ultimately not be handed down or guaranteed by the existing structures of national governance but would have to be created, struggled for, and sustained through their own self-activity. As wide-ranging as Californians' attitudes were on the subject of removal from the United States, they tended to share a common impulse—to push back against the restrictions that impinged on them, to expand the space they had to maneuver, and to rework prevailing channels of politics to serve their own needs and aspirations, to whatever extent they were able. Their struggles in the face of prevailing nationalisms expressed their political desires both below and above the level of the nation.

Not all the practices engaged by the populations targeted by expulsion measures fit the rubrics of agency and resistance often deployed in analyses of grassroots struggles. The political terrain these groups navigated was intensely fraught; the demands of survival varied, and pursuits of a dignified existence followed no uniform path. The conditions faced by targeted communities were not of their own design, and the political choices available to them were limited and often contradictory. Within this context, political actions required negotiation with a keen eye toward the risks and potential consequences involved. Yet, in the space between resistance and compliance, grassroots responses to expulsion revealed a wide field of activity through which people sought to refashion social and political arrangements, to exercise what autonomy they could, and to reclaim a sense of dignity and belonging that prevailing structures of national membership denied them.

Those who overtly resisted the pressures for expulsion did so at significant risk to themselves and their families. One of the more common practices by which people defied immigration and expulsion policies was by illicitly entering—or even, in defiance of deportation orders, reentering—the United States. While the drives for immigrant removal reduced the presence of targeted populations within the United States and contributed to a drastic reduction of immigration overall, they did not stop targeted populations from crossing the border on their own terms.[42] In fact, rather than halting unlawful border crossings, anti-immigrant measures prompted new methods for opposing immigration policies and evading border enforcement. Those who crossed the border without authorization at times sought to avoid capture by falsifying documents.[43] Others altered their appearance. One such migrant, Fausto Escalante, arrived in California from Mexico illegally in 1932, after having been deported on three prior occasions for illicit entry. He attempted to disguise himself and shaved his beard, hoping not to be recognized. Alas, in April 1934, after he was arrested for the fourth time on the same charge, the federal district court convicted and sentenced him to fifteen months in prison.[44]

While some risked imprisonment in their defiance of expulsion policies, others consciously chose to serve extended sentences behind bars to avoid being removed from the United States. As authorities relied on the state's penal system in their efforts to suppress mounting political unrest, California's incarcerated population quickly outgrew the holding capacity of its jails and prisons and sent public officials in search of new cost- and space-saving measures. Removing or expatriating prisoners—often by offering to commute their sentences if they agreed to "voluntary" departure from the United States—thus emerged as a practical and relatively inexpensive solution to the problem of jail and prison overpopulation.[45] For instance, during the fiscal year 1932/33, the Los Angeles County Jail estimated that deporting or repatriating its Mexican population alone would save approximately $2,552 per day. Countering such plans, however, some of the prisoners who received such offers declined them. Rejecting the offer of release-plus-repatriation was especially common among Filipinx prisoners, who recognized that their return to the Philippines would amount to permanent expulsion from the United States without the option of return. Between 1933 and 1935, San Quentin State Prison received numerous appeals from Filipinx prisoners who wished to serve their parole terms in California instead of in the Philippines. Prison administrators frequently denied their requests.[46] Those marked for expulsion who were "not amenable to deportation," as the prison records put it, sometimes opted to stay in prison past their eligibility for parole, some reportedly by two and a half years or more.[47] The choice of prison time versus repatriation required Filipinx and other foreign-born prisoners to weigh their present conditions behind bars against those they would encounter in their receiving countries. They had to balance immediate imperatives for release against the longer-term hopes and desires of their lives. As limited as their options may have been, refusing parole to avoid expulsion was a means by which people sought to determine the conditions of their own lives.

Some found ways to evade expulsion while en route to depart the country, often by fleeing the caravans and trains that carried them south.[48] Such actions may have reflected a change of heart among those who initially intended to make the journey to Mexico. For some, however, these were forthright acts of defiance against prevailing pressures to depart the United States, against the demands of the authorities who uprooted them from their communities, and against the oversight of the U.S. immigration inspectors whose duty it was to accompany them on the trains and buses and deliver them to Mexico. Escaping repatriates also risked punishment. Escapes became common enough that the officials administering repatriations had to adapt their practices to suppress the potential for rebellion in transit. For example, Los Angeles County officials designated a fleet of vehicles to travel alongside the repatriates and hired employees to check them in upon arrival at the border. Some trains carrying repatriates also began traveling directly to the Mexican border towns, removing stops on the U.S. side from their routes to reduce the possibility of escaping passengers.[49] These shifts in the daily functioning of repatriations revealed not only authorities' hopes that enhanced escort and surveillance activities would help ensure repatriates' departure and prevent their return but also the gaps in the power of the expulsion regime—gaps that the targeted ethnic populations utilized to their own ends.

Not everyone targeted by the expulsion sweeps was able to avoid removal from the United States. Nor did everyone involved necessarily wish to remain in the United States. Whatever their attitudes toward the expulsion regime and the exclusionary nationalist logic that underpinned it, many of the Californians targeted by expulsion policies saw in repatriation certain possibilities for enhancing their autonomy and advancing their aspirations beyond the constraints they faced in the United States. In this respect, for many of those who joined the exodus in this period, repatriation represented a viable, even preferable, alternative to life in California. This was as true for the Corcoran strikers highlighted earlier as it was for many others who understood the strains of subordination and the vicissitudes of life in the United States.

Historian Benny Andrés Jr. has helped to illuminate some of the ways in which ethnic Mexicans north of the border seized upon the channels made available to them by the U.S. and Mexican governments in the repatriation era in their efforts to improve the circumstances of their lives. As Andrés has shown, as early as 1930, the Mexican government began to receive a wave of letters from Mexican workers in California and elsewhere in the United States, expressing interest in repatriation and requesting assistance with the transition. The requests varied but typically included appeals for financial assistance with transportation and resettlement, land, and other resources to help them make a new start south of the border.[50] By the time California's agricultural strike wave reached its peak in 1933–34, as the backlash against labor organizing efforts reached new heights and as the Mexican government indicated its intentions to recruit repatriates to settle and develop the country's rural regions, the number of ethnic Mexicans in California seeking to take advantage of the opportunity rose exponentially.[51] By 1934 a report by a Brawley-based mutualista, the Mexican Social Welfare Committee, announced that a movement for "mass repatriation" was underway among campesinos in the Imperial Valley and that "similar groups with identical ideas were formed practically all over the State of California, particularly in Southern California."[52] According to historian Fernando Saúl Alanís Enciso, at least seven different Mexican-led organizations in California appealed to the Mexican government for support in coordinating the return migration of Mexican nationals during this period.[53]

Although their comparatively small numbers have contributed to their marginalization in the historical record, some Filipinx also saw repatriation as preferable to life in the United States. While the scarcity of sources makes it difficult to fully assess the Filipinx repatriates' desire to return, it is clear that the horrific levels of violence that confronted Filipinx in California, the promises attached to the prospect of Philippine independence, and a general yearning for home shaped their positions on the issue.[54] For some, repatriation offered an expedient escape from ongoing unemployment in the mainland United States or access to the support of family and kin on the islands. For others, the possibility of political inclusion and access to political participation in the Philippines figured prominently.[55] For example, Rudolph Arizibal, who was imprisoned in San Quentin between June 1931 and October 1934, expressed "ambitions to enter into a political career when he does return to the Philippines," which guided his efforts to navigate California's expulsion regime.[56] Indeed, such political aspirations would have been unattainable in California at the time, where he was regarded as a U.S. national rather than a citizen and then, after 1935, as an alien.

While Mexican and Filipinx populations were the main targets of repatriation drives, people of various other ethnic and racial backgrounds also sought to take advantage of the outflow of migrants from the United States to seek a better life elsewhere. In August 1930 one news source reported that hundreds of African American expatriates had unlawfully arrived in Mexico's Yucatán Peninsula. According to *La Opinión*, twenty of them were bound for Cuba, while most of them flooded into the fields of rural Mexico. Their presence roused concern among local Mexican residents and the Mexican government and prompted an effort to detain and deport them.[57] In addition to African Americans, the Mexican government reportedly received appeals from Russians, Slavs, Chinese, and Anglo-Americans in the United States who wished to emigrate to Mexico. As the Mexican government became overwhelmed by such requests, officials began ignoring altogether appeals for asylum from non-Mexican-origin populations in order to privilege those of Mexican descent.[58]

The enthusiasm and aspirations that California's ethnic Mexicans invested in repatriation found perhaps their fullest expression in the organizing efforts of the Vanguardia de Colonización Proletaria (Vanguard of Proletarian Colonization), which formed in Brawley in the aftermath of the 1930 lettuce strike. In the same moment that local farmworkers and U.S. Communist organizers collaborated to form the Agricultural Workers' Industrial League as a multiracial labor organization, the Vanguardia was organized by a collection of workers who became convinced that their needs would be better served by leaving the United States altogether. The Vanguardia not only proposed that emigration to Mexico was a viable route to expanding autonomy and dignity in the face of racial and class oppression but also advanced an agenda for channeling the repatriation process to serve "the agrarian work of the revolution."[59] While it is difficult to know how sizable the Vanguardia's following was, by April 1930, in an appeal to the Mexican government for financial assistance with its relocation plan, the organization reported that it had forty thousand members, including Mexican Americans as well as Mexican nationals. It also claimed to have raised $40,000 and projected raising a total of $12–$15 million within five months in order to implement its objectives.[60]

The hopes that many migrants attached to repatriation were bolstered further by the Mexican government's promises to lend support to those resettling south of the U.S.-Mexico border. In practice, however, the repatriates' expectations drastically exceeded the government's intentions. Although President Pascual Ortiz Rubio made overtures about facilitating the colonization of Baja California by making land available to return migrants beginning in 1930, a concrete plan never cohered under his administration.

When President Lázaro Cárdenas came to power in 1934, his administration developed a more thorough settlement program for specified areas of Baja California, the Yucatán Peninsula, and several states across the country. He initiated three major irrigation projects and in 1937 purchased the landholdings of the Colorado River Land Company to make the program a reality. However, many of those who sought to benefit from the project never received the funds or land that had been promised to them. Beyond this, repatriates faced a host of additional challenges, including difficulties accessing basic necessities, medical care, and jobs, as well as anti-immigrant hostilities not unlike those they had encountered in the United States. Their experiences illustrated Mexican policy makers' overall ambivalence toward welcoming back Mexican nationals from north of the border. Moreover, the disjuncture between these repatriates' hopes and the realities they encountered also reflected the distance between their own goals for repatriation (as a route to autonomy and empowerment) and the government's designs for repatriation (in service of nation building and industrialization).[61]

Thus, a sense of belonging did not wait readily in receiving countries for those who left the United States during this period. Rather, repatriates and deportees had no choice but to alleviate the strains of dislocation and sustain a sense of dignity through their own self-activity as they made their way from one system of oppression to another. Whether their migration was voluntary, forced, or some mixture of the two, the populations departing the United States during this period engaged a wide range of strategies for survival as they sought to make their lives livable amid deep uncertainty and rupture. In their efforts to endure the trauma of resettlement or, when possible, to take some amount of ownership over their journey, repatriates brought with them personal belongings that invoked feelings of security, preparedness, and home. The items they brought along on repatriation trains included pets, tools, plants, bedding, treasured mementos, musical instruments, and Singer sewing machines.[62] Some of the items represented migrants' hopes for carrying on a trade as they established themselves in a new land. Many also served as instruments for nurturing a sense of selfhood and belonging that had been denied them by prevailing institutions and the societies they moved between. More than artifacts of crass consumerist materialism, the goods that repatriates packed along on their journey functioned as palliatives in an experience that was in many other respects frightening and alienating.

In addition to the belongings they brought along, repatriates also found ways to forge social connections amid shared experiences of dislocation.

To be sure, trauma, turmoil, and grief defined the emotional dimensions of repatriation for many of those involved. Amid the woeful goodbyes and final pleas to stay, reports from the loading stations of repatriation caravans described the dispositions of the repatriates, ranging from those who looked "very quiet and pensive" to those who were outwardly sorrowful and crying.[63] The ordeal doubtlessly triggered a mixture of fear, anger, sadness, and helplessness, which those who boarded the caravans experienced and expressed in a variety of ways. For many, the coercive tactics that officials deployed and the pains of separation from family and home could indeed have had overwhelmingly isolating effects. At the same time, for some, the situation appears to have urged an outward reach for human connection. Observers' accounts tell of passengers wandering the trains in search of familiar faces. Young children reacted to the frightful scenario by "grasping each other's hands." Many appealed to a higher power, beseeching blessings and fellowship and offering prayers to the Virgen de Guadalupe. Such expressions fused repatriates' desperation and apprehensions with desires for communion and support. In these and myriad other practices that were recorded by observers—from making conversation to reciting poetry and other readings, to composing ballads and making music together, to serenading each other—repatriates leaned on each other in search of solace and coped together with their uprooting.[64] Through these practices that facilitated the exchange of stories, personal experiences, fears, and desires, the repatriates constructed a sense of community for themselves in the wake of their expulsion.

After their arrival, the repatriates worked to construct and sustain community and family ties and to counter the disruptive impact of the expulsions. As historian Romeo Guzmán has shown, through letter writing these transborder migrants sustained connections to their families and communities amid their experiences of dislocation and alienation. Through personal correspondence, those who repatriated or were deported nurtured a sense of transnational belonging that was not readily available to them in the places they settled.[65] Guzmán's work reveals how repatriates and their loved ones who remained in the United States wrote not just directly to each other across borders but also to the U.S. government and Mexican consuls, appealing for resources as well as assistance in reuniting with family members.[66] Nongovernment organizations, mutual aid societies, and newspapers also offered crucial support to these communities. For example, beginning in May 1933 and continuing throughout the 1930s, *La Opinión* maintained a specific column, "Respuestas desde México" ("Answers from Mexico"),

FIGURE 3.1 Mexican repatriates await a train to depart the United States at Central Station in downtown Los Angeles, March 8, 1932. Herald Examiner Collection/Los Angeles Public Library.

devoted to seeking answers to readers' questions regarding issues related to individuals in Mexico.[67] It appeared in the paper every Wednesday, and one of its primary functions was to locate and connect people presumed to be in Mexico with loved ones north of the border who were searching for them. Whether editors were able to provide a specific address or a town name or region, or whether it was impossible to locate the person sought, the column functioned as an important channel for salvaging personal connections in the wake of the era's expulsions.

Far from cohering around a singular, common response to the pressures for expulsion, the survival strategies and decision-making practices of people affected by the repatriation drives underscore the multifaceted character of grassroots identities, priorities, and aspirations. Their efforts to navigate the Depression era did not conform to prevailing paradigms of Americanism and were not reducible to a simple preference for one nation over another. In fact, to a significant extent, their struggles reveal the capacity of the nation to serve as a source of fragmentation as much as of unification. Rather than a unifying identity or nation-state loyalty, what linked their responses was a shared sense of vulnerability and a shared desire to maintain dignity in the face of prevailing patterns of racialized expulsion. Their struggles also collectively energized alternative ways of thinking about and organizing for social justice that departed from the dominant currents of labor and civil rights activism at the time.

Being and Belonging beyond the Nation

As the populations targeted by the era's repatriation and deportation campaigns sought to endure the hardships of the expulsion regime, their maneuverings also fueled modes of political analysis and organization that breached the limits of assimilationist efforts for national inclusion. Historical scholarship has widely highlighted how during the interwar era, citizenship, Americanization, and assimilation guided ethnic politics in the United States. There were practical reasons why this approach did indeed take hold within some communities. On one level, the legal infrastructure of citizenship, which crystallized in the late nineteenth century and expanded with the welfare state during the early twentieth century, both enabled and encouraged a citizenship-oriented politics while intensifying the stigmatization of noncitizen communities. On another level, many second- and third-generation immigrants who came of age during the interwar era, including those born on U.S. soil and those who had naturalized, found it strategically useful to make claims on the promises of citizenship in their efforts for civil rights reform, even if doing so required distancing themselves from recent immigrants and noncitizens. The intensification of anti-immigrant hostilities in the midst of the Great Depression confronted immigrant-descended communities with difficult decisions about their ethnic identities, social and cultural affiliations, and a pragmatic way forward, politically speaking. Some doubled down on an assimilationist and citizenship-driven politics, at times supporting the exigencies of the expulsion regime in hopes of safeguarding their own claims to citizenship. The League of United Latin American Citizens, Japanese American Citizens League, and Chinese American Citizens Alliance were just some of the most prominent organizations that pursued this line of civil rights advocacy in California during the 1930s, reflecting a broader impulse that historian James R. Barrett has described as "Americanization from the bottom up."[68] Yet these currents hardly represented the totality of grassroots ethnic and immigration-related politics.

For many foreign-born and ethnically marginalized Californians, especially those targeted by the era's repatriation drives, the transnational realities of life and the fragility of their own claims to national membership in the United States militated against a politics that privileged citizenship above other legal and political statuses. The strike that swept the San Joaquin Valley's cotton fields in 1933, mentioned at the opening of this chapter, is a case in point. In an era when many civil rights organizations and most labor unions barred recent immigrants and noncitizens from membership, the 1933 strike linked workers with widely varied identities, legal statuses, and relationships to American nationhood. Beyond treating noncitizen workers as constitutive players in the struggle for economic justice—and thus refusing the exclusionary boundaries of prevailing patterns of organizing—the strikers also made the rights of foreign-born workers central to their demands. In circulars among themselves and in appeals to employers and state officials, the strikers called for better wages, sick pay, Social Security, and an end to child labor, and they insisted that such rights belonged to all workers regardless of race, color, religion, or citizenship status.[69]

The 1933 cotton strike was not exceptional in this historical moment but was rather a key flash point within a wider surge of grassroots movements in which foreign-born workers and their rights figured prominently. The action had roots in a string of agricultural work stoppages that joined workers across lines of race, trade, nationality, and citizenship in and beyond California, stretching back to a lettuce strike in the Imperial Valley in January 1930 and forward to the organizing activities of the United Cannery, Agricultural, Packing, and Allied Workers of America, which formed as an agricultural arm of the Congress of Industrial Organizations (CIO) in 1937. Beyond agriculture, on the heels of the 1933 strike, the coastwise waterfront strike and San Francisco general strike in 1934 presented one of the era's most dramatic displays of multiracial and transnational industrial solidarity. While the battles waged by workers in each instance were shaped by the particularities of their respective local contexts, they commonly combined demands for livable wages and working conditions with an insistence that all strikers deserved the rights to presence, participation, and movement whatever their race, religion, or legal status. As they appealed to the state for vital legal protections and social welfare benefits, they resisted pressures to treat the existing boundaries of American nationhood and citizenship as the horizon of their political visions. Rather than binding workers' politics to a frame of Americanism, in other words, the major strike actions of this era expressed a politics that treated labor rights and immigrant rights as inextricable and that prioritized differentiated constructions of human dignity over bounded categories of nationality.[70]

Beyond the front lines of industrial confrontation, repatriation policies themselves became the subjects of political criticism and touchstones for the elaboration of alternative logics of social membership and justice. Advocates of immigrant rights in this period recognized the nuances and complexity of repatriating populations' decision-making practices and, accordingly, mobilized to enhance targeted communities' capacity to determine for themselves the course of their own lives. Rather than opposing repatriation outright, some activists focused on the top-down manner in which repatriation policies were carried out, as a managerial strategy that excluded the involvement, voices, or choices of the repatriated populations themselves. This approach found one of its most assertive articulations in the organizing efforts of El Congreso de Pueblos de Hablan Española (the Congress of Spanish-Speaking Peoples). Founded in 1938, El Congreso built on the legacies of multiracialist and internationalist strike actions earlier in the decade and drew directly on the Mexican American, Mexican national, and other Latinx activists who had been involved in CAWIU; the United Cannery, Agricultural, Packing, and Allied Workers of America; and affiliated labor organizations. The group elaborated its position on repatriation in a 1939 statement. According to El Congreso, the problem was not the abstract principle of facilitating Mexicans' removal from the United States to Mexico. Rather, it was that, in practice, repatriation "has been distorted by forces hostile to the interests of the Mexican and Spanish-American people in the United States, and . . . such distortion leads to abuses upon our people not familiar with this policy."[71] While denouncing the coercive character and destructive effects of the repatriation drives, Congreso activists neither assumed that all would prefer to remain in the United States nor condemned those who ultimately wished to depart the country. Rather than halt the exodus of Mexicans from the United States altogether, then, they resolved to "use every avenue of publicity to truly explain the Repatriation procedure and policy to its affiliated members and the public at large" and set up a bureau of information devoted to that purpose.[72] In doing so, they strove to support the targeted communities' efforts to make informed decisions for themselves and to navigate the expulsion regime in whatever ways best served them.

Empowerment, more than inclusion, defined not only El Congreso's response to repatriation but also its broader vision of social membership. To be sure, El Congreso became one of the era's most vocal advocates for the expansion and enrichment of citizenship as a route to procuring rights and affirming the humanity of all Latinx people. The organization modeled an ethic of organizing that refused the distinctions that mainstream organizations drew between U.S. citizens and the foreign-born and simultaneously argued for treating people's presence and labor within the U.S. economy as a basis for their membership and participation in the U.S. polity. As Guatemalan-born leader Luisa Moreno famously captured in a 1940 speech before the American Committee for the Protection of Foreign Born, "These people are not aliens." Moreno insisted with respect to Spanish-speaking people in the U.S. Southwest, "They have contributed their endurance, sacrifices, youth, and labor to the Southwest. Indirectly they have paid more taxes than all the stockholders of California's industrialized agriculture, the sugar beet companies, and the large cotton interests that operate or have operated with the labor of Mexican workers."[73] With Moreno, the activists and organizers of El Congreso insisted that the contributions of migrant noncitizen workers, rather than their cultural conformity, conferred on them the rights to participate and move freely within American society. They neither dismissed the social value of citizenship nor elevated it as a cure-all for the conditions of exploited workers. They refused migratory workers' marginalization from American society; further, rather than regarding migrants' assimilation as the hinge of inclusion and access to rights, Moreno and El Congreso insisted that the narrow definition of citizenship and rights arbitrated by the U.S. government needed to change.[74]

The labor and civil rights organizing taking place within ethnic Mexican communities in the shadow of the expulsion regime was part of a wider circulation of grassroots reimaginations of belonging and citizenship. Filipinx similarly criticized the repatriation process based on its denial of Filipinx dignity and its violation of the rights and respect they felt they deserved. One repatriate wrote to the Salinas newspaper *Philippines Mail* to warn readers that although repatriation was "supposed to be a Santa Claus gift to the Filipinos," in practice it entailed such "shabby, shameful, and most inhuman treatment" that it "reminds us of a CROCODILE's affection and caresses."[75] In the Stockton-based newspaper *Filipino Pioneer*, a local Filipinx wrote in, condemning the process by which repatriation was carried out and imagining an alternative ethic of rights and entitlement: "If the United States really want us to go home as repatriates, this free transportation is in no way called a favor because we have more than paid for it with our labor in this country—we must at least be given a decent treatment from the officials who are concerned."[76] Professions of benevolence meant nothing, in other words, without respect for the dignity of the Filipinx the policy purported to serve.

Efforts to organize on the basis of these criticisms and in pursuit of a more expansive, democratic vision of citizenship gave rise to the Committee for the Protection of Filipino Rights, which formed in San Francisco in the wake of the 1935 Filipino Repatriation Act. The committee condemned not only the treatment of repatriates under the program but also the program's destructive effects on Filipinx who remained in the United States. According to the committee's organizers, the paradoxical combination of Philippine independence, immigration restriction, and repatriation placed Filipinx Americans in an "anomalous status"; ultimately, the policies "deprived [them] both of the right of citizenship and the status of an alien" and effectively "den[ied] to these Filipino-Americans every vestige of the equal opportunity inherent in real democracy." Not unlike El Congreso, and in fact with El Congreso's express political support, the committee worked to advance the right of Filipinx immigrants to naturalize in the United States, without requiring a "declaration of intention and a certificate of arrival." For these activists, the right to naturalize was a means to attain "the right of franchise, [and] redress of grievances through the court," along with other civil rights that could defend against "the most ruthless and brutal economic exploitation" and the "indignities of segregation and discrimination in the routine, commonplace phases of everyday life" that Filipinx were forced to endure in the United States.[77] Their efforts for citizenship rights, in this respect, reflected more than a plea for inclusion; they set forth a social warrant insisting on the embrace of difference and the empowerment of aggrieved subjects to participate in the processes that impacted their lives.[78]

Significantly, the populations most explicitly targeted by repatriation policies were not the only ones engaged in critiquing them and advocating a broadened construction of civil and human rights in this period. As Los Angeles–based lawyer, writer, and Black newspaper editor Loren Miller underscored, Mexican and Filipinx repatriation had an important bearing on the lives of African Americans and all others struggling against racial subordination and exclusionary constructions of citizenship. He simultaneously compared Mexican, Filipinx, and African American experiences with each other and with those of Jews in Nazi Germany when he condemned the policy of repatriation as a "piece of Hitlerism" that was "about as fair as the 'equal accommodations' bills in the South." Miller asserted that Jim Crow laws directed at African Americans, as policies authorizing racialized discrimination and state violence, were "testimonies to the theory that the Negro is held to be an inferior as the Filipino [repatriation] resolution is a testimony to the 'inferiority' of Islanders."[79] Miller saw in these connections important insights for grassroots struggles and potential solidarities. He warned against the interethnic antagonisms and anti-immigrant hostilities that so often set racialized working populations against each other. He argued that "California Negroes can no more solve their unemployment problem by sending Filipinos back home than could New Jersey (which tried it) solve its problem by urging that Negroes be sent back to the south." Instead of attempting to conserve resources by reducing the relief costs devoted to purportedly unwanted immigrants, Miller proposed, it made more sense to support measures for wealth redistribution, alongside such programs as unemployment insurance, which would support all of those struggling economically within the state. Without casting such policy solutions as wholesale remedies for racial inequality or injustice, Miller proposed them as practical alternatives to repatriation, promising immediate material benefits for subordinated populations and simultaneously serving broader objectives of social justice.[80] Rather than tightening the restrictions of national membership to benefit some at the expense of others, such an approach was based on a more expansive vision of social belonging, participation, and rights that was interracial and transnational in nature.

For Miller, as for the activists of El Congreso and the Committee for the Protection of Filipino Rights, efforts to expel and repatriate Mexicans and Filipinx from California brought into relief the interconnections and interdependencies that linked the fates of oppressed communities within and beyond the United States. These activists collectively emphasized the necessity of a fuller democratization of citizenship, including widened access to state-backed legal protections, political participation, social welfare programs, and freedom of movement. Yet they did not treat the nation as the horizon of politics. In fact, in the arenas of everyday struggle as well as the realm of organized political activity, racially marginalized working-class communities fighting to survive and to preserve a sense of dignity amid the depredations of the era's expulsion campaigns generated notions of selfhood and belonging that were transnational in nature and multiracial in orientation. Their struggles contained possibilities for fusing struggles for civil and human rights, for democracy and global justice, marking a departure from mainstream assimilationist and anti-immigrant initiatives.

While these contestations occurred largely outside of official political channels, many people across California hoped that established channels might lead to a similar social transformation. The next chapter highlights how electoral politics became a key site of struggle for many working-class Californians during the Depression, presenting both possibilities and limitations for grassroots movements.

Radicalism at the
Ballot Box

4

As Edith Keyser, Ishmael P. Flory, Alfred Green, Leon H. Washington Jr., and Augustus F. Hawkins looked out on California's political scene from South Los Angeles in 1932, they saw an opening. The cohort had gotten to know one another during their college years at the University of California, Los Angeles (UCLA). Their shared concerns about the challenges facing South Los Angeles's Black community and their common frustrations with what they saw as the ineptitude of established leadership bonded them well past their time on campus.[1] Their affinities also energized a collective impulse to seek a new approach to politics—to redefine the relationship between Black Los Angeles and its elected leadership by diminishing the disconnect between the two and by creating an avenue to make government serve and respond to the will of the people, rather than the other way around.[2] Unknown among politicians and largely anonymous beyond their own friends and families, the group began attending gatherings in and around Central Avenue, speaking with people at the YMCA, the Elks Club, and elsewhere about utility rates, segregation practices, and a host of other issues affecting the daily lives of people in the community. They discussed the problems confronting South Los Angeles residents with local audiences and highlighted the political alignments behind the challenges at hand. "We found reception at some of these places," Hawkins recalled. "We would have individuals who would say, 'Let him speak, let him speak,' things like that." As they continued to expand these conversations, Hawkins noted, "we soon found converts" and noticed a growing number of people "who began to speak out as well."[3]

Sensing the momentum gathering at the grassroots, the group constructed a plan to unseat the Republican Fred Roberts, the incumbent State Assembly representative for California's Sixty-Second District and the state's first African American elected to public office, by running one of their own against him in the 1934 election. They decided together that Hawkins would make the best candidate for the position. They further agreed that their best route to victory was through the Democratic Party. The approach was an unlikely one for several reasons. To begin with, for an African American to run for office as a Democrat countered the tradition of Black loyalty to the party of Lincoln, which dated back to the Reconstruction era. That he was running against the only elected African American official in the state, moreover, also flew in the face of some political circles' attempts to pursue racial democracy by expanding Black political representation. Beyond this, from an institutional standpoint, the Democratic Party was far from a promising vehicle for electoral success. Despite widening support for the Democratic Party at the national level, which accompanied Roosevelt's rise to the presidency, California had been a "virtual one-party state" since the 1890s, with practically no substantive Democratic Party influence or following.[4] Yet, in choosing to use the Democratic Party to advance their political aims, Hawkins and his comrades were less preoccupied with the party's past than fueled by their own visions for its future. In it they saw a latent resource that could provide political access and material assets for disfranchised communities. Instead of focusing narrowly on increasing the number of Black representatives in government, they aimed to alter the process by which the Black community was represented and governed. As Hawkins put it, "We didn't have strong organization. In a sense, what we saw ourselves doing was taking over the group or organization, but we could not really build one ourselves. We didn't have the means of doing it."[5]

Their vision for taking over and transforming the local Democratic establishment resonated across the Sixty-Second District. Hawkins's campaign gained traction among White unionists, impoverished African Americans, the Sleeping Car Porters, Black college graduates, spiritual adherents of Los Angeles's budding Peace Mission Movement, co-op movement builders, Utopian Society members, and people who were active in an array of other multiracial and left-leaning coalitions. His diverse following propelled him to the Democratic nomination in the August 1934 primary and to victory in the general election that November.[6] Hawkins's election was not an anomaly but a bellwether of a larger political shift that was reshaping California's political landscape, transforming the role of the Democratic Party and pushing the New Deal to the left. During the same election cycle that saw Hawkins's rise to State Assembly, candidates across the state, similarly to the left of the political mainstream, surged into local and state-level positions as affiliates of the Democratic Party. In that same year, the lifelong socialist and muckraking author Upton Sinclair swept the Democratic gubernatorial primary with his campaign End Poverty in California, also on the Democratic ticket. Although he did not clinch the governorship in the general election, Sinclair's campaign roused the enthusiasm of a broad working-class constituency, unsettled the hold of established political leadership, and forced a response from advocates of social order from across the political spectrum. All in all, the election proved a key hinge in the transformation of California's Democratic Party from a party with 456,096 members in 1930 (in comparison to 1,638,575 Republicans statewide) to one with 2,419,629 members by 1940.[7]

Beyond its implications for the future of the Democratic Party and the New Deal in California, the 1934 election registered deeper processes of political negotiation among Californians. More specifically, the political realignments around the 1934 election reflected a reworking of basic expectations regarding the rights of citizens and the responsibilities of the state, adjusted in light of shifting perceptions concerning the limits and possibilities of politics in this historical moment. Just as Hawkins and his colleagues turned Los Angeles's wing of the Democratic Party into a vehicle for rechanneling resources and political influence toward their communities, the people who made up the broader electorate also recrafted their relationship to the state's political institutions, participating politically in new ways and actively helping to define the terms of citizenship, participation, and social membership. Reflecting on the changing relationship of working people in general and African Americans in particular to the Democratic Party during this period, Hawkins emphasized, "It wasn't that they became dyed-in-the-wool Democrats." Rather, he emphasized, it was "unemployment insurance and Social Security [and other] programs like that that attracted blacks."[8]

Rather than marking the limit of grassroots social visions, popular support for Democratic Party politicians and progressive policy measures registered that many Californians were maneuvering along routes of struggles with a longer endgame. Whether one considers Hawkins's agenda for "prosperity for the masses," Sinclair's "production for use," or Roosevelt's New Deal, the programs and policies that made the Democratic Party a magnet for popular support took into account grassroots demands for a fairer distribution of resources and for a social safety net capable of addressing the severest forms of material deprivation, promising conditions in which fuller democracy might be possible. None of these programs or policies—not even all of them together—ever reflected the sum total of grassroots political aspirations. They offered no guaranteed or unanimously supported definitions as to what democracy actually meant or how it would be experienced in practice; much less did they provide blueprints for implementing such concepts. Nonetheless, they had the potential to serve as points of convergence for a wider array of constituencies with a diverse range of political interests.[9] The electoral campaigns and initiatives of 1934 galvanized grassroots efforts to utilize electoral politics as a vehicle for their own struggles. They revealed the potential for electoral politics to serve as a site for contesting and redefining the terms of political participation, citizenship, and social membership. They also served as a means by which Californians recalibrated their relationship to the state during the Great Depression.

As the millions of people who gravitated into California's Democratic Party during the 1930s recognized, electoral politics was an important site for securing meaningful structural changes, with a direct bearing on the conditions of their lives. At the same time, it was also an inherently limited arena for oppositional political activity. Not only did electoral movements not reflect the totality of grassroots political aims, but, in fact, such movements in themselves could not have been wholly effective in achieving those aims. What gave the era's electoral movements their progressive political potential was their connection to grassroots struggles, their anchoring in the pulse and participation of the people. Yet this connection was fragile. It was vulnerable to disruption and dissociation. The institutional constraints of the electoral system, combined with the overwhelming influence of political groups that had historically dominated that system, militated against any sudden, thoroughgoing, or radical political change. Progressive campaigners in California faced external pressures not only from conservative Republicans seeking to defend the status quo but also from more moderate New Dealers representing the new mainstream of the national Democratic Party, who aimed to control the pace, directions, and extent of reform from the top down. As these forces escalated their efforts to guide electoral politics, political progressives experienced rising tensions between their own democratizing principles and the pragmatic necessity of obtaining votes.

By the end of the decade, New Deal moderates would overtake the insurgent left-progressive forces to become the dominant shapers of the Democratic Party. As a result, as many historians of the era have shown, the party itself would absorb radical elements and consolidate grassroots political energies around a corporatist, social democratic agenda. The party would help secure a New Deal order that contained both important gains and serious constraints for working people. The New Deal authorized and energized struggles for unionization. It also provided a structural foundation for a social safety net and a redistribution of wealth downward, making possible the growth of a sizable middle class in the decades to come. But it also created new challenges for the pursuit of multiracialist, internationalist, and surrealist social visions. It encouraged modes of corporatist negotiation that would politically distance union leadership from the rank-and-file workers. It also divided workers against each other by benefiting some at the expense of others, and it encouraged loyalty to the state over transborder affiliations and affinities. In the end, the Democratic Party in general and the New Deal in particular would militate against the broad, multifaceted coalitions and radical political imaginations that energized the party's ascendance in California in the first place.[10]

Yet in 1934 this future was neither foreseeable nor foreordained. Exploring how the Democratic Party emerged as a political force in 1930s California helps to illuminate how electoral politics could be a site of both possibility and contradiction, how it had the potential to open up some avenues for political engagement while constraining others. Electoral politics never encompassed the political hopes of grassroots Californians or promised a cure-all for their concerns and struggles. Yet, during the 1930s, Californians found formal political channels to be an important route for impacting the conditions of their lives, making claims on the societies in which they lived, and advancing their social visions.

State of Uncertainty, State of Possibility

In California the terrain of left politics had historically comprised a multitude of progressive forces, without a single dominant or unifying force. In this respect, the 1930s was no different. During the decade, the deepening polarization between reactionary and progressive forces, combined with the upsurge of grassroots energies making claims on the state, propelled a leftward shift of politics overall and remade the Democratic Party into a new, serious, and broadly influential political force.

Still, Californians' gravitation toward the Democratic Party was neither natural nor inevitable.

The roots of Republican dominance in the state ran deep. Even as the Great Depression reached its nadir in 1933, there was little reason to expect that to change. California had not had a Democratic governor since the turn of the twentieth century. It had not had a Democratic senator since World War I. As late as 1931, the state's eleven-member delegation to the House of Representatives included just one Democratic representative, while its State Assembly contained zero. Even as Roosevelt gained popularity during the 1932 presidential race, Republicans continued to dominate state-level politics.[11]

As Democratic Party registrations surged during the lead-up to Roosevelt's election, progressive political forces presenting alternatives to the two-party electoral system simultaneously proliferated. Labor and community organizations, civil and immigrants' rights groups, and local and regional affiliates of nationwide radical organizations like the Communist and Socialist Parties all grew in strength and influence alongside the party of Roosevelt. To these were added new upstarts. California saw the expansion of barter and cooperative movements that promoted a communalist ethos of self-help over more standard systems of charity or relief. A burgeoning technocratic movement advocated the liberating potential of technology as a route to more efficient production and more just distribution of resources. Utopian Societies sprouted up across the state, seeking to harness the productive capacities of industrialism for an inclusive, communitarian social vision. The Townsend movement advanced an old-age pension plan that fused imperatives for economic revival with social justice for the elderly. Meanwhile, a West Coast rendition of Father Divine's Peace Mission Movement combined goals of spiritual emancipation with moral living and cooperative economics. In these initiatives and others, California experienced not a consolidation but a multiplication of progressive political channels during the first two years of Roosevelt's presidency.[12]

Varied as these initiatives were, they shared some underlying impulses. On one level, the proliferation of progressivisms in early 1930s California reflected a widespread lack of confidence in the presiding political leadership's capacity to address the challenges many people faced. The hold of the state's economic elites over its political institutions and the generally hands-off approach of Governor James Rolph Jr.'s administration toward social problems gave many Californians little reason to view their government as a vehicle for redressing their grievances. Moreover, despite whatever enthusiasm existed for Roosevelt's administration at the national level, the early New Deal had only a limited impact in California. Californians felt the impact of FDR's administration mainly in the form of relief. However, even federal relief efforts were constrained, owing in part to the cultural stigma that accompanied the acceptance of government handouts but also to the direct monopolization of many relief agencies by elites seeking to minimize their impact.[13] At both the state and federal levels, then, government-led recovery efforts provided little recourse to struggling Californians, prompting many to seek out alternative routes to improve their circumstances.

On another level, in addition to a general lack of faith in existing leadership, the array of third-party and nonelectoral movements that took shape at this time also revealed a powerful participatory political ethos among many Californians. Rather than awaiting top-down answers from political leaders, these burgeoning movements across the state provided pathways for grassroots self-activity and for the building of political solutions from the bottom up. As diverse and seemingly disparate as they were, the unconventional political channels that Californians created during this period reflected a level of political energy, engagement, and common concern that carried a latent potential for integration and larger-scale mobilization. Once tapped, these forces could help remake California's political scene from the ground up.

If grassroots progressivisms helped set the stage for a wider political mobilization, the gubernatorial campaign led by the unorthodox candidate Upton Sinclair in 1934 provided the galvanizing spark. The earliest preparations for the 1934 state election might have seemed relatively unremarkable. Given the Republican stronghold within state-level politics, any serious contention in the campaign would typically have been among GOP candidates over the nomination in the primary, not between a Republican nominee and a challenger from another party. So it shocked the political scene when in September 1933 the renowned socialist and muckraking novelist announced his candidacy for governorship in California as a new registrant of the Democratic Party and quickly developed a following among voters.

With his End Poverty in California (EPIC) campaign, Sinclair laid out a bold political platform that aimed to abolish unemployment and redistribute wealth through a variety of economic measures. The plan included a system of state income and property taxes that targeted large corporations and utilities, along with a fifty-dollar-per-month pension for the elderly and the disabled. Its true hallmark and centerpiece, however, lay in its provisions for reorganizing the state's economy around the principles of what Sinclair called "production for use." Under this system, Sinclair envisioned that defunct farms and factories would be turned into cooperatives worked and run by the unemployed, providing their own subsistence and engaging in a system of exchange among cooperatives. In the immediate term, the EPIC plan provided a blueprint for delivering relief to the poor and jobless across California. In the long run, it could be seen as starting a larger shift away from a profit-driven economy of endless accumulation and wealth concentration, toward a state-run system of cooperative enterprise. Sinclair painted the future he envisioned in his pamphlet, *I, Governor of California, and How I Ended Poverty.* Writing from an imagined position in the aftermath of his term as governor, Sinclair depicted his expectation that EPIC would cause private industry "to crumble," much like "a swiftly flowing river eating into a sand bank. . . . And as quickly as any productive enterprise failed," he anticipated, it would be "made over into a public institution. Nothing could withstand the current of co-operation."[14] Sinclair's envisioned change, in other words, reached beyond palliative measures that might ease the burden of the Depression for the poor. According to Sinclair, what California needed and what EPIC promised was a more substantive transformation of the economy and its relationship to the state and its citizens.

Sinclair's EPIC plan combined initiatives for economic justice, a downward redistribution of wealth, and the empowerment of labor and the unemployed in ways that appealed broadly to struggling Californians. Hawkins recalled that the campaign garnered "a very strong economic base" because of its commitment to "fighting against monopolies and fighting against the exploitation of individuals based upon the fact that the prosperity should be spread around."[15] Yet the resonance among EPIC supporters went beyond the political outcomes promised by the plan. In centering the needs of the downtrodden and the impoverished and speaking directly to them, EPIC offered a platform for treating political engagement as a means to self-empowerment. Carey McWilliams captured it succinctly when he reflected on EPIC years later: "What Sinclair did—superbly—was to give victims of the Depression a feeling that they could do something about their miseries, and that they did not need to suffer in silence until the business cycle took an upward turn."[16]

Observers from both the right and the left during the 1930s, and historians for decades afterward, largely dismissed Sinclair's campaign as either the work of a crazed extremist or an expression of a disoriented, "broken down middle class."[17] In fact, Sinclair's EPIC garnered the support, enthusiasm, and political hopes of wide segments of working-class and lower-middle-class people across the state, proving to be a truly mass movement.[18]

The campaign was a participatory venture. It relied heavily and directly on the work of local-level volunteers, outside the official circles of EPIC leadership. Volunteers helped form over six hundred, and possibly as many as a thousand, EPIC clubs across the state during the election cycle. The clubs functioned as virtually autonomous, locally driven operations, with little more than a nominal relationship to EPIC headquarters in Los Angeles. Alongside them, EPIC-affiliated women's clubs, youth clubs, sports teams, drama groups, chorus lines, and film screenings also sprouted up to support the campaign from the grassroots. Volunteers circulated campaign literature and led unofficial advertising campaigns by hanging homemade window signs and painting EPIC slogans on rocks. They organized fundraising picnics, rummage sales, auctions, and barbecues, gathering donations of nickels and dimes.[19] They initiated voter registration drives, helping add hundreds of thousands of voters to the Democratic Party. In some contexts, volunteers undertook significant risks in carrying out their work. From a Los Angeles department store to the Imperial Valley's agricultural fields, workers hid their campaign activities from employers and local forces of law and order in an effort to evade retaliation.[20] The drive and resourcefulness of EPIC volunteers grew in part from their assessment of the high stakes of their political movement. At least as important, it reflected their sense of ownership over the campaign, along with their confidence in their own capacity to impact its outcomes.

The EPIC campaign's decentralized structure and reliance on grassroots energies distinguished it from most other electoral campaigns of its day. The difference was deliberate, based on political principles that prioritized the poor and the struggling over the already powerful and well-to-do. Campaign leaders acknowledged, "Money is needed to assure [the EPIC] program." However, they felt strongly that such funds could not properly come from sources who already possessed immense wealth and political influence. Instead, they insisted, "it must come from a great number of people giving small sums . . . from the great majority of people who will benefit by the operation of the EPIC Plan."[21] Activists with EPIC prided themselves that their main organ, EPIC News, was "a newspaper supported not by the bribes of plutocrats and monopolists, the gentlemen of the House of Have, but financed entirely by the subscription nickels, dimes, and dollars of its readers among the common people."[22] Such small-scale contributions along with the voluntary labor of EPIC supporters fueled the campaign. While other campaigns "hired precinct workers, campaign managers, and had very elaborate signs, literature, and stuff like that," Los Angeles–based lawyer and EPIC organizer

Robert Clifton affirmed that "there was very little money in the [EPIC] campaign. . . . If we wanted a sign, we made it ourselves or raised the money" for it. According to Clifton, it was as though "no one [in the EPIC movement] had ever heard of the idea of a paid campaign worker in the Sinclair organization." Instead, their "campaign was strictly 'from hunger.'"[23]

Between September 1933 and November 1934, the broad coalition of working-class and middle-class Californians who supported EPIC not only carried Sinclair into Democratic Party leadership in the state but also supported dozens of other EPIC-sponsored candidates running for positions at all levels of state and local government. These included many newcomers to campaign politics, which itself testified to the way in which EPIC offered a point of entry for people who might have otherwise remained alienated from the electoral realm. Some of those who cut their teeth in the EPIC campaign would subsequently become regular fixtures of the Democratic Party. They included journalist John Anson Ford, who ran for supervisor in District 3 of Los Angeles, along with high school teacher Lee Geyer of Gardena, whose campaign was managed by a saxophone player and fellow teacher, Ralph Dills. Also among the EPIC candidates was John B. Pelletier, a homeless man from skid row, who was recruited by Democratic lobbyist Artie Samish to run for State Assembly and proceeded to defeat his competitors for the nomination by a landslide. Meanwhile, Hawkins and his colleagues were pursuing their plans for seizing the reins of the Democratic Party in the Sixty-Second District and unseating Republican stalwart Fred Roberts.[24] More than an effort to elect an individual to the governorship, the EPIC movement sought to upend the state's conservative hegemony and to transform its political economy by securing authority across its governmental system. Sinclair himself conceded, "It would be a waste of my time and the people's votes to elect me Governor, and at the same time elect a Legislature which would not support the Plan, and to elect other State or County officials who would not work to carry out the Plan." For this reason, the goal of EPIC was not only to elect Sinclair but also to "make certain that the machinery of the [Democratic] party is turned in every district" to facilitate the implementation of the plan.[25] In principle at least, the election was a means to democratization rather than an end in itself.

For activist Florence McChesney, as for many others involved, the EPIC campaign stood out as "a real people's thing."[26] It was driven by, and aimed to serve, California's social majorities rather than an existing political elite or party machinery. Carey McWilliams dubbed it "perhaps, the outstanding example of a genuine grassroots political movement in recent history."[27] As effective as the campaign was in linking a popularly oriented and working-class-driven constituency, its political base was far from homogeneous, and its place within the political imaginations of its advocates was far from uniform. For this reason, its composition deserves fuller exploration.

EPIC's Constituency

The political alliance that formed the EPIC movement was extensive, diverse, and mass based, though it also proved to be delicate. People supported the campaign for widely different and sometimes contradictory reasons, and with varying levels of enthusiasm. The internal disagreements and differences that defined the campaign were pivotal to its political strength, even if they also made it vulnerable to fragmentation under pressure from both within and without. Examining the support base of EPIC in general and Sinclair in particular helps shed light on the contours of the movement, including points of resonance and tension.

Some unifying elements linked EPIC's most consistent constituency, especially in terms of geography and socioeconomic positioning. As historian James Gregory has shown in his study of EPIC's political anatomy, the campaign's strongest base of support came from urbanized working-class communities in Los Angeles County and the San Francisco Bay Area. The campaign drew some support from outside these metropolitan regions, though it was more scattered and limited. On the whole, EPIC voters tended to hold blue-collar jobs and to live in neighborhoods where housing costs were low. These included San Francisco's South of Market, Mission, Outer Mission, and Visitacion Valley; Alameda County's waterfront neighborhoods in Albany, Berkeley, and South Oakland; Los Angeles County's Boyle Heights, East Los Angeles, North Hollywood, and Burbank, as well as the industrial suburbs of South Gate, Torrance, Hawthorne, Huntington Park, Bell, Maywood, Compton, Signal Hill, and North Long Beach; and a few nonmetropolitan districts in Colton, Roseville, and Needles, as well as railroad towns and places where miners and timber workers struggled with high unemployment rates.[28]

The electorate backing EPIC in each of these regions was heterogeneous, and the support they lent to the campaign was more steadfast and widespread among some than others. The demographic most responsible for voting Sinclair into prominence was White working-class men. The EPIC movement drew expansive support from the new arrivals who were reshaping California's working class leading into the middle of the decade:

blue-collar workers from the Midwest and the South, mostly Protestant, mostly White, and mostly born in the United States. The campaign relied especially on the large proportion of these new migrants who lived and worked in Los Angeles County, where they constituted about 45 percent of the blue-collar male population.[29]

The strong resonance of EPIC among White midwesterners and southerners, and among White working-class men in general, might seem to suggest a generally left-wing orientation among this demographic. Indeed, in some places—in Arvin, California, for example—pockets of Okie migrants shared an inclination toward radical and left politics and supported left-of-mainstream Democratic candidates like Sinclair as a means of advancing a fuller set of progressive political aims.[30] For many others, however, the draw of EPIC had less to do with its radical potential than with its engagement of a populist discourse that more conservative White workers could identify with owing to their anti-elitist sensibilities and that did not preclude or disturb many of these workers' parallel commitments to antiunionism, nativism, racism, and patriarchal values.[31] While more radical EPIC supporters viewed Sinclair as a vehicle for transitioning away from capitalism, many others could support him because he spoke to their traditionalist values of self-help and engaged their language of plain-folk Americanism.[32] As historian Becky M. Nicolaides has shown, among many working-class voters in suburban neighborhoods like Southgate, the EPIC campaign lent political energy to an emergent strain of blue-collar conservatism that hinged on values of self-help, hard work, frugality, individualism, and the promise of private homeownership.[33] These individuals welcomed the turn toward a more activist government, as did much of the nation during the New Deal era, while maintaining a relatively conservative view as to who the proper beneficiaries of such a shift ought to be.[34] They could laud such measures as a graduated income tax, unemployment insurance, and the construction of a social safety net to the extent that these initiatives served those they deemed deserving, while at the same time harboring mixed feelings about "production for use" and distancing themselves from communism, socialism, and other radical movements that promised valuable resources to "undeserving" individuals.[35]

Many Protestants supported Sinclair despite an explicit and aggressive effort by Republicans to deter them. Conservative opponents worked hard to paint Sinclair as an antireligious extremist, for example, by broadcasting lines from his early writings in which he dubbed Christianity to be "one of the chief enemies of social progress." While such characterizations turned away some religious voters, others reasoned that the propaganda misrepresented him; that the statement was an artifact of the past, taken out of context; and that Sinclair had since changed his position and was perhaps even "sorry he wrote it."[36] One pro-Sinclair Protestant even offered the tongue-in-cheek proposition "that Mr. Sinclair's statement was a typographical error, that what he really wrote was that 'Frank Merriam is one of the chief enemies of Christianity.'"[37]

Recent immigrant White "ethnics"—many of whom were of Italian or Russian descent and of Catholic or Jewish faith—also demonstrated significant support for EPIC in 1934. They too, on the whole, resisted Republican efforts to steer off religious voters. For some believers, the affinity between the EPIC campaign and Judeo-Christian beliefs was irrefutable and provided a major reason to back Sinclair. Those campaigning for EPIC worked hard to promote this perspective. For example, in *The Catholic Plea*, an organ of California's progressive-leaning Catholic community, one writer stressed that the present "national crisis" took "local form . . . in the contest between Democrats and Republicans for control of California" and that, within that contest, Catholics "can fall back upon the teachings of the Holy Mother church for guidance." Treating Pope Pius XI's recent encyclical as a "yardstick" for Catholic principles and comparing it with Sinclair's EPIC program, the author highlighted their congruent critique of the limits of private property, shared emphasis on serving the common good, and similar valuation of the right to work and to a living wage. In short, the writer concluded, "it cannot be denied that [the EPIC campaign's] programs strikingly approach the just demands of Christian social reformers."[38] Another Catholic EPIC advocate, author and playwright Frank Scully, highlighted continuities from "the Sermon of the Mount . . . to Pope Pius XI's Encyclical of 1932 and Upton Sinclair's EPIC Plan of 1934." Scully wrote that each had "a similar basic point of view and develop[ed] a similar economic philosophy. In brief, they are pointing the same way and a vote for one is a vote for the other."[39] Certainly not all Catholic believers saw such a seamless connection between EPIC and religious doctrine. That Catholic and Jewish voters collectively leaned toward Sinclair might suggest that, for some, political and economic concerns outweighed religious ones. It may also indicate the consolidation of a working-class White racial identity over an ethnocultural and religious identity.[40] Most likely, Jewish and Catholic voters supported EPIC for a wide variety of reasons that reflected the diversity of the broader campaign.

Support for EPIC was less widespread and less consistent among those for whom the stresses of economic strife were inextricable from the stresses of racial and gender injustice. For instance, Sinclair received less support from women of all races, ethnicities, classes, and generations than he did from men.[41] The modestly lower numbers of female EPIC supporters might have indicated a more generalized gender gap in the political orientations of California voters. At the same time, they could also have signaled the influence of a common strain of progressive politics, not unique to Sinclair's campaign or to California's liberal-left movements, that treated economic injustice primarily as an affront to White manhood, potentially alienating many women voters.[42] For some women, the problem with Sinclair was not only the way he marginalized their personal needs and interests, subordinating them to those of men, but also the way his program appeared to threaten the sanctity of the domestic sphere and the stability of the heteronormative nuclear family more generally. For example, Eleanor Banning McFarland, who proudly identified as a "life-long Democrat," condemned Sinclair for his criticism of California's public school system, parent-teacher associations, and Boy Scouts, three "beloved institutions" that she regarded as vital to "the future status of California home life." According to McFarland, Sinclair's "vicious attack" on these institutions represented an "utter repudiation" of the "true ideals of democracy" and "should be the cause of burning indignation on the part of every mother of children in California."[43] For more conservative Democrats like McFarland, the problem with Sinclair was not his relative disregard for issues of gender equality or women's rights but rather the risk he appeared to pose to prevailing values of domesticity.

Although they never represented a majority of female voters, the women who did back EPIC played an important role in organizing for the campaign. The movement had a strong cohort of female political activists in its leadership, four of whom ran successful campaigns for congressional office in the 1934 election.[44] At the grassroots level, female organizers constructed forums for EPIC speakers and coordinated fundraising activities in support of the campaign. Their activism proved especially critical in politically and racially marginalized communities, areas that contained historically fewer registered voters compared to White communities, and where there was no preexisting base for the Democratic Party. For example, in September 1934 Los Angeles's Women's Democratic Club organized a banquet in support of Sinclair's EPIC campaign within the predominantly African American Central Avenue district. According to the local Black newspaper, the *Los Angeles Sentinel*, the event drew 250 people.[45] The organizers and attendees did not match the profile of the majority of Sinclair's supporters. Nor did they reflect the political preferences of women or communities of color writ large. Yet these individuals displayed a significant level of engagement and enthusiasm for EPIC's political potential and revealed its appeal beyond White masculinist currents in progressive-left circles.

While it is difficult to tell with certainty on the basis of available statistics, on the whole African Americans appear to have voted for Sinclair at rates comparable to the general electorate and to have favored the Republican candidate and incumbent Frank Merriam for governor overall.[46] The main base of Black support for EPIC was in Los Angeles, at the time home to just under fifty thousand African Americans. Of the thirteen census tracts where African Americans represented a demographic majority, Sinclair won in just three.[47] The reasons for this were many. In part, the limits of Black support for EPIC could be attributed to conservative and traditionalist sensibilities among African Americans. Many who had historically voted for the party of Lincoln maintained this loyalty into the 1930s.[48] Attitudes toward EPIC were likely also shaped by the channels of mobilization that African American communities had established outside of electoral politics, such as churches and community organizations; they trusted these and continued to lean on them in hard times rather than turning to elected leadership.[49] Still others opposed Sinclair out of a carefully considered skepticism about the racial implications of Sinclair's economically oriented program and the longer history of harm done by White labor and left circles to the Black community. Civil rights activist and *Los Angeles Sentinel* editor Leon Washington Jr., for example, warned African Americans not to be wooed by the "glib promises of the socialist Epic plan" or by any "professional politicians merely seeking our voting support" while offering little in return to the Black community. Voters too easily swayed by such "political parasites" risked driving African Americans "back where we were a century ago, in serfdom, practically in slavery." Washington argued that "from a purely selfish standpoint," that is, prioritizing the particular needs of Black Californians, "we should analyze which candidate for governor gives the best assurance of safety for those who now have jobs, and the best assurance of employment for those who are now unemployed," ultimately offering "the greatest assurance for the future welfare of the colored people in this state of California." For Washington, and for many other African American Californians, the most trusted candidate in this respect was Sinclair's Republican opponent.[50]

Sinclair himself made only minimal efforts to address the particular problems facing Black people in California, which did not help his reputation among African Americans. Beyond appealing to key leaders in Los Angeles's Black communities and hiring someone to coordinate outreach to Black voters, Sinclair did little to bridge the disconnect between African Americans and EPIC.[51] Just two weeks before the November 1934 general election, *Collier's* ran an article addressing Sinclair's persistent reticence on the race question. The author wrote, "Offhand it would seem that EPIC is made to order for Negroes. The majority of them are poor and jobless and EPIC is primarily designed to help the poor and jobless. . . . EPIC is for modern social legislation, and no group needs that more than the Negroes. But," the author asserted, "Sinclair is mum on the Negro."[52] For all the speeches that Sinclair had given concerning the detriments of the economy and the plight of the common person, and for all the books he had written on "almost every subject imaginable," the same writer observed, on the issue of problems facing African Americans, "Sinclair has said nothing at all."[53] For some, such silence translated into ineptitude on the subject of race relations, if not outright support for the racial status quo. Lawyer and *California Eagle* editor Loren Miller highlighted that "Sinclair has made few direct promises to Negroes. . . . Nor does Sinclair plan any sweeping reform of existing inequalities against Negroes." In fact, when Miller pressed Sinclair in a public forum on the question of whether he would support the abolition of anti-intermarriage laws and restrictive residential covenants, "his answer was 'no' based on his claim that he would have to stick to his Epic plan."[54] Sinclair's hesitation where race was concerned might have been strategic, part of an attempt to avoid alienating more conservative White voters, many of whom would have been turned off by a more assertive antiracist platform. It might also have reflected his own ignorance or a more deeply seated racism. Whatever the case may have been, his lack of clarity on the issue indicated to many the racial limits of his progressivism and likely played an important role in curbing enthusiasm for EPIC among Black Californians.

The support that Sinclair did have among Black voters came much less from his own outreach or from the organizing efforts of his official EPIC leadership than from the self-initiated activism of African Americans who promoted EPIC as a vehicle for Black struggles. The same calculus that Leon Washington suggested, of thinking "selfishly" in the interest of the Black community, led a good number of African American Californians to the opposite conclusion than the one he suggested—that is, to support rather than oppose the EPIC program. Community-based EPIC advocates used available channels and created new ones to promote EPIC's potential to advance African American interests. Black EPIC supporters took the stage in public forums, spoke up in organizational meetings, and utilized informal conversations with friends and neighbors to defend Sinclair from prevailing criticisms and make the case for voting for him.[55] Well-known and influential figures in the community also utilized their positions to advocate for EPIC. For example, countering conservative claims that Sinclair was a threat to Christian believers, Reverend H. E. Jones sought to reassure Black Angeleno church-goers that "Sinclair is a man of God, and a friend of man, and will sweep the colored Eastside on election day in spite of all that his opponents do to deceive and hoodwink the voters."[56] Prominent Los Angeles–based civil rights advocate William Pickens similarly hoped to drum up Black support for Sinclair when he issued a statement that "Colored citizens are faced by two alternatives. . . . To choose the heir and successor of James Ralph, Jr., or to choose Upton Sinclair, a stainless and incorruptible leader who is un-compromised by the exploiters of white and black people." Pickens added that "it will be a glorious achievement if Rolphism can be supplanted even for the next four years by Sinclairism" and, further, that "it will redound to the credit and respect of colored people if . . . their voting power contrib-uted to that achievement."[57] Other EPIC promoters in the African American community were more half-hearted, if still ultimately supportive of Sinclair's candidacy. For example, one reasoned in writing, "Although Sinclair has never said anything FOR the Negro, at the same time he has never been a Negrophobe. . . . In voting for him and his EPIC plan, Negroes will at least be going in the right direction."[58] Whether they cast him as a savior for the Black community or simply the lesser of two evils, self-initiated promoters of EPIC helped fill in the gaps left by Sinclair's silence on the race issue and, according to the *Sentinel*, "aroused the imagination of Eastsiders" in Los Angeles and other politically marginalized constituencies in California.[59]

One of the biggest advocates of EPIC in Black Los Angeles, and a key figure in ushering in a more general grassroots shift toward the Democratic Party, was Augustus Hawkins. Hawkins's run for State Assembly in 1934 dis-tinguished him as a harbinger of a new, younger generation of Black leader-ship within the Sixty-Second District, a region encompassing the hub of Los Angeles's Black community and one of the largest concentrations of African Americans in the West.[60] Hawkins, a vocal supporter of Sinclair, was widely recognized as an "Epic candidate" and promoted a platform that similarly included old-age pensions, unemployment insurance, and progressive so-cial legislation.[61] Even more than Sinclair's campaign, however, Hawkins's was driven by his particular commitment to the local concerns of African Americans and other working-class communities in the Sixty-Second Dis-trict. He appealed to "those who were let down by the present administra-tion," those who wished to see "a real housecleaning" of Sixty-Second

District politics, and, perhaps most important, those who desired more "direct representation of the Eastside" in local and state government.[62] Support for Hawkins's Democratic campaign for State Assembly came not only from fellow EPIC supporters, Black labor unions like the Pullman porters, White unionists, Utopians, Townsendites, and followers of Father Divine but also from people like Leon Washington who distrusted Sinclair and were skeptical of EPIC.[63] Many of his supporters saw Hawkins's candidacy as part of a "battle for the masses," as the Los Angeles Sentinel put it, and a route toward reshaping the relationship between government and the Black community.[64] In Hawkins's own view, what propelled the "shift of sentiment" among Black voters toward support for the Democratic Party reached beyond individual politicians or specific policy measures.[65] He emphasized, "It was not really the great love for the Democratic party itself that caused blacks to change; it was just a matter of economic survival."[66] The new pools of Democratic Party voters had no intentions of assimilating or conforming to the standards of the party as it existed, in other words. They sought to adapt EPIC, the New Deal, and the Democratic establishment to serve their own needs, rather than the other way around.

Ethnic Mexicans in California appear to have held a mixture of attitudes toward EPIC and the Democratic Party. Quantitative studies of Mexican American voting patterns in 1934 are inconclusive, and the attitudes of ethnic Mexicans toward EPIC and the Democratic Party are difficult to assess with certainty.[67] As with other politically marginalized populations, several factors seem to suggest that ambivalence and opposition to state-level Democratic candidates likely persisted among ethnic Mexicans. To be sure, the large proportion of recent immigrants from Mexico and generally low levels of naturalization militated against investment in electoral politics generally speaking. Moreover, as with African Americans, EPIC did not give a great deal of attention to the particular needs and struggles of these communities, even though the campaign did acknowledge the plight of ethnic Mexicans in Los Angeles in its newspaper and did some minimal outreach to these populations.[68] It is also possible that support for Sinclair among ethnic Mexicans shifted as the campaign unfolded. Particularly after the primaries, Sinclair took an increasingly strong anti-immigrant stance. Responding to critics who condemned him for earlier statements that purportedly encouraged immigration, and hoping to endear himself to Californians who feared the ongoing influx of new arrivals especially from the Midwest and southern Plains, Sinclair's position increasingly synchronized with attitudes that supported sweeping projects of Mexican and Filipinx repatriation.[69] As racialized depictions of ethnic Mexicans cast them as foreigners and confronted them with anti-immigrant hostilities whether they were born in the United States or not, many within these populations were likely sensitive to, and alienated by, Sinclair's crystallizing attitude on the subject.[70]

At the same time, however, there appear to have been significant clusters of ethnic Mexican supporters of EPIC, who also contributed to the leftward shift of the Democratic Party. The proportion of ethnic Mexicans who sought naturalization (and thus eligibility to vote), which had remained low overall during the 1930s, saw a notable surge between 1934 and 1936.[71] The rising numbers of people seeking naturalization suggested a new relationship to American politics and new claims on social membership and political participation, corresponding with the timing of the EPIC campaign and other progressive-left electoral movements. Historians have chronicled a general enthusiasm for the Democratic Party among Mexican American voters at this time. Historian Rodolfo Acuña remarked, "Most Chicanos have been nurtured to believe in the Virgin of Guadalupe, the Sacred Heart, and the party of Franklin D. Roosevelt."[72] While it is difficult to assess how pervasive their political support was for Sinclair or the EPIC program, there is evidence that those who supported the campaign in 1934 did so enthusiastically.[73] As early as May 1934, Los Angeles–based civil rights activist Tom Raphael signed on to EPIC's campaign team as a Spanish translator and organizer within the ethnic Mexican community.[74] As he worked to familiarize the community with the EPIC plan, Raphael underscored the particular promise that the plan held for ethnic Mexicans in California. "I don't believe another candidate can offer to the Spanish speaking *colonias* of California, and what is more, carry out, the improvement of conditions . . . that Mr. Sinclair promises," Raphael asserted.[75] According to him, Sinclair's campaign not only provided a practical route for addressing the concerns of ethnic Mexicans but also created an "opportunity for Spanish-speaking voters" to participate politically in new ways and "to demonstrate that they are with the general sentiments of the public in California."[76]

Mexican American citizens were not the only people of Mexican descent who were involved in advancing Sinclair's gubernatorial candidacy and transforming the Democratic Party in California. Some noncitizens and Mexican nationals also expressed their political investment in the outcome of the 1934 election, even if they did not have access to the vote. For example, Mexican national and Los Angeles resident Dr. Aristrides Mayorga wrote a piece for *La Opinión* entitled "How California's Electoral Crisis Looks in Mexico." In it, Mayorga wrote, from the perspective of a non-U.S. citizen,

"In California, as in the rest of the states, the two old parties of the Democrats and Republicans have been controlled by the big financial interests, the invisible government that makes its presence and power felt in all aspects of the economy." The article highlighted the ways in which Sinclair departed from this political status quo, calling particular attention to the transformative potential of "production for use" and underscoring the significance of his pursuit of such a program not through an ancillary or "outmoded" institution but "instead with the Democratic Party." In doing so, Mayorga explained, "Sinclair proposes breaking the antiquated electoral charade and turning it into a strong instrument of positive democracy."[77] For Mayorga, EPIC's effort to transform the Democratic Party embodied a fusion of bold progressive vision with smart political strategy. It marked a departure from politics as usual and held promise for substantive social change.

Despite the skepticism that persisted within some communities, Sinclair and EPIC commanded a remarkable following among Californians and swept the primary election on August 28, 1934. Sinclair received 436,220 votes in all, more than the Republican nominee Frank Merriam and more than all six of his Democratic primary opponents combined. Alongside Sinclair, forty-nine other EPIC-backed candidates won nominations for the state legislature. Among them was Hawkins, who surpassed several established, old-guard leaders of Black Los Angeles to claim the Democratic nomination for the Sixty-Second District.[78] In many regions of the state, the race was close. In some key areas, EPIC candidates lost to old-line Democrats and more moderate New Dealers.[79] Yet the victory for the campaign was decisive. Moreover, its implications reached beyond the ballot for the upcoming general election.

Navigating the Postprimary Political Terrain

In some respects, the August primary marked the height of EPIC's success, and the months leading up to it contained the most radical political possibilities. The campaign would continue to attract new followers in the primary's aftermath. However, it would also encounter new challenges. During the postprimary period, as EPIC faced off directly with the Republican opposition and prepared for the general election, EPIC's advocates found themselves straining to balance their progressive political aims with the quantitative necessity for votes. Before the primary, EPIC campaigners could address themselves more openly to a left-of-center constituency, and the movement as a whole could serve more readily as a channel for advancing political aspirations far more radical than those espoused by Sinclair himself. After the primary, however, the campaign faced escalated pressures to moderate its platform and reorient its messaging toward more conservative segments of the electorate, including more conservative Democrats, New Dealers, and people who had historically voted Republican. During this period, EPIC's own internal limitations, compounded with the institutional constraints of the electoral system and an intensified political assault from the right, constrained the campaign's terrain for political maneuvering.

The odds were stacked against EPIC from the start. With preponderant control over the major channels of mass media in the state and an overwhelming supply of capital at their disposal, conservative opponents of Sinclair wasted no time in launching a full-fledged smear campaign against him. Seeking to halt EPIC's influence by undermining Sinclair's support base, pro-Merriam forces flooded the radio waves, the pages of newspapers, and motion picture newsreels with stories that painted Sinclair as a Communist, atheist, philanderer, and polygamist.[80] They trumpeted EPIC's disastrous implications for the economy, highlighting especially its threat to consumers in the form of inflation and rising prices. They appealed to voters' prejudices, equating the prospect of Sinclair's election with the downfall of Christian morality, the erosion of the sanctity of marriage, and the opening of California to a torrent of unwanted immigrants.[81] Summing up his own argument about Sinclair, Merriam charged, "Mr. Sinclair is not a Democrat" but a "radical Socialist" who "carries their party banner."[82] While he strove to lure voters by touting the false promise of ending poverty in California, what Sinclair truly offered, according to Merriam, was nothing short of an "attack on [the] fundamental principles of American life."[83] At a time when uncertainty and insecurity pervaded Californian society, EPIC's conservative detractors cast Sinclair as a composite of a multitude of popular fears and a harbinger of social, economic, political, and cultural havoc. As exaggerated and bizarre as many of their claims were, the Republican-led smear campaign helped place EPIC on the defensive, pressuring Sinclair to prove his moderate credentials and narrowing the range of political debate.

While Sinclair was in many ways the most likely target, conservatives recognized that the threat lay not simply in the prospect of Sinclair's election but in the more sweeping mass mobilization that EPIC represented. Discrediting the gubernatorial candidate was thus part of a broader counterinsurgency that also aimed to obstruct the election of EPIC candidates to legislative positions across the state and to issue "a stinging rebuke to the Epic philosophy of government in California."[84] As the *Los Angeles Times* reported, the election of Republican nominees across the ballot was necessary not just to ensure "harmony and a chance for progress in the next Legislature" but to deliver a "rebuff" to the full slate of "nominees who were hot for Epic."[85] Far beyond the defeat of Sinclair as an individual, the anti-Sinclair forces rallied to extinguish all traces of EPIC's influence and the ideas and principles that fueled it.

The Republican-led assault made the final months of the election cycle the most trying for EPIC, though it was far from the only challenge that the movement faced during this period. The campaign also received fierce criticism by New Deal liberals within the Democratic Party, not only in California but also nationwide. The ascendance of EPIC and Sinclair's nomination drew the attention of national Democratic Party leaders and provoked a split among them. While some Democrats saw the potential for an alliance between EPIC and New Deal advocates, others repudiated the EPIC movement as a threat to the party and its national recovery agenda. For the latter camp, the victory of Sinclair and other EPIC-affiliated candidates in the California primary reflected the creeping influence of socialism, a trend that would cause Democrats across the country to "rapidly lose confidence in the New Deal." Ultimately, some feared, EPIC's ascendance could lead "to disintegration of the party and Socialist control throughout the United States."[86] As EPIC campaigners recognized, winning the support of New Deal liberals was critical to electoral success in November. Yet such support did not flow naturally or readily even after EPIC's landslide victory in the primary.

As the EPIC campaign contended with condemnation from both the political right and moderate Democrats, its supporters felt it was urgent to widen their constituencies beyond working-class voters and progressive-left circles if they were to have any hope of winning in November. Given the deluge of partisan propaganda that shaped the postprimary political terrain, the task was inherently an uphill battle. Moreover, the ways EPIC leaders responded to the challenges at hand added to the potential for confusion in the movement. More specifically, the efforts of Sinclair and other candidates and organizers to endure the right-wing attack while expanding their ranks among political moderates involved reining in some of their further-reaching proposals and recasting themselves as New Dealers who were going to bring "Roosevelt's new brand of liberalism" to California.[87] On the one hand, tapping into the wider support base for Roosevelt's New Deal could help translate the general leftward shift in politics that was sweeping the nation into the state of California. On the other hand, likening EPIC to the New Deal also meant toning down the more radical elements of the campaign and risked alienating some of the segments of the California electorate that had helped drive EPIC into prominence in the first place.

Sinclair's strategic shift toward the political center was traceable in his public statements about the Roosevelt administration, the New Deal, and the limitations of both. When he first published his campaign pamphlet, *I, Governor of California, and How I Ended Poverty*, Sinclair freely criticized what he saw as the "inadequacy" of the National Recovery Administration (NRA) and New Deal and sought to distinguish EPIC from them.[88] Although, "like all good Americans," he overall supported the political direction that the New Deal represented, Sinclair stressed, "I cannot shut my eyes to its failures."[89] He accused President Roosevelt of "trying the futile Hoover idea, of extending bank credit to businessmen who had no customers." He also highlighted "the failure of the NRA" and the insufficiency of New Deal programs to alleviate problems of unemployment and wage cuts.[90] Under the New Deal government, Sinclair contended that "the nation seemed to be heading toward another collapse," and he anticipated that "the crisis was going to get worse, not better." Ultimately, he contended, "there was no remedy under the present system."[91] Following the primary, however, Sinclair's public discussions of the New Deal rang a strikingly different tune. He touted in a radio address that "the President had the right ideas about the recovery."[92] Elsewhere, he lauded Roosevelt: "His heart is warm in the people's cause [and] Roosevelt will act in your behalf as fast as you will let him."[93] Sinclair went so far as to liken EPIC to the New Deal and cast it as a register of the New Deal's success. Through EPIC's rising influence, he proclaimed in celebration, "the New Deal is vindicating itself here in California."[94]

In his effort to mollify tensions between EPIC and the New Deal and to bridge the divide within the Democratic Party that his nomination had provoked, Sinclair promptly sought the support of the Roosevelt administration following his primary victory. He wrote to the president requesting a meeting, urging "that we should win next November not merely for California but to keep California in line two years later."[95] While Roosevelt granted the request and invited Sinclair to visit him in Hyde Park in early September, he purposely avoided taking a position on EPIC so as not to isolate his supporters on either side of the party's split over the matter. He imposed strict conditions on the visit, insisting that it remain a purely social affair and refusing to talk politics with the aspiring governor. After Sinclair returned to California, Roosevelt maintained his silence on the subject and declined to offer any support or disapproval either for Sinclair's candidacy in particular or for the EPIC platform in general. Reactions within the wider administration were mixed. Some individuals came out harshly against Sinclair and warned the president against consorting with the controversial candidate, even socially. Others, however, including prominent, more left-leaning New Dealers such as Harry Hopkins and Henry Wallace, openly endorsed him. For instance, Hopkins rejected portrayals of Sinclair as a socialist and an extremist, insisting in a statement to the press, "He's a good Democrat. He's on our side." Moreover, Hopkins asserted, Sinclair's EPIC program contained some elements that were "very good" for California and the country at large.[96] While such approval was never as widespread within the administration as EPIC folks would have liked, it was key to countering reactionary propaganda and broadening the base of EPIC in California as the November election approached.

Back in California, EPIC leadership worked to mainstream the campaign by garnering acceptance from more conservative Democrats, especially by finding grounds for compromise with them. The statewide Democratic convention in Sacramento on September 20 tested the relationship between the party's competing factions. The support that EPIC received from at least some members of Roosevelt's administration, combined with EPIC's role in expanding the party's ranks by hundreds of thousands, gave the campaign a degree of clout that could not simply be dismissed by the party's more conservative wing. At the same time, for their part, Sinclair and EPIC recognized that setting differences aside and finding common ground with fellow Democrats were key to securing their position within the party. The political leadership on both sides of the Democratic Party divide, in other words, found reasons to compromise. In the days leading up to the convention, Sinclair met with his recently defeated competitor for the Democratic gubernatorial nomination, George Creel. In that meeting Sinclair yielded to Creel's urging that he accept a more generalized party platform, one that curbed EPIC-identified rhetoric and sidelined any explicit reference to EPIC's distinguishing economic and social programs. Doing so, Creel proposed, would "attract the broadest support" and enable "non-EPIC Democratic candidates [to] run on the platform as well."[97] Creel further declared his intention to write the bulk of the platform himself. Sinclair accepted this as well, without any overt contestation.[98]

At the convention itself, the platform that the Democratic Party voted through reflected the influence of both strains of politics within the party—old-line and new, more conservative and more progressive. It affirmed the party's rejection of communism and its defense of private property, religious freedom, and a normative ideal of American domesticity and said nothing of old-age pensions, farm colonies, state-run factories, or production for use. It did, however, express a commitment to goals that aligned, at least in broad strokes, with some of EPIC's core principles. Specifically, it emphasized the importance of employing the unemployed in "productive work" and "enabling them to produce what they themselves are to consume." Further, it deemed these objectives to be "a means of industrial and social rehabilitation" and ultimately "of ending poverty in California."[99] While the platform clearly dissociated itself from EPIC's defining programs, it upheld the ideas on which they were based closely enough to elicit an ovation from EPIC supporters at the convention.[100]

Outside the convention, responses to the political maneuvering of EPIC leadership were mixed. Supporters and observers of the campaign debated whether the new party platform marked the Democrats' embrace of EPIC or their co-optation of it—or, as one press writer put it, "whether Sinclair took the Democratic Party or the party assimilated Sinclair."[101] For his part, Sinclair lauded the platform as a signal of a new sense of "harmony in the Democratic Party in California."[102] According to him, the compromises that the platform embodied included provisions that both EPIC supporters and old-line Democrats could celebrate. Yet some EPIC supporters resented what they saw as the uneven and limited incorporation of EPIC by the party. According to one journalist for the *Sacramento Bee*, the platform paid lip service to EPIC while reducing it to the margins of a more moderate, New Deal agenda. The same author blamed EPIC leadership, as much as old-line Democrats, for the outcome. They charged, "Upton Sinclair and his EPIC planners grabbed control of the Democratic State Convention . . . and jammed through a compromise platform in which the essentials of the EPIC scheme, while included in modified language, are subordinated to the policies of President Roosevelt and the New Deal."[103] To the extent that the platform incorporated some elements of EPIC into a multifaceted "composite," the same author held, such elements were "considerably toned down to keep the Democratic Party in line and allay public distrust of left wing extremists."[104] Onlookers could widely agree that the convention and platform registered the shift of EPIC from radical fringe to mainstream acceptance within the Democratic Party. Yet, for some, the compromises that made this transition possible muddied the relationship between the campaign and its own political and social foundations. By deprioritizing some of the plank's more radical provisions, EPIC candidates and leaders sought to garner more votes within moderate circles. However, in doing so they also limited the terms on which EPIC advocates could elaborate and advance their visions.

Efforts to mainstream EPIC drew criticism from people across the political spectrum. The campaign's shift provided fodder for a new wave of attacks from the political right, including some who wished to stoke tensions and widen the breach within the Democratic Party. Sinclair came under fire for what one writer slammed as his "attempts to straddle the fence between the two groups; those who voted for him and his Epic scheme in the primaries and the overwhelmingly larger group who favor the AMERICAN plan of the New Deal." The same author argued that Sinclair could be caught "continually contradicting himself," such that it became difficult to discern where he stood on key issues, precisely because he was driven less by genuine principles than by "pure political expediency" and an "effort to be all things to all men."[105] Criticisms emanating from the Democratic Party's conservative wing in this moment cast him as a political "chameleon" and an "opportunist" and accused him of "insincerity" in his "endeavor to ingratiate himself with 'regular' Democrats."[106]

For others who critiqued him from the far left, the trouble with Sinclair reached beyond a lack of clarity or consistency to the impression that he had sold out the campaign to political moderates. One Young People's Socialist League activist concluded that "instead of capturing the Democratic Party," Sinclair had essentially "surrendered to the Democratic Party." He had given up what radical potential he once represented and "adopted the New Deal in its entirety. If elected to the office of Governor," the writer surmised, "the party machinery would hold him well in hand."[107] In other words, Sinclair's pragmatism not only obscured his connection to the EPIC platform but also, in the eyes of skeptics on the left, sacrificed values for votes and made him more easily manipulated by established power elites.

Although he was the most prominent, Sinclair was not the only EPIC candidate seeking a wider constituency as the general election approached. Virtually all candidates affiliated with the movement engaged in political maneuvering of a parallel sort, working to attract support from beyond the Democratic Party's emergent left wing. Augustus Hawkins was no exception. As he set out to broaden his base, Hawkins worked determinedly to extend his message into new venues. His outreach efforts reportedly involved giving at least two speeches every night during the period between the primary and the general election.[108] Yet sheer tirelessness was just one element of his approach. The nature of the alliances he built was another. The distinguishing feature of Hawkins's campaign strategy, and ultimately the key to his electoral success, was his constituency's wide-ranging, interracial character. On one level, Hawkins represented a new wave of African

American political leadership within Los Angeles's Black belt. Incidentally, however, his political ascendance hinged on the support of White working-class voters, including racist labor leaders on the district's west side. His efforts to secure White voters' support relied in part on toning down the racial dimensions of his program and emphasizing its pro-labor features when speaking to White audiences. In addition, he used the lightness of his own complexion to his advantage, passing as White when it seemed useful and embracing many White voters' assumption that he, too, was White. Remarking on the way his racial presentation figured into his political strategizing, Hawkins explained that, on the east side of the district, "my complexion was not identifiable with blacks, many of them didn't know I was black—so I lost votes. On the other side, on the white side, however, it was an asset, so it was a gamble as to which would be the greater loss."[109] In the end, Hawkins's active pursuit of White support probably did cost him some portion of the Black vote. Yet he maintained sufficient support among African Americans across the Sixty-Second District, while building a following among White Angelenos and other racialized communities, to beat out other contenders for the Democratic Assembly ticket in the primary and to unseat longtime Black Republican leader Fred Roberts in the general election (figure 4.1).

While the tack of downplaying key values to maximize votes worked for Hawkins, it was not enough to enable Sinclair to overcome the skepticism of certain circles of voters, to counter the onslaught waged by Republicans and moderate Democrats, or to edge out Republican contender Frank Merriam. On November 6, 1934, Sinclair amassed 879,537 votes. This doubled the number of votes he had garnered during the primary. It amounted to 38 percent of the total votes in the general election. It was a substantial showing, to be sure, but fell short of an electoral victory. Merriam won the election with 49 percent of the vote. Another 12 percent of the vote went to Raymond Haight.[110]

Despite Sinclair's loss, forty-one EPIC-backed candidates won their respective races for positions in the legislature. Nine won seats in Congress and would represent EPIC's influence at the national level. Additionally, several key seats on the Democratic Party's Central Committee fell under EPIC control, creating a direct route for EPIC to shape the future directions of the party.[111] While the Republicans maintained numerical dominance in state government overall, the Democratic Party had gained a stronger presence than it had had in decades, and it was turning to the left.

Together, the results of the 1934 election signaled a shifting of the political winds. Culbert Olson—an EPIC supporter, California Democratic Party

FIGURE 4.1 Augustus F. Hawkins, pictured here as a newly inducted member of the California State Assembly, 1935. Courtesy of California State Library.

chairman, and newly elected member of the State Senate—likened the situation of California Democrats in 1934 to that of the nation's Republicans in 1856. In that election, just two years after its formation, the Republican Party lost the presidency but gained political momentum that would continue to shape national politics in the years to come. In 1860, the following election, the party would win with the election of Abraham Lincoln. "This is our election of '56," he proclaimed. "Upton Sinclair has re-founded the Democrats in this state, and we take up where he left off."[112] The claim was perhaps even more prescient than Olson himself recognized, as Olson would go on to win the governorship in 1938, taking the post from California's Republicans for the first time since 1899.

Beyond its immediate electoral outcomes, EPIC helped energize a broader reimagining of the relationship between government and society and impacted the future directions of the Democratic Party. The campaign galvanized the grassroots, providing a lightning rod for growing dialogues about social justice and creating a channel by which California's working populations could imagine influencing the state's formal political domains. In doing so, EPIC altered the calculus of partisan politics within and beyond the state. As Carey McWilliams put it, EPIC "brought a Democratic party into existence [in California]."[113] Within approximately ten months of Sinclair's declaration of candidacy, Reuben Borough affirmed, EPIC carried the state's Democratic Party "from obscurity to an important position in the political life of the nation" and, in turn, placed "California Democracy at the forefront of the Roosevelt New Deal army."[114] Key to EPIC's political influence was its capacity to serve as a vehicle for the social visions of a wide-ranging popular constituency. As diverse as its proponents—and their social visions—were, they collectively advanced a social warrant that demanded a government more responsive to their needs, one that would facilitate a redistribution of wealth and serve as a bulwark against autocratic government. In doing so, they remade California's Democratic Party and pushed it further to the left than it might otherwise have reached.

At the national level, the New Deal, too, moved leftward and assumed more boldly progressive forms. In the following year, 1935, the Roosevelt administration instituted the Wagner Act, which established protections for organized labor; the Works Progress Administration, which expanded access to jobs; and the Social Security Act, which provided for old-age pensions and unemployment insurance. Of course, even these important gains had their limits. The Wagner Act excluded agricultural and domestic workers from its benefits and did little to discourage discrimination and racial segregation within unions. At the same time, the Social Security Act excluded farm labor, city and county employees, and common laborers—effectively, most people of color. The Federal Housing Administration, a product of the 1934 National Housing Act, standardized the practice of refusing to insure mortgages in and near communities of color, while at the same time financing the construction of new housing subdivisions that were reserved exclusively for White residents. These measures helped to guarantee that cities like San Francisco, Oakland, San Diego, and Los Angeles, well beyond the bounds of the Jim Crow South, would serve as sites of increasingly entrenched racial segregation and racialized economic inequality leading into the mid-twentieth century. In effect, even as it provided an important new social safety net for a majority of White Americans, the New Deal as a whole reinforced racial and social divisions in California and across the nation and ensured that a more thoroughly inclusive and participatory vision of democracy would require ongoing struggle and continued political pressure from the grassroots.[115]

Hawkins's own political career reflected the possibilities and challenges of that ongoing struggle as it was waged in the halls of government. Hawkins's election in 1934 signified the political potential of a broad-based, multiracial campaign. Especially when he was reelected by a landslide in 1936, his success also signified a larger set of political realignments—that of Los Angeles from a Republican-dominated to a Democratic-majority city, and of African Americans from an established loyalty to the party of Lincoln toward an influential bloc within the party of Roosevelt. For many, the Democratic Party in particular and the federal government in general seemed especially promising channels for advancing civil rights as part of a broader agenda for racial and social justice. Hawkins himself used his position in California's State Assembly to promote a host of initiatives that aimed to address the racial limitations of the New Deal and to support a more inclusionary vision of democratic governance. He introduced legislation to extend social welfare benefits to domestic workers, to prohibit discrimination in housing and hiring, and to expand support for low-cost housing, mass transportation, day care, and disability insurance. He would become best known for his tireless efforts to address employment inequality and for the role he would later play as a congressional representative in authoring Title VII of the 1964 Civil Rights Act. Yet, throughout his time in the California State Assembly, and in his career more generally, Hawkins faced immense personal and political challenges. He not only confronted explicit racism from his colleagues in government but also faced obstinate opposition to many of his civil rights initiatives, including from economic liberals who supported the New Deal. In fact, most of the measures Hawkins introduced with hopes of democratizing the New Deal in California failed to win the support of his own political party.[116]

Despite the limitations of the leftward-shifting New Deal, and despite the ongoing attempts of moderate Democrats to tame the more rebellious elements of the newly reconstructed party, marginalized and working-class Californians continued to look for openings in the political landscape that surrounded them. Alongside formal domains of political activity, they turned to other avenues of political engagement to claim space for themselves and to envision modes of participatory citizenship beyond the constraints of the electoral system. Just as labor unions could not contain or encapsulate the totality of grassroots hopes and desires, neither could official domains of electoral politics. Grassroots struggles relied on a wider-ranging war of position, a war that was fought most fully on the terrain of culture.

Part III.

EXPRESSIVE CULTURE AND THE POLITICS OF THE POSSIBLE

5

The Art of Opposition in the Culture Industry's Capital

On the evening of the Fourth of July, 1934—the eve of the violent clash in San Francisco that would become known as Bloody Thursday—a crowd gathered in the auditorium of Los Angeles's downtown Cultural Center for a theatrical production featuring select scenes from Paul Peters and George Sklar's play, *Stevedore*. The show was a quintessentially community affair, staged by and for local residents of Central and South Los Angeles. It drew to-gether an eclectic community of middle-class activists as well as impoverished working and unemployed residents of the racially mixed Black, Asian, Latinx, and White neighborhoods that surrounded the city's major industrial districts, between South Los Angeles's Central Avenue corridor, Boyle Heights to the east, and Little Tokyo to the north.[1] *Stevedore* had opened on Broadway in April of that year, and the amateur performers, community members, and organizers who had coordinated the night's events were preparing their own rendition of the show for a full run in Los Angeles in the fall. In a sense, then, the Fourth of July performance previewed what was to come. Yet the troupe's reasons for staging an incomplete and minimally rehearsed set of segments from the show reached beyond generating anticipation for the full-length debut: the event's organizers recognized the show's particular relevance for Central and South Los Angeles residents during the summer of 1934. That summer rounded out a year that had confronted these communities with the deepest and most widespread deprivation in the city's history, the most intense political repression they had experienced in over a decade, and new levels of interethnic rivalry and targeted racial scapegoating. In presenting a few portions of the play at such an early stage of the production process in response to these developments, the show's coordinators seized an opportunity for performers and audience members to grapple collectively with social problems that were both present and pressing.[2]

The play itself depicts the story of a White woman in contemporary New Orleans who is beaten by her illicit lover and, rather than tell the authorities the truth and expose the scandal, claims that she was raped by a Black man. In the upwelling of racial hostility that ensues, as police round up as many Black men as they can and force them into lineups, waterfront employer Jeff Walcott recognizes an opportunity to oust one of the leading organizers of a movement for union rights and workplace equality that was taking shape on the levees, Lonnie Thompson. After Walcott has Thompson arrested and the White woman alleges he was her assailant, Thompson manages to escape and go into hiding. The incident stirs up a White mob, which riots through the streets and begins raiding the homes of Black residents. Ultimately, the men from the waterfront, in solidarity across racial lines, fight them off.[3]

Foregrounding the criminalization of Black masculinity; the impulse to protect White womanhood; the terror of racism; the twisted relationship among justice, law, and power; and the difficulties of navigating racial and class divisions amid broader struggles against oppression, the show not only registered such highly publicized contemporaneous events as the Scottsboro trial and the coastwise waterfront strike as key political coordinates but also told a story that working-class Angelenos could identify as "typical" in a local sense, "true to life in every detail."[4] As the local Black weekly, the *California Eagle*, put it, the scenes from the play performed at the Cultural Center that Fourth of July evening resonated with the lives and struggles of the people who filled the auditorium with a degree of "realism that makes one shudder and squirm."[5] Significantly, Los Angeles did not give rise to the multiracialist brand of labor unionism that took hold in San Francisco in this same moment. The Southern California metropolis's more mixed economic base, the wider spatial scattering of its working-class populations, the firm grasp of eugenic, White supremacist thinking on its dominant political culture, and the severity of antiunion repression in the city—epitomized most notoriously by the Red Squads of the Los Angeles Police Department (LAPD)—militated against making the workplace a site for broad-based political mobilization. Perhaps more visibly and persistently than any other major western metropolis, Los Angeles emblemized the reliance of urban capitalist development on the forms of violence and racial terror that *Stevedore* depicted onstage. Moreover, as evidenced by the local International Longshoremen's Association intransigent resistance to inclusionary unionism along the docks in San Pedro, the city also offered a grim illustration of the common tendency for labor's spokespeople to secure their own partial gains at the expense of significant segments of the working population. These conditions made the kind of solidarity invoked in *Stevedore*'s conclusion simultaneously as urgent and as challenging as ever.[6]

The significance of the evening's performance derived not strictly from the ways it reflected conditions and experiences that were familiar to working-class Angelenos, however, but from the ways it enabled forms of affiliation and social imagination that were unwelcome—perhaps unthinkable—in other venues throughout the city. In defiance of the racial limits of organized labor's main institutional channels and dominant notions of proper civic behavior, the Cultural Center performance linked Black, Brown, and White residents from Central and South Los Angeles in the construction of a shared past, one shaped by patriarchal racist violence and antiunionism. It nurtured a sense that their personal struggles and respective stakes in the future were intimately linked. The people onstage and in the seats of the Cultural Center that evening were urged by the performance to actively and collectively work through questions to which there were no immediate answers—questions about how solidarities might be built and nurtured in the face of prevailing social divisions, how grassroots struggles might be carried forth against the seemingly overwhelming forces of racial capital, what democracy meant in practice, and what a dignified existence comprised. Against a dominant culture that sought to manage popular desires by binding them to a trajectory of racial capitalist development, grassroots cultural expressions like the *Stevedore* performance encouraged imagining alternative possibilities—blueprints of "another Los Angeles," as George Sánchez has put it.[7]

Far more than benign entertainment, artistic expressions were critical to the structuring of power relations and the crafting of visions for the future development of California generally and Los Angeles specifically during the 1930s. Art was a key terrain on which understandings of the past and present were worked out and on which the horizons of the imaginable and the possible were drawn. For Southern California elites throughout the early twentieth century, art provided a fruitful avenue for the production of ideas about what kind of city Los Angeles ought to be. They worked hard to fashion an urban aesthetic capable of supporting their aspirations for regional capitalist development. What emerged from their endeavors was a dominant culture that combined conventional notions of high art with boosterist imagery that promoted the city as an Eden of leisure and prosperity, particularly for a narrowly defined imagined community of White Protestant migrants, consumers, national investors, and financiers.[8]

For a majority of the international migrants and non-White workers who helped build the city—including many of those who filled the Cultural Center on the Fourth of July—the art of the powerful offered little beyond tokenization, denigration, and erasure. Yet racial capitalist elites never exerted a monopoly over cultural production in the city, and art proved a distinctly malleable, and uniquely valuable, tool for those pushing back against the forces seeking to subordinate them. Just as it carried the potential to fortify municipal power hierarchies and enforce exclusionary social boundaries, artistic production also held the capacity to widen the conditions of political possibility for people seeking to challenge those same boundaries and to make their lives livable.[9]

In forms that ranged from theater performances to murals to music, expressive culture linked diverse communities across the city and helped generate new kinds of relationships among them. It helped foster modes of historical memory and insurgent knowledge that could empower people in the face of seemingly overwhelming forces of subordination. Different from more directly confrontational modes of politics, which drew people together around strategic forms of political unity and hopes of securing immediate, agreed-upon objectives, art functioned as a prism through which differentiated struggles in the city redefined themselves and their relationships to each other. Hinging less on the construction of strategic essentialisms than on forthrightly open-ended anti-essentialisms, expressive culture mediated more flexibly than most other political domains between the commonalities of working-class experiences and the constitutive particularities of local ethnic communities and individual subjectivities. Less viable than organized politics for the task of securing concrete concessions from power, art was nonetheless vital to cultivating the grassroots self-empowerment on which more organized movements relied.

During the 1930s, Los Angeles gave rise to a grassroots counterculture that placed art at the center of struggles for liberation. Multiracial, interethnic, and cross-generational, Los Angeles's oppositional culture was animated by the shared, albeit varied and sometimes conflicting, struggles of local communities for dignity, self-definition, and empowerment. It reflected a surrealist refusal of the social discipline and systems of classification imposed by the dominant culture, along with an intuitive sense of the integral relationship between creative practice and social change. The city's counterculture was expressed in major works of public visual art by left-leaning professional artists, who used murals to critique the city's development narrative and contribute to a popular historical countermemory. It included a community-based, community-oriented, and largely female-led arts movement that flourished through overlapping networks of community activists, who saw theatrical performance as a crucial avenue for empowerment and public dialogue. It was also animated by the creative expressions of the local youth culture, which energized the city's jazz scene and underscored the centrality of collaboration, experimentation, and improvisation to the pursuit of emancipation.

This chapter examines how grassroots artistic expressions helped expand political possibilities for people facing tremendous barriers to social inclusion and political participation, while contributing to an oppositional, surrealist cultural milieu in 1930s Los Angeles. It highlights the nonnegotiable grassroots priorities of creative autonomy and democratic participation and reveals the distinctly vital role that grassroots artistic expressions had to play in securing these priorities. Ultimately, this chapter demonstrates that many Angelenos found in culture a widened terrain for nurturing anti-essentialist visions of themselves and a means for sustaining and regenerating broader dreams for the future of social relations.

Culture and Power in the Open-Shop City

Throughout the late nineteenth and early twentieth centuries, expressive culture in general, and art in particular, had served as a key terrain for political contestations within Los Angeles and for battles over the city's development future. From its early transformation from a backcountry town in the 1880s to a booming center of citrus groves, tourism, and real estate speculation by the 1910s, to its emergence as a sprawling industrial metropolis by the end of the 1920s—complete with one of the world's most ambitious irrigation systems, its most productive oil derricks and refineries, and the fastest-growing manufacturing district in the country—the production of narratives about the city and what it had to offer the world was central and indispensable to its political economic development.[10] As much as Los Angeles's urban growth drew on the natural resources that would provide the raw material for its infrastructure, it also relied on city builders' and boosters' efforts to appeal to the desires of prospective investors, residents, home buyers, tourists, and entrepreneurs—to enable the city to be seen as fertile ground for unfilled promises, a "last best hope" for people seeking a wide range of opportunities. As writer and satirist Morrow Mayo wrote in 1933, "Los Angeles, it should be understood, is not a mere city. On the contrary, it is, and has been since 1888, a *commodity*; something to be advertised and sold to the people of the United States like automobiles, cigarettes, and mouth wash."[11] During the first three decades of the twentieth century, the expansion of Los Angeles went hand in hand with the construction of a dominant vision of the city as a land of sunshine and prosperity, where residents could be free of the squalor and cultural degeneracy associated with eastern cities and where business growth could proceed without the troublesome interference of union activity.

Far from a naturally occurring phenomenon, the vision of Los Angeles as a land of sunshine and prosperity had to be constructed and sold by the city builders. As historian William Deverell has shown, Los Angeles's emergence as a symbol of racial capitalist progress—a celebrated "city of the future"—required the construction of a whitewashed mythology of its past, the disavowal of the contributions made by Native and Mexican populations to the historical development of the region, and the suppression of alternative and oppositional visions of the city.[12] At the same time that lynch mobs and vigilante raiders worked to purge undesirable elements from public spaces and the mainstream of civic culture, tourist pamphlets and real estate advertisements re-created the city in the popular imagination as ripe for new business ventures, a place where folks on the make could find wealth and good health in a life of leisure on the beach.[13] As Deverell notes, that Los Angeles became a booming industrial metropolis structured by White dominance by the 1920s was not a manifestation of "a city that got what it wished for"; rather, this was "a city that wished for what it worked diligently to *invent*."[14] By 1934 the *Los Angeles Times* heralded the city as "the new cultural center of the world," a status it had acquired by becoming "a land not fettered by custom or tradition" but instead "giving the world something new, permeated by California sunshine."[15]

A central pillar of Los Angeles's development during the first three decades of the twentieth century was the city builders' construction of the metropolis as an open-shop city. In the most basic sense, the open shop was a policy that aimed to cripple union power by affirming employers' right to hire nonunion members. In early twentieth-century Los Angeles, this policy did more than regulate union activity within specific work sites; it served as a core element of the broader hegemonic order governing the metropolis.[16] It was the fulcrum of local boosters' campaign to grow the city's industrial base by attracting entrepreneurs, industrial branch plants, and investors to the region and a vital means for maintaining a cheap and flexible supply of industrial labor. Los Angeles was neither the first nor the only city in the United States to organize its infrastructure around the open shop. In fact, the open shop became common practice in many cities across the country following the upsurge of labor in the late 1910s and early 1920s. Nonetheless, city boosters loved to boast about Los Angeles's role in setting a precedent for capitalist modernization nationwide. In 1930 the *Los Angeles Times* proudly declared that "the one great difference which has outweighed all natural handicaps and has made this city one of the first manufacturing centers of the country—is the fact that, from its beginnings, Los Angeles industry has been maintained under the open shop as against union rule in San Francisco, in Portland, and in Seattle."[17]

Both accompanying and facilitating the tremendous expansion of Los Angeles's economic infrastructure on the basis of the open shop during the early twentieth century was the ascendance within the city of one of the most highly centralized arrangements of employer power that the world had ever seen. The cornerstone was the Merchants and Manufacturers Association (M&M). Founded in 1896 under the leadership of *Los Angeles Times* editor Harrison Gray Otis and his son-in-law, Harry Chandler, the M&M coordinated the efforts of local magnates in industry, banking, and transportation to safeguard industrial freedoms and prosperity against disturbances from below. Especially after the metal trades strike and bombing of the *Times* building in 1910, the M&M devoted itself explicitly and entirely to the struggle against trade unionism. Along with their political allies in the Chamber of Commerce, M&M-affiliated employers in Los Angeles stood at the front lines of the city's industrialization campaigns. Collectively, they worked to ensure the exclusion of existing trade unions from the political process, the virtual prohibition of picketing, and the outlawing of political dissension.[18]

The political successes of the M&M and its allies in promoting the city's industrialization reshaped Los Angeles's urban geography during the 1920s. Burgeoning motion picture, aircraft, oil, and aggregate producers gave rise to clusterings of very large plants in the city's agricultural and suburban periphery. Meanwhile, the bulk of industrial activity—including sweatshop-style production of apparel, furniture, and processed foods as well as newer Fordist-style production of tires and automobiles—concentrated around the city's urban core. From the old industrial district just east of downtown, sprawling southward along Alameda Street and eastward along the Union Pacific line, cheap land, access to road and rail networks, and abundant electric and water power made possible the emergence of a dense archipelago of factories, branch plants, and warehouses. Correspondingly, an array of businesses, saloons, nightclubs, churches, and employment agencies sprang up in adjacent districts to cater to the working populations who flooded into the city in massive numbers to fill its demand for industrial labor.[19] Surrounding these districts, neighborhoods filled with subdivided lots, and relatively low-cost bungalow-style homes sprang up to house these same populations.[20]

The open shop formalized employers' control over production and authorized the implementation of discriminatory hiring practices and wage rates that helped keep workers divided and vulnerable. Such practices provided Los Angeles business leaders with a crucial mechanism for managing a workforce that grew and changed rapidly along with the city's industrial base.[21] To be sure, for those who preferred to view Los Angeles as a place where "Anglo-Saxon civilization must climax in the generations to come," industrial expansion in the region proved a mixed blessing.[22] The industrialization of Los Angeles not only contributed to the overall growth of the local population, from 50,000 in 1890 to 1.2 million in 1930 (2.3 million if one includes the surrounding metropolitan districts), but also transformed its composition. The active recruitment of low-cost labor from across the Pacific, south of the U.S.-Mexico border, and the far reaches of the continent contributed to remaking Los Angeles as not only the fastest-growing but also the most ethnically diverse city in the country. The number of African Americans in Los Angeles doubled between 1920 and 1930, and the ethnic Mexican population more than tripled during that same period. The region was also the main entrepôt for Japanese-origin immigrants. By the 1930s, Los Angeles's non-White population constituted 14.2 percent of the total population, exceeding the proportion of non-White residents in such major cities as San Francisco, New York, Chicago, and Philadelphia.[23] On the one hand, the diversity of Los Angeles's workforce was necessary to the city's growth and economic modernization. On the other, it also disturbed the racialized visions that Los Angeles's builders and boosters had cultivated about the city as a stronghold for White supremacy.[24]

At the same time that Los Angeles became one of the most ethnically diverse cities in the world, it also became one of the most racially polarized. One of the great migrations to Los Angeles during the early twentieth century was that of Anglo-Protestants from the Midwest. Lured to the city by myriad forces, including a supposedly endless supply of jobs and freedom from the presence of large numbers of Jewish and Catholic immigrants from southern and eastern Europe that increasingly characterized other major cities, these transplants helped bolster the image of Los Angeles as a haven of White racial purity and the destined "world capital of Aryan supremacy."[25] Unlike in San Francisco, where racial restrictions on housing were mostly informal, Los Angeles's patterns of segregation were overt, explicit, and pervasive. Some researchers have estimated that as much as 95 percent of Los Angeles housing was subject to racially restrictive housing covenants during the period, prohibiting the sale of property to non-White residents.[26] Local boosters sought to capitalize on the appeal of these racially restrictive and Anglo-only neighborhoods, boasting that various enclaves contained "no Negroes and very few Mexican and Chinese" or that their resident populations were "100% American of the White race."[27]

The relatively few neighborhoods that were open to poor, immigrant, and non-White residents became densely concentrated hubs of working-class life. Segregated and multiethnic enclaves that included ethnic Chinese, Japanese, Filipinx, Mexican, African American, Italian, Russian, and Jewish residents expanded in the areas surrounding the city's industrial core, especially in the districts that stretched between the downtown neighborhoods of Chinatown and Little Tokyo, Boyle Heights to the east, the neighborhoods surrounding Central Avenue, and Watts to the south.[28] Interactions across ethnic and racial groups within these neighborhoods are well documented and could lead to new interethnic tensions as well as collaboration. In spaces ranging from schools to markets to nightclubs and dance halls, Central and South Los Angeles neighborhoods provided a setting in which the lives of the city's multiracial workers became interwoven with each other.[29] They were "economic and cultural meeting point[s] for many ethnic groups," not only for those who lived within them but also for many "who passed through them on their way downtown."[30]

Changing demographics and the emergence of newly non-White spaces in the city raised anxieties about the possible directions of Los Angeles's future, and city builders intensified their efforts to control that future. Within this context, tightened segregation and zoning policies aimed not only to control human movement across the urban landscape but also to determine the accessibility of public spaces, resources, and modes of civic participation for different segments of the local population. Residents of non-White neighborhoods in the city came increasingly to occupy a second-class citizenship, distanced from dominant definitions of social membership and from the main channels of civic life and participation. They also became primary targets of a new policing offensive. In the wake of the Mexican and Russian Revolutions and the upsurge of domestic radical movements at the end of World War I, fears about the threat that foreign and dissident subjects posed to the health and stability of the city provoked a wave of political repression. Aggressive assimilationist projects and anti-Red raids ensued, making working-class Angelenos in Central and South Los Angeles the main subjects of efforts to secure local power blocs, fortify the open shop, preserve the sanctity of White spaces, and subdue seditious political activity.[31] Seeking to crush unionization efforts and other perceived threats to employer power, the M&M expanded and reorganized its operations, establishing its own hyperpatriotic offshoot, the Better America Federation. It also backed the militarization of the local police force and the creation of the LAPD Red Squads. Explicitly aiming to eradicate disturbances to the social order, the Red Squads and broader M&M and LAPD activity severely constrained available avenues for political engagement in the city by attaching a high price and potentially harrowing consequences to oppositional activity.[32]

Official law enforcement bodies were by no means the only ones responsible for maintaining the hegemony of the open shop and racial capitalist development in Los Angeles. The wider climate of racial hostility on which the open shop relied drew on reactionary currents among working- and middle-class Angelenos during the 1920s. During this period, the city became a capital of the eugenics movement and a bastion for the rapidly growing Southern California section of the Ku Klux Klan (KKK). These forces terrorized the city's growing non-White populations, reinforced established regional hierarchies, and helped bind definitions of social progress to the preservation of White racial dominance.[33] Together, the many forces of racial and political repression—both official and unofficial varieties—severely limited the political possibilities for immigrant and non-White working people in early twentieth-century Los Angeles, especially in the realms of formal municipal politics and labor unions.

While threats of physical violence and repression were critical components of the open-shop city's municipal power structure, these forces relied for their legitimacy on a broader civic culture that upheld Los Angeles's image as a land of leisure, prosperity, and consumer pleasure. In this respect, the making of social order in the city was in significant part an artistic task. Art was as critical to the work of policing social boundaries as were the LAPD's Red Squads, and as vital to advancing the city's position on the global stage as were the wealth and goods it produced. For these reasons, throughout the early twentieth century, Los Angeles's power brokers made the cultivation of a civic identity through art a top political priority. Los Angeles business leaders and boosters joined forces with classically trained professional and amateur artists to form the California Art Club and other art clubs, which dominated the local artistic scene for most of the 1910s and 1920s. These exclusive, patrician-led bodies acted as gatekeepers to the local art world, controlling much of the city's exhibition space and establishing the parameters for its urban aesthetic. They promoted traditional notions of a transcendent high art that separated thought from experience, seeking idealized refinement over organic expressions of life, alongside a commercial culture that could help market the city on a national and global stage. The dominant artistic culture was, above all, a visual culture, emphasizing landscape and representational styles of painting along with boosterist modes of commercial imagery. Rather than expressing the concerns and imaginations of Angelenos themselves, it sought to enlighten and uplift them in ways that suited elite notions of proper citizenship. In other words, this art aimed to serve the city's booster machine while spreading culture among those who presumably lacked it.[34]

The transformations of the 1920s brought new challenges to the dominance of Los Angeles's conservative art elite. For one thing, growing local interest in the concerns of modernism raised new questions about elitist high art and gave rise to new institutional spaces—organizations as well as art schools—which loosened the grip of elite-led clubs on artistic production in the city. For another, new technologies of cultural production and consumption created new avenues for Angelenos to define for themselves their relationship to the world around them, to each other, to the past and the future. The increasing prevalence of mass cultural forms—from movie theaters to radio programs and records—contributed to the formation of new public spheres and new vehicles for popular expressions of identity. Neither necessarily conservative nor inherently oppositional, the ascendant mass culture reflected the contradictions of life in early twentieth-century America. Fordist mass production, the deskilling of labor, and the tendency toward vertical integration, standardization, and Taylorization contributed to the tightened concentration of wealth and power and to new levels of inequality in all areas of society. In the industries of cultural production and distribution, these developments generated new avenues for the making and maintenance of hedonistic forms of consumerism and racial capitalist hegemony. At the same time, the rise of mass culture and consumerism also helped widen the field of possibility for new forms of engagement, congregation, interaction, and identification by and among working people.[35] As Lizabeth Cohen describes, "Although they did not always recognize it, workers [during the 1920s] increasingly were shopping at the same chain stores, buying the same brand goods, going to the same chain theaters, and listening to the same radio programs on chain networks."[36] The experiences that accompanied these developments contained the raw material from which people could construct and circulate new systems of meaning and memory, new languages of struggle, and new social visions.

Cultural production was as vital to dominant efforts to fashion a white-washed narrative of the city as a bastion of urban racial capitalist progress as it was to working people's efforts to make sense of the world around them, to experiment with alternative visions of themselves and the world, and to forge ties of community and collective struggle. The rich literature on culture and community formation in Los Angeles has shown how cultural production and consumption served as crucial channels for the struggles of insubordinate immigrant populations in the face of displacement, dislocation, racial hostility, segregation, and dehumanization. Until recently, much of this excellent literature has focused on specific ethnic and racial group-oriented histories.[37] Recent studies of multiracial community formation have highlighted how the 1930s marked a high point of interethnic collaboration both within the organized left and in the broader consolidation of a non-White identity.[38] Yet we have a great deal more to learn about the social visions and practices that emerged at the intersection between culture and politics during this period. Scholars who have examined the politics of culture and multiraciality in Los Angeles in the World War II and postwar eras have shed light on the interconnections among differently racialized populations in the city.[39] Far fewer works have looked at the role of culture in shaping interethnic relations in Los Angeles before World War II.[40]

This study builds on the extant literature as it seeks a fuller picture of multiracial cultural politics in Los Angeles during the Great Depression. This chapter underscores how the intensely constrained nature of the formal political arena in 1930s Los Angeles requires that we look more in depth at the political visions that were generated and pursued in grassroots cultural politics. It shows how, during the Depression, as conditions of deprivation and suffering grew deeper and became more widespread, the people of Los Angeles drew on the resources available to them, including those provided by the culture industry, as they built dialogues and affinities across cultural and racial difference. As they engaged in innovative forms of artistic production, beyond traditional points of industrial production, these communities expressed a collective critique of racial capitalist power in Los Angeles and their shared, though differentiated, desires for autonomy and dignity.

Subversive Spectacles

As the main artistic arena in which city leaders constructed narratives of Los Angeles as a land of sunshine, the visual arts were a critical site of cultural contestation. They were also one of the most conspicuous arenas where the city's countercultural expressions took shape during the Great Depression. As historian Sarah Schrank has shown, the 1930s marked a period of transition in Los Angeles's visual art world, away from the classical landscape painting and kitschy boosterist imagery that had dominated the preceding decades and toward a modernist approach that combined American commercial culture and socialist avant-garde aesthetics.[41] While local elites were eager to tap into these artistic streams in order to establish the city as a world "cultural center," they struggled to control cultural production in its fast-evolving forms. City builders' efforts to link the production of modern art to the promotion of Los Angeles's development facilitated the opening of new platforms for artistic production and display—from gallery spaces, to art schools, to the commissioning of public works of art, especially murals. It also eased the entry of previously marginalized artists onto the local art scene's center stage. Between 1932 and 1933, Mexican revolutionary muralist David Alfaro Siqueiros accepted a series of commissions to produce massive public works of art in the heart of the city. Painters Luis Bastar, Philip Guston, Reuben Kadish, Harold Lehman, and others followed in Siqueiros's wake, contributing to a growing presence of ethnic Mexican and Jewish artists in the city. In 1935 sculptor Beulah Ecton Woodard became the first African American artist to display work in a one-person show at the celebrated Los Angeles County Museum.[42] The inclusion of new communities of artists in the civic art world did not dignify a trend toward democratization within the city as a whole. The city leaders never intended for the shifting parameters of artistic participation to challenge the basic structures of Anglo capitalist dominance and development in Los Angeles. Some conservative elites opposed the new measures of racial inclusion outright, viewing the increasingly multiethnic character of the local art world as a threat to the status quo. Others perceived in such changes the opportunity to fortify existing hierarchies by incorporating the city's diverse popular elements into a nationalist, "middlebrow" American culture.[43] Despite such efforts, however, local elites never fully controlled the modes of artistic production and expression over which they presided, and visual arts provided an important channel for cultural politics among the artists and audiences who obtained access to them. As we shall see, during the 1930s a growing cohort of left-leaning artists in the city used these channels toward transgressive, countercultural ends.

For many Los Angeles–based artists, the city's art galleries, museums, and mural walls were sites where it was possible to fuse struggles for access to and inclusion in dominant institutions with efforts to promote grassroots self-definition and self-representation. In these venues, some Angeleno artists helped to advance ideals of cultural democracy at the same time that they affirmed the particularities of grassroots experiences and identities. In varying ways and contexts, their work used visual imagery to subvert dominant discourses of development, resignify established definitions of progress, and challenge bounded notions of national cultural unity. In the process, they contributed to making a popular historical memory that critiqued the city's power structure while linking its multiracial working communities around shared, differentiated, and open-ended struggles for dignity.

The interconnection between grassroots struggles for cultural inclusion and self-definition in 1930s Los Angeles was perhaps nowhere more visible to the public than in the battles over murals in the city. Of course, public muralism in Los Angeles was shaped to a significant degree by the commissioners' desires to see the city at the helm of modern arts movements and to take advantage of the widened audience for visual art that had been created by the circulations of mass culture. To the extent that muralism carried the potential to generate and reinforce narratives about the city as an embodiment of racial capitalist modernity, city leaders hoped that completed murals could represent Los Angeles's preeminent status to the public and the world. While muralists sometimes conformed to these desires, they also challenged them in some cases.

The artist who was perhaps most responsible for exposing the radical possibilities of public muralism to Angelenos was David Siqueiros. A Mexican revolutionary artist who helped launch a mural renaissance in Mexico along with contemporaries Diego Rivera and Jose Clemente Orozco, Siqueiros was particularly driven to use muralism as a vehicle for building dialogues about the disavowed histories of oppressed peoples. According to him, contemporary artists had a responsibility to learn and "borrow from the synthetic energy" of "Negro art" and "primitive art" in the Americas—traditions whose "clarity and depth [had been] lost for centuries," obscured by the forces of colonialism and imperialism. While he insisted that it was critical to "avoid lamentable archaeological reconstructions so fashionable" and fetishized as "Indianism," "Primitivism," and "Americanism," Siqueiros saw that deep lessons could be drawn from their "admirable human content."[44]

Siqueiros's relocation to Los Angeles in the spring of 1932 was driven partly by pressure from the Mexican government and the threat he faced as an internal exile in Mexico. Yet he was also moved to a significant degree by a sense of the city itself as a generative site for radical art.[45] After accepting an invitation from the Chouinard Art Institute to teach a fresco course and to paint a mural in the institute's courtyard, he set about producing his first mural north of the border. With the sponsorship of Nelbert Chouinard, he enlisted the latest technologies of the motion picture industry in the project. Film projectors as well as airbrushes, blowtorches, waterproof cement, and spray guns, all of which had become commonplace tools for building movie sets, enabled Siqueiros to produce a mural massive enough to occupy the entire twenty-four- by nineteen-foot wall he was allotted and durable enough to survive the outdoor elements. Rather than painting the mural on separate smaller canvases to be fixed onto the wall, Siqueiros insisted on painting directly on the wall itself, incorporating older methods of fresco painting within a contemporary context. The finished product could not be broken down, bought, or sold. Rather, he intended it to be free and accessible to the public.[46] In appropriating modern industrial technologies to produce such a work within the capital of the film industry and a key nerve center of the mass consumer economy, Siqueiros's mural embodied what he called "dialectic-subversive painting."[47]

As his description suggested, Siqueiros conceived of muralism as an artistic practice with transformative political potential in the context of 1930s Los Angeles. The Chouinard mural, which he entitled *Workers' Meeting*, was an opportunity to experiment with that potential. The mural itself depicted workers, including a Black man and a White woman who each hold children in their arms, taking a break from their jobs to listen to a speech by a labor agitator. The painting centered themes of political activism, interracial affinity, the relationship between industrial production and social reproduction, and disrupted labor discipline. As such, it attracted the ire of art critics and local civic elites. It was whitewashed by an unknown source shortly after its unveiling in July 1933.[48] Yet a critical aspect of its production outlasted the mural's destruction. To complete the project, Siqueiros called on a cross section of the city's most skilled and innovative resident artists. They included Luis Bastar, a resident painter from Mexico and cofounder of the radical Liga de Escritores y Artistas Revolucionarios (League of Revolutionary Writers and Artists) and, later, Taller de Gráfica Popular (People's Print Workshop); Reuben Kadish, a Chicago-born Jewish radical sculptor and painter who was active in opposing U.S. imperialism in Nicaragua; Philip Guston, a Canadian-born Jewish painter (Siqueiros regarded Guston and Kadish as "the most promising painters in either the US or Mexico"); Harold Lehman, a radical surrealist painter who helped found a postsurrealist school and artistic movement in Los Angeles; and Paul Sample, a watercolorist known for his social realist style and rendering of popular struggles, among many others. The mural project nurtured the formation of new ties among these artists and lent new creative energy to their work. The experience galvanized a number of them to form a muralist bloc of their own, in order to continue experimenting with the medium beyond the direction of Siqueiros himself. Many of them would also become leading figures in the Public Works of Art and Works Progress Administration arts projects.[49]

The capstone, and most controversial, work that Siqueiros completed in Los Angeles during his stay there in 1932 was a commissioned mural on the second story of the old Italian Hall on Olvera Street, entitled *América Tropical* (figure 5.1).

Siqueiros was commissioned for the work by Plaza Art Center director F. K. Ferenz, who hoped the project would help propel Los Angeles into the national spotlight as a leading site in a growing civic arts movement. The assigned theme—an idealized tropical landscape representative of California's imagined premodern past, complete with colorful flora, fauna, and Native peoples—intended to serve and support the commercial culture of the mural's venue. Olvera Street, after all, was an invention of civic boosters, who aimed to create an Anglo commercial tourist destination through the commodification of Mexican culture and the cultivation of popular nostalgia for an "authentic" Mexican past. It boasted "70-odd stores and booths," lined with "gay decorations and displays of Mexican foods, pottery, and trinkets."[50] In the minds of its funders, *América Tropical* would not only boost tourism in the district but also bolster the image of contemporary, Anglo-dominated Los Angeles as a model of urban modernity vis-à-vis its juxtaposition to romantic, primitivist fantasies of the region's history.

The finished product, however, diverged starkly from the commissioner's intentions and aimed instead to drum up a different, darker memory of the region's past. Unveiled on October 9 in its completed form, Siqueiros's *América Tropical* was an insurgent indictment of the racial violence and settler colonialism that accompanied the advancement of dominant notions

FIGURE 5.1 David Alfaro Siqueiros, *América Tropical*, 1932.

of civilization and progress in the Americas. Stretching a massive eighteen by thirty-two feet overlooking the plaza, and viewable from three different streets, the public spectacle centered a crucified Indigenous subject against the background of an ancient temple. In the upper right corner of the painting, amid the serpentine branches that surround the central subject, a Mexican campesino and a Peruvian Indian are ready to shoot down an eagle, an emblem of American nationhood and empire. According to Siqueiros, "It is the violent symbol of the Indian peon of feudal America doubly crucified by the nation's exploitative classes and, in turn, by imperialism. It is the living symbol of the destruction of past national American cultures by the invaders of yesterday and today. It is the preparatory action of the revolutionary proletariat that scales the scene and readies its weapons to throw itself into the ennobling battle of a new social order."[51]

Although *América Tropical* did not survive long before being whitewashed, and Siqueiros was forced to leave Los Angeles in the fall of 1933 after the government refused to renew his visa, experiments with radical muralism continued to reverberate through the work of the artists who collaborated with him, and others drew inspiration from the innovative art form and the movement it created. Harold Lehman recalled how his participation in the Siqueiros murals along with his peers gave rise to a newly politicized collective. According to Lehman, while working with Siqueiros, he and his artist colleagues "had at our disposal this shed, which we used for the fresco paintings. So we all got together every chance we could" to collaboratively learn the methods of fresco painting and large-scale canvas construction, to experiment with techniques as well as the political and thematic content of their work. Lehman described, "We learned how to construct these things up to the finished surface of the fresco paintings. And we painted these things in a group—we each had our own sets of the paint—but we painted them together along the wall. We would line one up after another."[52] Their work focused on themes of multiraciality and inter-sectional working-class struggle that marked their interpretation of contemporary social movements. "Each of us had a subject to paint," Lehman recalled, "in fact we had two subjects to paint. One was the exploitation of labor by capital in America, and the other was the persecution of the Blacks, or at that time whom we called the Negro in America: those two subjects. So we each painted frescoes on each one of those subjects. I did too." The experience they gained "instigated us to come and form this group [the Bloc of Mural Painters], and we were eager to get going and do it because we all wanted to be mural painters."[53]

As city leaders and boosters well understood, the movement that emerged around radical muralism in 1930s Los Angeles, and the explicit political messages that its artwork frequently conveyed, posed a threat to the city's dominant culture. For precisely this reason, elite forces sought to eradicate the cultural influence of radical muralists. On February 11, 1933, shortly after artists from the Bloc of Mural Painters had transported a collection of their paintings to the John Reed Club in Hollywood for what was to be their first official exhibit, the city's Red Squad raided the club and broke up a gathering that was being held there by members of the radical Japanese-language paper *Rodo Shimbun* (Labor News), the Japanese Proletarian Cultural League, and the International Labor Defense. The officers went to extra lengths to destroy the artwork that covered the walls. The mutilated murals included three large portable mural panels that the bloc had devoted to the Scottsboro Nine—one depicting the Scottsboro defendants in a courtroom setting with an electric chair in the background, one with a Black man tied to a post being whipped by a masked member of the KKK, and another of a Black man with his hands and feet bound lying on the floor of a prison cell. Photographs of the paintings taken in the aftermath of the raid show the canvases ridden with gashes and bullet holes, including bullet holes deliberately placed in the forehead and groin of the Black subjects.[54] This was far from an arbitrary act of destruction: the LAPD officers who raided the John Reed Club not only sought to ensure that the murals would not see the light of day but also issued a clearly legible threat to club-affiliated activists who dared to challenge the racial status quo. In typical fashion, the press narrated the incident not as an act of aggression by the LAPD but as a measure taken to secure public safety against left-wing political subversives. Days after the raid, the *Illustrated Daily News* warned readers of the insidious threat of radical art in the city, underscoring that the "so-called harmless writers' and artists' club—the John Reed club of Hollywood—is in reality just another communist tentacle, reaching into the artistic and intellectual life of Los Angeles."[55]

The impulse to manage radical elements in the city that drove the repressive tactics of Los Angeles's Red Squads also shaped municipal efforts to institutionalize a Public Works of Art Project (PWAP) in the city. A precursor to the Works Progress Administration's Federal Art Project, the PWAP was coordinated by civic officials with relatively conservative intentions for the program. In contrast with public arts programs in other cities across the United States, where arts administrators encouraged popularly rooted, middlebrow notions of art and American culture, Los Angeles's PWAP officials clung overwhelmingly to transcendent visions of high art.[56] They encouraged the production of the conventional landscape paintings and historical scenes that were the hallmarks of California's dominant narrative—scenes such as the arrival of Spaniard Juan Rodriguez Cabrillo to the region's shores and the state's 1849 Constitutional Convention.[57]

However, some of the PWAP's commissioned artists seized the opportunity of mural making to critique prevailing power relations and development patterns. For example, in 1935 artist Hugo Ballin was commissioned by the Section of Fine Arts to paint a mural depicting the early, gold rush–era days of the mail system on an interior wall of an Inglewood post office. Although he ultimately accepted the task, Ballin fiercely criticized the boosterist nature of the project in the context of the Great Depression. Ballin remarked in a letter to the project's commissioners, "It seems a shame that any group of men should be so naive as to ask any serious painter to waste $680 of government money [on such a project]. . . . The people need many things more than a depraved painting of a '49 gold rush bar room episode, which you have asked me to do."[58] After ultimately accepting the terms of the commission, Ballin pulled a stunt on the arts program to critique what he saw as a misuse of funds by a misguided, antidemocratic, patrician-led hierarchy of the civic art world and elitist notions of high art. The mural he produced offered a satirized countermemory of Los Angeles's history and the culture of the city's pioneers and founders. The Los Angeles Times spurned the finished product as "a dream-like satire of the fat capitalists," tinged with "vulgarity and a splatter of revolutionary sentiment."[59] As the Times described, "A group of heavily caricatured miners, gamblers and bartenders are seen in a saloon with two frowsy girls. At the bar a sick drunk is hoisting another shot of red-eye while a worthy behind him draws his knife to stab his companion in the back."[60] Much to the dismay of the Times editors and other business interests in the city, Ballin's mural offered a glaring indictment of the greed, patriarchal entitlement, and violent lust for power that he perceived as hallmarks of Los Angeles's civic leadership.

Another PWAP artist, Gordon K. Grant, was commissioned by the Section of Fine Arts to produce a mural in the Alhambra post office depicting "the development of California."[61] Bending the assigned theme in a critical direction, beyond the commissioners' intentions, Grant covered his post office wall with depictions of an oppositional narrative of California's development. Rather than celebratory images of the region's Americanization, Grant's mural highlighted continuities in regional power relations that shaped structures of Indian, Mexican, and Anglo labor. The fresco included panels devoted to Native American workers engaged in mission construction, Mexican farmers and ranch hands, and Anglos panning for gold and branding a horse. While the physical characteristics of the subjects and the specific activities in which they were engaged differed across each of the panels, they all performed work that bent their backs in a similar stooping posture.[62] The mural thus expressed commonalities across the differentiated populations of workers, calling attention to the ways in which historical patterns of colonialism commonly relied on bodies at work. Rather than depicting a linear trajectory of development as progress, Grant's work underscored the historical continuity of the oppression of labor and the dignity of laboring people. At a time when popular insurgencies of colonized and working people were gaining momentum across California and the globe, Grant's mural can be seen as representing a longer genealogy of grassroots struggle. Perhaps not surprisingly, Grant's mural provoked conservative reactions from the public. One complaint characterized the mural as "entirely inappropriate," sure to "detract from the appearance of a post office lobby," and an aberration that should be replaced with something "in keeping with the nature of the business transacted in such places."[63] Another declared that the post office's "beautiful lobby will be ruined by the murals."[64] In the contestation over Grant's post office murals, competing notions of California's development and competing notions of aesthetic beauty were intertwined.

While radical muralism was an important current of oppositional cultural formation in 1930s Los Angeles, it did not by any means represent the totality of the region's oppositional culture, nor did it exhaust the full range of radicalisms taking shape among working-class Angelenos in this period. In fact, the privileged access that professional artists had and that enabled them to produce commissioned murals in public spaces made them a relatively unique segment within the spectrum of Los Angeles's creative communities. Most of the popular struggles in the city did not have such resources at their disposal, and the inclusion of non-White and female artists within formal channels remained severely limited. Moreover, the exposure that muralism garnered—a result of its distinctly public, spectacular form and often explicitly political content—also carried its own inherent political constraints. In many cases, the very boldness with which muralists articulated a counternarrative of regional history and identity made them readily legible to civic authorities as a threat to the dominant order, ensuring they would become targets of the city's repressive forces. For this reason, they can and must be considered as partial, incomplete, nontotalizing expressions of the oppositional culture that emerged in the city at the time.

A wider range of radical art was emerging in Los Angeles during this moment, beyond the domains of city-sanctioned art clubs, schools, galleries, and mural commissions. Much of the work of Los Angeles's artistic communities hinged less on the advancement of clearly articulated political messages and occurred in spaces less heavily surveilled by civic authorities than the murals examined here. Much of it fell beyond the purview of repressive campaigns by LAPD's Red Squads and beyond the scope of dominant definitions of politics, taking place within the neighborhoods of working-class communities themselves.

Community Theater and Community Making in South Los Angeles

While oppositional and surrealist political currents animated struggles for cultural democracy in the city and contributed to the making of a popular countermemory of Los Angeles's development, they also figured prominently in local movements that utilized art as a vehicle for community building. The community arts movement that took hold in Los Angeles during this period drew heavily on the leadership and social networks built by local women of color. Activating the social ties and political resources they had fostered in the course of their everyday lives and work, South Los Angeles–based Black women in particular helped give rise to a creative community that linked local working- and middle-class residents across racial and ethnic lines, around participatory forms of social organization and cultural production. Proceeding from a shared recognition of the interconnections between material survival and dignified grassroots autonomy, the city's community arts organizers helped encourage critical dialogue about the functions of power and possibilities of social relations in the city. Placing the arts, especially theater, at the center of their organizing efforts, these activists created new spaces and opportunities for Angelenos to explore alternative imaginings of life in Los Angeles.

A central fixture in the city's community arts movement during the peak years of the Great Depression was the Hawthorne House. The Hawthorne House was, first and foremost, a community center. It first opened its doors at 837 East Twenty-Fourth Street in the spring of 1934 "to provide a community center for Eastside activities" and to address what its organizers saw as "an actual need in the community."[65] In a basic and immediate sense, Hawthorne House participants sought to meet needs related to the material deprivation experienced by local neighborhood residents, which had reached new levels between 1933 and 1934. While poverty, unemployment, and hunger had characterized South Los Angeles's multiethnic neighborhoods throughout the 1910s and 1920s, the Depression intensified conditions of deprivation for local residents, confronting them with rising food prices, heightened levels of joblessness, and limited access to the relief programs that emerged to serve other areas of the city.[66] At the same time, the Hawthorne House organizers recognized that an effective response to the material needs of South Los Angeles residents had to go hand in hand with a further-reaching and more open-ended project for community empowerment. The district in which the new community center emerged—comprising an African American majority but also including a diverse scattering of European, Asian, and Mexican immigrants—not only experienced some of the highest levels of unemployment and poverty in the city but also faced some of the most stringent forms of segregation, harassment, and dehumanization.[67] In contrast with other projects across the city that were oriented more narrowly around the distribution of relief, the Hawthorne House sought to provide South Angelenos with a resource center that could equip them to challenge the forces of social division, fragmentation, and subordination that they experienced in their daily lives.

The center itself was an outgrowth of, and a nexus for, collaboration among overlapping community networks and progressive activists from across the city. At the center of its administrative corps were "some of Los Angeles' leading women," many of whom were veteran professional and amateur artists with backgrounds in the culture industry.[68] For example, Sarah DeCoursey Page, coordinator of Hawthorne House activities from its earliest stages, was an established writer, producer, singer, and teacher and a leading figure in Los Angeles's community theater movement. After garnering a reputation in New York as "the first Race woman to crash Broadway as a promoter and producer" and "the only Race person in New York to have an hour on the air bearing her name," DeCoursey returned to Los Angeles with her husband, the composer and teacher Eugene Edgar Page, and reopened their studio on East Forty-Sixth Street to continue teaching piano, voice, and drama lessons to neighborhood residents.[69] Another of the center's key organizers, Sanoma DeBeal, was a student at the University of Redlands and a gifted singer and stage performer. Originally from Roswell, New Mexico, DeBeal and her family were among the first African American residents to settle in Corona, California.[70] DeBeal was active in civic affairs throughout the Los Angeles and San Bernardino County region in the years preceding her involvement with the Hawthorne House. She frequently lent her talents to civic and progressive causes, ranging from singing "popular Spanish so-loes" for the Corona High School Spanish Club, to singing "Negro spirituals" for the Cope Cooperative Club in Redlands, to singing solos at a rally pro-testing the exploitative practices of the Southern California Telephone Com-pany.[71] Other major figures in the organizing and running of the Hawthorne House included South Los Angeles residents and activists Margaret and Earl Jackson; engineer, poet, and community organizer John H. Owens; and fel-low activists Barbara Capers, Carl Gross, and Harry Penn.[72] Support and resources for the house and its various activities and events regularly came from the Workers' International Relief, the League of Struggle for Negro Rights, the *California Eagle*, and an array of Hollywood progressives.[73]

On one level, the Hawthorne House's organizers and participants sought to meet needs in the community that were basic, material, and immediate. For example, one ongoing program involved collecting and distributing do-nations of food, clothing, and other necessities.[74] In an era marked by intense material deprivation and widespread suffering, the delivery of such things to people not adequately served by relief programs was no small matter.

But its objectives reached beyond filling a gap in the state-sponsored New Deal relief. On a broader plane, the Hawthorne House was an experiment in democratic and participatory forms of social organization that prioritized the autonomy of grassroots communities while encouraging their creative self-expression and empowerment. The collaborating organizers, and the constituency it served, breached many of the divisions imposed by the wider society in which it operated, crossing lines of race, ethnicity, and gender, with women playing crucial leadership roles.[75] House organizers welcomed "all residents in the community," including "strangers in the city," to "avail themselves of its facilities" and resources and to participate in its programs. Its ongoing weekly agenda included child care services; a mother's clinic; lectures on personal health and dietetics; classes in Black history, social problems, art, writing, dance, music, fashion design, and drama; and dialogues about contemporary events in a House-sponsored citywide forum. All of these programs were "free of charge."[76] Providing resources at no cost, made possible by the "support for the house coming from those who felt the need for such an institution in the community," dramatized the House organizers' investment in grassroots autonomy and community building over and against the profit-driven impulses of the market. It also underscored the center's guiding political priorities of access, inclusion, and collective democratic participation.[77]

The centrality of the arts to the Hawthorne House project indicates the organizers' sense of the integral relationship between creative practice and social change. In addition to the range of art classes that the House offered on an ongoing basis, its organizers and participants also screened motion pictures and staged plays in the open-air theater of the facility's front lawn as well as other venues around the city, such as the Los Angeles Cultural Center and the Elks Hall. These events included films like *The Song of the Marketplace*, based on a story by radical Russian writer Maxim Gorky. They featured such plays as Fyodor Dostoyevsky's *Crime and Punishment* and Swedish writer August Strindberg's *The Stronger*, a one-act play that provoked deep questions about normative gender roles, domesticity, and dependency. Other theatrical productions included *Miss Liberty and Little Red* and *The Father*; the latter depicts a woman who defies her husband's adherence to discipline and flees to raise her daughter the way she pleases, potentially as an artist.[78] The performances sometimes drew crowds of up to three hundred people.[79] The works put questions about social norms, hierarchies, power, and patriotism on the table for community discussion. They opened up discursive space for collective social and cultural criticism and contributed to a potentially subversive body of shared knowledge and historical memory. Much like the works by radical muralists in other parts of the city, these screenings and exhibitions contributed to a countercultural dialogue that nurtured practices of self-definition among working-class Angelenos.

Far from being an isolated example of art-based community making, the Hawthorne House was part of a network of creative communities across the city. Hawthorne House participants collaborated with other community arts groups in shows and performances in venues outside South Los Angeles and hosted those groups at the neighborhood community center. Groups with whom they collaborated included the Los Angeles Japanese Players, the Hollywood Blue Blouse Players, the Finnish Workers Choral Group, the Ukrainian Russian Chorus, and Jose Martinez's Spanish Orchestra.[80]

The diverse groups and participatory practices engaged by the Hawthorne House's organizers and constituents reflected a politics that valued multi-vocality, difference, and dialogue over unity and conformity. Events such as International Theatre Group Night, held at the Los Angeles Cultural Center, and the Workers International Solidarity Day, held at the Hawthorne House itself, presented organizers, community members, and the broader public with opportunities not only for entertainment and celebration but also for collective learning and dialogue.[81] As one Hawthorne House representative explained, these events presented opportunities to build a "finer type of ra-cial expression." While such a statement might be interpreted as suggesting the pursuit of a purified or civilized mode of expression in accordance with dominant notions of high art, it might also be read as signifying a more fully situated collective knowledge capable of empowering community members and equipping them to confront the forces of racial oppression.[82]

On October 15, 1934, the local full-length rendition of *Stevedore* debuted at the Musart Theater, on Figueroa in downtown Los Angeles, under the auspices of the Hawthorne House. The cast comprised members of the Hawthorne House's theater troupe, "the Hawthorne Players, a cooperative group of unemployed Negroes and whites and ought to answer some of the questions of those jittery people who whine about the jobless wasting their time."[83] According to the *Los Angeles Times*, "The Hawthorne Players present a unique perspective inasmuch as one half of the company are white people, while the remainder of the cast consists of twenty Negro players."[84]

The show was a hit among local working-class people. As the local Black paper *Los Angeles Sentinel* underscored, criminalization of Black people and false accusations of rape were "all too familiar" to local African Americans.[85] One editor affirmed the connection between the theatrical production and the lived reality of South Angelenos, reporting, "By a curious coincident the play revolves partially around another such incident as that which occurred here last week when a hysterical white woman told a story of attack by Negroes."[86]

The Hawthorne Players kept prices for the show between twenty-five cents and one dollar, depending on the day and time of the performance, in order to "attract the largest possible crowd."[87] They announced on Octo-ber 18 "that 25 tickets will be given free each day to unemployed Negroes. Clubs and organizations wishing to see the drama may purchase 35 cent seats in blocks of 12 or more for 25 cents each. Seventy five cent seats bought on a similar scale will be sold for 45 cents each."[88] The show was a huge success and spurred requests for a repeat production after it closed. "This demand has come from many people who have heard the play discussed, but did not get an opportunity to see it."[89] Los Angeles residents' widespread interest and participation in the Hawthorne Players' showing of *Stevedore* reflected and contributed to an emergent counterculture in the city. This counterculture was rooted in an oppositional worldview and collaborative critique of racial capitalist power and driven toward the collaborative pursuit of multiracial working-class autonomy. At the same time that South Los Angeles's community arts movement encouraged grassroots creativity and self-definition, it also helped foster a sense that dominant patterns of development—dehumanization, division, and marginalization—were not the only ones possible.

Jazz and the World of Popular Front Youth Culture

If the radical muralism of David Siqueiros and those inspired by him disrupted the city's dominant narrative with a political language that was readily legible to civic authorities as subversive, and the Hawthorne House's community theater worked to cultivate community dialogues among Angelenos, the improvised creation of new languages of struggle by working-class communities themselves was epitomized by the local jazz scene that took hold in the city, especially among South and East Los Angeles youth. Less shockingly controversial than the murals of radical artists, and less scripted and choreographed than the plays that community organizers created with South Los Angeles residents, the music of young jazz players in the city charted new paths for expanding the boundaries of political activity and for generating and enacting new visions of a dignified social existence.

For young people growing up in South and East Los Angeles during the 1930s—where unemployment and poverty rates were exceptionally high, access to relief was severely constrained if it existed at all, and the city's dominant narrative offered little place for them and little hope for the future—musical improvisation helped to expand the horizons of what was politically possible. Jazz music provided a model for empowerment, dialogue, and social action. With historical roots in Afrodiasporic traditions, jazz was part of a musical genealogy that linked the blues, ragtime, gospel, and swing in a common "poetry of revolt." To borrow from Paul Garon's analysis, jazz was "a language of the richest complexity," defined by its distinct capacity to articulate dreams "for gratification of repressed wishes."[90] In this sense, the young Angelenos who took up jazz as a practice and a way of life carried forth a repository of historical oppositional knowledge at the same time that they employed it to situate themselves in the present and to reinvent the future. As Daniel Fischlin, Ajay Heble, and George Lipsitz have argued, "Adaptability, improvisation, and invention are the weapons of the weak."[91] In this respect, examining the improvisational musical culture of young working-class Angelenos can help us to uncover practices of grassroots self-activity and self-definition in Depression-era Los Angeles.

Of course, examining the cultural practices and politics of youth in 1930s Los Angeles requires attending to the distinct position of young people within the open-shop city and the emergent movements taking shape within it. On the one hand, young people's lives were shaped by the same economic and structural forces, and patterns of exclusion and exploitation, that shaped those of their parents. They similarly faced racial segregation, discrimination, and economic deprivation in their daily lives. Yet their relationship to the world around them, to capital, and to the creative process also differed from their elders'. As Robin D. G. Kelley describes, "Unlike more mature adults, young people are in the process of discovering the world as they negotiate it. They are creating new cultures, strategies of resistance, identities, sexualities, and in the process generating a wider range of problems for authorities whose job it is to keep them in check."[92] As Lizabeth Cohen has shown, working-class youth in the 1930s engaged mass culture more readily and more fully than their parents. They often used the spaces of theaters, clubs, and dance halls as arenas to forge new identities for and among themselves, not only against the prescriptions of dominant culture but also against the expectations of their parents and ethnic communities.[93] Generally less constrained by the inhibitions that encumbered older residents, youth culture was an important site for the production of Los Angeles's culture of opposition during the 1930s. It also offers a valuable site for exploring grassroots surrealist political imaginings amid the crisis of the Great Depression.

Music was integral to the lives of young people growing up in Los Angeles during the 1930s and also to the circuitry of everyday life and struggle. The creation and circulation of music was part of the process of community formation and part of the dialogue that occurred across generations. In the words of drummer William Douglass, "The music was always around."[94] Born in Sherman, Texas, Douglass moved with his parents to Los Angeles before his first birthday and considered himself a "native of Los Angeles." For him, familial bonds and musical collaborations had a close and symbiotic relationship. Douglass grew up in the care of parents and extended family members for whom music provided both emotional and financial sustenance. Douglass recalled how his father made time outside his schedule as a parent and a custodian in the local school system to sing regularly in a vocal quartet. Douglass's grandfather was a skilled professional violinist, and his uncle, a guitarist. Douglass credited his uncle with teaching him "a few little chords" early on and introducing him to a musical community that included such famed musicians as saxophonist Floyd Turnham and alto sax player Marshall Royal, with whom his uncle played in Les Hite's orchestra.[95] "So I used to see and hear all this kind of stuff at the family picnics and things," Douglass recollected.[96]

Across the diverse neighborhoods of South Los Angeles, music assisted patterns of community making and identity making among residents. In La Colonia, an ethnic Mexican enclave in Watts where saxophonist Anthony Ortega grew up, a mixture of live music and radio regularly filled the streets for formal and informal gatherings among residents. Neighborhood festivals such as La Jamaica drew people who lived in the vicinity to the grounds of the local church, where they socialized and danced to a soundtrack that ranged from traditional Mexican songs and polkas to popular swing tunes like Glenn Gray and the Casa Loma Orchestra's "No Name Jive" and Artie Shaw Orchestra's "Frenesí." Such gatherings not only created spaces of leisure and laughter for people who faced pressures and restrictions in other parts of the city but also fostered the bonds of community and facilitated the production of multivalent, cross-generational identities among ethnic Mexicans within the multiracial city.[97]

In addition to musical traditions fostered by families and communities, proximity to Central Avenue, the main hub of the West Coast's jazz scene, ensured that South Los Angeles residents were connected to the jazz world. Central Avenue ran through the heart of Los Angeles's racially mixed and predominantly Black residential districts. It was a main artery on which South Los Angeles residents traveled to get to other parts of the city, and along which Angelenos from other districts passed to get between the city's industrial centers, downtown, neighborhoods further south and to the west, and the San Pedro waterfront. As Douglass explained, from the house he grew up in on East Fifty-Sixth Street, just two blocks from Central Avenue, "I had to go down Central to get wherever I was going. If I wanted to go downtown, I had to get the 'U' car on Central and take it all the way downtown."[98] For young people like Douglass, however, Central Avenue was more than a passageway to someplace else. It was a global cultural and artistic center they could rightly identify as their own. It was "a way of life," as Douglass put it.[99] Trumpeter Clora Bryant moved with her father from Denison, Texas, to Los Angeles in 1945. Her father moved to work in the shipyards, and she enrolled to study music at the University of California, Los Angeles. As she described, "There was so much activity on Central Avenue when I got there. It was like a beehive. It was people going in and out of everywhere, out of the clubs, out of the restaurants, the stores." There were "a lot of young kids just hanging there just to be on the scene and to learn."[100]

Many young people growing up in the vicinity worked at venues along or near Central Avenue while going through school, and these jobs provided an entry into the local music scene.[101] For example, tenor sax and clarinet player Buddy Collette recalled that he began working alongside Vernon Slater as a shoeshiner around the age of eleven or twelve.[102] From the neighborhood in Watts where they lived, Collette and Slater would ride up through Central Avenue and downtown to offer shoeshines to passersby. According to Collette, shoeshining enabled young men from South Los Angeles to feel good about "earning our own thing," but it also "helped us musically, because we found all the music stores."[103] Between shines, "we'd go hang out in music stores or something and meet the people who would come in from the bands. . . . We were fascinated by the music stores and the musicians and the mouthpieces and the horns and everything."[104] It was often through their jobs that young South Angelenos met each other and forged lasting friendships. For example, Collette met bass player Charles Mingus while they were both shoeshining.[105] Through the work they performed in these early years, South Los Angeles youth built relationships, acquired firsthand knowledge of the city, and developed strategies for navigating racial and class boundaries outside their home neighborhoods, all of which proved to be valuable resources and skills that they carried into their musical careers.

The ways in which young South Angelenos utilized circuits of labor to navigate the city's racial and spatial boundaries reveal that their work was about much more than earning an income. Saxophonist and clarinetist Jackie Kelso (Jack Kelson) grew up on East Twenty-Sixth Street, just across the railroad tracks from the Long Beach Avenue thoroughfare. Kelso got hooked on playing the clarinet after seeing some family friends playing the woodwinds. He became friends with drummer Forest "Chico" Hamilton in grade school, whom he described as "a creative artist from the word go."[106] Hamilton and Kelso began shoeshining together around the same time they started playing music together. While shoeshining and music may seem disparate arenas of activity, Kelso's experience suggests that the spontaneous, creative spirit that animated their music also shaped their activities and experiences as shoeshiners. According to Kelso, shoeshining offered an enhanced sense of autonomy. It was a good way not only to "pick up some change" but also "to have untold adventures."[107] As he described, "You build a little box and you walk around town anywhere, hopping trucks, stealing rides, jumping on streetcars, not having to pay, you know, in the days they had streetcars."[108] There was a certain performative artistry to the way they approached their job that enabled them to evade and defy certain racial and social restrictions. "A shoeshine boy can go in and out of everywhere," Kelso explained. "It's almost like down South. Put a white coat on a black man, he can go anywhere, because that white coat indicates, 'He's a good one. He's got a job. He can be trusted.' It's like *The Invisible Man*."[109]

While South Los Angeles youth were exposed to a range of musical forms across their homes, neighborhoods, and jobs, developing their own personal tastes in music, their likes and dislikes, was a key part of their self-definition and identity formation. Many young people seeking to define their musical preferences began by rejecting the forms either inherited from or imposed on them by their parents, grandparents, or teachers. Bass player Don Tosti, for instance, described how he grew up surrounded by traditional *ranchera* and mariachi music but never liked them. He found these styles to be "too simple, too stupid. . . . We used to call it 'shit-kicking' music."[110] In contrast, jazz music appealed to him as something "more advanced, more interesting."[111] Buddy Collette remembered feeling stifled by his grandmother's insistence that he learn piano. "She was so set on me being a pianist. She could see me as a classical pianist," he reflected. Around the age of ten, when his grandma started picking him up from his parents' house to bring him to piano lessons every weekend, he found it to be "a lot of pressure" and overwhelmingly "boring." Trying to find a way out of piano lessons, Collette discovered his desire to play the saxophone. "Now, that would be a nice way to go," he recalled thinking. In addition to giving him access to a style of music that appealed to him, a saxophone meant "I'd have something to take to school and show off."[112]

Young Angelenos who gravitated toward jazz and swing styles developed role models among the icons who frequented joints along Central Avenue. As Douglass noted, "Like our idols were the Count Basies, Jimmie Luncefords, Duke Ellingtons, and what have you."[113] Star jazz players displaced the heroes celebrated by civic nationalists in the city—the European explorers, settlers, and urban developers—and provided an alternative source of identification for local youth. More than trite celebrity worship, young Angelenos' reverence for such musicians gave them a connection to creative communities that enhanced their own sense of creative and political possibility. As Douglass recalled, "All of us as young kids, when we got out of school and were on our way home, we would walk right down Central Avenue just for a chance to pass by the Dunbar Hotel, because that's where all the big bands stayed. . . . It might be Basie or whatever." He explained, "We'd watch these guys climb off the bus and go upstairs to their hotel rooms, and we just hung around. And then, if they opened in a theater, you know, no school for us! . . . We'd just sit through that movie over and over again just to catch the next show. . . . We'd run out in the alley and watch them come out of the backstage entrance, in and out. That kept on until we got a chance to get acquainted with the guys, and then they knew we were musicians."[114] To have their role models recognize and acknowledge them as musicians provided these young people with an alternative form of affirmation and belonging to what was offered by family, school, or other neighborhood or civic institutions.

Of course, young people also had their hometown heroes and a corresponding sense of connection to locally based creative communities. For example, the Woodman brothers, who were from Watts, and their band, Woodman Brothers Biggest Little Band in the World, jumpstarted much of the local swing scene during the 1930s. According to Collette, the Woodman brothers were responsible for "setting the stage" for South Los Angeles youth in the 1930s. They helped Collette to see "what musicians could do" and to establish "what kind of musician I had to be."[115] Having role models from their own community helped local youngsters to expand their visions of their own capabilities as well as of the potential that existed for their future. The affiliations and aspirations that emerged from these relationships challenged the boundaries of the social visions celebrated by Los Angeles's elites in this era.

Many youth utilized the resources at their disposal to make music. For example, William Douglass recalled how he and tenor saxophonist Dexter Gordon learned to drum by using chairs, tin cans, and a washtub.[116] Anthony Ortega honed his skills on the saxophone by following the lead of Charlie Parker records on his family's windup Victrola. "I'd put the old 78 [rpm record] on there, and if a run was real fast, I could just slow it down," he explained.[117] Improvised jam sessions using the raw materials of everyday life disrupted the dominant rhythms of the city and gave expression to new ones. These forms of cultural production also diverged starkly from the forms of production that dominant forces in the city would have preferred working people of color to perform.

By the 1930s, South Los Angeles, Watts, and East Los Angeles had developed a vibrant community infrastructure of music instruction and education, which nourished the creativity and cultivated the skills of local youth.

Through the available channels of music instruction, they not only learned basic rudiments of music but also developed the links between creativity and life. Many working-class young people's first introduction to playing an instrument was through the public school system, and the schools in these communities had no shortage of talented and generous music teachers. "We had voice lessons and instrumental lessons and music theory and all that sort of thing," with instruments provided by the schools, Leroy Hurte recalled.[118] In the words of Buddy Collette, who attended Jordan High School in Watts, the teachers who came to work in the area "were very special people" in part because they "had to be special people. . . . They didn't just come for the money, because, you know, long ride, no freeways, and they knew they had to really teach," since they were given plenty of warnings by school administrators that the area was "rough," with "a lot of black kids" and "a lot of Mexicans."[119] According to Collette, and the descriptions of other students from Jordan and Jefferson High Schools, the music instructors in the local area shared and transmitted the same spirit of community building and grassroots empowerment that animated the Hawthorne House, as described earlier in this chapter.[120] They were "dedicated," the kind of teachers who "knew they had their work cut out for them" but were committed to "see if [they] can build" and not just give lessons and assign homework.[121]

It was not uncommon for instructors to stay after class to train their students or help their students organize bands beyond the regular orchestra or forge valuable connections in the music world.[122] In Douglass's words, "they sort of looked out for our needs quite a bit."[123] By the late 1930s, legendary instructors Samuel Browne and Lloyd Reese were also teaching in the area. As Ortega noted, in exchange for private lessons with Reese that typically cost about three dollars per hour, "Eric Dolphy used to cut Lloyd's grass or do the work around there like washing dishes. . . . He used to do chores for his lessons."[124]

Music was fundamentally a collective practice for Los Angeles's young musicians. Collaboration, of course, was at the heart of forming and playing as a band. One had to be "concerned about the whole orchestra" and not just oneself as an individual, as Buddy Collette described.[125] The collaborative ethos reflected in the bands that these youth formed went beyond music itself, however. As these young people grew up in the community together, their experiences and struggles were intimately bound up in each other's. This reality seems to have fostered a sense of mutual interdependence among many of them, albeit if sometimes with a dose of "healthy competition."[126] After all, in Douglass's words, everyone was in the "same school,

FIGURE 5.2 The Al Adams Band, pictured here at Elks Hall on Central Avenue ca. 1939, served as an early site of musical collaboration for South Los Angeles teenagers Buddy Collette (on alto sax, front row, second from right), Jackie Kelso (Jack Kelson; alto sax, front row, third from right), and Forest "Chico" Hamilton (on drums, back row). Courtesy of Steven Isoardi.

same band. . . . Everybody played. Everybody was working jobs at night."[127] As Collette explained, whether they lived in South Central and attended Jefferson High School or in Watts and attended Jordan, the young musicians who came of age in the 1930s "had a kinship," one that stemmed as much from mutual respect as from collaborative learning. "Nobody was making any records or anything, but every now and then, for example, maybe we'd do something up in the L.A. area or maybe one of the guys would hear us, or then, later on, as we got a little older, then we'd remember Ernie Royal or somebody. And the influences would go back and forth." One band member might "bring us a little something that we'd think, 'Oh he does something different.' And then the same thing: he might see that I would. So that was all a part of us growing closer together."[128]

Collette reflected on the experience of forming a band with Vernon Slater, Minor Robinson, Charlie Martin, and Crosby Lewis during the mid-1930s, when they were all in their early teenage years. "We had to have that band," he asserted. It was not the most tightly organized affair, and "a couple of them weren't serious about playing." Yet, as he put it, "kids will do it. When you get older you got to have everything just right, but kids will say, 'Well, this is two altos, we'll play.' 'An alto and a drum, we'll play.' And that's what it's all about. It doesn't have to be perfect. You will learn more by getting together than playing alone." Collette's memories of his early band days reflected an alternative approach to learning than the dominant model that suggested practicing in isolation was the key to mastery. Someone used to playing an instrument in solitude was of little use when it came to the task of "interplay," that is, "playing with one more or two more people." As Collette put it, "A lot of people say, 'Well, let's practice and practice and you'll be good.' Yeah, but there's a line that's stronger than that." What was most important was "to listen." Listening was key to musical collaboration and collective modes of improvisation. It was "part of the discovery period" that enabled them to recognize "'Hey, I got that with you, haven't I?' . . . 'Oh, I got "ta-da ta-da ta-da-da" with you.' And I'd say, 'Yeah, you got it.' So we were smart at the time, but I'm saying togetherness. We learned a lot."[129]

The collaborative ethos of the jazz world had its limits. As a generally masculinized arena of cultural activity, it reflected the tendency of many grassroots struggles for dignity to advance the autonomy of some while reinforcing the marginalization of others. As Clora Bryant explained, jazz on Central Avenue and in the broader South Los Angeles region was overwhelmingly a "male thing." "They weren't looking for any females to be a part of that," she noted. "Nobody was knocking the door down to record women. . . . There was no push for us, for women, to do it. And the men were trying to get themselves in, so they definitely did not want that kind of competition."[130]

The resistance that female jazz players like Bryant encountered in Los Angeles did not come strictly from male musicians and producers, however. Frequently, audiences and the broader public frowned on, or were even outright hostile toward, women who entered the jazz world. Racialized assumptions about female musicians as sexually promiscuous, or as embodying gender impropriety, subjected them to rude treatment and sometimes violence.[131] Bryant recalled how the seemingly mundane experience of calling her male musician companions on the telephone to coordinate gigs and rehearsals provoked wild reactions from her friends' significant others. "You'd call the fellows up about rehearsal or something and they'd [the wife or girlfriend would] say, 'Well, who's that bitch?'" she recollected. Once when Bryant called saxophonist Clifford Scott for such a reason, she overheard his wife in the background, "You know, 'Is that your bitch?'" to which she quipped back, "Tell that bitch I ain't no bitch."[132] In another instance, Bryant remembered playing at the Onyx Club on Fair Oaks Avenue in Pasadena: "I was playing drums and trumpet at the same time, when Charles Norris was on guitar and Elyse was on piano and George Morrow was the bass player. . . . I played with my eyes closed. I never saw what was going on, you know." Apparently a man in the audience was looking at Bryant in a way that led his wife to believe Bryant was "going with her husband." As the woman sat there "and just g[ot] very upset," Elyse noticed the woman "pulling her knife out of her purse . . . and I had my eyes closed, and Elyse said, 'Look out, Clora!' I said 'Oh, my God.'"[133] She added, "I wasn't the only one. I mean, any girl musician you know can tell you stories like that."[134]

The hostility that women jazz players encountered did not necessarily define their experience of the jazz scene as a whole, however. In certain spaces, the jazz community provided what Bryant characterized as "a lot of camaraderie" and "caring." "That's why I became a part of it," she asserted.[135] Just as it relied on musical experimentation and innovations, the jazz world also contained a certain openness to unconventional social and gender behavior that was unavailable in other areas of society. That women like Bryant managed to carve out space for themselves within the jazz world indicates that the music scene was defined loosely enough to nurture alternative expressions of femininity and masculinity. This relative openness to social experimentation, and the general ethos of collectivity that nurtured it, was undoubtedly no small factor in keeping Bryant and other female musicians in the jazz world despite the harsh reactions they confronted.

In a variety of ways and contexts, the relationships that young Angelenos forged around music challenged the norms of social division and competition promoted by wider society as they joined people across race and gender. For example, Leroy Hurte formed an a cappella choir while attending Jefferson High School. They called the choir the Four Blackbirds and billed themselves as "three boys, a girl, and a guitar." The choir included a young woman named Geraldine Harris as first tenor, David Patillo as second tenor, Richard Davis as bass, and Hurte himself as baritone and guitarist. The choir itself was a product of relationships forged in the local interracial school system and also had a life beyond school. After graduating from high school, the Four Blackbirds continued meeting to rehearse at each other's houses and sang at such celebrated venues as Frank Sebastian's Cotton Club and the 1935 California Pacific International Exposition in San Diego.[136] Jackie Kelso recalled having some success playing with Chico Hamilton and ethnic "Mexican piano player" Jesus "Chuy" Reyes while in junior high school. Especially after Hamilton and Reyes took home first prize in an amateur contest in the Burbank Burlesque Theatre, music increasingly enabled their band to transgress the city's racial and generational boundaries and to secure gigs in different neighborhoods around town. As Kelso described, "While still in junior high school, somebody in Jesus Reyes's family gets married, so Chico, Jesus, and I provide the music. I play the clarinet [at the] reception or house party. At night, too. Twelve, thirteen years old. . . . I don't think we made any money. We were just happy playing together." They so enjoyed the event that they made an agreement, "Chuey, we played free for you, so, Chuey, you're going to play free for a Hamilton party and a Kelson party."[137] Such convergences and collaborations across normative social boundaries created potential for new subjectivities and resonances between different struggles.

Young musicians in South Los Angeles recognized that music enhanced their autonomy and mobility—geographically and socially—and actively sought opportunities to play in different parts of the city. Collette recalled doing jaunts around thirty to forty miles outside his home neighborhood, even down to San Diego.[138] Hurte seized the opportunity to sing on "just about every radio station in Los Angeles" and performed in motion pictures.[139] Ortega and the Frantic Five played at a Hollywood nightclub and got their names in the paper, an experience he recalled as just about the "greatest thing that ever happened."[140] Douglass also recalled how playing music around town provided a source of autonomy from parents' regulations, as he remembered his own parents' disapproval when he played late at places where booze was being served.[141]

Much like the innovations they engaged in musically when they rearranged music and played their own style to create something new, as they moved into spaces such as dance halls and nightclubs, they, along with the audiences and attendees, transformed those spaces. As historians Luis Alvarez and Anthony Macias have shown, informal clubs and dance halls were sites where multiethnic working-class youth created new social spaces and often subverted the city's dominant racial order and norms of gender and sexual propriety. Within these sites, swing music nourished a wider youth subculture that combined zoot suit fashions with pachuco slang and a politics of self-expression that challenged the social and cultural norms of middle-class Anglo-Americanism.[142] The activities that went on in these spaces so disturbed the status quo that they frequently provoked reactions from civic officials. For example, one of the city's dance halls got shut down because it was going to allow Black, Mexican, Filipinx, and White youth to dance together.[143]

A Central Avenue State of Mind

In a 1990 oral history interview, Clora Bryant described Central Avenue not just as a place in her life and in the world but as a "spirit" and a "history" that helped her to redefine her own place in the world. "It became more than a street, you know," Bryant explained. "The street was over there, but it was all over L.A. . . . . Wherever we congregated, that was our Central Avenue." Bryant's description could be generalized beyond the jazz community that Central Avenue so famously fostered, to characterize the surrealist ethos that animated Los Angeles's culture of opposition more broadly. As she noted, it was not the bricks and mortar, the buildings, or the bandstands that defined Central Avenue's significance, even if these physical structures and roots nurtured the modes of gathering she described. "There was an aura. There was a feeling" about the place. "And it's something that I think only people who are really in tune to whatever—No matter whether it's music or if you're a clerk or a steel mill worker, when you get around certain things, it's something that you—If you're really into that and you feel it, you know that this is where you're supposed to be. . . . It's just a feeling. It really is." In times of chaos and in the face of glaring injustice, "it gave me the motivation, the inspiration, enthusiasm, the desire, joy, you name it." It was "where I found out who Clora was and what Clora wanted to be."[144]

In describing Central Avenue as a source of self-definition and social belonging, Bryant calls attention to a key aspect of the relationship between place and politics that defined the circulation of surrealist politics and oppositional culture in 1930s California. While surrealist imaginings emerged out of and were fundamentally shaped by specific local conditions and on-the-ground experiences, they contributed to a broadened way of knowing and viewing the world. As Bryant put it, "I can get my Central Avenue in a lot of different places. . . . I was in Russia and I heard some music. That was Central Avenue. I've had it in New York . . . [and in] Kansas City." As she explained, "There's a Central Avenue in every large city or any city that had a black congregation where they started their music. . . . It might be called Main Street or whatever, but, you know, like 125th [Street] was Central Avenue."[145] Less important as a geographic place than as an epistemological vantage point, Bryant's Central Avenue provided her with a means of understanding and navigating the world around her. It helped her define her relationship not only to immediate local conditions but also to broader arrangements of power and circulations of struggle.

Like the Central Avenue that Bryant described, grassroots countercultural currents differed significantly across localities, while at the same time they contributed to a wider, translocal culture of opposition that linked divergent struggles for dignity and liberation. Cultural politics in general and surrealism in particular, like Central Avenue, helped people facing varied forms of subordination across California to redefine their relationship to the world around them not strictly as one of oppression but one of affirmation, to see themselves not strictly as a regional or national majority but as part of a global social majority.

The oppositional culture that crystallized in Los Angeles during the 1930s, while shaped by the specific local context of the city in this period and by the specific practices of local actors, should not be seen as a parochial or exclusively local phenomenon. Rather, it was part of a wider circulation of grassroots struggle throughout and beyond California, which linked popular struggles for dignity and self-definition among Angelenos not only with the mass movements in the fields and on the docks but also with the cultural struggles of other aggrieved populations. Turning to Northern California's Round Valley Indian Reservation gives us an opportunity to bring this fuller circulation of struggle into view.

6

Native Jazz and Oppositional Culture in Round Valley Reservation

At the night school near the hop fields in Covelo, California, likely during the late spring planting season in 1937, Pomo–Little Lake Indian Elizabeth Willits began learning to play the trumpet. She would have been in the eighth grade at the time, had she not recently dropped out of the reservation school following an argument with her teacher.[1] Instead, she took to spending her days training the fields for growing season, and her evenings taking music lessons from an instructor who was in charge of entertaining local farm working children who "didn't have too much to do" while their parents took adult classes in a separate room.[2] There was "a bunch of us," Willits recalled. It was "quite a big class [the music teacher] had of Indian people."[3] Willits eventually picked up a "little ABC's" on the banjo, guitar, violin, and drums from her brother and a few others in the community and "formed a group" with her friends, Concow-Yuki-Wailacki brothers Albert and Everett McLane and a local "Hawaiian man" who went by the name of Buck Potter.[4] The group played at house parties around the reservation and at several venues in the town of Covelo itself. They played "all kind [of] music . . . [w]altzes an' two-steps an' . . . in jazz world what they call Bye-Bye Blues and all that stuff."[5] They worked with special focus to advance their technique in "more a rhythm type of jazz music."[6] She noted, "It was more of a jazz [that appealed to her and her friends] in those days when we learned to play."[7]

The musical collaborations of Willits and her friends serve as a register of changes underway in Indigenous and immigrant communities in the vicinity of Mendocino County's Round Valley Reservation during the 1930s.[8] At a time when assimilationist pressures and homogenizing notions of Americanism threatened the survival of nonconforming subjects, the modes of cultural production embodied by Willits's band and their music charted an alternative path toward social belonging. The reservation school that Willits had left behind was a cornerstone of dominant efforts to secure the "total assimilation" of Native Americans during the early twentieth century. It intended to function as a laboratory for cultural uplift that would rearrange Native habits of mind and behavior to mold young women like Willits into proper subjects of head-of-household patriarchy and Victorian domesticity.[9] The music Willits took up and the band she helped form, in contrast, rejected impositions of cultural conformity and consensus in favor of forms of cultural experimentation and cocreation that confounded conventional boundaries of race, gender, nation, and genre.

Historian and cultural critic George Lipsitz has done much to illuminate the potential for popular culture in general and music in particular to serve as "a site for experimentation with cultural and social roles not yet possible in [formal domains of] politics."[10] Cultural critic Josh Kun has similarly underscored music's capacity to function as "a mode of relation, a point of contact," for cartographies and cultural formations that are traditionally regarded as wholly distinct.[11] For Native communities in Round Valley and its vicinity during the 1930s, who were largely excluded from dominant channels of political participation and variably silenced and satirized by dominant culture, cultural production played a crucial role in sustaining struggles for a dignified existence and expressing affinities with other ethnic working communities.[12] At the same time that multiethnic organizing in more formal coalitions prompted fierce crackdowns from government officials and business leaders, popular culture enabled forms of collaboration, social organization, dialogue, and intersubjectivity that often flew under the radar of elites.[13] Through music Willits and her band helped raise funds for a variety of Native clubs and organizations and for Native activists traveling to Washington, DC, to fight "for Indians' rights and to be recognized as people."[14] Also through music the same band expressed its solidarity with anticolonial struggles beyond the United States, including efforts for independence in the Philippines.[15] Willits recalled that she "played with the Filipinos' band there [near Hopland Rancheria]. . . . Played for their organization and they were sending money over to their land [because the United States had] invaded the Philipines [sic] island over there. They had an organization to raise money to send to their people. Played with Mr. [Aguilar] down there. He had a band with three Filipinos and I played banjo with them. So I was playing around making my life with them, playing music every other Saturday night."[16]

Attending to grassroots cultural politics in Round Valley gives us a window on how Round Valley Indians experienced, navigated, and altered the world around them amid the chaos and crisis of the Great Depression. Compared to cities like Los Angeles or San Francisco, Round Valley may seem peripheral to, if not altogether separated from, the main centers of California's capitalist development and Depression-era crisis. It has certainly never attracted the attention from scholars that other sites discussed in this book have. It is overlooked in most scholarship on the Great Depression.[17] Nonetheless, Round Valley—an Indian reservation located within the overwhelmingly rural county of Mendocino, in the northern reaches of the state—in fact played a pivotal role in California's global capitalist modernization. Round Valley was the site of some of the worst bloodshed resulting from Anglo colonization and home to one of the vastest cross sections of the tribes forcibly removed from their lands during the gold rush. By the early twentieth century, it had also become one of the nation's largest hop-producing regions and an important source of wealth from agriculture, ranching, and logging for the broader California region. In this respect, at crucial historical conjunctures, Round Valley stood at the front lines of battles over California's development future in both a physical and a geographic sense. It was also foundational to the construction of popular imaginings of what constituted modernity for California. Contrasting them with Indians in more central and southern regions of the state, who were allegedly more readily assimilated or subdued, Anglo settlers cast Round Valley Indians as distinctively "wild tribes."[18] Purportedly uncivilizable and culturally irredeemable, Round Valley Indians provided a main counterpoint against which Anglo settlers constructed dominant visions of California's development future. They also generated some of the most innovative countervisions of California as the crossroads of an alternative modernity and globality. Among the earliest of California's displaced peoples, Round Valley Indians experienced Depression-like conditions and the endemic crisis of capitalism before, and for a longer time than, most other Californians. During the Depression era, they drew on this longer history of struggle as they adapted to the shifting contours of life on and beyond the reservation. The imaginative and improvisational practices they engaged as they fought to endure in an inhospitable world provide us with a vista on the alternative possible futures they hoped to build.

In this chapter I consider the music that Elizabeth Willits and her band performed in and around Round Valley as part of a broader matrix of leisure, spiritual, and other cultural practices that mediated local Indigenous populations' efforts to make their lives livable and to situate themselves in relation to wider circulations of struggle during the 1930s. As I examine how Native Californians experienced and responded to the upheavals of the era, I illuminate how they redefined their relationship to the land, tribal affiliations, and other ethnic working populations and contributed to making a broader oppositional culture in the process. I argue that, at the same time as the federal government, under the aegis of the New Deal's Indian Reorganization Act, sought to confine Native populations geographically on the reservation, and politically within Bureau of Indian Affairs (BIA)-authorized modes of governance, Round Valley Indians pursued a politics of dignity and self-definition that situated them within a wider circulation of emancipatory struggles. As they affirmed a distinct Indigenous epistemology based on ancestral traditions and collective memories of conquest, settler colonialism, and genocide, Round Valley Indians expressed visions of Indigenous autonomy that were intersectional in nature, linking Indigenous and immigrant working communities in the face of prevailing forces of imperialism and racial capitalism. Their autonomy reached outward, not just inward, embracing rather than suppressing difference and underscoring the necessity of Native self-determination while also supporting broader multiracial and transnational grassroots struggles for liberation.

Genealogies of Multiracial Struggle in the Lands of the Round Valley Indians

The world that witnessed Elizabeth Willits's early introduction to the trumpet, her affinity for jazz, and the music she played to advance Native rights and transnational grassroots self-determination had roots in a longer history of struggles for autonomy founded in cultural difference and practices of cultural innovation. As inhabitants of one of the most densely populated and culturally diverse regions in North America before European contact, the Indigenous populations of California had cultivated methods for negotiating linguistic, cultural, and regional differences in tribal relations, alliances, and conflicts over the course of centuries.[19] Between 1812 and 1850, those who lived north of San Francisco Bay, in the homelands of the Native tribes that would ultimately constitute the bulk of Round Valley Reservation's residents (regions that anthropologists have designated as the central California and northeastern Indigenous cultural areas), found themselves at the crossroads of the succeeding and overlapping forces of Spanish, Russian, and Mexican colonization.[20] While the impact of these divergent colonialisms varied across specific local contexts, they generally and collectively subjected Native populations in the northern regions of Alta California to projects of Christianization, racial subjugation, land and resource confiscation, environmental and health devastation, and labor exploitation, which were transforming the broader Western Hemisphere and the non-Western world.[21] At the same time that these forces worked to alienate Indigenous people from their ancestral homelands and lifeways, they also made them part of an emergent transnational and multiethnic workforce that included diverse tribes from across Northern California along with Russian, Mexican, Creole, Native Alaskan, and Native Hawaiian people who were brought to the region as workers by colonial settlers and merchants.[22]

The gold rush solidified Northern California's position as a key node in the globalizing economy during the 1850s and turned the ancestral homelands of Round Valley Indians into some of the most violent battlegrounds on which conflicts over the development and future of the region unfolded during the late nineteenth century. As fortune-seeking migrants flooded into California's mining regions from across the globe, a complex web of law, custom, and culture facilitated Anglo attempts to shore up social boundaries that marginalized non-White immigrant and Indigenous populations, barring many from access to resources for survival and channels of political participation. As legal scholar Cheryl I. Harris notes, the seizure of Native lands and dispossession of Native subjects in particular served as pivotal components of the process by which Anglo settlers reordered property rights and relations and facilitated the institutionalization of White supremacy and racial capitalism on the frontier.[23] As historian Tomás Almaguer has shown, these processes were both enabled and justified by a dominant culture that constructed Native peoples and traditions as irredeemably backward, primitive, and incompatible with modernity and American nationhood.[24] Across Northern and Central California during this period, the same logic that determined Native territories to be free for the taking cast Native peoples as obstacles to White visions of political economic development in the region, to be subordinated and exploited when possible and exterminated when necessary.[25]

California's northern and central mining regions experienced some of the most gruesome violence ever waged against Native Americans by Anglo settlers in the history of American nation building. Indians in these coveted territories became targets of extralegal and state-sponsored killings and extermination campaigns, along with disease, kidnappings, varying forms of coerced labor, and sexual violence. As a whole, California's Native population plummeted from an estimated 300,000 at the turn of the nineteenth century, to 150,000 by the eve of the gold rush in 1848, to just 30,000 in 1860.[26] The genocidal imperatives and devastating consequences of Anglo colonization have led many scholars to characterize the history of California Indians in general and the Round Valley Indians in particular as a linear story of physical destruction and cultural decline.[27] Yet, as historian Albert L. Hurtado has emphasized, "the same numbers that illustrate the destruction of native populations also show where and how some Indians survived in a land that was starkly different than the one their grandparents had known."[28]

Round Valley Indians struggled for survival amid American colonization both physically and culturally. Even after the mass racial violence against Indians subsided, surviving populations had to cultivate modes of endurance and subsistence in response to removal and allotment programs that sought to undermine Native identities and traditions by transforming them into obedient subjects of American empire and racial capitalism. Attending to Native struggles for cultural endurance should not suggest efforts to preserve fixed identities and lifeways as distilled remnants of some distant past, however. Rather, survival inherently and necessarily required constant innovation, accommodation, and collective re-creation of identities, affiliations, modes of life, and systems of meaning. Anglo settlers, policy makers, reformers, and industrial employers consistently characterized Native peoples as existing outside modernity, as antimodern, throughout the late nineteenth and early twentieth centuries. Yet Native Californians themselves worked hard to carve out space for themselves—to remain alive and to make their lives livable—within a rapidly modernizing world that simultaneously changed the circumstances of all its inhabitants. Instead of clinging to an existence outside modernity and its attendant institutions of race, nation, and the market, as dominant social forces imagined, Round Valley Indians appropriated and accommodated these, and impacted their evolution, as they fashioned identities for themselves and worked to resist their own dehumanization or obliteration.[29]

In their struggles under Anglo-American rule, Round Valley Indians continually ran up against a system of cultural representation that portrayed

Native Americans as anomalies of the modern world, as people frozen in time, and as obstructions to liberal capitalist progress.[30] As Mendocino County worked to develop as a center of agribusiness, lumber, and tourism, its self-designated regional identity as the heart of the "Redwood Empire" relied on the production of conceptualizations of "Whiteness" and "Indianness" that supported its triumphalist narrative of regional development. Like other developing regions across the country in the aftermath of the Civil War, Mendocino County hosted traveling shows, expositions, tourist attractions, and, from the 1910s on, screenings of Hollywood films that commonly celebrated White valor and conquest on the frontier, while either erasing or caricaturing Native peoples. Appropriations of Native culture abounded in the local region, from tokenized enactments of "Indian war dances" that accompanied civic organizational events and parties, to the naming of local "Redmen" and "Pocahontas" lodges, to the orchestrations that surrounded annual Fourth of July "Frontier Days" festivals, a tradition that civic leadership in the town of Willits invented in 1927 to capitalize on widespread popular yearnings for frontier imagery in the form of "a real old-fashioned wild-west celebration."[31] The emerging dominant culture of racial representation enabled White participants to indulge and inhabit fantasies of conquest while fetishizing Native culture and shoring up norms of White racial and patriarchal domination and Native subordination.

Of course, Round Valley Indians always defined their own lives and identities in far more complex ways. The history of Indian removal in Northern California and the creation of Round Valley Reservation stand as a case in point. The federal legislation that established Round Valley Reservation (originally Nome Cult Farm) was based on racialized assumptions that treated northern and central tribes as culturally homogeneous and part of a collective racial, political, and social problem. However, as the removal process turned the Yukis' Indigenous homeland into a reservation and forcibly brought Indigenous peoples as diverse as the Concows, Pit Rivers, Nomlackis, Nisenans, Wailackis, and Pomos to the region from across central and northeastern California, these same policies also conditioned the formation of multifaceted affinities and identities among Round Valley Indians.[32] In fact, from its inception Round Valley Reservation was home to not only Indigenous Californians but also a small number of Anglo people who had rejected their former lifestyle in favor of living with Native communities, and at least one Native Hawaiian who had forged kinship and familial ties with Concow Indians in the years before their removal.[33] The historical record suggests that an immigrant descendant of Hawaiian royalty, by the name of Iona, who came to work on John Sutter's New Helvetia ranch in 1839 had married a Concow woman by the name of Su-my-neh. Despite their claims to royal Hawaiian ancestry, they and their two children were forced on the hundred-mile journey, the so-called Concow trail of tears, to Round Valley. Eventually, after appealing to the king of Hawai'i for support, Iona, Su-my-neh, and their children were released and returned to live on the native soil of the Concow but maintained ties to Round Valley through the twentieth century.[34] Round Valley Reservation's pan-Indigenous and multiethnic character helped to shape the multiracial and transnational politics that crystallized in the 1930s and were made visible in the band and music discussed at the beginning of this chapter.

Round Valley Indians engaged simultaneously in practices that sustained tribal identities—for instance, passing down tribe-specific myths, creation stories, and traditions—and practices that forged ties across tribal lines. They built intertribal social networks and engaged in some spiritual and cultural rituals together. They also circulated shared memories of Anglo conquest and Native devastation and survival. They recalled how Anglo settlers "made slaves of Indians," treating them "just like cattle," and how Indians endured forced removal, disease, massacres, and other forms of calculated cruelty.[35] Such memories contributed to an oppositional body of historical knowledge about the region's Americanization. They also inculcated a sense of the long history of struggle shared by local Native people, aiding the production of multivalent, pan-Indian identities.

The very school system that aimed to tighten Anglo control over Native behavior provided an additional avenue for intertribal convergence. This was particularly true of the boarding school system, which brought Round Valley Indians into contact with Native Americans from other reservations. In a description of Riverside, California's Sherman Institute, Adaline Figueroa explained, "It [the school] was big. There was people from all over the United States. From New York, you know. There were even people look like full Black; even [Indians who were light-skinned enough to pass as] White people, but they came anyway."[36] In drawing together Indigenous populations of diverse backgrounds from disparate geographic locations, the Sherman Institute and other boarding schools like it proved to be sites of contestation. There, efforts to impose a homogenizing discipline on Indian populations could be transgressed by students seeking to learn about nuances, differences, and affinities among them. In a sense, the school created a unique lens through which Native students could view the interconnectedness between Round Valley and other Indigenous struggles across the broader imperialist landscape.

Just as they constructed identities and historical narratives outside the terms dictated by the dominant culture, Round Valley Indians also struggled to enhance their autonomy within the local economy. Capitalist advancement in Mendocino County transformed the region into a booming site for industrial development, especially for agriculture, forestry, and, increasingly by the 1920s and early 1930s, tourism. The discourse of assimilation on which the allotment system relied conflicted with the evolving demands of the region's growing industrial economy. Indeed, the Indian Agency officials who touted the self-reliant family farm as an idealized future for Native Americans did so just as that ideal was becoming eclipsed by large-scale industrial agricultural enterprises. Advancements in irrigation and intensive farming practices boosted the power of large farms and made the average eight-and-a-half-acre plots that the agency distributed to California Indians insufficient for competition in the agricultural market.[37] While allotment aimed to confine Round Valley Indians to individualized private parcels and to promote a spirit of individualism and self-sufficiency among them, they routinely supplemented production on their allotments with wage work off the reservation, planting and harvesting crops, shearing sheep, and raising cattle on farms and *rancherías* across the broader Mendocino and Lake County regions, where the demand for cheap and flexible labor expanded rapidly.[38] Although Native populations never became a primary source of labor in California generally speaking, they formed a significant proportion of laborers in Mendocino County, often preferred by employers.[39] By the 1890s, Indian populations constituted approximately 6 percent of Mendocino County's total population yet an estimated 25 percent of its waged workforce.[40] They continuously outnumbered the combined total of ethnic Mexican, African American, Chinese, and Japanese populations in the local area between 1870 and 1940.[41]

As historian William Bauer has shown, patterns and practices of work, both paid and unpaid, were key channels through which Round Valley Indians situated themselves in relation to each other and the world around them. According to Bauer, Round Valley Indians utilized a mixture of waged and nonwaged labor, on and off the reservation, "to maintain one foot in the growing economy and one foot in an older subsistence economy and to create community."[42] Many traveled the local circuit, following seasonal demands for agricultural and ranch work, while some traveled to cities, especially in the San Francisco Bay Area, for jobs in domestic service and other industries.[43] The same circulations of labor that were so central to the making of racial capitalism were, in fact, a contested terrain that also contributed to

FIGURE 6.1 Young Pomo women picking hops in Ukiah Valley, n.d. Circuits of agricultural labor expanded the range of places and people with whom Round Valley Indians interacted. Robert J. Lee Photographic Collection, Mendocino County Historical Society.

the formation of new ties among Indigenous and non-Indigenous working-class communities. Wailacki June Britton noted that, beyond providing a means to a wage, working on hop farms around the local region enabled her to socialize with people with whom she would otherwise not have had the chance to interact, including Indians from distant areas as well as non-Indian workers who were drawn to the region by the labor demands of developing industries (see figure 6.1).[44] "I enjoyed the company of being out amongst people [picking hops]," she explained. "We were raised up on [the north] end of [Round Valley]. . . . [Our parents] never took us no place. . . . If I could get out and pick hops I could see different people."[45]

As Concow John Cook described, "It was a mixture [of people working in the hop fields], it wasn't all Indians; it was Black and Mexicans."[46] The persistent engagement of Round Valley Indians in the regional labor circuit troubled BIA officials, not only because it meant that these populations did not conform with the assimilationist imperatives of Indian policy but also because their interactions and collaborations with other ethnic working communities blurred the boundaries of racial divisions that were so crucial to maintaining structures of subordination. In a 1936 report, BIA-commissioned anthropologist Gordon MacGregor expressed concern that Round Valley Indians who left the reservation tended to spend their free time mingling across racial lines and "mostly with the lowest class" of people. He explained that "they . . . play[ed] cards with certain [low] classes of white people" and intermarried with non-Indian populations. According to his own estimate, "as far as blood goes, it is centering around the three-quarter mark. . . . Ten to fifteen per cent of the Indians in the area are less than one half blood."[47]

Mendocino-area Indians socialized with differently racialized working populations not only at work, in labor camps, and on rancherías but also after hours in a variety of settings. The emergence of an intertribal, multiethnic, and interracial working-class leisure culture in the area demonstrated that the ways working communities chose to spend their time, energy, and money departed from the expectations held for those communities by the BIA and regional industrial employers. Although relations among racialized working-class populations in the region were by no means free from the competition and conflict that nurtured the ascendance of racial capitalism, spaces of leisure frequently joined working-class communities across racial lines.[48] Like many working-class communities, Round Valley Indians unwound from their workdays over drinks at the same pool halls, movie houses, and house parties that non-Indian workers also attended. They made moonshine, bootlegged, and gambled together.[49] These practices not only helped working people in Round Valley and the broader Mendocino County region to make their lives a bit more livable but also situated them in a broader cultural world that prioritized values of leisure, pleasure, and dignity.

By the time the Great Depression unfolded in Mendocino County, Round Valley Indians had not become the independent, self-sufficient farmers that the allotment's crafters, as well as local elites and reformers, had envisioned. Instead, they were part of broader multiethnic and transnational grassroots struggles, fighting to survive and resist the indignities and dehumanizing forces of racial capitalist development. Their sense of the past and present was shaped more by collective memories of colonialism and the racist directions of regional industrialization than by a process of civilization, assimilation, and progress. They had more in common with other displaced working people of different tribal, racial, and national backgrounds than with the farmers and other regional employers whom BIA officials had imagined as their role models.

The Shifting Contours of Struggle
in the Great Depression

The Great Depression deepened existing polarizations of wealth and power in Round Valley and the broader Mendocino County region—intensifying efforts among employers and political leaders to manage social conditions in the area while also enhancing a sense of cultural and political affinity among aggrieved Indigenous and immigrant working communities. Depression-era conditions combined with state and federal law to further undermine Round Valley Indians' ability to supplement their families' food supply by hunting and fishing. Declining agricultural prices not only made it exceedingly difficult for those living on allotted lands to hold on to what remained of their property but also led employers to pass on their financial burden to workers, contributing to reductions in wages and rising unemployment among both Native and non-Native working-class communities.[50] By the early 1930s, one White observer noted that "the Indians fall in the same social class as the white fruit tramps."[51]

The decade also ushered in a transformation in federal Indian policy. By the 1930s, it was clear that allotment had failed to turn Native Americans into the obedient, assimilated subjects that the policy's architects hoped they would become. Within Round Valley, government officials also recognized that the allotment program had created administrative problems of its own. Authorities complained that "the Indians of the Sacramento jurisdiction, outside the true reservations, are too scattered for administration, educational and health services, or cooperative enterprise."[52] Their grievances revolved as much around the manageability of a spatially dispersed population as the antagonism that the policy had fueled between Native residents and government officials. According to a government report covering the effects of Indian policy in Round Valley, beyond failing its intended purpose, allotment threatened the social order because it "thrust the Indians into an economic, spiritual, and social no-man's land, and reduced some of them to almost psychopathic resentment."[53] These concerns encouraged Mendocino County administrators and elites to view the Great Depression at the local level as fundamentally "a social problem rather than an economic one."[54] They hoped that a restructuring of Indian policy might help to stabilize unrest and resolve "the Indian problems we have here in California."[55]

The federal response to the failures of allotment came in the form of the Indian Reorganization Act (IRA) in 1934. The IRA was the brainchild of Commissioner of Indian Affairs John Collier and the core element of what became known as the "Indian New Deal." It brought an end to the allot-ment program, established Indian community control over unalloted and trust-status lands, and provided for the establishment of tribal governments and corporate charters. Driven in part by Collier's vision of granting more control to Native Americans over their own politics and resources, the IRA created important new opportunities for organizing tribes politically, ex-panding reservation land holdings, and developing tribal economies. Still, the paternalism that permeated many of the BIA's operations was also pres-ent in the IRA. The BIA created the templates for tribal constitutions and set the terms for many other aspects of tribal governance. BIA agents also determined who would have access to the opportunities made available by the IRA and who would not. The policy was inextricable from efforts to quell unrest and opposition among Native populations and to consolidate the po-litical activities of those living on reservations. It ultimately embodied the federal government's effort to resolve the so-called Indian problem from the top down.[56] Beneath the rhetoric of promoting Native self-determination, the IRA functioned, as ethnic studies scholar Thomas Biolsi has argued, as "a technique of domination."[57]

Responses to the IRA among Round Valley Indians were mixed. Some opposed the measure outright, viewing it as part of a system that would un-dermine Native autonomy by deepening their reliance on the government and resubordinating them to the authority of the Sacramento Agency and the BIA.[58] Others saw the act as an improvement on the allotment program and considered it an opportunity to obtain fuller control over their land, resources, and lives. After its enactment at the federal level, many indi-viduals in Round Valley wrote letters to the BIA, appealing for financial assistance with homes, building supplies, and school grounds or for access to historical tribal land claims, though many of their requests exceeded the intentions and provisions of the measure.[59] Two years later, in a federally mandated election in November 1936, Round Valley Indians voted to ac-cept the IRA's implementation locally, with an approval rate of 69 percent in an election whose turnout composed just 24 percent of eligible voters. The Covelo Indian Community Council, the new tribal government that resulted from the measure, instituted initiatives ranging from a housing project to the provision of loans supporting agricultural and ranching ac-tivities.[60] Significant as these undertakings were in attempting to alleviate some of the strains that afflicted the Round Valley community, they fell far short of what was needed to advance Round Valley Indians' own under-standings of their livelihood and dignity.

Alternative Visions and Circulations
of Struggle in Round Valley

Against dominant efforts to define the terms of Indian life, land, and identity, Round Valley Indians continued to define themselves and to engage in social and cultural practices outside the discretion of BIA officials and the broader political establishment. In the process, they asserted themselves as participants in a broader culture of grassroots opposition against racial capitalist articulations of power. They expressed forms of Indigenous subjectivity that exceeded the narrow definitions imposed by the BIA and that hinged instead on a more open-ended conceptualization of the struggle for dignity that linked aggrieved communities across lines of race, gender, nationality, and locality.[61]

At the same time that local society and dominant culture promoted narrow and tokenizing depictions of what authentic "Native culture" was and ought to be, Indigenous communities engaged in and contributed to a wider world of transnational, multiracial cultural struggle. Culture, as Stuart Hall has urged us to see, is itself "a sort of constant battlefield. A battlefield where no once-for-all victories are obtained but where there are always strategic positions to be won and lost." It is an arena where struggles both "for and against a culture of the powerful" are engaged, and at the same time, "it is also the stake to be won or lost *in* that struggle."[62] During the 1930s, Native self-assertions and identifications with other ethnic and racial working communities—in the vicinity of Round Valley Reservation and far beyond it—acquired their fullest expression on the terrain of culture. Round Valley Indians did not dismiss formal political channels as necessary sites for addressing the limits and failures of dominant institutions and pursuing important concessions from elites. Yet they did recognize that the political possibilities available to them within these channels were inherently confined by the terms of the powerful.[63] Where the politics of dominant institutions gave them little room for maneuver, little meaningful participation or opportunities for self-representation, cultural forms provided the space and tools they needed to generate what C. L. R. James has characterized as "new words, new verse, new passwords" of struggle and what Paul Gilroy describes as "qualitatively new desires, social relations, and modes of association"—new kinds of relations both among aggrieved communities and between those communities and the dominant bloc.[64] For Round Valley Indians amid the crisis of the 1930s, cultural politics provided an avenue for expressing and enacting an alternative vision of the world—of the past, present, and possible futures of development—that departed starkly from that which was imposed on them by forces beyond their control. The vision brought to life by their art, their music, and their spiritual and religious practices revolved around a politics of dignity and autonomy that did not subsume or marginalize difference but embraced it, that did not seek to erect boundaries between the struggles of different people but rather was anchored in a sense of their fundamental interconnectivity.

Music was a necessary and constitutive element in forging an alternative history, identity, and epistemology in Round Valley and in imagining alternative avenues of belonging, social membership, and participation in the 1930s. Scholars of music have long acknowledged its role in building and sustaining dialogues and collective memories among people and communities across disparate geographies and generations, especially for nondominant and aggrieved groups. From the blues people of the Mississippi delta to the *corrideros* (folk singers) of the U.S.-Mexico borderlands, historically marginalized groups have fashioned identities and circulated ideas, values, and emotions through music.[65] This is equally true for the Native Californians who had survived American colonization and removal and were living in and near Round Valley during the 1930s. As Round Valley resident William Oandasan, of Yuki and Filipinx descent, explained, Round Valley Indians have long harbored a deep-rooted appreciation for the intimate relationship between "song and story." The link was more than aesthetic, however. "On the broadest level it is a kind of entertainment," Oandasan notes. "But it is also a way of teaching lessons," conveying "stories of origin," of "creation," and "implement[ing] history in the telling."[66] In the words of Hopi-Miwok anthropologist and artist Wendy Rose, the knowledge that has emerged from the historical struggles of those descended from the first people of California entails a recognition that "song and dance and story are one; together they are life itself." As Rose explains, songs simultaneously carry the voices of "ancestor, individual, and descendant" and pulses "of sensation, inspiration, expression and awareness." She urges attention to the fact that musician, artist, and poet alike are "not blind to what is happening elsewhere" but are animated by "voices [that] pray in suffering and pain" and, through it all, usher forth "the knowledge of continuance."[67]

Yet music's potential to serve as a source of identification, historical narration, and sustained struggle reaches beyond the sustenance of group-based identities. As Josh Kun writes, music can provide us with "identificatory 'contact zones,'" that is, "sonic and social spaces where disparate identity-formations, cultures, *and* geographies historically kept and mapped separately are allowed to interact with each other as well as enter into relationships whose consequences for cultural identification are never predetermined."[68] Historian Luis Alvarez has illuminated music's capacity to nourish transnational political subjectivities and affinities, to form a kind of diaspora "based not on any single race, ethnic, or place-based identity, but on their shared and ongoing struggles for dignity."[69] In Depression-era Round Valley, music provided a contact zone and catalyst that linked local Indigenous people with a broader diaspora and circulation of struggle among a multiracial, transnational, and intercolonial social majority.

When Elizabeth Willits decided to drop out of the reservation school and pick up the trumpet, as described at the beginning of this chapter, it is, of course, not entirely clear what personal imperatives motivated her shift in course. Perhaps she refused to endure the rigid discipline that structured the reservation's educational system. Perhaps she desired to seek or build an arena in which she could define more fully the contours of her life. Whatever motivated her, she ultimately found in music a channel for creating, improvising, and experimenting on her own terms and for fashioning new relationships with her peers and local community. For Willits, and for others with whom she lived, worked, and played, music provided a soundtrack for a different way of being in the world, a different way of relating to local society and translocal circulations of struggle. It was an essential feature of Round Valley residents' efforts to set the rhythm and temporality of their own lives. It animated scenes at rancherías during after-work hours and filled the house parties, bars, pool halls, and dances where Round Valley residents congregated and socialized.[70] Joe Happy recalled, "They sing all night, you know. . . . Eat, then sing and sing." According to Happy, music facilitated efforts to "have [a] good time" in a world otherwise filled with harsh realities.[71]

Grassroots musical production in Round Valley not only helped constitute an alternative temporality but also reflected and fostered forms of collectivity that deviated from those the BIA had historically sought to encourage among local Indians. While the reservation school and the broader logic of Indian policy aimed to secure a gendered division of social roles that revolved around male-headed nuclear families and values of female domesticity, playing music with her male friends enabled Willits to assert her own creativity in potentially transgressive ways. The social space that their band produced opened up possibilities for nurturing alternative constructions of gender relations, and for her to hone her skills while contributing to a larger collective creative project. "So we would all join together and change over and play," Willits explained. "The boys would play one song or two for a [quadrille] and then we'd play a waltz," sometimes "just to entertain ourselves," and other times "for the dance to go on—our old time dances and parties."[72]

The instruments and genres that Round Valley musicians played reflected a transregional and transnational cultural dialogue that reached across seemingly distant geographic localities and racial and ethnic communities, well beyond the boundaries of the reservation to which policy makers hoped to confine them, and beyond the boundaries of the nation-state within which reformers hoped to incorporate them. To be sure, the fiddles, guitars, trumpets, and banjos that were commonly used in the music that Round Valley residents played during the 1930s had historical roots in grassroots struggles far beyond the local region. The tunes that local bands played contributed to a dialogue that linked working-class cultures and communities in Mendocino County with those in the Deep South, the Appalachian Mountains, Harlem, and Los Angeles's Central Avenue. In addition to jazz, waltzes, and gospel, they played "western dances, a lot of that."[73] The freedom with which Round Valley players employed different instruments and moved across boundaries of musical genre suggests a definition of art that centered on collaborative and improvised modes of creativity and performance, rather than mastery of a specific, compartmentalized craft or canon.[74] Moreover, the variety of popular and folk musics that they performed, with roots in different ethnic and cultural traditions, challenged boundaries of racial essentialism and authenticity and belied the alleged cohesion of American national cultural forms. For example, at the same time that jazz music in particular was increasingly commodified and minstrelized in American mass culture, registering and celebrating the formation of a multiethnic but still racially exclusive (White) melting pot, the affinity that Willits and her band felt for a "rhythm type of jazz" registered an oppositional jazz epistemology that linked them less with a dominant national body politic than with a transnational circulation of grassroots struggle.[75]

At the same time that the music played by Round Valley residents linked them to a broader intergenerational and transregional dialogue of struggle, it also enabled them to move about in physical space at the local level in new ways and to transform the spaces they entered. While Native musicians were excluded from many local venues, they created their own spaces to practice and play. Armstead Want noted that "they played down . . . at the dance down there in the grove" and, according to Acklan Willits, in "those little cabins back there."[76] Leland Fulwider Jr. noted, "[We] use to have dances all the time."[77] Against the pressures of Indian policy to consolidate Indigenous life within the space of the reservation, Round Valley Indians used music to carve out an alternative social geography. On the odd occasion when a segregated venue would allow Native residents to enter, it was typically to play music for Anglo audiences. Most often, however, Native bands played for working-class and non-White audiences. "I traveled up and down the country working for different ranches and different places and playing music," Willits noted.[78]

As they contributed to a dialogue among seemingly disparate working-class communities, Round Valley musicians also challenged the hegemony of a local culture that had historically hinged on the silence and compliance of Native populations. At a time when radio stations "were for white people," Willits described how "we Indians went up there, had to pay so much, . . . so much a half an hour. We had to pay to get time on the station. . . . So we played. We got on the station to preach the gospel to the Indians. Let them know we were doing something."[79] According to Willits, she played

> in the ole, this KHSL station over in Chico, California for the American Indian Association with Mr. Freeman's group for the Pentecostal Association over there. I an, an another girl by the name of Marylin Mitchell. . . . We played in that little ole radio station there for half an hour an sing a few gospel songs. . . . We went on the air over there an we had to, ah, like you, you have a piano sitting here, what you was going to play. Then you had the instruments, played over there in that radio station when I was young. When we was going around preaching the gospel, we was, and helping the gospel, helping spreading.[80]

To the extent that radio widened the circulation of music by young Native women like Willits and Mitchell, the medium contained generative possibilities for challenging the constraints of race, class, and gender that impinged on those who lived at the intersection of multiple patterns of social and political oppression. Despite its usually exclusionary boundaries, the KHSL station's radio broadcasts perhaps unwittingly provided a vehicle for differentiated visions of dignity and grassroots empowerment. Moreover, as a channel for spreading local grassroots articulations of Pentecostal religion, Willits's and Mitchell's radio engagements also draw attention to the intimate interconnection between, on one hand, the ways Round Valley Indians' cultural struggles bridged the distinction between art and politics and, on the other, their deep-seated struggles for spiritual liberation.

On the surface, spreading the gospel to Indigenous communities through radio might have seemed a tame and unthreatening act to some observers. However, as a conduit for the construction of grassroots epistemologies and practices, Pentecostalism in fact held transgressive political potential for Round Valley cultural struggles during the Great Depression. Alongside, and sometimes central to, grassroots music and other cultural and leisure practices, Pentecostalism flourished as a religious movement in the vicinity of Round Valley during this period. Given the confluence of multiethnic musicking and Pentecostalism as modes of cultural practice in the region, it is not surprising that Willits gained a significant part of her musical education in the Pentecostal Church and played for the church for a number of years. As she put it, "That's where I got a lot of training from sitting an playing in old Pentecostal Church."[81] Examining more fully the role of Pentecostalism in shaping and nurturing Round Valley cultural struggles urges consideration of how grassroots struggles for dignity and autonomy were for many as much a spiritual as a political and cultural endeavor.

From deep-rooted animistic beliefs that emphasized the interconnectivity and interdependency of all living things to the proliferation of the Earth Lodge Religion (a variant of the Ghost Dance, whereby dancing and living in subterranean houses protected participants from the apocalypse) between the late nineteenth and early twentieth centuries, spiritual and religious beliefs had long been part of the way Round Valley Indians established their relationship to the world around them, generated and circulated moral and political values, and defined the contours of their communities.[82] The Depression era witnessed the burgeoning of a Pentecostal movement in Round Valley that not only situated reservation residents within a tradition of worship and fellowship that was embraced by multiethnic working populations across the globe but also helped nurture and sustain emancipatory struggles in everyday life at the local level.[83]

Pentecostalism first came to Round Valley in the spring of 1929, when Pit River Indian and African American Pentecostal preacher E. F. Wilkes led a revival in the assembly hall of the reservation's Methodist church (see figure 6.2).[84] Wilkes came at the invitation of Methodist preacher Reverend Leon Schillinger, a longtime Indian rights advocate who had a reputation among local government officials as one who was "not in sympathy with the administration."[85] Pentecostalism spread rapidly not only among Indian communities "representing all tribes on the reservation" but also among both Indian and non-Indian communities beyond the reservation.[86] Among those drawn to the Pentecostal movement in this period were many who had led Native protests in the region during the 1920s, suggesting that participation in the church might be seen as an extension of long-standing struggle and oppositional subjectivity.[87] By 1931 local adherents of Pentecostalism

FIGURE 6.2 Round Valley Methodist Church. Built in 1869 as a U.S. government warehouse, the building was remade into a church in 1900. Here the Round Valley Indians were introduced to Pentecostalism in 1929. G. E. E. Lindquist Papers, Burke Library Archives, Columbia University Libraries.

pooled their energy and resources to build a church building of their own. A humble, "barnlike" structure on a half-acre parcel donated by Yuki residents Lucy and Ralph Moore, the church was both an outgrowth of and an engine for community life in Round Valley throughout the 1930s.[88] In 1937 the church reportedly had around a hundred regularly attending members, representing an intertribal, multiethnic, and interracial cross section of the local working-class population.[89]

Not all local residents welcomed the growth of Pentecostalism in Round Valley. Some Round Valley Indians rejected the movement on racial grounds, frowning particularly on the fact that the church's preacher was of mixed "Indian Negro blood."[90] Others saw the church as a cultural aberration and insisted that it was "not preaching or teaching on educating principles."[91] The most hostile reactions, however, came from more well-to-do Anglo residents in the region surrounding the reservation. While many applauded that Pentecostalism seemed to encourage more conservative social behavior among Round Valley Indians—including a decline in drinking, gambling, and the enjoyment of other "worldly pleasures"—the interracial congregation and the lack of internal hierarchy among members disturbed the region's racial order and upset dominant notions of proper gender and social behavior. As a whole, the movement appeared to many a serious "detriment to the morals and peace," as well as the overall stability, of local society.[92]

Broadly speaking, the appeal of Pentecostalism among Round Valley Indians and other working people in the Round Valley region resulted in part from aspects of the religion that made it popular among working-class communities worldwide.[93] From its inception in the Azusa Street Revival, Pentecostalism drew its congregations overwhelmingly from economically, racially, and culturally marginalized communities. The Pentecostal Church's rejection of the forms of hierarchy that structured other churches and its insistence on the potential for all people to have a direct and unmediated relationship with God offered an inclusive and participatory environment to people who faced exclusion in many other arenas of life.[94] Moreover, its liturgical emphasis on the poor, uneducated, and working-class character of Jesus's disciples and the corrupting power of wealth bolstered its aura as a religion of the people. That most Pentecostal preachers in the early twentieth century hailed from poor and working-class communities and had little or no formal education reinforced Pentecostal churches' tendency to operate with minimal financial resources, in buildings that ranged from storefronts, to private homes, to granary buildings, located in the portions of cities and towns that were home to aggrieved communities.[95]

While part of a global working-class movement, Round Valley's Pentecostal movement also took on a unique shape of its own, as local adherents both built on and enlisted local traditions of struggle and spirituality in their practice of the religion. In his study of Pentecostalism's ascendance in Round Valley, Gordon MacGregor observed in 1936 that local Indians actively and assertively "identified the old Indian religion with the Pentecostal Christian religion." According to MacGregor, Pentecostal churchgoers and nonchurchgoers alike were accustomed to viewing supernatural figures of Indigenous cosmology like the Silver Fox, "representative of the 'Great Spirit,'" and Coyote, "a mischievous figure in old legends," as "only Indian terms for God and the Devil."[96] There were also continuities between Native healing practices and Pentecostalism's emphasis on faith-based healing. One woman who attended Round Valley's Pentecostal church witnessed the curing of a fellow member by a Native healer in the congregation who used "ancient medicine and preaching." According to the woman, the healer "got his power through Jesus Christ" and cured "just like the men in the Bible, by laying on his hands."[97] The continuities were also clear to anthropologist George Foster, who came to observe the Pentecostal movement in Round Valley for two months in 1937. In Foster's words, the Pentecostal Church in Round Valley "is interesting both because it is the one really vital force in Indian life today, . . . and because it is, in my opinion, merely the latest recurrence of an aboriginal religious pattern which made the Yuki susceptible to the Ghost Dance of the seventies as well as to foreign beliefs associated with the little understood Central California Kuksu cult."[98] As they engaged syncretic practices that combined older forms of spiritualism with newer ones, Indigenous adherents of Pentecostalism in Round Valley made the religion their own while also giving it new meaning in the process.[99]

At the same time that its broader transnational appeal and continuities with Native spiritual traditions help to illuminate the resonance of Pentecostalism among Round Valley Indians, its significance for these communities cannot be fully understood without considering its implications for their daily lives and subjectivities during the late 1920s and 1930s. Pentecostalism offered an outlet for forms of self-expression, spiritual exploration, and creativity that were discouraged, prohibited, and even punished in broader society. The church's demonstrative style of worship; the way the congregation sang, shouted, and danced "with wild and uncontrolled bodily and emotional action"; and the fervor with which members spoke in an "unknown tongue" contrasted strikingly with the practices of the longer-established local Catholic and Methodist churches and defied normative codes of gender and social behavior.[100]

The church also promoted forms of social relations that deviated from—and in the views of some observers threatened—the forces of individualism and competition that settlers and elites had imposed on Native people in Round Valley during the allotment era. The church's notion of fellowship hinged on "brotherly love toward all."[101] Even with the church's masculinist language, the value Pentecostal congregations placed on mutuality, cooperation, and a collective struggle for salvation served as a powerful counterforce to the individualism that often structured other evangelical traditions as well as the discourse of political economic advancement in the region. The collective and communitarian emphasis of the Pentecostal Church perhaps can be seen most readily in its regular practice of the testimonial service. Testimonial services entailed members offering personal stories about the workings of God in their lives, while the group offered support and prayers to each participant. For the aggrieved communities who composed the local Pentecostal congregation, testimonial services and similar practices formed a kind of dialogue in which members leaned on each other and helped each other to get through the challenges of the day. In this and many other ways, the church built trust and fostered community among the diverse constituents who attended.[102]

Music played an especially critical role in virtually all of the Pentecostal Church's activities. Music was a means of gathering the congregation's expressions of praise, sorrow, desire, and tribulation into a common creative endeavor, with a synchronized rhythm and a loose-enough structure to allow for spontaneous shifts in emotion to shape the songs and service as the service proceeded. As was common practice in almost all Pentecostal churches, Round Valley services opened, closed, and were interspersed with songs. Next to the pulpit at the front of the church, a choir orchestra helped guide the melody for the congregation, though members in the congregation frequently initiated songs that moved them, "suggesting numbers from well-worn hymnals" and altering the course of the gathering as they did so.[103] The instruments that the Round Valley congregation incorporated in their services included a pipe organ, a guitar, and a whole bunch of tambourines. Members without instruments "tapped [their] feet in time to the music and [clapped their hands,] thighs as well as hinds."[104] According to George Foster, the music served as accompaniment to "prayers [that] were simple, for the most part repetitions of snatches of the Lord's prayer, bits of other prayers, original and spontaneous additions, all interspersed with [such praises as] 'Glory to God,' 'Praise the Lord,' 'Hallelujah.'"[105] Songs expressed desires for and pursuit of salvation, emancipation, and empowerment. For example, one hymn went as follows: "Oh, there's power, power, wonder-working power, in the blood, in the blood of the lamb, of the lamb. Oh, there's power, power, wonder-working power, in the precious blood of the lamb."[106] Another hymn of Round Valley's Pentecostal Church was "Paradise Valley," a variation on the classic folk tune "Red River Valley," which also inspired a Woody Guthrie recording and a version about the Spanish Civil War titled "Jarama Valley."[107]

Altogether, Round Valley Pentecostal musical practices might be considered a means of seeking transformation in the current moment while fostering hopes for a brighter future ahead. According to Foster, "The valley whites are much opposed to the entire movement, feeling that the strange antics that go on are neither religious nor conducive to quiet among the Indians."[108] Yet those drawn to the movement saw in it a world of transformative and liberatory possibilities. Reservation resident Maggie Dorman explained in 1937, "I've been a lifelong Methodist, and was married in the church fifty-three years ago. But I go to the service, and come out feeling just the way I did when I went in. But when I go to the Pentecostal Church,

I come out feeling free and uplifted." This, Dorman asserted, constituted what she considered to be "true religion."[109]

Although Round Valley Indians' cultural and religious practices addressed and exceeded the limits of dominant political institutions, they should not be regarded as separate or wholly distinct from the domains of those institutions. In fact, as an arena that nurtured new imaginings of the norms of political participation, cultural production in 1930s Round Valley in many cases reshaped and energized concerted grassroots efforts for structural social change in formal and electoral channels. On the one hand, the cultural worlds generated by Round Valley's Pentecostal Church, its music scene, and other cultural formations during the 1930s reflected and nurtured the multivalent political identities that Round Valley Indians had constructed over the longer fetch of their historical struggles. On the other hand, these cultural worlds also encouraged new forms of political collaboration and mobilization among local communities in a variety of political valences.

The cultural politics that Round Valley Indians forged in schools, at work, in pool halls, and in churches animated their coordinated efforts to challenge structures of oppression and imperialism at the local level and beyond. For instance, Elizabeth Willits recalled how she and her band linked their aesthetics to progressive and anticolonial struggles in the Round Valley region during this period:

> All the Indians then at that time was beginning to fight the . . . United States government . . . fighting for their hundred and fifty, whatever they call it on there. . . . So that's how we ah, begin to form again our band, begin to form to play music to raise money to send our delegates back to Washington to talk for our Indians' rights and to be recognized as people. So that we could get some benefits out of the government or see this government for what they was holding back from us. Such as education . . . and schools and not letting us ah, ah, being, going to into public places. . . .
>
> Mr. Cordova down in the Sonoma County area [was] working to help us Indians getting ahead on these bills to go to Washington, D.C. so that the younger generation of Indians could get their rights to go to school, to get these programs set up an they knew when they went into it and study it for while, these things were set up that the Native Americans had the right to have these educational systems set up for them. . . . These other Indians organized and found out an

they had lawyers. So they all went in, that's how they begin to move and that's how our band got interested in playing music for different organizations.[110]

For Willits and for other Native women in Round Valley, the struggle against settler colonialism and racism was inseparable from the struggle against sexism and patriarchy. She participated in and played music for several local women's clubs, including the Pomo Women's Club, which formed during this period to address the cumulative vulnerabilities of Round Valley Indian women. Despite the tribal orientation of its name, the Pomo Women's Club linked Indian women across tribal lines "to promote the political and social welfare of our race."[111] As she described, "They formed their little clubs there and we played music there. I and my brother, Richard Willits, an Inez Oliver, she played with us."[112]

At the same time that they organized around the particular needs and aspirations of Native women and those of the pan-Indian community, Willits and her bandmates also recognized political linkages between Native struggles for justice and autonomy in Round Valley and battles for liberation in colonized territories beyond U.S. borders. The collaboration between Willits's band and the local band of Filipinx musicians described at the beginning of this chapter offers a case in point. In playing banjo with Aguilar's band "every other Saturday night" and "making [her] life with them," Willits defined for herself a sense of identity and belonging that departed from that envisioned by the political establishment and the main currents of White society in the transition from allotment to the IRA. Furthermore, in "play[ing] with the Filipinos' band there," "sending money over to their land," and actively supporting people struggling against American imperialism in the Philippines, Willits and her friends contributed to the making of new expressions of liberatory politics. They enacted an emergent vision of intercolonial solidarity and multiethnic working-class autonomy that revolved around an awareness of the interdependence of differentiated grassroots struggles for dignity, against the subordinating forces of racial capitalist development.[113]

The definitions of crisis and visions of liberation that Round Valley Indians constructed through their aesthetic, religious, leisure, and other cultural practices presented a radical alternative to those that dominated major channels of political debate and economic planning during the Great Depression. While political leaders at the local and national levels clamored to enhance their ability to manage the region's working-class populations, restore stability to the regional economy, and achieve some semblance of social equilibrium, Round Valley Indians intensified their defiance of the social boundaries and divisions that so profoundly shaped their lives. Against the IRA's attempt to tighten structures of political control by spatially consolidating their communities on the reservation, Round Valley Indians continually looked across social divisions to recognize the history of struggle they shared with other aggrieved communities. Without dismissing or eliding the differentiated nature of gender, tribal, ethnic, racial, and national affiliations, the emancipatory visions advanced by Round Valley Indians in this period cast their local struggles as part of a broader, multifaceted struggle that was internationalist in orientation and global in scope.

The oppositional culture that took shape in Round Valley during the 1930s shared with other political and cultural formations across California's factories, fields, city streets, and docks not a common political agenda but a collective liberatory impulse. Like the political currents that energized grassroots movements in San Francisco, Los Angeles, Imperial Valley, and elsewhere across the state, Round Valley's oppositional culture reflected a more widespread, surrealist-inflected refusal of the conditions and classifications imposed by prevailing development patterns, along with an impetus to move beyond them. Round Valley Indians rejected the boundaries of national, racial, and industrial categorizations so frequently ascribed to them and created ways of being and belonging that underscored their multiplicity, variability, and interdependence with those around them. They fostered a multiracialist politics of working-class autonomy that challenged the social divisions of capital locally while also supporting efforts to combat American imperialism and racial capitalism beyond U.S. borders. Through an array of creative and imaginative political practices, the movements of the Round Valley Indians, like those of other working-class Californians during the Great Depression, engaged a poetics of opposition that treated freedom and democracy not merely as aims to be sought in some distant future but as things to be enacted and experienced in the process of political struggle.[114]

Conclusion

Philippine-born author, farmworker, and labor organizer Carlos Bulosan wrote dozens of poems and stories over his years living and working in California's fields and cities during the 1930s. He penned the short story "My California" to convey something of the spirit that animated his writings during that era. As the title suggests, Bulosan's story is driven largely by a desire to reclaim the land of California for its people. Refusing prevailing structures of property ownership and entitlement, as well as dominant systems of capitalist value and virtue, Bulosan reimagined the industrial landscape on his own terms. Bulosan described his California as "a magic world," shaped as much by his own "enchanting vision" and deep "feeling of affinity" as by the "signs of industry" that brought him to the place and stretched "for miles around." Where entrepreneurs, planners, and policy makers saw commodifiable resources and potential for profit, Bulosan "found beauty and poetry in every living thing." As he described, "The lettuce fields in Salinas, where I had worked with Mexicans and members of my own race for a while, were like a deep valley inundated with glittering dews. The grapevines in Bakersfield resembled the inimitable symmetry of the Sierra Madre mountains in my own province. The cantaloupe patches in Imperial Valley were like a motionless, sleeping son, especially at night when the moon and the stars shone brilliantly in the sky." In Los Angeles, Bulosan "walked around the city a great deal," taking in the sights of its "streets and buildings and places." In San Francisco, "I would follow Market Street to the end and then take a bus to the Embarcadero, smelling the salty tang of the sea and hearing the expressive speech of the dock workers." From Pismo Beach, to Santa Barbara, to San Diego, "I would walk on the beach and look across the water, watching the small ships and barges moving in the wind. . . . I would remember my native land beyond the wide ocean" with a mixture of "great sadness" and "secret pride." As Bulosan described, "I was beginning to feel that California . . . was not a part of the United States" but rather "a complete world in itself."[1]

Bulosan's vision of California was defined to a significant degree by the interconnections among its geographic features, natural resources, and people. For him, California was a place where land and ocean, fields and cities, and diverse populations from across the globe met. Rather than an exemplar of American nationhood, California was for him a global intersection, a site of transnational crossing and cultural convergence. Rather than a model of social progress or modernity, it was a place where the past shaped the present and where the future was not predetermined. Yet the sense of place in California that Bulosan described was inseparable from the sense of belonging that his story conveyed. This was *his* California, after all. "Not a part of the United States" but "a complete world unto itself," this was a California in which Bulosan situated himself not within tidy categories of national, racial, or place-based identity. Rather, Bulosan saw himself, in California, as part of a wider circulation of grassroots struggle.

This book has pursued the central question of how working-class people and communities in California made sense of prevailing conditions, pursued self-defined needs and aspirations, and sought to make their lives livable during the Great Depression. While most literature on the topic emphasizes the emergence of a unifying social democratic politics and multicultural American identity among working-class people during the 1930s, this book suggests that significant currents of grassroots movements engaged an alternative politics of working-class autonomy, animated by overlapping strains of multiracialism, internationalism, and surrealism. Rather than mobilizing around a unifying class-based agenda or a homogenizing national identity, the people and communities at the center of this project coalesced around their shared insubordination to the varied forms of dehumanization they faced. Their multiracialist politics of dignity and autonomy was transregional and international in its scope and open-ended in its ideological orientation. It was grounded in opposition to forces of racism, imperialism, and capitalism in the everyday lives of working people. It pursued social change not solely through efforts to negotiate with employers at the workplace or to lobby government officials in municipal, state, and national channels but through the assertive self-activity and self-definition of grassroots communities.

The political expressions of California's aggrieved communities assumed different forms in different local contexts, with different limits and possibilities for emancipatory struggles. Evolving reciprocally with the direct-action campaigns, strikes, and electoral initiatives that punctuated the era, the political imaginations under scrutiny here relied fundamentally on political work that occurred on the terrain of culture. While grassroots cultural politics in themselves were not adequate to wrest concessions from elites, much less topple structures of power, the direct-action campaigns that proved so critical to enacting structural political and economic change during the 1930s would have been unimaginable without them. Cultural forms sustained and regenerated grassroots struggles for dignity, challenged the legitimacy of prevailing power relations, and generated social visions that fueled social movements.

Just as attention to multiracialist, internationalist, and surrealist currents in California's Depression-era oppositional culture highlights the interplay between culture and politics in struggles for social change, it also underscores the interdependence of movements, places, and people that scholars have tended to treat in isolation. Urban and rural spaces; industrial, agricultural, and commercial work; and the lives of the diverse people who performed these types of work were fundamentally intertwined in both the political economic synthesis that governed regional capitalist development in California on the eve of the Great Depression and the oppositional culture that crystallized there during the 1930s. Many of the people and communities who composed California's multiethnic working class during the 1930s intuitively saw the differentiated grassroots struggles for survival and dignity as interdependent. Their multifaceted efforts for liberation engendered and affirmed alternative aspirations for the future of development, as well as alternative visions of modernization.

Attending to the ways in which grassroots struggles for dignity and autonomy threatened prevailing patterns of regional development in the 1930s underscores the social foundations of the era's crisis and the endemic tendency of capitalism toward crisis. Rather than being a strictly economic event, precipitated by the crash of 1929, the crisis of capitalism that marked the 1930s had roots in the problems that capitalist development created for people during the late nineteenth and early twentieth centuries. For the displaced, impoverished, and racially aggrieved populations who composed the region's social majorities, the Great Depression marked not the inauguration but the intensification and generalization of long-standing patterns of dehumanization. It also entailed a breakdown of control among prevailing political and economic institutions, opening up space and possibility for change. For elites and leaders of the racial capitalist development regime, this breakdown of control, dramatized and exacerbated by the upsurge of grassroots insubordination, defined the era's crisis. The task of developing new strategies for effective social management drove the redefinition of liberalism and the making of the New Deal order.

As one of the most politically polarized regions of the country throughout the 1930s, California lent urgency to broader national efforts to resolve the crisis and restabilize the capitalist economy. In the summer of 1934, Lorena Hickok, a veteran journalist and chief investigator for the Federal Emergency Relief Administration, traveled to California to document relief efforts across the western states in the early stages of Roosevelt's New Deal. What she found was a political situation she described as "a pretty hopeless mess."[2] In her view, the main problem was not the poverty and inequality she witnessed but Californians' unruliness in the face of federal programs that aimed to restore order. Beyond "heat, depression, bitterness, more heat, terrible poverty, [and] confusion," Hickok chronicled a widespread absence of confidence in or loyalty to national leadership among Californians across the political spectrum. She decried that large numbers of moderate progressives, union organizers, and rank-and-file workers had virtually "lost faith in their leaders." At the same time, she expressed frustration with the "violently anti-administration" attitudes of merchants, business leaders, middle-class conservatives, and journalists, all of whom had failed to control the grassroots insurgency while actively resisting federal efforts to alleviate the crisis.[3] The problem, in other words, was Californians' disobedience toward national imperatives and the degree of autonomy they claimed for themselves. Hickok's general impression of the impact of federal programs was "so far, very bad. . . . It's a mess. . . . It's California politics. . . . God damn it." She declared in a letter to Federal Emergency Relief Administration supervisor Harry Hopkins, "I think we ought to let Japan have this state. Maybe they could straighten it out."[4]

Hickok's sarcastic commentary about giving California to Japan aside, her assessment of the intractable character of California society and the unsustainability of its political antagonisms reflected concerns that were shared by many liberal politicians and intellectuals who were hard at work seeking to save capitalism from itself. During the Depression decade, California became the focus of a flurry of intellectual production by social scientists of varying sorts who aimed to diagnose and prescribe solutions for the conglomeration of "social problems" that converged within the state. For some, the most pressing priority was to subdue labor unrest in order to "restore the controllability of production," as economist Murray Reed Benedict put it. For others, the greatest urgency lay in alleviating what sociologist Carl Kraenzel described as the more general "difficulties of social control," which accompanied conditions of material deprivation and ranged from "crime and delinquency" to "[s]uicide and insanity." Some expressed a moral obligation to fulfill the nation's democratic promises, emphasizing as economist George B. Herington did the need to find "a decent and democratic solution [to the problems at hand] in an American way," at least for those who fit within the scope of prevailing definitions of the "American people."[5] While the particularities of their analyses varied, the professional intellectuals studying California in this era generally agreed that the state stood at the crux of efforts to avert the threat of either fascism or revolution, and that for the sake of the nation as a whole its problems "must certainly and soon be solved . . . now, not after an explosion." Along with the New Deal policymakers whose decisions they informed, California's intellectual authorities turned for solutions to the levers of "national policy [to] keep society on a middle path."[6]

The New Deal had complex implications for Californians. On the one hand, it offered substantial concessions to working people. It established collective bargaining rights, redistributed wealth through the introduction of a graduated income tax, and created a new social security system and broader social safety net, which made possible the growth of the nation's middle class leading into World War II and the postwar era.[7] On the other hand, its benefits and protections were deeply circumscribed along lines of race and gender. New Deal programs directed the benefits of unemployment insurance, federal home-loan assistance, and other workforce protections enshrined in the Wagner Act primarily to White Americans, especially White men. Owing in no small part to the efforts of southern Democratic legislators to safeguard Jim Crow segregation, they explicitly excluded agricultural and domestic workers from minimum-wage standards and work-hour regulations, unionization rights, and the benefits of the Social Security Act. The New Deal did not prohibit racial and gender discrimination in public life. In fact, it reinforced residential segregation by standardizing racially discriminatory home-loan and subsidy procedures under the Federal Housing Administration. Consequently, New Deal policies helped to resurrect many of the social divisions that had been destabilized by grassroots movements in the early and mid-1930s. They shored up geographic, gender, and racial divisions in the labor market, supporting the overall stability of capitalism while ensuring the endurance of gender and racial inequities.[8]

While New Deal policies drove a wedge into multiracial coalitions that had crystallized amid the crisis, the entry of the United States into World War II further fragmented California's oppositional culture while accelerating the rise of a patriotic mobilization to defend the American state. Especially in the wake of the Japanese attack on Pearl Harbor, the upwelling of nativist sentiments and racist suspicions about the supposed presence of enemy aliens fueled the mass incarceration of Japanese Americans and reinforced the boundaries of American national culture. Meanwhile, the pressures of defense mobilization, deployment of troops, demands for national unity, and widespread repression of political dissent constricted or closed many of the channels through which Californians had mobilized throughout the 1930s. As the Depression-era victory of the right to strike gave way to a wave of no-strike pledges by labor leaders, the workplace shifted from a site of confrontation between workers and employers to a site for the production of discourses of common purpose and home-front unity. It became increasingly clear throughout the 1940s that the new corporatist relationship among unions, employers, and government would do less to support the political participation of rank-and-file working people than to solidify the power of ruling blocs through the military industrialization of California's economy. In the words of longshore worker and labor organizer Stan Weir, "The coming of war did not strike dumb the people who built the new unionism of the 30s, but it did remove them from the workplaces and the social combinations inside the shops that were the basis of the organizing drives. . . . Also, it geometrically accelerated the bureaucratization of their unions." In short, "social unionism was a war casualty."[9]

Despite these closures, the shifting contours of the wartime economy should not undercut our sense of the significance of the oppositional culture that Californians built during the 1930s, or its lasting impact. As George Lipsitz reminds us, within struggles for social change "victory and defeat are not mutually exclusive categories," and any assessment of the successes and failures of movements should consider not merely the outcomes

of the "short-term institutional struggle for power" and "specific concessions" wrested from ruling classes but also the "long-term ideological work
of constructing counterhegemonic ideas and institutions."[10] As sociologist
Larry Isaac has similarly urged, social movements can never be fully understood in terms of their role in changing immediate structural realities.
Instead, he emphasizes that, "at root, movements are cultural production
agents. Regardless of whatever else they accomplish, they produce new cultural forms in the course of the struggle; they often change and augment
mainstream cultural stock in the process, and sometimes live on for generations in collective memory." Beyond their immediate impacts on power relations, movements "change our awareness, perceptions and sensibilities. . . .
They *move* our culture."[11]

Despite the reassertions of racial capitalist power that marked the 1940s,
the modes of self-activity engaged by grassroots Californians during the Depression era changed the way people understood themselves and the world
around them. The thoughts and actions of people struggling for dignity both
manifested and affirmed the emancipatory desires of California's social majorities against the universalizing principles of racial capitalist modernization and U.S. imperialism. Moreover, the social ties, cultural affinities, and
differentiated notions of working-class dignity that they advanced provided
vital sustenance for the protracted struggles of grassroots communities
throughout the World War II and postwar eras. In the face of demands for
home-front unity and McCarthyite political purges that swept progressive
organizations in the war's aftermath, the networks of friendship and political affiliation that activists forged in the 1930s served as crucial resources
for those who continued to challenge racism, imperialism, patriarchy, and
class inequality into the Cold War era. Against the bureaucratic, centralized
structure of corporatist political organizations, the creative communities
that took shape in 1930s California provided models of participatory democracy and community-based organization that continued to shape ongoing grassroots struggles for liberation. Against emergent discourses of racial
liberalism, which bolstered structures of White supremacy beneath a veil of
fairness and equal opportunity, the languages of struggle that proliferated
in Depression-era California—from swing tunes to Pentecostal rituals—
served as repositories for collective historical countermemories and sources
of cultural affirmation.[12]

The expressions of working-class dignity and autonomy that Californians
advanced in the midst of the Great Depression laid the foundations for
new modes of transnational, interethnic, and multiracial engagement and

solidarity that shaped social justice struggles throughout the long civil rights era. While Depression-era Californians did not remake the world according to their desires, they offered a counternarrative that subsequent generations could reference and draw on as they confronted evolving structures of power and oppression. Depression-era Californians widened the frame for the construction of new visions of liberation by people in other times and places by reimagining forms of struggle and solidarity in their own time. While in the throes of uncertainty, they breathed life into possibilities. In the midst of turbulence and turmoil, calamity and crackdown, they made traceable a glimpse of another horizon.

PROLOGUE

1. *Western Worker*, January 2, 1933, 1–2; *Western Worker*, January 9, 1933, 1; and Sam Darcy, radio address for station KTAB San Francisco, January 5, 1933, box 2, folder 25, Sam Darcy Papers, TAM 124, Tamiment Library and Wagner Labor Archives, New York University.

2. *Western Worker*, January 2, 1933, 2.

3. Clinton Clark, *Remember My Sacrifice: The Autobiography of Clinton Clark, Tenant Farm Organizer and Early Civil Rights Activist* (Baton Rouge: Louisiana State University Press, 2007), 26–27; Judy Yung, *Unbound Feet: A Social History of Chinese Women in San Francisco* (Berkeley: University of California Press, 1995), 342; *Western Worker*, January 16, 1933, 1; and *Western Worker*, January 23, 1933, 4.

4. "Returning Marchers Write of Bitter Struggle in Washington," *Western Worker*, December 26, 1932, 2; "Negro, White Workers Unite behind Sharecroppers," *Western Worker*, January 16, 1933, 1; "Street Fighting in Spain," *Western Worker*, January 23, 1933, 2; "Revolt in India Province," *Western Worker*, January 23, 1933, 2; "2,000 Arrested in Japan Raids," *Western Worker*, January 30, 1933, 2; and "Insurrection in Nicaragua," *Western Worker*, January 9, 1933, 2.

5. Social Science Research Conference of the Pacific Coast, Report to Plenary Session by the Committee on Social Planning, July 16–17, 1932, 11, carton 7, folder 11, Murray Reed Benedict Papers, BANC MSS 2009/109, Bancroft Library, University of California, Berkeley; and meeting minutes, Social Science Research Conference of the Pacific Coast, June 15, 1932, morning session, Clift Hotel, San Francisco, 1, carton 7, folder 11, Murray Reed Benedict Papers.

6. Social Science Research Conference of the Pacific Coast, Third Annual Meeting program and advance summaries of opening addresses, June 14, 1933, "How Far Are Social Forces Controllable?," carton 12, folder 16, Murray Reed Benedict Papers; and meeting minutes, Social Science Research Conference of the Pacific Coast, June 15, 1932, morning session, 2.

7. Bernard Baruch, quoted in John Holloway, *Change the World without Taking Power* (New York: Pluto, 2010), 196.

8. Richard A. Walker, "California's Golden Road to Riches: Natural Resources and Regional Capitalism," *Annals of the Association of American Geographers* 91, no. 1 (2001): 172–73.

9. Mike Davis, "Sunshine and the Open Shop: Ford and Darwin in 1920s Los Angeles," in *Metropolis in the Making: Los Angeles in the 1920s*, ed. Tom Sitton and William Deverell (Berkeley: University of California Press, 2001), 103–4.

10. Major works on California art include Stephanie Barron, Ilene Fort, and Sheri Bernstein, *Made in California: Art, Image, and Identity, 1900–2000* (Berkeley: University of California Press, 2000); Daniel Hurewitz, *Bohemian Los Angeles and the Making of Modern Politics* (Berkeley: University of California Press, 2007); Paul Karlstron, ed., *On the Edge of America: California Modernist Art, 1900–1950* (Berkeley: University of California Press, 1996); Peter Plagens, *Sunshine Muse: Art on the West Coast, 1945–1970* (Berkeley: University of California Press, 1999); Richard Cándida Smith, *Utopia and Dissent: Art, Poetry, and Politics in California* (Berkeley: University of California Press, 1995); and Daniel Widener, *Black Arts West: Culture and Struggle in Postwar Los Angeles* (Durham, NC: Duke University Press, 2010). Regarding California's role in the making of mass culture and consumerism, see, for example, Lary May, *Screening Out the Past: The Birth of Mass Culture and the Motion Picture Industry* (Chicago: University of Chicago Press, 1983); Lary May, *The Big Tomorrow: Hollywood and the Politics of the American Way* (Chicago: University of Chicago Press, 2000); Kevin Starr, *Material Dreams: Southern California through the 1920s* (Oxford: Oxford University Press, 1990); and Kevin Starr, *Inventing the Dream: California through the Progressive Era* (Oxford: Oxford University Press, 1985).

11. Walker, "California's Golden Road to Riches"; and Paul A. David and Gavin Wright, "Increasing Returns and the Genesis of American Resource Abundance," *Industrial and Corporate Change* 6, no. 2 (1997): 203–45. Regarding the impact of Los Angeles and the Southern California region on the national and global political economy, see Edward W. Soja, *My Los Angeles: From Urban Restructuring to Regional Urbanization* (Berkeley: University of California Press, 2014); Edward W. Soja, *Postmodern Geographies: The Reassertion of Space in Critical Social Theory* (New York: Verso, 1989), chap. 8; Allen John Scott and Edward W. Soja, *The City: Los Angeles and Urban Theory at the End of the Twentieth Century* (Berkeley: University of California Press, 1996); Mike Davis, *City of Quartz: Excavating the Future in Los Angeles* (New York: Vintage Books, 1992); and Carey McWilliams, *Southern California: An Island on the Land* (1946; Salt Lake City: Gibbs Smith, 1973). Regarding the particular contributions of California's cities to patterns of metropolitan and military development, see Roger W. Lotchin, *The Bad City in the Good War: San Francisco, Los Angeles, Oakland, and San Diego* (Bloomington: Indiana University Press, 2003); and Roger W. Lotchin, *Fortress California, 1910–1961* (New York: Oxford University Press, 1992).

12. Karl Marx to Friedrich Sorge, November 5, 1880, trans. and ed. Leonard E. Mins, in *Karl Marx and Frederick Engels: Letters to Americans, 1848–1895* (New York: International

Publishers, 1953), 126. Mins's translation was previously published in *Science and Society* 2, no. 2 (Spring 1938).

13. Soja, *Postmodern Geographies*, 190.

14. Walker, "California's Golden Road to Riches."

15. See especially Patricia Limerick, *The Legacy of Conquest: The Unbroken Past of the American West* (New York: W. W. Norton, 1987); Tomás Almaguer, *Racial Fault Lines: The Historical Origins of White Supremacy in California* (Berkeley: University of California Press, 1994); Lizbeth Haas, *Conquests and Historical Identities in California, 1769–1936* (Berkeley: University of California Press, 1996); and James N. Gregory, "The West and Workers, 1870–1930," in *A Companion to the American West*, ed. William Deverell (Malden, MA: Blackwell, 2004), 240–55. For early seminal works on this subject, see Mario Barrera, *Race and Class in the Southwest: A Theory of Racial Inequality* (Notre Dame, IN: University of Notre Dame Press, 1979); and Alexander Saxton, *The Indispensable Enemy: Labor and the Anti-Chinese Movement in California* (Berkeley: University of California Press, 1971). Significantly, patterns of resource and population management in the region were not isolated experiments but provided a model for the rest of the nation and its imperial ventures abroad. See David R. Roediger and Elizabeth D. Esch, *The Production of Difference: Race and the Management of Labor in U.S. History* (New York: Oxford University Press, 2012).

16. Almaguer, *Racial Fault Lines*, 120–30.

17. Almaguer, *Racial Fault Lines*, 120–30; and Alexander Saxton, *The Rise and Fall of the White Republic: Class Politics and Mass Culture in Nineteenth-Century America* (New York: Verso, 1990), esp. 269–91.

18. Carey McWilliams, *California: The Great Exception* (1949; Westport, CT: Greenwood, 1971), 129–30, 138–39.

19. U.S. Senate Committee on Education and Labor, *Violations of Free Speech and Rights of Labor, Report No. 1150, Part 1* (Washington, DC: U.S. Government Printing Office, 1942), 64–65; and McWilliams, *California*, 129–30.

20. Roediger and Esch, *Production of Difference*, 155–62; and Almaguer, *Racial Fault Lines*, 13–14.

21. These calculations are based on the 1930 census, which counted "Mexicans" as non-White. This was revised in the 1940 census, which included people of Mexican heritage/ethnicity as part of the White race. Data come from U.S. Census Bureau, *Fifteenth Census of the United States, 1930: Population* (Washington, DC: National Archives and Records Administration, 1931–33), vol. 2, *General Report*, table 17, 12, and vol. 3, *Reports by States*, pt. 1, table 2, 233.

22. McWilliams, *California*, 774–75; data come from U.S. Census Bureau, *Fifteenth Census: Population*, vol. 3, *Reports by States*, pt. 1, table 2, 233.

23. McWilliams, *California*, 81. During the 1850s male California residents outnumbered female California residents by a ratio of twelve to one. By 1850 women constituted just 30 percent of the state's total population, and by 1870 that figure had risen just slightly, to 37 percent.

24. McWilliams, *California*, 81; and U.S. Census Bureau, *Fifteenth Census: Population*, vol. 3, *Reports by States*, pt. 1, table 2, 233.

25. Roediger and Esch, *Production of Difference*, 193–204.

26. See especially Saxton, *Indispensable Enemy*; Nayan Shah, *Contagious Divides: Epidemics and Race in San Francisco's Chinatown* (Berkeley: University of California Press, 2001); Mae M. Ngai, *Impossible Subjects: Illegal Aliens and the Making of Modern America* (Princeton, NJ: Princeton University Press, 2004); and Peggy Pascoe, *What Comes Naturally: Miscegenation Law and the Making of Race in America* (London: Oxford University Press, 2010).

27. Regarding this central antagonism between forces of subordination and insubordination, see Karl Polanyi, *The Great Transformation: The Political Origins of Our Time* (1944; Boston: Beacon, 2001); and Holloway, *Change the World*.

28. McWilliams, *California*, 17, 20.

29. Polanyi, *Great Transformation*, 210–11.

30. Robert W. Cherny, Gretchen Lemke-Santangelo, and Richard Griswold del Castillo, *Competing Visions: A History of California* (Boston: Houghton Mifflin, 2005), 248–49.

31. Loren B. Chan, "California during the Early 1930s: The Administration of James Rolph, Jr., 1931–1934," *Southern California Quarterly* 63, no. 3 (1981): 268.

32. James N. Gregory, *American Exodus: The Dust Bowl Migration and Okie Culture in California* (New York: Oxford University Press, 1989), 6–7.

33. Kevin Starr, *Endangered Dreams: The Great Depression in California* (Oxford: Oxford University Press, 1996), esp. chaps. 6 and 7; Richard Lowitt, *The New Deal and the West* (Bloomington: Indiana University Press, 1984), 172; and Robert E. Burke, *Olson's New Deal in California* (Berkeley: University of California Press, 1953), 230.

34. Lowitt, *New Deal and the West*, 175.

INTRODUCTION

1. Quoted in Carlos Bulosan, *America Is in the Heart* (Seattle: University of Washington Press, 2014), 186.

2. Charlotta Bass, November 1939 radio broadcast, "Next week we celebrate the 'Roosevelt Thanksgiving . . . ,'" 2, Additions—box 1, folder: "Articles, 1930s," Charlotta Bass Collection, MSS 002, Southern California Library for Social Studies and Research, Los Angeles.

3. Regarding "revolutionary time," see David R. Roediger, *Seizing Freedom: Slave Emancipation and Liberty for All* (New York: Verso, 2014), 14.

4. Regarding the formation and composition of California's urban and rural power blocs, see, for example, Carey McWilliams, *Factories in the Field: The Story of Migratory Farm Labor in California* (1935; Berkeley: University of California Press, 2000); Mike Davis, "Sunshine and the Open Shop: Ford and Darwin in 1920s Los Angeles," in *Metropolis in the Making: Los Angeles in the 1920s*, ed. Tom Sitton and William Deverell (Berkeley: University of California Press, 2001), 96–122; Devra Anne Weber, *Dark Sweat, White Gold: California Farm Workers, Cotton, and the New Deal* (Berkeley: University of California Press, 1996); and William Issel and Robert W. Cherny, *San Francisco, 1865–1932: Politics, Power, and Urban Development* (Berkeley: University of California Press, 1986).

5. See, for example, Kevin Starr, *Endangered Dreams: The Great Depression in California* (Oxford: Oxford University Press, 1996), esp. chap. 6; and Laura Renata Martin, "'California's Unemployed Feed Themselves': Conservative Intervention in the Los Angeles Cooperative Movement, 1931–1934," *Pacific Historical Review* 81, no. 1 (February 2013): 33–62.

6. George Lipsitz, *Rainbow at Midnight: Labor and Culture in the 1940s* (Urbana: University of Illinois Press, 1994), esp. 59–60, 157–81, 341–43; Steve Fraser and Gary Gerstle, eds., *The Rise and Fall of the New Deal Order, 1930–1980* (Princeton, NJ: Princeton University Press, 1989); and Nelson Lichtenstein, *Labor's War at Home: The CIO in World War II* (Philadelphia: Temple University Press, 2003).

7. Becky M. Nicolaides, *My Blue Heaven: Life and Politics in the Working-Class Suburbs of Los Angeles, 1920–1965* (Chicago: University of Chicago Press, 2002); Starr, *Endangered Dreams*; David G. Gutiérrez, *Walls and Mirrors: Mexican Americans, Mexican Immigrants, and the Politics of Ethnicity* (Berkeley: University of California Press, 1995); James N. Gregory, *American Exodus: The Dust Bowl Migration and Okie Culture in California* (New York: Oxford University Press, 1989); and Bruce Nelson, *Workers on the Waterfront: Seamen, Longshoremen, and Unionism in the 1930s* (Urbana: University of Illinois Press, 1988).

8. My use of the term "racial capitalism" draws on Cedric J. Robinson, *Black Marxism: The Making of the Black Radical Tradition* (Chapel Hill: University of North Carolina Press, 2000).

9. Magonistas were part of a current of anarchosyndicalism that grew out of early twentieth-century Mexico and that was based on the ideas of Ricardo, Enrique, and Jesús Magón.

10. Shelley Streeby, *Radical Sensations: World Movements, Violence, and Visual Culture* (Durham, NC: Duke University Press, 2013); Douglas Monroy, "Fence Cutters, Sedicioso, and First-Class Citizens: Mexican Radicalism in America," in *The Immigrant Left in the United States*, ed. Paul Buhle and Dan Georgakas (Albany: State University of New York Press, 1996), 11–44; Daniel Rosenberg, "The IWW and Organization of Asian Workers in Early 20th Century America," *Labor History* 36, no. 1 (1995): 77–87; Michael Kazin, "The Great Exception Revisited: Organizer Labor and Politics in San Francisco and Los Angeles, 1870–1940," *Pacific Historical Review* 55, no. 3 (August 1986): 371–402; and Fay M. Blake and H. Morton Newman, "Upton Sinclair's Epic Campaign," *California History* 63, no. 4 (Fall 1984): 305–12.

11. Works in this vein range widely in their orientations and approaches. Key examples include Theodore Draper, *The Roots of American Communism* (New York: Viking, 1957); Harvey Klehr, *The Heyday of American Communism: The Depression Decade* (New York: Basic, 1984); Harvey Klehr and John Earl Haynes, *The American Communist Movement: Storming Heaven Itself* (New York: Twayne, 1992); Maurice Isserman, "Notes from Underground," *Nation* 260, no. 23 (June 12, 1995): 846–56; and Michael Denning, *The Cultural Front: The Laboring of American Culture in the Twentieth Century* (New York: Verso, 1996).

12. Robin D. G. Kelley, *Hammer and Hoe: Alabama Communists during the Great Depression* (Chapel Hill: University of North Carolina Press, 1990), xiii–xiv. See also

Robert W. Cherny, "Prelude to the Popular Front: The Communist Party in Califor-
nia, 1931–35," *American Communist History* 1, no. 1 (2002): 5–42; Michael K. Honey,
*Southern Labor and Black Civil Rights: Organizing Memphis Workers, Working Class
in American History* (Urbana: University of Illinois Press, 1993); Gerald Horne,
Communist Front? The Civil Rights Congress, 1946–1956 (Rutherford, NJ: Fairleigh
Dickinson University Press, 1988); Vicki L. Ruiz, *Cannery Women, Cannery Lives:
Mexican Women, Unionization, and the California Food Processing Industry, 1930–1950*
(Albuquerque: University of New Mexico Press, 1987); Bruce Nelson, "Unions and
the Popular Front: The West Coast Waterfront in the 1930s," *International Labor and
Working-Class History* 30 (Fall 1986): 59–78; and Mark Naison, *Communists in Harlem
during the Depression* (Urbana: University of Illinois Press, 1983).

13. My framing of the 1930s political left in California as a "movement of many
movements" draws on the theoretical contributions of late twentieth- and early
twenty-first-century antiglobalization movements. See, for example, Tom Mertes, ed.,
A Movement of Movements: Is Another World Really Possible? (New York: Verso, 2004).

14. Seminal works on the political culture of popular front movements include
Irving Bernstein, *The Turbulent Years: A History of the American Worker, 1933–1941*
(Chicago: Haymarket Books, 1969); Lizabeth Cohen, *Making a New Deal: Industrial
Workers in Chicago, 1919–1939* (Cambridge: Cambridge University Press, 1991); Denning,
Cultural Front; Fraser and Gerstle, *New Deal Order*; and Lichtenstein, *Labor's War
at Home*.

15. Cherny, "Prelude to the Popular Front."

16. Grower, quoted in Benny J. Andrés Jr., *Power and Control in the Imperial Valley:
Nature, Agribusiness, and Workers on the California Borderland, 1900–1940* (College
Station: Texas A&M University Press, 2015), 147. See also Elizabeth E. Sine, "Grassroots
Multiracialism: Imperial Valley Farm Labor and the Making of Popular Front California
from Below," *Pacific Historical Review* 85, no. 2 (May 2016): 227–54.

17. For additional examinations of multiracialism in 1930s social movements, see
Christina Heatherton, "Relief and Revolution: Southern California Struggles against
Unemployment in the 1930s," in *The Rising Tide of Color: Race, State Violence, and
Radical Movements across the Pacific*, ed. Moon Ho Jung (Seattle: University of
Washington Press, 2014), 159–87; and Robert Zecker, "A Road to Peace and Freedom":
*The International Workers Order and the Struggle for Economic Justice and Civil Rights,
1930–1954* (Philadelphia: Temple University Press, 2018).

18. W. E. B. Du Bois, *Black Reconstruction in America, 1860–1880* (1935; New York:
Free Press, 1992), 728.

19. W. E. B. Du Bois, "The Color Line Belts the World," in *W. E. B. Du Bois: A
Reader*, ed. David Levering Lewis (New York: Henry Holt, 1995), 42.

20. Regarding the international and transnational dimensions of 1930s social
movements and the politics of racial, ethnic, and working-class internationalisms
more generally, see Zecker, "Road to Peace and Freedom"; Rachel Ida Buff, *Against
the Deportation Terror: Organizing for Immigrant Rights in the Twentieth Century*
(Philadelphia: Temple University Press, 2018); Benjamin Balthasar, *Anti-imperialist
Modernism: Race and Transnational Radical Culture from the Great Depression to the*

Cold War (Ann Arbor: University of Michigan Press, 2016); Kenyon Zimmer, *Immigrants against the State: Yiddish and Italian Anarchism in America* (Urbana: University of Illinois Press, 2015); Jennifer Guglielmo, *Living the Revolution: Italian Women's Resistance and Revolution in New York City* (Chapel Hill: University of North Carolina Press, 2012); Josephine Fowler, *Japanese and Chinese Immigrant Activists: Organizing in American and International Communist Movements, 1919–1933* (New Brunswick, NJ: Rutgers University Press, 2007); Nikhil Pal Singh, *Black Is a Country: Race and the Unfinished Struggle for Democracy* (Cambridge, MA: Harvard University Press, 2004), esp. chap. 2; and Brent Hayes Edwards, *The Practice of Diaspora: Literature, Translation, and the Rise of Black Internationalism* (Cambridge, MA: Harvard University Press, 2003).

21. In the words of David Gascoyne, cofounder of the Surrealist Group in England in 1936, "It is the avowed aim of the surrealist movement to reduce and finally to dispose altogether of the flagrant contradictions that exist between dream and waking life, the 'unreal' and the 'real,' the unconscious and the conscious, and thus to make what has hitherto been regarded as the special domain of poets, the acknowledged common property of all." Gascoyne, *A Short Survey of Surrealism* (San Francisco: City Lights, 1982), viii, quoted in Franklin Rosemont and Robin D. G. Kelley, eds., *Black, Brown, and Beige: Surrealist Writings from Africa and the Diaspora* (Austin: University of Texas Press, 2009), 3.

22. Malcolm de Chazal, quoted in F. Rosemont and Kelley, *Black, Brown, and Beige*, 2.

23. John Holloway, "Dignity's Revolt," in *Zapatista! Reinventing Revolution in Mexico*, ed. John Holloway and Eloína Peláez (London: Pluto, 1998), 169, 183.

24. Suzanne Césaire, "1943: Surrealism and Us," in Penelope Rosemont, ed., *Surrealist Women: An International Anthology* (Austin: University of Texas Press, 1998), 136–37.

25. Here I paraphrase Czech surrealist Karel Teige, who proclaimed, "When freedom becomes reality, poetry becomes life." Quoted in Franklin Rosemont, "Notes on Surrealism as a Revolution against Whiteness," in "Surrealism: Revolution against Whiteness," spec. issue, *Race Traitor*, no. 9 (Summer 1998): 19.

26. How and why working people became oriented around a social democratic politics and corporatist agenda, and what happened as a result, has been a central question pursued by scholars of the era's social movements. See, for example, Lichtenstein, *Labor's War at Home*; Fraser and Gerstle, *New Deal Order*; Cohen, *Making a New Deal*; and Denning, *Cultural Front*. While more recent departures in historiography of the New Deal era have tended to shift the focus from social and cultural histories of the working class to higher levels of New Deal policy making, established analyses of working-class culture that revolve around working-class unity and Americanism continue to shape the narrative. For example, see Jefferson Cowie, *The Great Exception: The New Deal and the Limits of American Politics* (Princeton, NJ: Princeton University Press, 2016); and Jefferson Cowie and Nick Salvatore, "The Long Exception: Rethinking the Place of the New Deal in American History," *International Labor and Working-Class History* 74 (Fall 2008): 3–32. For a sample critique of Cowie and Salvatore's analysis, see Nancy MacLean, "Getting New Deal History Wrong," *International Labor and*

Working-Class History 74 (Fall 2008): 49–55 (MacLean's article is part of the round-table "Rethinking the Place of the New Deal in American History").

27. Denning, *Cultural Front*, xvi–xvii.

28. Denning, *Cultural Front*, 129–32, 238–39. Paul Buhle makes a parallel argument about the role of ethnicity and ethnic subordination in the making of working-class solidarities in Buhle, *Marxism in the United States: A History of the American Left* (New York: Verso, 2013).

29. David R. Roediger, *History against Misery* (Chicago: Charles H. Kerr, 2006), 27 (italics mine). Roediger's fuller critique of Denning's work can be found in pages 12–27 of this same text. See also George Lipsitz, *American Studies in a Moment of Danger* (Minneapolis: University of Minnesota Press, 2001), 31–56. For additional analysis regarding the limits of labor as a frame for examining grassroots struggles and culture, see Paul Gilroy, *Small Acts: Thoughts on the Politics of Black Cultures* (New York: Serpent's Tail, 1993), 137–38.

30. Roediger, *History against Misery*, 19–20; Robin D. G. Kelley, *Freedom Dreams: The Black Radical Imagination* (Boston: Beacon, 2002), 4–6; and Gavin Grindon, "Surrealism, Dada, and the Refusal of Work: Autonomy, Activism, and Social Participation in the Radical Avant-Garde," *Oxford Art Journal* 34, no. 1 (2011): 79–96.

31. F. Rosemont and Kelley, *Black, Brown, and Beige*, 3.

32. In the words of Robin D. G. Kelley, the conceptual tools that surrealism provides have "no birth date, no expiration date, no trademark." Kelley sees a surrealist genealogy as traceable from "the ancient practices of Maroon societies and shamanism back to the future, to the metropoles of Europe, to the blues people of North America, to the colonized and semicolonized world that produced the like of Aimé and Suzanne Césaire and Wilfredo Lam." Kelley, *Freedom Dreams*, 4–5. With Kelley, I argue that surrealist "dreams" are part of a protracted struggle that extends forward to the present as well and that bears a strong resonance with reconceptualizations of revolution by current antiglobalization movements, which also inform this work. Of particular note are theorizations by the Ejército Zapatista do Liberación Nacional (Zapatista Army of National Liberation) in Chiapas, Mexico. See John Holloway and Eloína Peláez, "Introduction: Reinventing Revolution," in *Zapatista! Reinventing Revolution in Mexico*, ed. John Holloway and Eloína Peláez (London: Pluto, 1998), 1–18.

33. Robin D. G. Kelley, *Race Rebels: Culture, Politics, and the Black Working Class* (New York: Free Press, 1996), 9. In addition to Kelley's work, my interpretation of the political is informed by the broader contributions of subaltern, feminist, and cultural studies. For seminal examples, see Stuart Hall and Tony Jefferson, eds., *Resistance through Rituals: Youth Sub-cultures in Post-war Britain* (London: Hutchinson, 1976); James C. Scott, *Weapons of the Weak: Everyday Forms of Peasant Resistance* (New Haven, CT: Yale University Press, 1985); Elizabeth Faue, *Community of Suffering and Struggle: Women, Men, and the Labor Movement in Minneapolis, 1915–1945* (Chapel Hill: University of North Carolina Press, 1991); Mary P. Ryan, *Women in Public: Between Banners and Ballots, 1825–1880* (Baltimore: Johns Hopkins University Press, 1992); Elsa Barkley Brown, "Negotiating and Transforming the Public Sphere: African

American Political Life in the Transition from Slavery to Freedom," *Public Culture* 7 (1994): 107–46; and Dick Hebdige, *Subculture: The Meaning of Style* (New York: Routledge, 1994).

34. For example, Kelley, one of the leading contemporary scholars of surrealism, has produced a rich and expansive body of work chronicling and interpreting modes of grassroots struggle and resistance that reach well beyond a strict understanding of surrealism per se. See, for example, Kelley, *Hammer and Hoe*; *Race Rebels*; and *Yo Mama's Dysfunktional! Fighting the Culture Wars in Urban America* (Boston: Beacon, 2008).

35. Cedric J. Robinson, *Terms of Order: Political Science and the Myth of Leadership* (Chapel Hill: University of North Carolina Press, 2016).

36. Regarding the rethinking of revolution, freedom, and democracy articulated here, see John Holloway, *Change the World without Taking Power* (New York: Pluto, 2010), 218–19, 224–25.

37. The dilemma of organizational discipline and working-class self-activity sat at the heart of such foundational texts of the political left as Vladimir Ilyich Lenin, "What Is to Be Done?," in *Essential Works of Lenin: "What Is to Be Done?" and Other Writings*, ed. Henry Christman (New York: Dover, 1987), 53–176; and Vladimir Ilyich Lenin, *"Left-Wing" Communism and Infantile Disorder: A Popular Essay in Marxian Strategy and Tactics* (Honolulu: University Press of the Pacific, 2001). For more contemporary analyses regarding the centrality and pervasiveness of this dilemma within struggles for social change, see, for example, Geoff Eley's work on the European left in Eley, *Forging Democracy: The History of the Left in Europe, 1850–2000* (Oxford: Oxford University Press, 2000); and Paul Gilroy's work on Black cultural politics in Gilroy, *Small Acts*, 15.

38. Regarding the social warrant advanced by 1930s social movements, see George Lipsitz's afterword to Stan Weir's memoir: Lipsitz, "Stan Weir: Working Class Visionary," in *Singlejack Solidarity*, by Stan Weir (Minneapolis: University of Minnesota Press, 2004), 351–52. Also see George Lipsitz, "Abolition Democracy and Global Justice," *Comparative American Studies* 2, no. 3 (2004): 273.

39. Ralph Ellison, "Harlem Is Nowhere," *Harper's Magazine*, August 1964, 54.

40. Gilroy, *Small Acts*; Kelley, *Race Rebels*; S. Hall and Jefferson, *Resistance through Rituals*; George Lipsitz, *Time Passages: Collective Memory and American Popular Culture* (Minneapolis: University of Minnesota Press, 1990); and George Lipsitz, *Footsteps in the Dark: The Hidden Histories of Popular Music* (Minneapolis: University of Minnesota Press, 2007).

41. James C. Scott, *Domination and the Arts of Resistance: Hidden Transcripts* (New Haven, CT: Yale University Press, 1990), 183.

42. Gilroy, *Small Acts*, 134.

43. Gilroy, *Small Acts*, 134, 137–38.

44. Antonio Gramsci, *Selections from the Prison Notebooks*, ed. Quintin Hoare and Geoffrey Nowell Smith (New York: International Publishers, 1971).

45. Josh Kun, *Audiotopia: Music, Race, and America* (Berkeley: University of California Press, 2005), 17.

46. Stuart Hall, "Notes on Deconstructing 'the Popular,'" in *Cultural Resistance Reader*, ed. Stephen Duncombe (London: Verso, 2002), 192.

47. Lipsitz, *Time Passages*, 16. As literary scholar Lisa Lowe puts it, "Some cultural forms succeed in making it possible to live and inhabit alternatives in the encounter with [dominant] prohibitions; some permit us to imagine what we still have yet to live." Lowe, *Immigrant Acts: On Asian American Cultural Politics* (Durham, NC: Duke University Press, 1996), x.

48. Earl Lewis, "To Turn as on a Pivot: Writing African Americans into a History of Overlapping Diasporas," *American Historical Review* 100 (June 1995): 765–87. Brent Hayes Edwards, "Shadow of Shadows," *Positions: East Asia Cultures Critique* 11, no. 1 (2003): 13. For seminal studies that underscore the West's importance as an illuminator of the role of racial difference in U.S. history, see Patricia Limerick, *The Legacy of Conquest: The Unbroken Past of the American West* (New York: W. W. Norton, 1987); and Richard White, "Race Relations in the American West," *American Quarterly* 38, no. 3 (1986): 396–416.

49. Juan Flores, "Reclaiming Left Baggage: Some Early Sources for Minority Studies," *Cultural Critique* 59 (Winter 2005): 187–206.

50. Eley, *Forging Democracy*, viii–ix.

1. MULTIRACIAL REBELLION IN CALIFORNIA'S FIELDS

An early form of Chapter 1 appeared in Elizabeth E. Sine, "Grassroots Multiracialism: Imperial Valley Farm Labor and the Making of Popular Front California from Below," *Pacific Historical Review* 85, no. 2 (May 2016): 227–54.

1. The story of the 1930 Imperial Valley lettuce strike has been told many times. For the most thorough and seminal accounts, see Benny J. Andrés Jr., *Power and Control in the Imperial Valley: Nature, Agribusiness, and Workers on the California Borderland, 1900–1940* (College Station: Texas A&M University Press, 2015), 139–42; Gilberto G. González, "Company Unions, the Mexican Consulate, and the Imperial Valley Agricultural Strikes, 1928–1934," *Western Historical Quarterly* 27, no. 1 (Spring 1996): 56–60; Cletus E. Daniel, *Bitter Harvest: A History of California Farmworkers, 1870–1941* (Berkeley: University of California Press, 1982), 111–17; Devra Anne Weber, "The Organizing of Mexicano Agricultural Workers: Imperial Valley and Los Angeles, 1928–1934, an Oral History Approach," *Aztlán* 3, no. 2 (1973): 319–21; Irving Bernstein, *The Turbulent Years: A History of the American Worker, 1933–1941* (Chicago: Haymarket Books, 1969), 147–50; Stuart Jamieson, *Labor Unionism in California Agriculture* (Washington, DC: U.S. Government Printing Office, 1945), 81–84; and Frank Spector, *Story of the Imperial Valley* (New York: International Labor Defense, n.d.), 15–19. Regarding the 1928 cantaloupe strike, other earlier work stoppages, and patterns of political repression, see Charles Wollenberg, "Huelga, 1928 Style: The Imperial Valley Cantaloupe Workers' Strike," *Pacific Historical Review* 38, no. 1 (February 1969): 45–58; Carey McWilliams, *Factories in the Field: The Story of Migratory Farm Labor in California* (1935; Berkeley: University of California Press, 2000), 212–13; Jamieson, *Labor Unionism in California Agriculture*, 75–78; Louis Bloch, "Report on the Strike of the Imperial Valley Cantaloupe Pickers," in *Mexicans in California: Report of Governor C. C. Young's Mexican Fact-Finding Commit-*

tee, dir. Will J. French, G. H. Hecke, and Anna L. Saylor (San Francisco: California State Printing Office, 1930), 135–47; and Paul S. Taylor, *Mexican Labor in the United States: Imperial Valley* (Berkeley: University of California Press, 1928), 45–52.

2. Regarding the longer history of interracial competition and exclusionary unionism as a central feature of racial capitalist development in the Imperial Valley and beyond, see David R. Roediger and Elizabeth D. Esch, *The Production of Difference: Race and the Management of Labor in U.S. History* (New York: Oxford University Press, 2012).

3. Regarding the confluence of Magonistas, Wobblies, Communist Party members, and other radicals in the Imperial Valley in 1930, see Douglas Monroy, "Fence Cutters, *Sedicioso*, and First-Class Citizens: Mexican Radicalism in America," in *The Immigrant Left in the United States*, ed. Paul Buhle and Dan Georgakas (Albany: State University of New York Press, 1996), 11–44; and Weber, "Organizing of Mexicano Agricultural Workers."

4. *Daily Worker*, January 6, 1930, quoted in Jamieson, *Labor Unionism in California Agriculture*, 81.

5. Andrés, *Power and Control in the Imperial* Valley, 140–41.

6. Of the ninety-nine strikes that occurred in the United States and involved 87,364 agricultural workers during 1933–34, forty-nine happened in California and involved 67,887 California farmworkers. Stuart Jamieson, quoted in I. Bernstein, *Turbulent Years*, 142. Regarding the formation and activities of CAWIU as well as the peak of strike activities in 1933–34, see Devra Anne Weber, *Dark Sweat, White Gold: California Farm Workers, Cotton, and the New Deal* (Berkeley: University of California Press, 1996); Rudy P. Guevarra Jr., *Becoming Mexipino: Multiethnic Identities and Communities in San Diego* (New Brunswick, NJ: Rutgers University Press, 2012), 107; Andrés, *Power and Control in the Imperial Valley*, 142–43; Daniel, *Bitter Harvest*, 128–39, chap. 5; and I. Bernstein, *Turbulent Years*, 153–70.

7. According to one report by the California State Division of Labor Statistics and Law Enforcement, "Statistical Summary of Agricultural Strikes in California 1933," CAWIU's strike activities involved an estimated 32,800 farmworkers in 1933 alone. "Statistical Summary of Agricultural Strikes in California 1933," typewritten manuscript, 1–7, box 20, folder 36, Carey McWilliams Papers, Card Files, 1930–1940, Special Collections, Collection 1243, Charles E. Young Research Library, University of California, Los Angeles.

8. According to the "Statistical Summary of Agricultural Strikes in California 1933," of the twenty-four walkouts that CAWIU led during 1933 alone, twenty achieved at least partial wage increases, and only four resulted in a total loss for the union. "Statistical Summary of Agricultural Strikes in California 1933," 1–7.

9. Grower, quoted in Andrés, *Power and Control in the Imperial Valley*, 147.

10. Cedric J. Robinson, *Black Marxism: The Making of the Black Radical Tradition* (Chapel Hill: University of North Carolina Press, 2000).

11. Andrés, *Power and Control in the Imperial Valley*, chap. 1.

12. Andrés, *Power and Control in the Imperial Valley*, 75–76; and Alan L. Olmstead and Paul W. Rhode, "The Evolution of California Agriculture, 1850–2000," in *California Agriculture: Dimensions and Issues*, ed. Jerome B. Siebert (Berkeley: University of California Press, 2004), 4–5.

13. Andrés, *Power and Control in the Imperial Valley*, 73–76; and Mark Reisler, *By the Sweat of Their Brow: Mexican Immigrant Labor in the United States, 1900–1941* (Westport, CT: Greenwood, 1976), 61. "Large-scale" farms were defined by the Departments of Commerce and Agriculture as those that raised produce amounting to an annual value of $30,000 or more. The growing dominance of large-scale farms in the Imperial Valley reflected a statewide trend. By 1929 California contained nearly 40 percent of all the large-scale farms in the United States. Although they constituted just 2.1 percent of all the farms in California at the time, these large farms produced roughly one-third of the state's agricultural output and fueled the expansion of the state's agricultural workforce from 109,000 in 1879 to 332,000 in 1929, approximately 15 percent of California's total waged workforce. See Reisler, *By the Sweat of Their Brow*, 78–79; and Olmstead and Rhode, "Evolution of California Agriculture," 4, 19.

14. Andrés, *Power and Control in the Imperial Valley*, 112–15; and Reisler, *By the Sweat of Their Brow*, 83.

15. Roediger and Esch, *Production of Difference*, 193–204; Monica Perales, *Smeltertown: Making and Remembering a Southwest Border Community* (Chapel Hill: University of North Carolina Press, 2010), chap. 1; and Katherine Benton-Cohen, *Borderline Americans: Racial Division and Labor War in the Arizona Borderlands* (Cambridge, MA: Harvard University Press, 2009).

16. The term "multiracism" comes from Vijay Prashad, "Bruce Lee and the Anti-imperialism of Kung-Fu: A Polycultural Adventure," *Positions: East Asia Cultures Critique* 11, no. 1 (2003): 59–90. Other seminal examples of this vast literature include Alexander Saxton, *The Indispensable Enemy: Labor and the Anti-Chinese Movement in California* (Berkeley: University of California Press, 1971); Mario Barrera, *Race and Class in the Southwest: A Theory of Racial Inequality* (Notre Dame, IN: University of Notre Dame Press, 1979); Ronald T. Takaki, *Iron Cages: Race and Culture in Nineteenth-Century America* (New York: Knopf, 1979); Reginald Horsman, *Race and Manifest Destiny: The Origins of American Racial Anglo-Saxonism* (Cambridge, MA: Harvard University Press, 1981); Mae M. Ngai, *Impossible Subjects: Illegal Aliens and the Making of Modern America* (Princeton, NJ: Princeton University Press, 2004); Peggy Pascoe, *What Comes Naturally: Miscegenation Law and the Making of Race in America* (London: Oxford University Press, 2010); Tomás Almaguer, *Racial Fault Lines: The Historical Origins of White Supremacy in California* (Berkeley: University of California Press, 1994); and Roediger and Esch, *Production of Difference*.

17. Roediger and Esch, *Production of Difference*, 15, 193–204.

18. Andrés, *Power and Control in the Imperial Valley*, 98–100.

19. Adam McKeown, "Global Migration, 1846–1940," *Journal of World History* 15, no. 2 (June 2004): 155–89; June Mei, "Economic Origins of Emigration: Guangdong to California, 1850–1882," *Modern China* 5, no. 4 (October 1979): 463–501; and Gilbert González and Raúl Fernández, *A Century in Chicano History: Empire, Nations, and Migration* (New York: Routledge, 2003), chap. 2.

20. James N. Gregory, *American Exodus: The Dust Bowl Migration and Okie Culture in California* (New York: Oxford University Press, 1989), 8–10.

21. Andrés, *Power and Control in the Imperial Valley*, 51–52.

22. Paul Taylor, quoted in Roediger and Esch, *Production of Difference*, 197. The estimate of ethnic Mexicans as constituting 90 percent of the Imperial Valley's farm labor force by 1928 comes from Wollenberg, "Huelga, 1928 Style," 47. For further information on demographics in the regional economy, see "Report on the Strike of the Imperial Valley Cantaloupe Pickers," in French, Hecke, and Saylor, *Mexicans in California*, 136; Guevarra, *Becoming Mexipino*, 100; and Karen Leonard, *Making Ethnic Choices: California's Punjabi Mexican Americans* (Philadelphia: Temple University Press, 2010), 38–40.

23. Roediger and Esch, *Production of Difference*, 197–98.

24. Woman secretary at Fresno Farms Company, Kerman, CA, September 10, 1928, "Mexican Labor in U.S., Field Notes: Series-E, Set-I," 190, carton 10, folder 8, Paul Schuster Taylor Papers, BANC MSS 84/38c, Bancroft Library, University of California, Berkeley.

25. Roediger and Esch, *Production of Difference*, 198.

26. Wilbur J. Hall, "Just like Dixie Land," *Sunset* 24, no. 2 (1910): 175.

27. Andrés, *Power and Control in the Imperial Valley*, 101.

28. Interview with farmer, conducted by Theodosia Samano, Hemet, CA, July 14, 1935, carton 15, folder 9, Paul Schuster Taylor Papers; interview with farmer, conducted by Theodosia Samano, Calexico, CA, July 12, 1935, carton 15, folder 9, Paul Schuster Taylor Papers; David G. Gutiérrez, *Walls and Mirrors: Mexican Americans, Mexican Immigrants, and the Politics of Ethnicity* (Berkeley: University of California Press, 1995), 46, 49; and Mark Reisler, "Always the Laborer, Never the Citizen: Anglo Perceptions of the Mexican Immigrant during the 1920s," *Pacific Historical Review* 45, no. 2 (May 1976): 231–54.

29. P. Taylor, *Mexican Labor in the United States*, 54; Reisler, *By the Sweat of Their Brow*, 178; and Gutiérrez, *Walls and Mirrors*, 49.

30. Andrés, *Power and Control in the Imperial Valley*, 99; Spector, *Story of the Imperial Valley*, 9–10; and P. Taylor, *Mexican Labor in the United States*, 8–12.

31. Andrés, *Power and Control in the Imperial Valley*, 75–76.

32. "Imperial Country, California," promotional brochure, n.d., carton 10, folder 21, Paul Schuster Taylor Papers.

33. James C. Scott, *Domination and the Arts of Resistance: Hidden Transcripts* (New Haven, CT: Yale University Press, 1990), 183. See also James C. Scott, *Weapons of the Weak: Everyday Forms of Peasant Resistance* (New Haven, CT: Yale University Press, 1985); and Robin D. G. Kelley, *Race Rebels: Culture, Politics, and the Black Working Class* (New York: Free Press, 1996).

34. Interview with Stillwell, interview, November 26, 1926, "Mexican Labor in U.S., Field Notes: Series-A, Set-I," 84, carton 10, folder 4, Paul Schuster Taylor Papers; interview with Giffen, Mendota, CA, September 7, 1928, "Mexican Labor in U.S., Field Notes: Series-E, Set-I," 84, carton 10, folder 8, Paul Schuster Taylor Papers; interview with Sr. Estrada, Calexico, CA, n.d., carton 10, folder 14, Paul Schuster Taylor Papers; interview with Mr. Pisquierra, Brawley, CA, April 26, 1927, carton 10, folder 15, Paul Schuster Taylor Papers; interview with Gladstone Reed, Los Angeles, CA, 1927, carton 10, folder 23, Paul Schuster Taylor Papers; and John Sánchez, oral history, interview

by Harvey Schwartz, March 31, 1998, tape 1, side 2 (B), Labor Archives and Research Center, San Francisco State University.

35. Interview with Giffen, Mendota, CA, September 7, 1928.

36. Interview with Mr. Martinez, conducted by Paul Taylor, Clovis, CA, September 5, 1928, 1, carton 10, folder 9, Paul Schuster Taylor Papers. Regarding time-work discipline, see E. P. Thompson's important work on this issue, in Thompson, "Time, Work-Discipline, and Industrial Capitalism," *Past and Present* 38 (December 1967): 56–97.

37. Interview with Mr. Rowe, Los Angeles, CA, March 30, 1927, carton 10, folder 24, Paul Schuster Taylor Papers.

38. Guevarra, *Becoming Mexipino*, 104.

39. Interview with Mexican laborer, conducted by Theodosia Samano, Brawley, CA, June 16, 1935, carton 15, folder 9, Paul Schuster Taylor Papers.

40. Interview with "humilde servidora," conducted by Theodosia Samano, Hemet, CA, July 12, 1935, carton 15, folder 9, Paul Schuster Taylor Papers

41. Manuel Luz, oral history, interview by Joan L. Zoloth, November 1976, 41–42, 45, "Oral Histories of Workers in California Agriculture: The 1930s," Labor Archives and Research Center, San Francisco State University.

42. Luz, oral history, 42–43.

43. John Sánchez, oral history, interview by Harvey Schwartz, March 31, 1998, tape 1, side 1 (A), Labor Archives and Research Center, San Francisco State University.

44. Sánchez, oral history, tape 1, side 1 (A).

45. Saenz, quoted in "Mutual Benefit Societies," Paul Taylor field notes, Brawley, CA, April 1927, carton 10, folder 12, Paul Schuster Taylor Papers.

46. Weber, "Organizing of Mexicano Agricultural Workers"; and Gutiérrez, *Walls and Mirrors*, 106.

47. For "La cause de la crisis . . . ," see "Corrido Nacional," carton 1, folder 26, Paul Schuster Taylor Papers. For "Aunque dicen que en México . . . ," see "Corrido de Pancho Villa," carton 1, folder 26, Paul Schuster Taylor Papers. Also see "Corrido de Obregón," carton 1, folder 26, Paul Schuster Taylor Papers.

48. Regarding the implications of the Mexican Revolution for revolutionary internationalisms and political convergences, see Christina Heatherton, "The Color Line and the Class Struggle: The Mexican Revolution and Convergences of Radical Internationalism, 1910–1946" (PhD diss., University of Southern California, 2012); and Monroy, "Fence Cutters, *Sedicioso*, and First-Class Citizens."

49. Carlos Bulosan, "The Growth of Philippine Culture," n.d., 1, 10, box 1, folder 18, Carlos Bulosan Papers, Accession No. 0581-011, Special Collections, University of Washington Libraries.

50. Dawn Bohulano Mabalon, *Little Manila Is in the Heart: The Making of the Filipina/o American Community in Stockton, California* (Durham, NC: Duke University Press, 2013); Rick Baldoz, *The Third Asiatic Invasion: Migration and Empire in Filipino America, 1898–1946* (New York: New York University Press, 2011); and Yen Le Espiritu, *Home Bound: Filipino American Lives across Cultures, Communities, and Countries* (Berkeley: University of California Press, 2003).

51. Moon-Kie Jung, *Reworking Race: The Making of Hawaii's Interracial Labor Movement* (New York: Columbia University Press, 2010).

52. Rudy P. Guevarra Jr., "Mabuhay Compañero: Filipinos, Mexicans, and Labor Organizing in Hawai'i and California, 1920s–1940s," in *Transnational Crossroads: Remapping the Americas and the Pacific*, ed. Camilla Fojas and Rudy P. Guevarra Jr. (Lincoln: University of Nebraska Press, 2012), 171–97; and Guevarra, *Becoming Mexipino*, 105–6.

53. Quintard Taylor, *In Search of the Racial Frontier: African Americans in the American West, 1528–1990* (New York: W. W. Norton, 1998), 192–96, 242–43; Steven Hahn, *A Nation under Our Feet: Black Political Struggles in the Rural South from Slavery to the Great Migration* (Cambridge, MA: Belknap Press of Harvard University Press, 2003), 466–74; and Delores Nason McBroome, "Harvests of Gold: African American Boosterism, Agriculture and Investment in Allensworth and Little Liberia," in *Seeking El Dorado: African Americans in California*, ed. Lawrence B. de Graaf, Mevin Mulroy, and Quintard Taylor (Seattle: University of Washington Press, 2001), 166.

54. Frank Maneze, oral history, interview by Joan L. Zoloth, November 1976, 81, "Oral Histories of Workers in California Agriculture: The 1930s," Labor Archives and Research Center, San Francisco State University. For additional reference to the relevance of historical memories of multiracial struggle, including the IWW's multiracial organizing as well as Mexican-Japanese collaboration in the 1903 Oxnard beet strike, see Jamieson, *Labor Unionism in California Agriculture*, 76.

55. Andrés, *Power and Control in the Imperial Valley*, 129–31; James A. Sandos, *Rebellion in the Borderlands: Anarchism and the Plan of San Diego, 1904–1923* (Norman: University of Oklahoma Press, 1992); and Linda B. Hall and Don M. Coerver, *Revolution on the Border: The United States and Mexico, 1910–1920* (Albuquerque: University of New Mexico Press, 1988).

56. McWilliams, *Factories in the Field*, 212.

57. Guevarra, *Becoming Mexipino*, 103; McWilliams, *Factories in the Field*, 212; and Andrés, *Power and Control in the Imperial Valley*, 133.

58. Regarding differential racialization, see Laura Pulido, *Black, Brown, Yellow, and Left: Radical Activism in Los Angeles* (Berkeley: University of California Press, 2006), 24. Regarding the pertinence of differential racialization for understanding race in the San Diego and Imperial County regions, see Guevarra, *Becoming Mexipino*, 93.

59. Gutiérrez, *Walls and Mirrors*, 97.

60. Interview with Juan Estrada, El Centro, CA, October 14, 1929, carton 10, folder 9, Paul Schuster Taylor Papers.

61. Interview with Juan Estrada, 2; interview with "Mexican Boy at Campomento Mejicano," Reedley, CA, September 8, 1928, "Mexican Labor in U.S., Field Notes: Series-E, Set-I," 180–81, carton 10, folder 8, Paul Schuster Taylor Papers; interview with Arturgo, Sanger, CA, September 11, 1928, "Mexican Labor in U.S., Field Notes: Series-E, Set-I," 198–99, carton 10, folder 8, Paul Schuster Taylor Papers; and P. Taylor, *Mexican Labor in the United States*, 54.

62. Leonard, *Making Ethnic Choices*, 140; and Weber, "Organizing of Mexicano Agricultural Workers," 316.

63. "Mexican Labor in U.S., Field Notes: Series-E, Set-I," 188, 192, 197, carton 10, folder 8, Paul Schuster Taylor Papers.

64. Interview with "Mexican Boy at Campomento Mejicano," 180; Theodosia M. Samano, interview with "Family living in Santa Fe Railroad section," Hanford, CA, June 26, 1935, carton 15, folder 9, Paul Schuster Taylor Papers; interview with W. C. Nestler and Trinidad Romero, November 7, 1928, "Mexican Labor in U.S., Field Notes: Series-A, Set-I," 16, carton 10, folder 4, Paul Schuster Taylor Papers; and interview with "Young Mexican laborer," conducted by Theodosia Samano, San Bernardino, CA, June 24, 1935, carton 15, folder 9, Paul Schuster Taylor Papers.

65. Interview with Mr. Martinez, 4; and interview with "Mexican Boy at Campomento Mejicano," 180.

66. Weber, *Dark Sweat, White Gold*, 11, 58–59, 66; and Devra Anne Weber, "Raiz Fuerte: Oral History and Mexicana Farmworkers," *Oral History Review* 17, no. 2 (Autumn 1989): 53–59.

67. Sánchez, oral history, tape 1, side 2 (B).

68. Sánchez, oral history, tape 1, side 2 (B).

69. Weber, *Dark Sweat, White Gold*; Nan Enstad, *Ladies of Labor, Girls of Adventure: Working Women, Popular Culture, and Labor Politics at the Turn of the Twentieth Century* (New York: Columbia University Press, 1999); and Elizabeth Faue, *Community of Suffering and Struggle: Women, Men, and the Labor Movement in Minneapolis, 1915–1945* (Chapel Hill: University of North Carolina Press, 1991).

70. Weber, *Dark Sweat, White Gold*, 60–61.

71. "Defensa de los Norteños," n.d., carton 1, folder 26, Paul Schuster Taylor Papers.

72. "Eleven Cent Cotton and Forty Cent Meat: A Sharecropper's Lament," song collected by Tom Collins, Bakersfield, CA, September 5, 1936, carton 5, folder 201, Works Progress Administration (WPA) Folk Music Project, Music Library, University of California, Berkeley.

73. Seminal works on the significance of folk ballads in the borderlands include Américo Paredes, *With a Pistol in His Hand: A Border Ballad and Its Hero* (Austin: University of Texas Press, 1958); and José Limón, *Mexican Ballads, Chicano Poems: History and Influence in Mexican-American Social Poetry* (Berkeley: University of California Press, 1992). Also, regarding the role of music in Okie subculture, see Gregory, *American Exodus*, chap. 8.

74. George Lipsitz, *Dangerous Crossroads: Popular Music, Postmodernism, and the Poetics of Place* (London: Verso, 1994).

75. Abel Patillo, interview, Brawley, CA, 1927, Paul Taylor field notes, carton 10, folder 13, Paul Schuster Taylor Papers.

76. "Unionization of Filipinos in Agriculture," quoted in Guevarra, *Becoming Mexipino*, 106.

77. "Worker," quoted in Andrés, *Power and Control in the Imperial Valley*, 148.

78. Gutiérrez, *Walls and Mirrors*, 106.

79. Andrew Hemingway, *Artists on the Left: American Artists and the Communist Movement, 1926–1956* (New Haven, CT: Yale University Press, 2002), 94–95.

80. Zakheim, quoted in Anthony Lee, *Painting on the Left: Diego Rivera, Radical Politics, and San Francisco's Public Murals* (Berkeley: University of California Press, 1999), 143.

2. "A DIFFERENT KIND OF UNION"

1. For accounts of the strike, see Irving Bernstein, *The Turbulent Years: A History of the American Worker, 1933–1941* (Chicago: Haymarket Books, 1969), 252–98; Charles P. Larrowe, *Harry Bridges: The Rise and Fall of Radical Labor in the United States* (New York: Lawrence Hill, 1972), 32–93; Bruce Nelson, *Workers on the Waterfront: Seamen, Longshoremen, and Unionism in the 1930s* (Urbana: University of Illinois Press, 1988), 127–55; Mike Quin, *The Big Strike* (Olema, CA: Olema, 1949); and David F. Selvin, *A Terrible Anger: The 1934 Waterfront and General Strikes in San Francisco* (Detroit: Wayne State University Press, 1996).

2. "Mike Quin" was the penname of sailor and author Paul William Ryan. Quin, *Big Strike*, 148. Sociologist Paul S. Taylor also described a "holiday mood in the air" in his observations of the strike. Paul S. Taylor, "Trouble on the Waterfront," August 1, 1934, 8, carton 6, folder 32, Paul Schuster Taylor Papers, BANC MSS 84/38c, Bancroft Library, University of California, Berkeley.

3. Revels Cayton, oral history, BBC interview, July 1975, transcript, 43, box 1, folder: "BBC interview, July 1975," Richard S. Hobbs Oral History Interviews with Revels Cayton, Accession No. 5483-001, University of Washington Libraries.

4. See, for example, Nelson, *Workers on the Waterfront*; Nelson, "The 'Lords of the Docks' Reconsidered: Race Relations among West Coast Longshoremen, 1933–61," in *Waterfront Workers: New Perspectives on Race and Class*, ed. Calvin Winslow (Urbana: University of Illinois Press, 1998), 155–92; and Nelson, "Unions and the Popular Front: The West Coast Waterfront in the 1930s," *International Labor and Working-Class History* 30 (Fall 1986): 59–78; Howard Kimeldorf, *Reds or Rackets? The Making of Radical and Conservative Unions on the Waterfront* (Berkeley: University of California Press, 1988); Nancy Quam-Wickham, "Who Controls the Hiring Hall? The Struggle for Job Control in the ILWU during World War II," in *The CIO's Left-Led Unions*, ed. Steven Rosswurm (New Brunswick, NJ: Rutgers University Press, 1991), 41–68; and Robert W. Cherny, "Prelude to the Popular Front: The Communist Party in California, 1931–35," *American Communist History* 1, no. 1 (2002): 5–42.

5. Quam-Wickham, "Who Controls the Hiring Hall?," 48; and Nelson, "'Lords of the Docks' Reconsidered," 157.

6. See, for example, Nelson Lichtenstein, *Labor's War at Home: The CIO in World War II* (Philadelphia: Temple University Press, 2003); Steve Fraser and Gary Gerstle, eds., *The Rise and Fall of the New Deal Order, 1930–1980* (Princeton, NJ: Princeton University Press, 1989); Lizabeth Cohen, *Making a New Deal: Industrial Workers in Chicago, 1919–1939* (Cambridge: Cambridge University Press, 1991); and Michael Denning, *The Cultural Front: The Laboring of American Culture in the Twentieth Century* (New York: Verso, 1996).

7. William Issel and Robert W. Cherny, *San Francisco, 1865–1932: Politics, Power, and Urban Development* (Berkeley: University of California Press, 1986), 116; and Brian J. Godfrey, "Urban Development and Redevelopment in San Francisco," *Geographical Review* 87, no. 3 (July 1997): 314.

8. Issel and Cherny, *San Francisco*, chap. 2, 83.

9. Tomás F. Summers Sandoval Jr., *Latinos at the Golden Gate: Creating Community and Identity in San Francisco* (Chapel Hill: University of North Carolina Press, 2013), 87.

10. T. Sandoval, *Latinos at the Golden Gate*, 88.

11. Issel and Cherny, *San Francisco*, 113; and Godfrey, "Urban Development and Redevelopment in San Francisco," 313–14.

12. James Bacigalupi, quoted in *San Francisco Business*, November 11, 1925. For additional discussion of the relationship between San Francisco's public culture and its imperial status, see Issel and Cherny, *San Francisco*, 109; and Judd Kahn, *Imperial San Francisco: Politics and Planning in an American City, 1897–1906* (Lincoln: University of Nebraska Press, 1979), 62.

13. Regarding larger trends in global migration during this period, see Adam McKeown, "Global Migration, 1846–1940," *Journal of World History* 15, no. 2 (June 2004): 155–89.

14. Issel and Cherny, *San Francisco*, 55–56.

15. Other sources suggest that the numbers might have been higher. Yong Chen, *Chinese San Francisco, 1850–1943: A Trans-Pacific Community* (Stanford, CA: Stanford University Press, 2000), 59–60; and Issel and Cherny, *San Francisco*, 56.

16. David R. Roediger and Elizabeth D. Esch, *The Production of Difference: Race and the Management of Labor in U.S. History* (New York: Oxford University Press, 2012), 174–75; Mae M. Ngai, *Impossible Subjects: Illegal Aliens and the Making of Modern America* (Princeton, NJ: Princeton University Press, 2004), 21–25; and Issel and Cherny, *San Francisco*, 55–59.

17. Roediger and Esch, *Production of Difference*, 186–204; Ngai, *Impossible Subjects*, 54–55; and Brian J. Godfrey, *Neighborhoods in Transition: The Making of San Francisco's Ethnic and Nonconformist Communities* (Berkeley: University of California Press, 1988), 68.

18. Albert S. Broussard, *Black San Francisco: The Struggle for Racial Equality in the West, 1900–1954* (Lawrence: University of Kansas Press, 1993), 22.

19. T. Sandoval, *Latinos at the Golden Gate*, 93.

20. Rick Baldoz, *The Third Asiatic Invasion: Migration and Empire in Filipino America, 1898–1946* (New York: New York University Press, 2011), 66.

21. U.S. Census Bureau, *Fifteenth Census of the United States, 1930: Population*, vol. 4, *Occupations, by States* (Washington, DC: U.S. Government Printing Office, 1931–33), table 4, 174–81.

22. U.S. Census Bureau, *Fifteenth Census: Population*, vol. 4, *Occupations, by States*, table 12, 208.

23. Cayton, oral history, 57; "Seamen Arrested during 1934 Strike," box 2, folder 5, Elaine Black Yoneda Collection, Accession Nos. 1992/033 and 1992/055, Labor Archives and Research Center, San Francisco State University; and Quin, *Big Strike*,

29. Regarding nationwide patterns of racial segmentation in waterfront work generally speaking, see Nelson, *Workers on the Waterfront*, 82–83.

24. U.S. Census Bureau, *Fifteenth Census: Population*, vol. 4, *Occupations, by States*, table 12, 208.

25. Victor Anthony Walsh, quoted in Broussard, *Black San Francisco*, 49.

26. Roediger and Esch, *Production of Difference*, 11; and Nelson, *Workers on the Waterfront*, 49–50, 85.

27. William Issel, "'Citizens outside Government': Business and Urban Policy in San Francisco and Los Angeles, 1890–1932," *Pacific Historical Review* 57, no. 2 (May 1988): 117–45.

28. Issel, "'Citizens outside Government,'" 143–44.

29. Richard A. Walker, "Industry Builds the City: The Suburbanization of Manufacturing in the San Francisco Bay Area, 1850–1940," *Journal of Historical Geography* 27, no. 1 (2001): 36–57; and Roger W. Lotchin, "The Darwinian City: The Politics of Urbanization in San Francisco between the World Wars," *Pacific Historical Review* 48, no. 3 (August 1979): 357–81.

30. Issel, "'Citizens outside Government,'" 127.

31. John Swett, quoted in Issel and Cherny, *San Francisco*, 102.

32. "Controlling Immigration: The Asiatic Problem Not the Only One Which Troubles," *San Francisco Chronicle*, October 11, 1907, 6.

33. Jerry Scanlon, "Immigration Laws Work to the Disadvantage of San Francisco," *San Francisco Chronicle*, August 9, 1922, 18. See also "Immigration a Big Problem Yet Unsolved: Commissioner-General Caminetti Tells of Conditions in Annual Report," *San Francisco Chronicle*, January 16, 1915, 86.

34. Hiram Johnson, quoted in Issel, "'Citizens outside Government,'" 127. The animus toward new immigrant populations reflects what Ambalavener Sivanandan has called "xeno-racism," that is, in the European context, "a racism that is not just directed at those with darker skins from the former colonial territories, but at the newer categories of the displaced, the dispossessed and the uprooted, who are beating at Western Europe's doors, the Europe that helped to displace them in the first place." Quoted in Liz Fekete, "The Emergence of Xeno-Racism," *Race and Class* 43, no. 2 (2001): 23–24.

35. See, for example, Douglas Henry Daniels, *Pioneer Urbanites: A Social and Cultural History of Black San Francisco* (Berkeley: University of California Press, 1991); Broussard, *Black San Francisco*; Judy Yung, *Unbound Feet: A Social History of Chinese Women in San Francisco* (Berkeley: University of California Press, 1995); Nayan Shah, *Contagious Divides: Epidemics and Race in San Francisco's Chinatown* (Berkeley: University of California Press, 2001); Tomás F. Summers Sandoval Jr., "Mission Stories, Latino Lives: The Making of San Francisco's Latino Identity, 1945–1970" (PhD diss., University of California, Berkeley, 2002), chap. 2.

36. Alexander Saxton, *The Indispensable Enemy: Labor and the Anti-Chinese Movement in America* (Berkeley: University of California Press, 1971), 156, 241–43, 261, 265. Other seminal analyses of racism and anti-immigrant hostilities within the labor movement during the late nineteenth and early twentieth centuries can be found in David R.

Roediger, *The Wages of Whiteness: Race and the Making of the American Working Class* (London: Verso, 1991); Theodore W. Allen, *The Invention of the White Race,* Vol. 1, *Racial Oppression and Social Control* and Vol. 2, *The Origin of Racial Oppression in Anglo-America* (New York: Verso, 2012); and Matthew Frye Jacobson, *Whiteness of a Different Color: European Immigrants and the Alchemy of Race* (Cambridge, MA: Harvard University Press, 1999).

37. Michael Kimmel, *Manhood in America: A Cultural History,* 3rd ed. (Oxford: Oxford University Press, 2011), chap 3.

38. Saxton, *Indispensable Enemy,* 259–61, 278; and Nelson, *Workers on the Waterfront,* 49–50.

39. Kevin Starr, *Endangered Dreams: The Great Depression in California* (Oxford: Oxford University Press, 1996), chap. 2; and Nelson, *Workers on the Waterfront,* chap. 2, 84–86.

40. Nelson, *Workers on the Waterfront,* 65–66, 79–80.

41. Broussard, *Black San Francisco,* 29–30.

42. Broussard, *Black San Francisco,* 35–36.

43. Broussard, *Black San Francisco,* 30.

44. T. Sandoval, *Latinos at the Golden Gate,* 93–95.

45. Godfrey, *Neighborhoods in Transition,* 70–71.

46. Lora Toombs Scott, oral history transcript, interview by Jesse J. Warr, August–November 1978, 4, 23–24, "Oral History Project: African Americans in San Francisco Prior to 1945," San Francisco Public Library.

47. Edward Alley, oral history transcript, interview by Jesse J. Warr, September 19, 1978, 18, "Oral History Project: African Americans in San Francisco Prior to 1945."

48. May and Edwin Low, oral history transcript, 3, box 1, folder: "May and Edwin Low," Combined Asian American Resources Project Interviews, BANC MSS 80/31C, Bancroft Library, University of California, Berkeley.

49. Chen, *Chinese San Francisco,* 199–200.

50. Broussard, *Black San Francisco,* 29–30.

51. Earl T. Watkins, oral history: "Earl T. Watkins: Jazz Drummer and Union Official," 13–14, Regional Oral History Office, Bancroft Library, University of California, Berkeley, 2003. See also Alley, oral history transcript, 30–31.

52. Alley, oral history transcript, 30–31. Also see Jane Lee, oral history transcript, 7, box 1, folder: "Jane Lee," Combined Asian American Resources Project Interviews; Frances and Howard Low, oral history transcript, 12, 15, box 1, folder: "Frances and Howard Low," Combined Asian American Resources Project Interviews; and Chalsa Loo, oral history transcript, 2, box 1, folder: "Chalsa Loo," Combined Asian American Resources Project Interviews.

53. Cayton, oral history, 43.

54. Cayton, oral history, 106.

55. Brent Hayes Edwards, "Shadow of Shadows," *Positions: East Asia Cultures Critique* 11, no. 1 (2003): 11–49.

56. Yung, *Unbound Feet,* 181; and Broussard, *Black San Francisco,* 114–17.

57. For example, "Sigue la huelga en Vacaville" and "A los huegistas de Vacaville," *El Imparcial* (San Francisco), December 9, 1932, 1; "Cordial recepció se hizo a México Liga de las Naciones," *Hispano América* (San Francisco), October 3, 1931, 1; "Los repatriados han encontrado trabajo," *Hispano América*, July 7, 1931, 1; and "Sigue la repatriación de mexicanos," *Hispano América*, December 5, 1931.

58. Regarding the concept of convergence spaces and their significance for social movements, see Christina Heatherton, "The Color Line and the Class Struggle: The Mexican Revolution and Convergences of Radical Internationalism, 1910–1946" (PhD diss., University of Southern California, 2012); and Christina Heatherton, "The University of Radicalism: Ricardo Flores Magón and Leavenworth Penitentiary," *American Quarterly* 66, no. 3 (September 2014): 557–81.

59. Trade Union Unity League and Unemployed Council, "Public Hearing— November 6, 1931, Fillmore District, San Francisco," transcript, and Trade Union Unity League and Unemployed Council, "Public Hearing—Nov. 7, 1931, Unemployed Workers, Held at San Francisco," transcript, box 2, folder 25, Sam Darcy Papers, TAM 124, Tamiment Library and Wagner Labor Archives, New York University.

60. Mrs. Springer, A. Gilpatrick, Martin Blank, and D. Merrihew, Trade Union Unity League and Unemployed Council, "Public Hearing—November 6, 1931"; and E. Madsen and Harry Logan, in Trade Union Unity League and Unemployed Council, "Public Hearing—Nov. 7, 1931."

61. I. R. Dawes and Floyd Torrence, Trade Union Unity League and Unemployed Council, "Public Hearing—November 6, 1931"; and John Bonavito and E. Madsen, in Trade Union Unity League and Unemployed Council, "Public Hearing—Nov. 7, 1931."

62. Floyd Torrence, in Trade Union Unity League and Unemployed Council, "Public Hearing—November 6, 1931."

63. P. Pauv, "Japanese worker," and Joe Comme, in Trade Union Unity League and Unemployed Council, "Public Hearing—November 6, 1931"; and McCormick and Alfred Fisher, in Trade Union Unity League and Unemployed Council, "Public Hearing— Nov. 7, 1931."

64. P. Pauv, in Trade Union Unity League and Unemployed Council, "Public Hearing—November 6, 1931."

65. "Japanese worker," in Trade Union Unity League and Unemployed Council, "Public Hearing—November 6, 1931."

66. W. Williams, in Trade Union Unity League and Unemployed Council, "Public Hearing—November 6, 1931."

67. Joe Comme, in Trade Union Unity League and Unemployed Council, "Public Hearing—November 6, 1931."

68. Pat Dougherty, in Trade Union Unity League and Unemployed Council, "Public Hearing—Nov. 7, 1931."

69. Floyd Torrence, Jack Perry, Wm. E. Tucker, Mr. and Mrs. Lindeman, I. R. Dawes, B. Silver, A. Gilpatrick, H. Adams, P. Pauv, Martin Blank, "Japanese worker," and P. Barker, in Trade Union Unity League and Unemployed Council, "Public Hearing—November 6, 1931"; and Harold Nauss and John Bonavito, in Trade Union Unity League and Unemployed Council, "Public Hearing—Nov. 7, 1931."

70. Martin Blank and P. Barker, in Trade Union Unity League and Unemployed Council, "Public Hearing—November 6, 1931."

71. John Bonavito, in Trade Union Unity League and Unemployed Council, "Public Hearing—Nov. 7, 1931."

72. Louis Truich, in Trade Union Unity League and Unemployed Council, "Public Hearing—Nov. 7, 1931."

73. J. M. Hafner, in Trade Union Unity League and Unemployed Council, "Public Hearing—Nov. 7, 1931."

74. Quin, *Big Strike*, 30.

75. International Longshoremen's Association, "The Maritime Crisis," 1936, quoted in Quin, *Big Strike*, 31.

76. Quin, *Big Strike*, 39.

77. *Waterfront Worker*, June 1933, 5; and Nelson, *Workers on the Waterfront*, 114–15, 120–22.

78. Quin, *Big Strike*, 40.

79. Nelson, *Workers on the Waterfront*, 122–26.

80. Sociologist Pierre L. van den Berghe used the concept of "*herrenvolk* democracy" to characterize the political systems of apartheid-era South Africa and the United States, "which are politically democratic for the master race but tyrannical towards the subordinate racial groups." David Roediger applied the concept of "*herrenvolk* republicanism" to the politics of nineteenth-century working-class White Americans, who "read African Americans out of the ranks of the producers and then proved more able to concentrate [their] fire downward on to the dependent and Black than upward against the rich and powerful." Pierre L. van den Berghe, *Race and Racism: A Comparative Perspective* (New York: Wiley, 1978), 126; Roediger, *Wages of Whiteness*, xxiii, 59–60.

81. Sam Darcy, address, "It is commonly agreed on the West Coast . . . ," 1934, 11–12, box 2, folder 38, Sam Darcy Papers; and Nelson, *Workers on the Waterfront*, 133. Support for the ILA among non-White populations came mainly from those already actively involved in the Bay Area's organized left. See, for example, letter from the East Bay chapter of the International Labor Defense, April 5, 1934, printed in *Waterfront Worker*, April 9, 1934, 2.

82. Some ILA members who recalled employers' success in utilizing this tactic in the strike of 1919 anticipated that this would likely be the case in 1934. *Waterfront Worker*, March 12, 1934, 3–4.

83. "Longshoremen Appeal to Negro for Strike Support; All-White Policy of Union Tottering?," *San Francisco Spokesman*, May 10, 1934, 1. Also see Nelson, *Workers on the Waterfront*, 133–34; and Quin, *Big Strike*, 50–51.

84. Darcy, address, "It is commonly agreed on the West Coast . . . ," 11–13.

85. "Longshoremen Appeal to Negro for Strike Support: All-White Policy of Union Tottering?," *San Francisco Spokesman*, May 10, 1934, 1. Also see "Bosses Spread Lies, Use Negroes as Scabs," *Waterfront Worker*, May 21, 1934, 3.

86. "Longshoremen Appeal to Negro for Strike Support; All-White Policy of Union Tottering?," *San Francisco Spokesman*, May 10, 1934, 1.

87. "To All Negro People," May 16, 1934, Coast Committee, Case-1934 Records, box 3, folder: "ILWU Case 1934 Correspondences (Misc.)," International Longshoremen's and Warehousemen's Union (ILWU) Archives; and "To All the Negro Peoples of the Bay Area Region," n.d., Coast Committee, Case-1934 Records, box 3, folder: "Strike Publicity Material and Notes—Press Releases, Radio, Speeches, Misc. Notes," ILWU Archives.

88. "To All Negro People," May 16, 1934; and Nelson, *Workers on the Waterfront*, 125.

89. Thomas C. Fleming, "Reflections on Black History: The Great Strike of 1934," *San Francisco Sun-Reporter*, January 5, 1999.

90. "Twelve Students from the San Mateo Jr. High College," n.d., Coast Committee, Case-1934 Records, box 3, folder: "Strike Publicity Material and Notes—Press Releases, Radio, Speeches, Misc. Notes," ILWU Archives; "Longshoremen Appeal to Negro for Strike Support; All-White Policy of Union Tottering?," *San Francisco Spokesman*, May 10, 1934, 1; Darcy, address, "It is commonly agreed on the West Coast . . . ," 12; and Quin, *Big Strike*, 51. Most of those who served as strikebreakers throughout the strike were brought in from the East Bay (especially white college students and football players from the University of California, Berkeley) and elsewhere. See Nelson, *Workers on the Waterfront*, 133.

91. *Waterfront Worker*, May 21, 1934, 1; and Nelson, *Workers on the Waterfront*, 134.

92. "To All Ship's Crews," Marine Workers Industrial Union (MWIU) flyer announcing Final Strike Conference, May 10, 1934, San Francisco Waterfront Strikes Scrapbooks, 1934–1948, vol. 2, BANC MSS 2004/187c, Bancroft Library, University of California, Berkeley. See also "The Seamen's Strike," *Waterfront Worker*, May 21, 1934, 3; and *Joint Marine Journal*, July 26, 1934, San Francisco Waterfront Strikes Scrapbooks, vol. 2.

93. "Seamen Endorse and Fight for One Union of All Seamen," pamphlet issued by MWIU, n.d., San Francisco Waterfront Strikes Scrapbooks, vol. 1; "Fellow workers—do you have to have fakers make a code . . . ," flyer issued by United Front Seamen's Strike Committee, n.d., San Francisco Waterfront Strikes Scrapbooks, vol. 2; "To All ISU Members!," flyer from United Front Seamen's Strike Committee, MWIU, n.d., San Francisco Waterfront Strikes Scrapbooks, vol. 2; "To All Bargemen, Ferryboatmen, and Harborworkers," n.d., San Francisco Waterfront Strikes Scrapbooks, vol. 1; "To All Striking Seamen, Organized or Unorganized Regardless of Affiliation," flyer issued by United Front Seamen's Strike Committee, MWIU, May 1934, San Francisco Waterfront Strikes Scrapbooks, vol. 2; and "To All Seamen, Organized and Unorganized, On Ships and on the Beach!," flyer from United Front Strike Committee, MWIU, May 26, 1934, San Francisco Waterfront Strikes Scrapbooks, vol. 2.

94. "To All Ship's Crews," MWIU flyer announcing Final Strike Conference, May 10, 1934. Also see "The Seamen's Strike," *Waterfront Worker*, May 21, 1934, 3.

95. Cherny, "Prelude to the Popular Front"; Nelson, "Unions and the Popular Front"; and Kimeldorf, *Reds or Rackets?*, 86.

96. "Final Strike Conference" flyer issued by the MWIU, May 10, 1934, San Francisco Waterfront Strikes Scrapbooks, vol. 2.

97. Carl Lynch, "Open Letter to Seamen," *Marine Joint Journal: Atlantic and Gulf*, August 4, 1934, 1, San Francisco Waterfront Strikes Scrapbooks, vol. 1; Herman Mills, "An Editorial," Joint Strike Committee of the International Seamen's Union Pacific Coast District, Strike Bulletin #4, June 29, 1934, San Francisco Waterfront Strikes Scrapbooks, vol. 1; and *ISU of A Journal*, vol. 2, no. 1, August 1934, 1, San Francisco Waterfront Strikes Scrapbooks, vol. 1.

98. John Pittman, editorial, *San Francisco Spokesman*, May 17, 1934, 6. Langston Hughes wrote a letter in response to Pittman's editorial, stating, "You did not differentiate or make your readers understand that it is always the A.F. of L. unions that discriminate against Negroes, or set up Jim Crow locals. This the Communists led unions have not and never did do, and some of their unions are already powerful—so you do not want to give the idea that all American labor unions discriminate against the Negro. Let him know that there are some that do not, and that the faster he joins them, the quicker will his own labor power be felt." Langston Hughes to John Pittman, May 28, 1934, box 1, folder 19, John Pittman Papers, TAM 188, Tamiment Library and Wagner Labor Archives, New York University.

99. Kenneth Finis, oral history transcript, interview by Jesse J. Warr, June 7, 1978, 46, "Oral History Project: African Americans in San Francisco Prior to 1945."

100. Thomas C. Fleming, "Reflections on Black History: The Great Strike of 1934," *San Francisco Sun-Reporter*, January 5, 1999.

101. "Lahat Ng Marino Filipino," flyer for the Filipinx section of the MWIU, n.d., San Francisco Waterfront Strikes Scrapbooks, vol. 2.

102. "Scalers' Section of the Marine Workers Industrial Union: Scalers' Demands," n.d., San Francisco Waterfront Strikes Scrapbooks, vol. 2.

103. *Waterfront Worker*, April 9, 1934, 2.

104. *Waterfront Worker*, May 21, 1934, 3.

105. Franklin D. Roosevelt to W. J. Lewis, Western Union telegram, March 22, 1934, box 1, folder 3, William J. Lewis Collection, Accession No. 1997/021, Labor Archives and Research Center, San Francisco State University; Joseph P. Ryan to William Lewis, Western Union telegram, March 22, 1934, box 1, folder 3, William J. Lewis Collection; and Robert Wagner to William Lewis, Western Union telegram, March 22, 1934, box 1, folder 3, William J. Lewis Collection.

106. Strike Bulletin #4, issued by Local 38-79 I.L.A. Publicity Committee, June 25, 1934, San Francisco Waterfront Strikes Scrapbooks, vol. 2.

107. Quin, *Big Strike*, 52.

108. "Joint Marine Strike Committee: Hear Why the Ryan Agreement Was Rejected, All Strikers, Every Union Man, Every Sympathizer, Invited to CIVIC AUDITORIUM," June 9, 1934, San Francisco Waterfront Strikes Scrapbooks, vol. 2; MWIU flyer, "Ryan Sells Out I.L.A.: Unity Our Only Weapon of Defence," June 1934, San Francisco Waterfront Strikes Scrapbooks, vol. 2; and Rank and File Committee flyer, "Frisco Rejects Sellout, Pedro Must Do the Same," June 1934, San Francisco Waterfront Strikes Scrapbooks, vol. 2.

109. Blackie Soromengo, quoted in Stan Weir, *Singlejack Solidarity* (Minneapolis: University of Minnesota Press, 2004), 127.

110. Quin, *Big Strike*, 68.

111. "Step in the Longshoremen's Fight—Scenes of the San Francisco Waterfront" and "5,000 Stevedores, Families, Sympathizers in S. F. Parade: Workers Cheer as Greetings Are Voiced from Other Organizations, Negroes, Chinese, Filipino Seamen," *Western Worker*, May 21, 1934, 4.

112. "Bosses Spread Lies, Use Negroes as Scabs," *Waterfront Worker*, May 21, 1934, 3. See also "Solidarity!," *Waterfront Worker*, August 28, 1934, 8; *Waterfront Striker* (MWIU publication), May 30, 1934, 2, San Francisco Waterfront Strikes Scrapbooks, vol. 2; "The Power on the Front," *Waterfront Worker*, May 21, 1934, 1; "Undaunted by Police Attack," *Western Worker*, June 11, 1934, 2; and "On Hunger Strike for Reduced Bail," *Western Worker*, August 13, 1934, 1.

113. I.L.A. Strike Bulletin #27, July 26, 1934, 1, box 2, folder 6, Archie Brown Collection, Collection No. larc.ms.0087, Accession No. 1992/005, Labor Archives and Research Center, San Francisco State University. Also see "5,000 Stevedores, Families, Sympathizers in S. F. Parade: Workers Cheer as Greetings Are Voiced from Other Organizations, Negroes, Chinese, Filipino Seamen," *Western Worker*, May 21, 1934, 4.

114. Telegram from San Francisco Industrial Association to Franklin D. Roosevelt, quoted in Quin, *Big Strike*, 82.

115. Harry Bridges, "Harry Bridges: An Oral History about Longshoring," ed. Harvey Schwartz, July 27, 2004, ILWU Oral History Collection, ILWU Archives, http://www.ilwu.org/?page_id=2616.

116. Regarding the "low-man-out" system of hiring, which replaced the shape-up, see Weir, *Singlejack Solidarity*, 263–67.

117. Weir, *Singlejack Solidarity*, 257.

3. REIMAGINING CITIZENSHIP IN THE AGE OF EXPULSION

1. Federal Writers' Project, "The California Cotton Pickers' Strike—1933," 47–48, in Monographs Prepared for a Documentary History of Migratory Farm Labor, 1938, BANC MSS 72/187c, Bancroft Library, University of California, Berkeley; and Devra Anne Weber, *Dark Sweat, White Gold: California Farm Workers, Cotton, and the New Deal* (Berkeley: University of California Press, 1996), 1–2, 89–90.

2. Federal Writers' Project, "California Cotton Pickers' Strike," 40–46; Weber, *Dark Sweat, White Gold*, 83, 90–92; and Cletus E. Daniel, *Bitter Harvest: A History of California Farmworkers, 1870–1941* (Berkeley: University of California Press, 1982), 180, 187–91.

3. Federal Writers' Project, "California Cotton Pickers' Strike," 12.

4. Federal Writers' Project, "California Cotton Pickers' Strike," 15.

5. Federal Writers' Project, "California Cotton Pickers' Strike," 47.

6. See especially Nelson Lichtenstein, *Labor's War at Home: The CIO in World War II* (Philadelphia: Temple University Press, 2003); Steve Fraser and Gary Gerstle, eds., *The Rise and Fall of the New Deal Order, 1930–1980* (Princeton, NJ: Princeton University Press, 1989); Lizabeth Cohen, *Making a New Deal: Industrial Workers in Chicago, 1919–1939* (Cambridge: Cambridge University Press, 1991); and Michael Denning, *The*

Cultural Front: The Laboring of American Culture in the Twentieth Century (New York: Verso, 1996).

7. Kiran Klaus Patel, *The New Deal: A Global History* (Princeton, NJ: Princeton University Press, 2016), 18–23.

8. Katherine Benton-Cohen, *Inventing the Immigration Problem: The Dillingham Commission and Its Legacy* (Cambridge, MA: Harvard University Press, 2018); Kunal Parker, *Making Foreigners: Immigration and Citizenship Law in America, 1600–2000* (New York: Cambridge University Press, 2015), chaps. 5–6; Kelly Lytle Hernández, *Migra! A History of the U.S. Border Patrol* (Berkeley: University of California Press, 2010), chap. 3; Mae M. Ngai, *Impossible Subjects: Illegal Aliens and the Making of Modern America* (Princeton, NJ: Princeton University Press, 2004); and Candice Lewis Bredrenner, *A Nationality of Her Own: Women, Marriage, and the Law of Citizenship* (Berkeley: University of California Press, 1998).

9. Parker, *Making Foreigners*, 166–69; Francisco E. Balderrama and Raymond Rodríguez, *Decade of Betrayal: Mexican Repatriation in the 1930s*, rev. ed. (Albuquerque: University of New Mexico Press, 2006), 63–64, 75–76; Natalia Molina, *How Race Is Made in America: Immigration, Citizenship, and the Historical Power of Racial Scripts* (Berkeley: University of California Press, 2014), chap. 4; and Melita M. Garza, *They Came to Toil: Newspaper Representations of Mexicans and Immigrants in the Great Depression* (Austin: University of Texas Press, 2018).

10. Statistics on this subject vary widely, ranging from as low as 400,000 to as high as 2 million. As Marla Andrea Ramírez contends, the combined waves of repatriation that spanned 1929–38 amounted to at least 900,000 and likely higher. If the 1939–44 period is incorporated, the numbers amount to at least one million and potentially more. Ramírez, "The Making of Mexican Illegality: Immigration Exclusions Based on Race, Class Status, and Gender," *New Political Science* 40, no. 2 (2018): 325. See also Balderrama and Rodríguez, *Decade of Betrayal*, 149–51; David G. Gutiérrez, *Walls and Mirrors: Mexican Americans, Mexican Immigrants, and the Politics of Ethnicity* (Berkeley: University of California Press, 1995), 72; Ngai, *Impossible Subjects*, 72–75, 122; and Rick Baldoz, *The Third Asiatic Invasion: Migration and Empire in Filipino America, 1898–1946* (New York: New York University Press, 2011), 192–93.

11. Regarding the deep-rooted relationship between nationalist racism and working-class formation and social inclusion, see Satnam Virdee, *Racism, Class, and the Racialized Outsider* (London: Palgrave Macmillan, 2014).

12. See especially Alexander Saxton, *The Indispensable Enemy: Labor and the Anti-Chinese Movement in California* (Berkeley: University of California Press, 1971); and Tomás Almaguer, *Racial Fault Lines: The Historical Origins of White Supremacy in California* (Berkeley: University of California Press, 1994). To situate California's anti-immigrant movements within the larger rubric of racial management across the U.S. West and the nation, see Patricia Limerick, *The Legacy of Conquest: The Unbroken Past of the American West* (New York: W. W. Norton, 1987); Peggy Pascoe, *What Comes Naturally: Miscegenation Law and the Making of Race in America* (London: Oxford University Press, 2010); David R. Roediger and Elizabeth D. Esch, *The Production of Difference: Race and the Management of Labor in U.S. History* (New York: Oxford

University Press, 2012); Ngai, *Impossible Subjects*; and Beth Lew-Williams, "Before Restriction Became Exclusion: America's Experiment in Diplomatic Immigration Control," *Pacific Historical Review* 83, no. 1 (2014): 24–56.

13. Parker, *Making Foreigners*, chaps. 5–6; and Bredrenner, *Nationality of Her Own*.

14. Ramírez, "Making of Mexican Illegality," 317–35; Balderrama and Rodríguez, *Decade of Betrayal*, 120; and Shelley Streeby, *Radical Sensations: World Movements, Violence, and Visual Culture* (Durham, NC: Duke University Press, 2013), 250–68.

15. Hernández, *Migra!*, 81; Parker, *Making Foreigners*, 168; and Balderrama and Rodríguez, *Decade of Betrayal*, 67.

16. Shana Bernstein, *Bridges of Reform: Interracial Civil Rights Activism in Twentieth-Century Los Angeles* (New York: Oxford University Press, 2010), 30–31.

17. Balderrama and Rodríguez, *Decade of Betrayal*, 71. See also George J. Sánchez, *Becoming Mexican American: Ethnicity, Culture, and Identity in Chicano Los Angeles, 1900–1945* (London: Oxford University Press, 1993), 123; Douglas Monroy, *Rebirth: Mexican Los Angeles from the Great Migration to the Great Depression* (Berkeley: University of California Press, 1999), 65; Carey McWilliams, *Factories in the Field: The Story of Migratory Farm Labor in California* (1939; Berkeley: University of California Press, 2000), 125; and Abraham Hoffman, *Unwanted Mexican Americans in the Great Depression: Repatriation Pressures, 1929–1939* (Tucson: University of Arizona Press, 1974), chap. 4.

18. Yen Le Espiritu, *Home Bound: Filipino American Lives across Cultures, Communities, and Countries* (Berkeley: University of California Press, 2003), 9.

19. Espiritu, *Home Bound*, 13–14; Baldoz, *Third Asiatic Invasion*, 193; Ngai, *Impossible Subjects*, 122; and Parker, *Making Foreigners*, 181–83.

20. Parker, *Making Foreigners*.

21. "14,000 Mexicans Returned to Homeland," newspaper clipping, February 13, 1936, in box 15, folder: "Migratory Workers: Miscellaneous articles," Carey McWilliams Papers, Card Files, 1930–1940, Collection 1243, Special Collections, Charles E. Young Research Library, University of California, Los Angeles; Rachel Ida Buff, *Against the Deportation Terror: Organizing for Immigrant Rights in the Twentieth Century* (Philadelphia: Temple University Press, 2018), chap 1; Parker, *Making Foreigners*, esp. 166–71; and Hernández, *Migra!*, chap. 3.

22. Honig, "Strike! . . . ," ca. 1933, 4–5, box 4, folder 26, Labor Research Association Records, TAM 129, Tamiment Library and Wagner Labor Archives, New York University; and Loren Miller, "On Second Thought," *California Eagle*, June 16, 1933, 12.

23. For more regarding discussions about African Americans' relationship to citizenship during the 1930s, see Nikhil Pal Singh, *Black Is a Country: Race and the Unfinished Struggle for Democracy* (Cambridge, MA: Harvard University Press, 2004).

24. Ngai, *Impossible Subjects*, 72; Baldoz, *Third Asiatic Invasion*, 156; and Hernández, *Migra!*, chap. 3.

25. "The 1930 Imperial Valley Case Defendants," *Rodo Shimbun-Labor News*, no. 45 (June 25, 1930), clipping in box 1, folder 7, Karl G. Yoneda Papers, Collection 1592, Special Collections, Charles E. Young Research Library, UCLA; "Mass meeting! Release the Imperial Valley Prisoners!" event flyer, April 14, 1931, box 1, folder 7,

Karl G. Yoneda Papers; financial report on Long Beach Deportation Fund, December 16, 1932, box 1, folder 7, Karl G. Yoneda Papers; individual and organization donations at "Deportation" Banquet, n.d., box 1, folder 7, Karl G. Yoneda Papers; Scott Kurashige, "Organizing from the Margins: Japanese American Communists in Los Angeles during the Great Depression," in *Race Struggles*, ed. Theodore Koditschek, Sundiata Keita Cha-Jua, and Helen A. Neville (Urbana: University of Illinois Press, 2009), 224–26; Vicki L. Ruiz, "Una Mujer sin Frontiers: Luisa Moreno and Latina Labor Activism," *Pacific Historical Review* 73, no. 1 (February 2004): 1–20; Buff, *Against the Deportation Terror*, chap. 1; and Hernández, *Migra!*, 76–77.

26. Ramírez, "Making of Mexican Illegality," 322.

27. Fernando Saúl Alanís Enciso, *They Should Stay There: The Story of Mexican Migration and Repatriation during the Great Depression*, trans. Russ Davidson (Chapel Hill: University of North Carolina Press, 2017); Benny Andrés Jr., *Power and Control in the Imperial Valley: Nature, Agribusiness, and Workers on the California Borderland, 1900–1940* (College Station: Texas A&M University Press, 2015), 133; Benny Andrés Jr., "Invisible Borders: Repatriation and Colonization of Mexican Migrant Workers along the California Borderlands during the 1930s," *California History* 88, no. 4 (2011): 6–8; Hernández, *Migra!*, chap. 3; and Ngai, *Impossible Subjects*, 72.

28. Baldoz, *Third Asiatic Invasion*, 179–80, 192–93.

29. See, for example, "2,000 repatriados llegaron a Aguascalientes: Manifestación contra EE.UU. en la estación," *La Opinión*, January 19, 1931, 5; "El problema de los repatriados," *La Opinión*, February 4, 1931, 3; "14,000 Mexicans Returned to Homeland," newspaper clipping, February 13, 1936, in box 15, folder: "Migratory Workers: Miscellaneous articles," Carey McWilliams Papers, Card Files; Isabel González, "Step-Children of a Nation: The Status of Mexican-Americans," 1947, 5, box 68, folder 1, California Ephemera Collection, Collection 200, Special Collections, Charles E. Young Research Library, University of California, Los Angeles; Loren Miller, "On Second Thought," *California Eagle*, June 16, 1933, 12; and Carey McWilliams, "Exit the Filipino," *Nation*, September 4, 1935, 265, clipping in box 15, folder: "Migratory Workers: Filipinos," Carey McWilliams Papers, Card Files.

30. Honig, "Strike! . . . ," 2.

31. I. González, "Step-Children of a Nation," 5.

32. I. González, "Step-Children of a Nation," 5.

33. Loren Miller, "On Second Thought," *California Eagle*, June 16, 1933, 12. Also see Honig, "Strike! . . . ," 13–14.

34. "El problema de los repatriados," *La Opinión*, February 4, 1931, 3.

35. Loren Miller, "On Second Thought," *California Eagle*, June 16, 1933, 12.

36. Parker, *Making Foreigners*.

37. Carey McWilliams, "The Coming Crisis in California," n.d., 2, box 15, folder: "Migratory Workers: Miscellaneous articles," Carey McWilliams Papers, Card Files.

38. Committee for the Protection of Filipino Rights, "An Appeal to Reason," pamphlet, 1940, box 15, folder: "Minorities: Filipinos," Carey McWilliams Papers, Card Files.

39. Gutiérrez, *Walls and Mirrors*, chap. 3.

40. I. González, "Step-Children of a Nation," 6. Carey McWilliams made a similar point in McWilliams, "Coming Crisis in California," 6.

41. Mark Reisler, "Always the Laborer, Never the Citizen: Anglo Perceptions of the Mexican Immigrant during the 1920s," *Pacific Historical Review* 45, no. 2 (May 1976): 231–54. Also, on deportability as an instrument of labor discipline, see Molina, *How Race Is Made in America*, chap. 4.

42. Balderrama and Rodríguez, *Decade of Betrayal*, 64–65.

43. On falsification of documents as a means to return, see Romeo Guzmán, "'My Dear Sir Mr. President': Repatriates, the Great Depression, and the Right to Return," forthcoming article shared with the author.

44. "Lo deportaron cuatro veces pero regresó," *La Opinión*, April 4, 1934, 8. Fausto's prison sentence reflected the recent criminalization of illegal entry, a product of both the Johnson-Reed Act of 1924, which inaugurated the country's first comprehensive quota system and created the Border Patrol, and a 1929 law that criminalized unlawful border crossings, making them punishable by hefty fines and prison time. See Ngai, *Impossible Subjects*, 4–5, 17, 59–60.

45. See Dept. of Corrections—Prison Terms, San Quentin Minute Books, 1932–1935, F3717: 1071–1073, California State Archives, Sacramento. Also see Hernández, *Migra!*, 75–77, 80.

46. See, for example, Dept. of Corrections—Prison Terms, San Quentin Minute Books, 1933–1934, F3717: 1072: 75, 125, 338, 449, 465; and Dept. of Corrections—Prison Terms, San Quentin Minute Books, 1934–1935, F3717: 1073: 57, 323.

47. Dept. of Corrections—Prison Terms, San Quentin Minute Books, 1934–1935, F3717: 1073: 323; "Changes in Filipino Paroles Are Suggested," publication and date unknown, marked as "Bee 8/7," box 15, folder: "Minorities: Filipinos," Carey McWilliams Papers, Card Files; and Carey McWilliams, research notes, "Offices Western Growers Protective Assn., June 8, 1935," 3, box 15, folder: "Migratory Workers: Miscellaneous articles," Carey McWilliams Papers, Card Files.

48. Balderrama and Rodríguez, *Decade of Betrayal*, 144.

49. Balderrama and Rodríguez, *Decade of Betrayal*, 144.

50. Andrés, "Invisible Borders," 9–10, 13–14; and Andrés, *Power and Control in the Imperial Valley*, 140.

51. Andrés, "Invisible Borders," 7; Andrés, *Power and Control in the Imperial Valley*, 140, 153; Balderrama and Rodríguez, *Decade of Betrayal*, 199, 203–4; and Enciso, *They Should Stay There*.

52. Andrés, "Invisible Borders," 9–10.

53. Enciso, *They Should Stay There*, 48.

54. See especially Carlos Bulosan, *America Is in the Heart* (Seattle: University of Washington Press, 2014).

55. Dept. of Corrections—Prison Terms, San Quentin Minute Books, 1933–1934, F3717: 1072: 75, 89, 465.

56. Dept. of Corrections—Prison Terms, San Quentin Minute Books, 1933–1934, F3717: 1072: 465.

57. "20 negros deportados de México," *La Opinión*, August 5, 1930, 1. Also see Enciso, *They Should Stay There*, xii.

58. Balderrama and Rodríguez, *Decade of Betrayal*, 205–6.

59. "Se organizará una sucursal en Brawley," *La Opinión*, April 6, 1930, 7.

60. "Una organización roja del Valle Imperial lanza duros ataques al Sr. Ortiz Rubio," *La Opinión*, April 6, 1930, 4; "Se organizará una sucursal en Brawley," *La Opinión*, April 6, 1930, 7; Andrés, "Invisible Borders," 9; and Balderrama and Rodríguez, *Decade of Betrayal*, 199–200.

61. Enciso, *They Should Stay There*; Balderrama and Rodríguez, *Decade of Betrayal*, 220–21; Andrés, *Power and Control in Imperial Valley*, 133; and Andrés, "Invisible Borders," 7–8.

62. Balderrama and Rodríguez, *Decade of Betrayal*, 139–40.

63. Balderrama and Rodríguez, *Decade of Betrayal*, 130–31.

64. Balderrama and Rodríguez, *Decade of Betrayal*, 130–32, 141–42.

65. Romeo Guzmán, "The Transnational Life and Letters of the Venegas Family, 1920s to 1950s," *History of the Family* 21, no 3 (June 2016): 457–82.

66. Guzmán, "'My Dear Sir Mr. President.'"

67. "Respuestas desde México" appeared for the first time in *La Opinión* on May 31, 1933.

68. James R. Barrett, *History from the Bottom Up and the Inside Out: Ethnicity, Race, and Identity in Working-Class History* (Durham, NC: Duke University Press, 2017), 122–44; Gutiérrez, *Walls and Mirrors*, 74–87; Cohen, *Making a New Deal*; and Gary Gerstle, *Working-Class Americanism: The Politics of Labor in a Textile City, 1914–1960* (New York: Cambridge University Press, 1989).

69. Gutiérrez, *Walls and Mirrors*, 106.

70. Buff, *Against the Deportation Terror*; and Alicia Schmidt Camacho, *Migrant Imaginaries: Latino Cultural Politics in the U.S.-Mexico Borderlands* (New York: New York University Press, 2008).

71. "Draft Program of the National Congress of Spanish Speaking People," 1939, 8, box 13, folder 9, Ernesto Galarza Papers, Coll. M0224, Department of Special Collections, Stanford University Libraries, Stanford, CA.

72. "Draft Program of the National Congress of Spanish Speaking People," 8.

73. Luisa Moreno, "Caravans of Sorrow: Noncitizen Americans of the Southwest," in *Between Two Worlds: Mexican Immigrants in the United States*, ed. David G. Gutiérrez (Wilmington, DE: Scholarly Resources, 1996), 119–24.

74. Gutiérrez, *Walls and Mirrors*, chap. 3.

75. Quoted in Ngai, *Impossible Subjects*, 124.

76. Quoted in Dawn Bohulano Mabalon, *Little Manila Is in the Heart: The Making of the Filipina/o American Community in Stockton, California* (Durham, NC: Duke University Press, 2013), 145.

77. Committee for the Protection of Filipino Rights, "An Appeal to Reason," pamphlet, 1940, box 15, folder: "Minorities: Filipinos," Carey McWilliams Papers, Card Files.

78. Regarding the role of social warrants within struggles for social change, see George Lipsitz, *American Studies in a Moment of Danger* (Minneapolis: University of Minnesota Press, 2001), xiv.

79. Loren Miller, "On Second Thought," *California Eagle*, June 16, 1933, 12.

80. Loren Miller, "On Second Thought," *California Eagle*, June 16, 1933, 12.

4. RADICALISM AT THE BALLOT BOX

1. According to Hawkins's oral history, Flory attended UCLA along with the others mentioned here. According to Flory's obituary, however, he attended UCLA for several years, left college to work in real estate and as a Pullman porter, and ultimately graduated from the University of California, Berkeley, in 1933. Augustus F. Hawkins, oral history, interview by Carlos Vásquez, January 15, December 10 and 12, 1988, transcript, 29–30, UCLA Oral History Program, for the California State Archives State Government Oral History Program, Special Collections, Charles E. Young Research Library, UCLA; and Tara Deering, "Ishmael Flory, 96," *Chicago Tribune*, February 12, 2004.

2. Hawkins, oral history, 28–41.

3. Hawkins, oral history, 38–40.

4. James N. Gregory, *American Exodus: The Dust Bowl Migration and Okie Culture in California* (New York: Oxford University Press, 1989), 90.

5. Hawkins, oral history, 38.

6. Douglas Flamming, *Bound for Freedom: Black Los Angeles in Jim Crow America* (Berkeley: University of California Press, 2005), 317–19.

7. Flamming, *Bound for Freedom*, 311.

8. Hawkins, oral history, 69–70.

9. Regarding the role of convergence spaces within early twentieth-century social movements, see Christina Heatherton, "The Color Line and the Class Struggle: The Mexican Revolution and Convergences of Radical Internationalism, 1910–1946" (PhD diss., University of Southern California, 2012); and Christina Heatherton, "The University of Radicalism: Ricardo Flores Magón and Leavenworth Penitentiary," *American Quarterly* 66, no. 3 (September 2014): 557–81.

10. Ira Katznelson, *Fear Itself: The New Deal and the Origins of Our Time* (New York: W. W. Norton, 2013); and Ira Katznelson, *When Affirmative Action Was White: An Untold History of Racial Inequality in Twentieth-Century America* (New York: W. W. Norton, 2005).

11. Gregory, *American Exodus*, 90; and James N. Gregory, "Upton Sinclair's 1934 EPIC Campaign: Anatomy of a Political Movement," *Labor: Studies in Working-Class History of the Americas* 12, no. 4 (December 2015): 57.

12. Richard Lowitt, *The New Deal and the West* (Bloomington: Indiana University Press, 1984), 172–73; Flamming, *Bound for Freedom*, 303–5; and Kevin Starr, *Endangered Dreams: The Great Depression in California* (Oxford: Oxford University Press, 1996), 130–36.

13. Devra Anne Weber, *Dark Sweat, White Gold: California Farm Workers, Cotton, and the New Deal* (Berkeley: University of California Press, 1996), 126–32; and Lowitt, *New Deal and the West*, chap. 11.

14. Upton Sinclair, *I, Governor of California, and How I Ended Poverty: A True Story of the Future*, 59, box 150, folder 13, Library of Social History Collection, Collection 91004, Hoover Institution Archives, Stanford University. See also "What Sinclair's

Epic Means to You," box 1, folder 1, Ed Mosk Papers, Collection MS 049, Southern California Library for Social Studies and Research, Los Angeles; and Starr, *Endangered Dreams*, 131–32.

15. Hawkins, oral history, 67.

16. Carey McWilliams, "Poverty, Pensions, and Panaceas: California in the Thirties," *Working Papers: For a New Society* 2, no. 3 (Fall 1974): 39, clipping in box 45, folder 2, Carey McWilliams Papers, 1894–1982, Collection 1319, Special Collections, Charles E. Young Research Library, UCLA.

17. George Creel, *Rebel at Large: Recollections of Fifty Crowded Years* (New York: Putnam, 1947), 268–88; Carey McWilliams, *Southern California: An Island on the Land* (1946; Salt Lake City: Gibbs Smith, 1973), 293–313; Starr, *Endangered Dreams*, 121–55; and Mike Davis, *City of Quartz: Excavating the Future in Los Angeles* (New York: Vintage Books, 1992), 37.

18. Gregory, "Upton Sinclair's 1934 EPIC Campaign."

19. Reuben Borough, "The Campaign Progresses," radio address transcript, June 24, 1934, box 40, folder 11, Reuben Borough Papers, Collection 927, Special Collections, Charles E. Young Research Library, UCLA; Richard S. Otto, End Poverty League Bulletin, March 3, 1934, box 40, folder 3, Reuben Borough Papers; Starr, *Endangered Dreams*, 138–39; and Gregory, "Upton Sinclair's 1934 EPIC Campaign," 56–59.

20. Chester Williams, "How Capitalism Fights," *Student Outlook* 3, no. 2–3 (November–December 1934): 18–19, clipping in box 40, folder 8, Reuben Borough Papers.

21. Otto, End Poverty League Bulletin, March 3, 1934.

22. Borough, "Campaign Progresses."

23. Robert Clifton, "The Democratic Party, Culbert L. Olson, and the Legislature," oral history, interview by Amelia R. Fry, October 6, 1972, transcript, 2c–3c, California Democrats in the Earl Warren Era, Earl Warren Oral History Project, Regional Oral History Office, Bancroft Library, University of California, Berkeley.

24. Greg Mitchell, *The Campaign of the Century: Upton Sinclair's Race for Governor of California and the Birth of Media Politics* (New York: Random House, 1992), 546.

25. Sinclair, *I, Governor of California*, 25–26; Upton Sinclair, "Epic Answers: How to End Poverty in California," box 150, folder 13, Library of Social History Collection; Gregory, "Upton Sinclair's 1934 EPIC Campaign"; and Flamming, *Bound for Freedom*, 313.

26. Florence McChesney Clifton, "California Democrats, 1934–1950," oral history, interview by Amelia R. Fry, August 9, 1972, transcript, 9, California Democrats in the Earl Warren Era, Earl Warren Oral History Project.

27. McWilliams, "Poverty, Pensions, and Panaceas," 39.

28. Gregory, "Upton Sinclair's 1934 EPIC Campaign," 61–64.

29. Gregory, "Upton Sinclair's 1934 EPIC Campaign," 68.

30. Gregory, *American Exodus*, 152–53.

31. Gregory, *American Exodus*, 154–71.

32. Gregory, *American Exodus*, chap. 5.

33. Becky M. Nicolaides, *My Blue Heaven: Life and Politics in the Working-Class Suburbs of Los Angeles, 1920–1965* (Chicago: University of Chicago Press, 2002), 121.

34. Nicolaides, *My Blue Heaven*, 169. Regarding the broader popular reorientation toward an activist government, see Lizabeth Cohen, *Making a New Deal: Industrial Workers in Chicago, 1919–1939* (Cambridge: Cambridge University Press, 1991).

35. Nicolaides, *My Blue Heaven*, 169, 172; Gregory, *American Exodus*; and Gregory, "Upton Sinclair's 1934 EPIC Campaign."

36. "Economic Evils Decried by Protestant Church: Author Discusses Religion of Merriam and Sinclair," *The Christian Plea*, n.d., 1, box 40, folder 1, Reuben Borough Papers.

37. "Economic Evils Decried by Protestant Church," 1.

38. "Pope's Message Urges Drastic Social Change: Liberty of Church Shown in Words of Holy Father," *The Catholic Plea*, n.d., 1, box 40, folder 1, Reuben Borough Papers.

39. Frank Scully, "Religion No Issue, Says Authority," *The Catholic Plea*, n.d., 1, box 40, folder 1, Reuben Borough Papers.

40. On working-class Whiteness in the interwar era, see Matthew Frye Jacobson, *Whiteness of a Different Color: European Immigrants and the Alchemy of Race* (Cambridge, MA: Harvard University Press, 1999); and David R. Roediger, *Working toward Whiteness: How America's Immigrants Became White; The Strange Journey from Ellis Island to the Suburbs* (New York: Basic Books, 2006).

41. Gregory, "Upton Sinclair's 1934 EPIC Campaign," 64–65.

42. Elizabeth Faue, *Community of Suffering and Struggle: Women, Men, and the Labor Movement in Minneapolis, 1915–1945* (Chapel Hill: University of North Carolina Press, 1991).

43. "Prominent Woman Broadcasts Warning to Mothers," *American Democracy*, October 11, 1934, 1, 3, box 40, folder 3, Reuben Borough Papers.

44. Gregory, "Upton Sinclair's 1934 EPIC Campaign," 64–65, 73.

45. "Women Democratic Club Fetes 250 with Party," *Los Angeles Sentinel*, September 27, 1934, 1.

46. Gregory, "Upton Sinclair's 1934 EPIC Campaign," 65, 79; and Flamming, *Bound for Freedom*, 315–16.

47. Gregory, "Upton Sinclair's 1934 EPIC Campaign," 65.

48. Flamming, *Bound for Freedom*, 311–12.

49. Hawkins, oral history, 67–68.

50. Leon H. Washington, "Awakened Colored Voters Shy at Fantastic Schemes," *Los Angeles Sentinel*, October 25, 1934, 1, 3. Also see Robert C. Emery, "Thunder over California," *Los Angeles Sentinel*, October 11, 1934, 4–5; October 18, 1934, 4–5; October 25, 1934, 4–5. Mark Wild notes that many African Americans also did not trust Sinclair because of his familial ties to southern White politicians. Wild, *Street Meeting: Multiethnic Neighborhoods in Early Twentieth-Century Los Angeles* (Berkeley: University of California Press, 2005), 260.

51. Reuben Borough did do some outreach on Sinclair's behalf in the Central Avenue district. "Forum Speakers to Discuss Candidates," *Los Angeles Sentinel*, October 4, 1934, 4.

52. "Mr. Sinclair Is Mum," *Collier's*, October 23, 1934, clipping in box 46, folder 8, Loren Miller Papers, mssMiller Papers, Huntington Library, San Marino, CA.

53. "Mr. Sinclair Is Mum," *Collier's*, October 23, 1934.

54. Loren Miller, "Aid Says He Will Give Race 'Break,'" originally published in Associated Negro Press, reprinted in *Collier's*, October 20, 1934, 6, clipping in box 46, folder 8, Loren Miller Papers.

55. "Debate Slated on Epic Plan," *Los Angeles Sentinel*, October 25, 1934, 2.

56. "Former Member of G.O.P. Will Assist Hawkins," *Los Angeles Sentinel*, October 11, 1934, 1.

57. "Negro Leader Urges 100% Sinclair Backing," *EPIC News*, November 5, 1934, 2, clipping in box 40, folder 9, Reuben Borough Papers.

58. "Mr. Sinclair Is Mum," *Collier's*, October 23, 1934.

59. "Former Member of G.O.P. Will Assist Hawkins," *Los Angeles Sentinel*, October 11, 1934, 1.

60. Flamming, *Bound for Freedom*, 306–8, 317.

61. "Voters End G.O.P. Rule in Assembly," *Los Angeles Sentinel*, November 8, 1934, 1.

62. "Former Member of G.O.P. Will Assist Hawkins," *Los Angeles Sentinel*, October 11, 1934, 1.

63. "Voters End G.O.P. Rule in Assembly," *Los Angeles Sentinel*, November 8, 1934, 1.

64. "Former Member of G.O.P. Will Assist Hawkins," *Los Angeles Sentinel*, October 11, 1934, 1; and "Voters End G.O.P. Rule in Assembly," *Los Angeles Sentinel*, November 8, 1934, 1.

65. "Former Member of G.O.P. Will Assist Hawkins," *Los Angeles Sentinel*, October 11, 1934, 1.

66. Hawkins, oral history, 69–70.

67. Gregory, "Upton Sinclair's 1934 EPIC Campaign," 66.

68. "Se pide que voten por Mr. Sinclair," *La Opinión*, October 6, 1934, 8; "Spanish Speaker Thomas Raphael Is Now Available," *EPIC News*, August 13, 1934, 5; and Gregory, "Upton Sinclair's 1934 EPIC Campaign," 66.

69. Upton Sinclair, "What I Shall Do If I Win/If I Lose: Two Paths Ahead," box 40, folder 3, Reuben Borough Papers.

70. Natalia Molina, *How Race Is Made in America: Immigration, Citizenship, and the Historical Power of Racial Scripts* (Berkeley: University of California Press, 2014), 34–38.

71. George J. Sánchez, *Becoming Mexican American: Ethnicity, Culture, and Identity in Chicano Los Angeles, 1900–1945* (Oxford: Oxford University Press, 1993), 222, 261.

72. Rodolfo Acuña, *Occupied America: The Chicano's Struggle toward Liberation*, 1st ed. (San Francisco: Canfield, 1972), 276; and Sánchez, *Becoming Mexican American*, 261.

73. Sánchez, *Becoming Mexican American*, 261–62.

74. "Spanish Speaker Thomas Raphael Is Now Available," *EPIC News*, August 13, 1934, 5; and "Se pide que voten por Mr. Sinclair," *La Opinión*, October 6, 1934, 8.

75. "Se pide que voten por Mr. Sinclair," *La Opinión*, October 6, 1934, 8.

76. "Se pide que voten por Mr. Sinclair," *La Opinión*, October 6, 1934, 8.

77. Dr. Aristrides Mayorga, "Cómo ven en México la crisis electoral en California," *La Opinión*, October 30, 1934, 3.

78. Flamming, *Bound for Freedom*, 317; and Mitchell, *Campaign of the Century*, 45.

79. Gregory, "Upton Sinclair's 1934 EPIC Campaign," 59.

80. Mitchell, *Campaign of the Century*; and Starr, *Endangered Dreams*, 143–48.

81. Thomas K. Case, "A Republican Viewpoint," *Independent Review*, September 6, 1934, 3, clipping in box 40, folder 1, Reuben Borough Papers; and Chester Williams, "How Capitalism Fights," *Student Outlook* 3, no. 2–3 (November–December 1934): 16–19.

82. "Candidates Fight for Bourbon Votes: Governor Merriam Pledges Non-partisan Administration in Bid for Democratic Sanction at Polls," *Independent Review*, September 6, 1934, 3, clipping in box 40, folder 1, Reuben Borough Papers.

83. "Candidates Fight for Bourbon Votes," *Independent Review*, September 6, 1934, 3.

84. "Anti-EPIC Legislature Must Be Named Tuesday," *Los Angeles Times*, November 4, 1934, pt. 1, 12, clipping in box 40, folder 4, Reuben Borough Papers.

85. "Anti-EPIC Legislature Must Be Named Tuesday," *Los Angeles Times*, November 4, 1934, pt. 1, 12.

86. The first quotation in this passage comes from a Tucson, AZ–based man quoted in Mitchell, *Campaign of the Century*, 27. The second quotation comes from Mitchell himself on the same page of this same source.

87. "Lawful Nuptials," *Illustrated Daily News*, September 22, 1934, clipping in box 40, folder 2, Reuben Borough Papers.

88. Sinclair, *I, Governor of California*, 12.

89. Sinclair, *I, Governor of California*, 12.

90. Sinclair, *I, Governor of California*, 12, 24.

91. Sinclair, *I, Governor of California*, 29–30.

92. "Sinclair Criticizes Roosevelt: Predicts Failure of New Deal," *American Democracy of California*, October 11, 1934, 1, clipping in box 40, folder 3, Reuben Borough Papers. As it tracked the shifting of Sinclair's public statements about Roosevelt and the New Deal, the article also criticized his "efforts to ingratiate himself with 'regular' Democrats" and "his effort to be all things to all men."

93. "Sinclair Lauds Roosevelt," *Sacramento Bee*, September 21, 1934, 10. See also "Sinclair Criticizes Roosevelt: Predicts Failure of New Deal," *American Democracy of California*, October 11, 1934, 1.

94. "Sinclair Lauds Roosevelt," *Sacramento Bee*, September 21, 1934, 10. See also "Sinclair Criticizes Roosevelt: Predicts Failure of New Deal," *American Democracy of California*, October 11, 1934, 1; and "Sinclair the Chameleon," *American Democracy of California*, October 11, 1934, 2, clipping in box 40, folder 3, Reuben Borough Papers.

95. Quoted in Mitchell, *Campaign of the Century*, 18.

96. Mitchell, *Campaign of the Century*, 27; and Starr, *Endangered Dreams*, 141–42.

97. Mitchell, *Campaign of the Century*, 181.

98. Mitchell, *Campaign of the Century*, 181.

99. Mitchell, *Campaign of the Century*, 212.

100. Mitchell, *Campaign of the Century*, 212.

101. "Lawful Nuptials," *Illustrated Daily* News, September 22, 1934.

102. "Sinclair Lauds Roosevelt," *Sacramento Bee*, September 21, 1934, 10, *American Democracy of California*, October 11, 1934, 1.

103. Herbert L. Phillips, "Democrats Subordinate EPIC Plan to New Deal," *Sacramento Bee*, September 21, 1934, 1, clipping in box 40, folder 3, Reuben Borough Papers.

104. Phillips, "Democrats Subordinate EPIC Plan to New Deal," *Sacramento Bee*, September 21, 1934, 1.

105. "Sinclair Criticizes Roosevelt: Predicts Failure of New Deal," *American Democracy of California*, October 11, 1934, 1.

106. "Sinclair the Chameleon," *American Democracy of California*, October 11, 1934, 2; and "Sinclair Criticizes Roosevelt: Predicts Failure of New Deal," *American Democracy of California*, October 11, 1934, 1.

107. "Sinclair Cannot End Poverty in California," Young People's Socialist League flyer, n.d., box 14, folder 2, Hyman Weintraub and William Goldberg Papers, Collection 831, Special Collections, UCLA.

108. Flamming, *Bound for Freedom*, 318.

109. Flamming, *Bound for Freedom*, 315.

110. California Secretary of State, *Statement of Vote in General Election on November 6, 1934* (Sacramento: State Printing Office, 1934), 5; Gregory, "Upton Sinclair's 1934 EPIC Campaign," 60; and Starr, *Endangered Dreams*, 154.

111. Gregory, "Upton Sinclair's 1934 EPIC Campaign," 60; Mitchell, *Campaign of the Century*, 546; and Starr, *Endangered Dreams*, 154.

112. Quoted in Mitchell, *Campaign of the Century*, 546.

113. Carey McWilliams, "Honorable in All Things Oral History Transcript: The Memoirs of Carey McWilliams," interview by Joel R. Gardner, July 10–19, 1978, transcript, 72, Collection No. 300/195, Special Collections, UCLA.

114. "Borough on EPIC Election," 1934, box 41, folder 1, Reuben Borough Papers.

115. Katznelson, *Fear Itself*; and Katznelson, *When Affirmative Action Was White*.

116. Josh Sides, *L.A. City Limits: African American Los Angeles from the Great Depression to the Present* (Berkeley: University of California Press, 2003), 33–34.

5. THE ART OF OPPOSITION IN THE CULTURE INDUSTRY'S CAPITAL

1. Mike Davis, "Sunshine and the Open Shop: Ford and Darwin in 1920s Los Angeles," in *Metropolis in the Making: Los Angeles in the 1920s*, ed. Tom Sitton and William Deverell (Berkeley: University of California Press, 2001), 100–101; and Mark Wild, *Street Meeting: Multiethnic Neighborhoods in Early Twentieth-Century Los Angeles* (Berkeley: University of California Press, 2005), 11.

2. L. S. H., "Group Gives 2 Scenes from 'Stevedore', 4th," *California Eagle*, July 6, 1934, 1. Since its New York debut, *Stevedore* had roused controversy over its representation of "human passions and race hatreds." It garnered fierce reactions from those who feared its "propaganda implications" and acclaim from those who admired the "crusading" manner in which it addressed "real people and real problems" of the day. "Three Contrasting New Plays," *New York Times*, July 15, 1934, BR13. For additional examples of popular reactions to *Stevedore*'s Broadway run, see Brooks Atkinson,

"The Play: The Drama of the Race Riot in 'Stevedore,' Put On by the Theatre Union," *New York Times*, April 19, 1934; Percy Hammond, "'Stevedore' Another Crusading Stage Play," *Los Angeles Times*, May 7, 1934, 9; and M. M., "A Vigorous Play," *Los Angeles Times*, June 17, 1934, A7.

3. Paul Peters and George Sklar, *Stevedore: A Play in Three Acts* (London: Jonathan Cape, 1935).

4. L. S. H., "Group Gives 2 Scenes from 'Stevedore,' 4th," *California Eagle*, July 6, 1934, 1.

5. L. S. H., "Group Gives 2 Scenes from 'Stevedore,' 4th," *California Eagle*, July 6, 1934, 1.

6. Bruce Nelson, "The 'Lords of the Docks' Reconsidered: Race Relations among West Coast Longshoremen, 1933–61," in *Waterfront Workers: New Perspectives on Race and Class*, ed. Calvin Winslow (Urbana: University of Illinois Press, 1998), 155–92.

7. George Sánchez, quoted in Daniel Widener, "'Perhaps the Japanese Are to Be Thanked?' Asia, Asian Americans, and the Construction of Black California," *Positions: East Asia Cultures Critique* 11, no. 1 (2003): 147.

8. Sarah Schrank, *Art and the City: Civic Imagination and Cultural Authority in Los Angeles* (Philadelphia: University of Pennsylvania Press, 2009), 12–13.

9. As George Lipsitz has put it, while cultural forms "engender accommodation with prevailing power realities, separating art from life, and internalizing the dominant culture's norms and values as necessary and inevitable," they also "create conditions of possibility, they expand the present by informing it with memories of the past and hopes for the future." Lipsitz, *Time Passages: Collective Memory and American Popular Culture* (Minneapolis: University of Minnesota Press, 1990), 16. Also regarding art as a contested, "elastic and exceedingly useful tool" for Los Angeles's diverse political struggles, see Schrank, *Art and the City*, 8.

10. A city that had produced negligible manufactured exports in 1905, Los Angeles became the nation's eighth-largest manufacturing center in 1924. By 1930 Los Angeles ranked as the fourth-largest metropolitan district nationwide. Mike Davis, *City of Quartz: Excavating the Future in Los Angeles* (New York: Vintage Books, 1992), 25, 117; and Davis, "Sunshine and the Open Shop," 96–97.

11. Quoted in Davis, *City of Quartz*, 17.

12. William Deverell, *Whitewashed Adobe: The Rise of Los Angeles and the Remaking of Its Mexican Past* (Berkeley: University of California Press, 2004).

13. Daniel Widener, "Another City Is Possible: Interethnic Organizing in Contemporary Los Angeles," *Race/Ethnicity: Multidisciplinary Global Contexts* 1, no. 2 (Spring 2008): 193; and Ken Gonzales-Day, *Lynching in the West, 1850–1935* (Durham, NC: Duke University Press, 2006), 207–8.

14. Deverell, *Whitewashed Adobe*, 4–5.

15. "A Center of Culture," *Los Angeles Times*, January 2, 1934, C15.

16. See Davis, "Sunshine and the Open Shop." Regarding the longer history of the open-shop movement, see Chad Pearson, *Reform or Repression: Organizing America's Anti-union Movement* (Philadelphia: University of Pennsylvania Press, 2015).

17. "An Open Shop Milestone," *Los Angeles Times*, January 1, 1930, quoted in Davis, "Sunshine and the Open Shop," 113–14.

18. Davis, "Sunshine and the Open Shop," 102; Davis, *City of Quartz*, 25; and Louis B. Perry and Richard S. Perry, *A History of the Los Angeles Labor Movement, 1911–1941* (Berkeley: University of California Press, 1963), viii, 5–6, 21. According to Perry and Perry, in 1910 the M&M counted as members nearly 750 firms, or about 80 to 85 percent of the larger establishments in the city. Perry and Perry, *History of the Los Angeles Labor Movement*, 21.

19. Davis, "Sunshine and the Open Shop," 98–101; and Wild, *Street Meeting*, 10–12.

20. Davis, "Sunshine and the Open Shop," 112–13.

21. Regarding discriminatory employment practices, see Wild, *Street Meeting*, 40–41; Douglas Flamming, *Bound for Freedom: Black Los Angeles in Jim Crow America* (Berkeley: University of California Press, 2005), 245–47; and Vicki L. Ruiz, *Cannery Women, Cannery Lives: Mexican Women, Unionization, and the California Food Processing Industry, 1930–1950* (Albuquerque: University of New Mexico Press, 1987), 15, 30–31. Regarding the broader implications of employer power and antiunionism for race management, see David R. Roediger and Elizabeth D. Esch, *The Production of Difference: Race and the Management of Labor in U.S. History* (New York: Oxford University Press, 2012).

22. Clarence Matson, quoted in Deverell, *Whitewashed Adobe*, 4.

23. Widener, "Another City Is Possible," 194; Rick Moss, "Not Quite Paradise: The Development of the African American Community in Los Angeles through 1950," *California History* 75, no. 3 (Fall 1996): 228; and Ruiz, *Cannery Women, Cannery Lives*, 5.

24. Davis, "Sunshine and the Open Shop," 117.

25. Davis, *City of Quartz*, 28, 114–15.

26. Widener, "'Perhaps the Japanese Are to Be Thanked?,'" 148.

27. Official descriptions of community labor markets, Industrial Department publications (1920s), collated in Davis, "Sunshine and the Open Shop," 117.

28. Wild, *Street Meeting*, 10–14; and Widener, "'Perhaps the Japanese Are to Be Thanked?,'" 148.

29. Luis Alvarez, *The Power of the Zoot: Youth Culture and Resistance during World War II* (Berkeley: University of California Press, 2008); Gaye Theresa Johnson, *Spaces of Conflict, Sounds of Solidarity: Music, Race, and Spatial Entitlement in Los Angeles* (Berkeley: University of California Press, 2013); Scott Kurashige, "The Many Facets of Brown: Integration in a Multiracial Society," *Journal of American History* 91, no. 1 (June 2004): 56–68; Anthony Macias, *Mexican American Mojo: Popular Music, Dance, and Urban Culture in Los Angeles, 1935–1968* (Durham, NC: Duke University Press, 2008); Widener, "'Perhaps the Japanese Are to Be Thanked?'"; and Wild, *Street Meeting*.

30. Wild, *Street Meeting*, 10.

31. Regarding the impact of revolutionary internationalisms in general and the Mexican Revolution in particular, see Christina Heatherton, "The Color Line and the Class Struggle: The Mexican Revolution and Convergences of Radical Internationalism, 1910–1946" (PhD diss., University of Southern California, 2012); and Douglas Monroy, "Fence Cutters, *Sedicioso*, and First-Class Citizens: Mexican Radicalism in America," in *The Immigrant Left in the United States*, ed. Paul Buhle and Dan Georgakas

(Albany: State University of New York Press, 1996), 11–44. Regarding public health concerns, see Natalia Molina, *Fit to Be Citizens? Public Health and Race in Los Angeles, 1879–1939* (Berkeley: University of California Press, 2006). Regarding labor radicalisms in Los Angeles during the World War I era, see Perry and Perry, *History of the Los Angeles Labor Movement*, chap. 6.

32. As Perry and Perry note, the business community's investment in the work of the M&M is evident in the fact that the organization doubled its membership between 1920 and 1923. Perry and Perry, *History of the Los Angeles Labor Movement*, 201.

33. It was not uncommon for Los Angeles's Red Squads and KKK to collaborate in the suppression of political dissenters and undesirables. See, for example, Perry and Perry, *History of the Los Angeles Labor Movement*, 190. Regarding the eugenics movement in Los Angeles, see Lily Kay, *The Molecular Vision of Life: Caltech, the Rockefeller Foundation, and the Rise of the New Biology* (Oxford: Oxford University Press, 1993), 63. Regarding the expansion of the KKK in Los Angeles and Southern California, see Davis, *City of Quartz*, 116, 162; and Flamming, *Bound for Freedom*, 200–202. Also see Wild, *Street Meeting*, 40–42, 60–61; and Becky M. Nicolaides, *My Blue Heaven: Life and Politics in the Working-Class Suburbs of Los Angeles, 1920–1965* (Chicago: University of Chicago Press, 2002), 157–58.

34. Schrank, *Art and the City*, 14–15.

35. Lipsitz, *Time Passages*, esp. chaps. 1 and 7; Nan Enstad, *Ladies of Labor, Girls of Adventure: Working Women, Popular Culture, and Labor Politics at the Turn of the Twentieth Century* (New York: Columbia University Press, 1999); and Kathy Peiss, *Cheap Amusements: Working Women and Leisure in Turn-of-the-Century New York* (Philadelphia: Temple University Press, 1985).

36. Lizabeth Cohen, *Making a New Deal: Industrial Workers in Chicago, 1919–1939* (Cambridge: Cambridge University Press, 1991), 157.

37. See, for example, George J. Sánchez, *Becoming Mexican American: Ethnicity, Culture, and Identity in Chicano Los Angeles, 1900–1945* (Oxford: Oxford University Press, 1993); Lon Kurashige, *Japanese American Celebration and Conflict: A History of Ethnic Identity and Festival, 1934–1990* (Berkeley: University of California Press, 2002); Flamming, *Bound for Freedom*; and Daniel Widener, *Black Arts West: Culture and Struggle in Postwar Los Angeles* (Durham, NC: Duke University Press, 2010).

38. Wild, *Street Meeting*; and Allison Varzally, *Making a Non-white America: Californians Coloring outside Ethnic Lines, 1925–1955* (Berkeley: University of California Press, 2008).

39. Alvarez, *Power of the Zoot*; Laura Pulido, *Black, Brown, Yellow, and Left: Radical Activism in Los Angeles* (Berkeley: University of California Press, 2006); Macias, *Mexican American Mojo*; Johnson, *Spaces of Conflict, Sounds of Solidarity*; and Widener, "Another City Is Possible."

40. An important contribution to the study of interracial cultural politics during the 1930s is Widener, "'Perhaps the Japanese Are to Be Thanked?'"

41. Schrank, *Art and the City*, 43–44.

42. Schrank, *Art and the City*, chap. 2; and Widener, *Black Arts West*, 84–86.

43. Victoria Grieve, *The Federal Art Project and the Creation of Middlebrow Culture* (Urbana: University of Illinois Press, 2009), 4.

44. Quoted in Laurance P. Hurlburt, *The Mexican Muralists in the United States* (Albuquerque: University of New Mexico Press, 1989), 196–97.

45. Schrank, *Art and the City*, 46.

46. Schrank, *Art and the City*, 46–48; and Hurlburt, *Mexican Muralists in the United States*, 206–7.

47. Schrank, *Art and the City*, 46.

48. Schrank, *Art and the City*, 48; and Hurlburt, *Mexican Muralists in the United States*, 207.

49. Schrank, *Art and the City*, 47, 51; and Hurlburt, *Mexican Muralists in the United States*, 206.

50. Federal Writers' Project of the Works Progress Administration, *Los Angeles in the 1930s: The WPA Guide to the City of Angels* (Berkeley: University of California Press, 2011), 153; and Deverell, *Whitewashed Adobe*, 43.

51. Quoted in Schrank, *Art and the City*, 49.

52. Harold Lehman, oral history, March 28, 1997, Archives of American Art, Smithsonian Institution, Washington, DC, originally recorded on seven sound cassettes, transcribed and digitized in 2010, http://www.aaa.si.edu/collections/interviews/oral-history-interview-harold-lehman-12894.

53. Lehman, oral history interview.

54. The photographs are from "Three of the Scottsboro Nine Paintings Mutilated 2/11/33," February 11, 1933, box 1, folder 6, Karl G. Yoneda Papers, Collection 1592, Special Collections, Charles E. Young Research Library, University of California, Los Angeles (UCLA).

55. "Reed Club Denied Hynes Indictment for Recent Raid," *Illustrated Daily News*, February 16, 1933, clipping in box 1, folder 6, Karl G. Yoneda Papers.

56. Regarding the advocacy of middlebrow culture in public arts projects beyond Los Angeles, see Grieve, *Federal Art Project*.

57. Schrank, *Art and the City*, 57.

58. Hugo Ballin to Edward Rowan, December 8, 1935, box 7, folder: "Inglewood, CA," Marlene Park and Gerald Markowitz New Deal Art Research Collection, Accession No. 00-11, Franklin D. Roosevelt Library Archives, Hyde Park, NY.

59. "Ballin Again in Art Hoax," *Los Angeles Times*, January 2, 1936, clipping in box 7, folder: "Inglewood, CA," Marlene Park and Gerald Markowitz New Deal Art Research Collection.

60. "Ballin Again in Art Hoax," *Los Angeles Times*, January 2, 1936. Also see Edward Rowan to Merle Armitage, January 17, 1936; Merle Armitage to Edward Rowan, January 7, 1936; Edward Rowan to Arthur Millier, n.d.; and "Hoax Painting That Charmed L.A. Brain Trusters," *Los Angeles Evening Herald Express*, January 14, 1936; all of the preceding are found in box 7, folder: "Inglewood, CA," Marlene Park and Gerald Markowitz New Deal Art Research Collection.

61. "Mural Painting by Gordon K. Grant: 'El Indio,' 'El Gringo,' 'El Paisano,'" box 7, folder: "Alhambra, CA," Marlene Park and Gerald Markowitz New Deal Art Research Collection.

62. Images of "El Indio," "El Paysano," and "El Gringo," marked as "Alhambra, Calif.: Grant, Gordon," box 26, folder: "California," Marlene Park and Gerald Markowitz New Deal Art Research Collection.

63. W. J. Beadle to Supervising Engineer, U.S. Treasury Department, March 17, 1938, box 7, folder: "Alhambra, CA," Marlene Park and Gerald Markowitz New Deal Art Research Collection.

64. S. W. Purdum to Procurement Division, Public Buildings Branch, U.S. Treasury Department, July 18, 1938, box 7, folder: "Alhambra, CA," Marlene Park and Gerald Markowitz New Deal Art Research Collection.

65. "Hawthorne House 'Get Acquainted' Tea Draws Crowd," *Los Angeles Sentinel*, May 24, 1934, 13; and "Hawthorne House Offering Varied Community Program," *California Eagle*, June 8, 1934, 2-B. See also "Hawthorne House Informal Opening Sunday Afternoon," *California Eagle*, May 18, 1934, 8; and "Popularity of Hawthorne House Winning Favor," *California Eagle*, May 11, 1934, 4.

66. "Young People's Clubs Rallying around Mrs. C. A. Bass Believing That They Will Benefit Should Final Victory Come," *California Eagle*, July 14, 1933, 1.

67. Wild, *Street Meeting*, 33.

68. "Hawthorne House Informal Opening Sunday Afternoon," *California Eagle*, May 18, 1934, 8.

69. "Prominent Artists Return to City after Two Years in New York," *California Eagle*, May 4, 1934, 8; and "Madame Page on Western School of Music Staff," *Los Angeles Sentinel*, November 27, 1934, 1. Sarah DeCoursey Page is interchangeably referred to by her married and maiden names, "Madame Page" and "Madame DeCoursey," in local newspapers. Because the use of DeCoursey is more frequent, I employ it for her here.

70. "DeBeal-Baugh-Critchlow," folder 28, Biographical Document File Collection, Manuscript Collection M024/1, Corona Public Library, Corona, CA; and "Recent Bride Former Californian," *California Eagle*, June 7, 1937, 1.

71. "Spanish Club of C.H.S. Enjoys Annual Banquet," *Corona Courier*, May 4, 1928, 2; "Summer Activities at Annual Picnic Held by Cooperative Club," *San Bernardino County Sun*, June 26, 1930, 14; and "Young People's Clubs Rallying around Mrs. C. A. Bass Believing That They Will Benefit Should Victory Finally Come," *California Eagle*, July 14, 1933, 1.

72. "Negro Art Group Scores at Downtown Center," *California Eagle*, June 8, 1934, 3; "Skit Wins Applause," *Los Angeles Sentinel*, June 7, 1934, 1; "Popularity of Hawthorne House Winning Favor," *California Eagle*, May 11, 1934, 4; "Little Theater Group Presents Strindberg Play," *Los Angeles Times*, May 24, 1934, 4; "E. W. Fisher to Lead L. A. Forum," *California Eagle*, June 30, 1933, 1; "John Owens at Art Reception," *Los Angeles Sentinel*, May 7, 1936, 6; "Fraternal Order Names John Owens Chairman," *Los Angeles Sentinel*, August 4, 1938, 5; and "Engineers Hear Poem by Owens," *Los Angeles Sentinel*, April 2, 1936, 1.

73. "Popularity of Hawthorne House Winning Favor," *California Eagle*, May 11, 1934, 4; "Green Speaks on Liberia Sunday," *Los Angeles Sentinel*, June 7, 1934, 7; "Hawthorne House Informal Opening Sunday Afternoon," *California Eagle*, May 18, 1934, 8; and

"Hawthorne House 'Get Acquainted' Tea Draws Crowd," *Los Angeles Sentinel*, May 24, 1934, 13.

74. "Hawthorne House Offering Varied Community Program," *California Eagle*, June 8, 1934, 2-B.

75. "Hawthorne House in Formal Opening Sunday Afternoon," *California Eagle*, May 18, 1934, 8; "Hawthorne House Will Entertain with Tea Sunday," *Los Angeles Sentinel*, May 17, 1934, 1; "Popularity of Hawthorne House Winning Favor," *California Eagle*, May 11, 1934, 4; and "Hawthorne House 'Get Acquainted' Tea Draws Crowd," *Los Angeles Sentinel*, May 24, 1934, 13.

76. Hawthorne House representatives frequently cast the center as a "non-political and non-religious institution, the facilities of which are open to all residents of the community." While I argue that the work of House organizers and participants was, in fact, deeply political, this statement highlights their self-conscious anchoring in a community-based politics of inclusion. Quotes in text come from "Hawthorne House 'Get Acquainted' Tea Draws Crowd," *Los Angeles Sentinel*, May 24, 1934, 13; "Hawthorne House Offering Varied Community Program," *California Eagle*, June 8, 1934, 2-B; and "Hawthorne House Will Entertain with Tea Tuesday," *Los Angeles Sentinel*, May 17, 1934, 1. See also "Popularity of Hawthorne House Winning Favor," *California Eagle*, May 11, 1934, 4; "Hawthorne House in Formal Opening Sunday Afternoon," *California Eagle*, May 18, 1934, 8; "Skit Wins Applause," *Los Angeles Sentinel*, June 7, 1934, 1; and "Green Speaks on Liberia Sunday," *Los Angeles Sentinel*, June 7, 1934, 7.

77. "Popularity of Hawthorne House Winning Favor," *California Eagle*, May 11, 1934, 4.

78. Hawthorne Neighborhood Center, advertisement for screening of *The Song of the Marketplace*, *California Eagle*, April 6, 1934, 11; "Popularity of Hawthorne House Winning Favor," *California Eagle*, May 11, 1934, 4; "Little Theatre Group Presents Strindberg Play," *Los Angeles Sentinel*, May 24, 1934, 4; "Skit Wins Applause," *Los Angeles Sentinel*, June 7, 1934, 1; and "Negro Art Group Scores at Downtown Center," *California Eagle*, June 8, 1934, 3.

79. "Skit Wins Applause," *Los Angeles Sentinel*, June 7, 1934, 1.

80. "Negro Art Group Scores at Downtown Center," *California Eagle*, June 8, 1934, 3; and "Hawthorne House Offering Varied Community Program," *California Eagle*, June 8, 1934, 2-B.

81. "Negro Art Group Scores at Downtown Center," *California Eagle*, June 8, 1934, 3; and "Hawthorne House Offering Varied Community Program," *California Eagle*, June 8, 1934, 2-B.

82. "Hawthorne House Offering Varied Community Program," *California Eagle*, June 8, 1934, 2-B.

83. J. A. C., "Stevedore, Water Front Drama, Is Exiting [*sic*] Play," *Los Angeles Sentinel*, October 18, 1934, 1.

84. Katherine von Blon, "Studio and Theatre Comings and Goings: Vitality Seen in Community Drama Season," *Los Angeles Times*, October 14, 1934, A2.

85. J. A. C., "Stevedore, Water Front Drama, Is Exiting [*sic*] Play," *Los Angeles Sentinel*, October 18, 1934, 1.

86. "Stevedore, Drama of Water Front, to Open Next Mon.," *Los Angeles Sentinel*, October 11, 1934, 1. Also regarding the role of the LAPD in reinforcing racial divisions within the city, see Report on Police Relations (1930), Additions—box 1, folder: "Articles, 1930s," Charlotta Bass Collection, MSS 002, Southern California Library for Social Studies and Research, Los Angeles.

87. "Stevedore, Drama of Water Front, to Open Next Mon.," *Los Angeles Sentinel*, October 11, 1934, 1.

88. J. A. C., "Stevedore, Water Front Drama, Is Exiting [*sic*] Play," *Los Angeles Sentinel*, October 18, 1934, 1.

89. "Group Plans to Repeat 'Stevedore,'" *Los Angeles Sentinel*, March 28, 1935, 1.

90. Garon, quoted in David R. Roediger, *History against Misery* (Chicago: Charles H. Kerr, 2006), 24–25. Also see Clyde Woods, *Development Arrested: The Blues and Plantation Power in the Mississippi Delta* (New York: Verso, 1998).

91. Daniel Fischlin, Ajay Heble, and George Lipsitz, *The Fierce Urgency of Now: Improvisation, Rights, and the Ethics of Cocreation* (Durham, NC: Duke University Press, 2013), xvi.

92. Robin D. G. Kelley, *Race Rebels: Culture, Politics, and the Black Working Class* (New York: Free Press, 1996), 11.

93. Cohen, *Making a New Deal*, 143–47.

94. William Douglass, oral history, interview by Steven L. Isoardi, February–March 1990, transcript, 9, Central Avenue Sounds, Oral History Program, Special Collections, Charles E. Young Research Library, UCLA. Virtually all of the musicians interviewed for UCLA's Central Avenue Sounds oral history collection share memories of growing up around music, including through their parents' and grandparents' traditions, community institutions and churches, and radio waves.

95. Douglass, oral history, 1–2, 5, 9.

96. Douglass, oral history, 9.

97. Anthony Ortega, oral history, interview by Steven L. Isoardi, September–November 1994, transcript, 7–8, Central Avenue Sounds, Oral History Program.

98. Douglass, oral history, 34.

99. Douglass, oral history, 34.

100. Clora Bryant, oral history, interview by Steven L. Isoardi, March–April 1990, transcript, 100–101, Central Avenue Sounds, Oral History Program.

101. Ortega, oral history, 76–77; and Don Tosti, oral history, interview by Anthony Macias, August 20, 1998, transcript, 12, box 1, folder 16, Don Tosti Papers, California Ethnic and Multicultural Archives (CEMA) 88, Department of Special Collections, University Libraries, University of California, Santa Barbara.

102. Buddy Collette, oral history, interview by Steven L. Isoardi, August 1989–January 1990, transcript, 62, Central Avenue Sounds, Oral History Program.

103. Collette, oral history, 62.

104. Collette, oral history, 63–64.

105. Collette, oral history, 42.

106. Jackie Kelso, oral history, interview by Steven L. Isoardi, March–May 1990, transcript, 23, Central Avenue Sounds, Oral History Program.

107. Kelso, oral history, 35–36.

108. Kelso, oral history, 35.

109. Kelso, oral history, 35–36. See also Ortega, oral history, 76–77; and Tosti, oral history, 12.

110. Tosti, oral history, 7.

111. Tosti, oral history, 7.

112. Collette, oral history, 23–26. Also see Leroy Hurte, oral history, interview by Steven L. Isoardi, July 1995, transcript, 4, Central Avenue Sounds, Oral History Program.

113. Douglass, oral history, 8.

114. Douglass, oral history, 21–22.

115. Collette, oral history, 58–59, 77.

116. Douglass, oral history, 6–7, 10–11.

117. Ortega, oral history, 26.

118. Hurte, oral history, 8–9.

119. Collette, oral history, 10.

120. Collette, oral history, 10.

121. Collette, oral history, 10.

122. Douglass, oral history, 8, 30–31.

123. Douglass, oral history, 30–31.

124. Ortega, oral history, 21–22.

125. Collette, oral history, 71.

126. Collette, oral history, 162.

127. Douglass, oral history, 16.

128. Collette, oral history, 68–69.

129. Collette, oral history, 35–36.

130. Bryant, oral history, 239.

131. Regarding the gendered dimensions of jazz culture in the popular front era, see Monica Hairston, "Gender, Jazz, and the Popular Front," in *Big Ears: Listening for Gender in Jazz Studies*, ed. Nicole Rustin and Sherrie Tucker (Durham, NC: Duke University Press, 2008), 64–89.

132. Bryant, oral history, 203.

133. Bryant, oral history, 202.

134. Bryant, oral history, 203.

135. Bryant, oral history, 100–101.

136. Hurte, oral history, 11, 15–17, 19–20.

137. Kelso, oral history, 37–38.

138. Collette, oral history, 78, 181–82.

139. Hurte, oral history, 17.

140. Ortega, oral history, 61–62.

141. Douglass, oral history, 20.

142. Alvarez, *Power of the Zoot*, 131–34, 138–52; and Macias, *Mexican American Mojo*, 17–18. Also regarding the politics of race and culture in multiethnic dance halls, see Kelley, *Race Rebels*, 168; and Les Back, "X Amount of Sat Siri Akal! Apache Indian,

Reggae Music, and Intermezzo Culture," in *Negotiating Identities: Essays on Immigration and Culture in Present-Day Europe*, ed. Aleksandra Alund and Raoul Granqvist (Amsterdam: Rodopi, 1995), 145.

143. Macias, *Mexican American Mojo*, 17.

144. Bryant, oral history, 229–34.

145. Bryant, oral history, 231–32.

6. NATIVE JAZZ AND OPPOSITIONAL
CULTURE IN ROUND VALLEY RESERVATION

1. Elizabeth Lenore Willits, oral history, interview by Acklan Willits, November 11, 1990, transcript, 1, 3–4, box 1, folder: "Elizabeth Willits," Round Valley Oral History Project, Round Valley Public Library, Covelo, CA. Regarding Willits's tribal ancestry, see William J. Bauer Jr., *We Were All like Migrant Workers Here: Work, Community, and Memory on California's Round Valley Reservation, 1850–1941* (Chapel Hill: University of North Carolina Press, 2009), 102; and *U.S. Census, 1930: Indian Census Roll: Census of the Round Valley Reservation of the Sacramento Agency*, Washington, DC, National Archives and Records Administration, June 30, 1930.

2. Willits, oral history, 4.

3. Willits, oral history, 5.

4. Willits, oral history, 5. While Willits's oral history transcript refers to an Albert and Everett McClean, the 1930 Round Valley census contains no such names. The census does, however, list an Albert and Everett McLane, Concow sons of John Wilsey and Carrie Heath McLane, as residents of the reservation. Most likely, this signals a slippage in the transcription, and these are the same people to whom Willits refers. *U.S. Census, 1930: Indian Census Roll*. Additionally, historian William Bauer notes that Carrie Heath McLane was of Yuki and Wailacki descent. Bauer, *We Were All like Migrant Workers Here*, 178.

5. Willits, oral history, 6–7.

6. Willits, oral history, 6.

7. Willits, oral history, 6.

8. Round Valley Reservation began as Nome Cult Farm in 1856, one of the five California Indian reservations that the federal government authorized in 1852. It is located on the ancestral homeland of the Yuki, in the northeastern region of what is now Mendocino County. Following the reservation's establishment in Yuki territory, the government removed diverse tribes from across central and northeastern California to the region, including Nomlackis, Nisenans, Pit Rivers, Concows, Wailackis, and Pomos. Bauer, *We Were All like Migrant Workers Here*, 2.

9. Wendy Wall, "Gender and the 'Citizen Indian,'" in *Writing the Range: Race, Class, and Culture in the Women's West*, ed. Elizabeth Jameson and Susan Armitage (Norman: University of Oklahoma Press, 1997), 202–9.

10. George Lipsitz, *Dangerous Crossroads: Popular Music, Postmodernism, and the Poetics of Place* (London: Verso, 1994), 17.

11. Josh Kun, *Audiotopia: Music, Race, and America* (Berkeley: University of California Press, 2005), 14.

12. Although initially the federal government's Round Valley Agency oversaw just the reservation established at Round Valley, during the early twentieth century its purview expanded to include Indians living and working on *rancherías* in Mendocino, Sonoma, and Lake Counties. In this chapter I use "Round Valley Indians" to refer broadly to all the Indians under the Round Valley Agency's supervision during the early twentieth century. This broader and more flexible usage of the term also reflects Native lives in the region better than one that confines itself to the physical space of the reservation. As Bauer has shown, the lives and subjectivities of Round Valley residents never fit neatly within the boundaries imposed on them by government agents and policy makers. Bauer, *We Were All like Migrant Workers Here*. For more on the establishment of rancherías, also see Albert L. Hurtado, *Indian Survival on the California Frontier* (New Haven, CT: Yale University Press, 1988), 129–30.

13. As George Lipsitz explains, popular music serves in significant ways as a "repository of collective memory and a vehicle for collective witness," an "alternative archive of history" that both reflects and transmits the "shared memories, experiences, and aspirations of ordinary people, whose perspectives rarely appear in formal historical archival collections." Lipsitz, *Footsteps in the Dark: The Hidden Histories of Popular Music* (Minneapolis: University of Minnesota Press, 2007), xi–xii.

14. Willits, oral history, 9.

15. Willits, oral history, 10.

16. Willits, oral history, 10.

17. An important exception is Bauer's work. See especially Bauer, *We Were All like Migrant Workers Here*; and Bauer, *California through Native Eyes: Reclaiming History* (Seattle: University of Washington Press, 2016).

18. Tomás Almaguer, *Racial Fault Lines: The Historical Origins of White Supremacy in California* (Berkeley: University of California Press, 1994), 146.

19. Over one hundred languages were spoken by the over 300,000 Indigenous people who inhabited California before contact and conquest. Bauer, *We Were All like Migrant Workers Here*, 17.

20. Beginning with the first mission and pueblo in San Diego in 1769, the Spanish colonial system in California consisted of twenty-one Franciscan missions, four military presidios, and three civilian pueblos. The last mission, San Francisco Solano, was established in Sonoma in 1823. Russian merchants established the first mercantile colony in California at Fort Ross in 1812, on the coast of what is now Sonoma County, and maintained a claim to this territory until 1841. The Mexican rancho era in California history began after Mexican independence in 1821 and peaked during the fifteen years that followed the 1834 secularization of the region's missions. Rancho Petaluma, the home of Mariano Guadalupe Vallejo and one of the largest and most powerful of all Mexican ranchos, was established just north of San Francisco Bay in 1834 and remained under Vallejo's control until 1857. Another of the Mexican era's largest ranchos, New Helvetia, was established by Swiss pioneer John Sutter in 1839 at the juncture of the American and Sacramento Rivers, in what became the city of Sacramento.

For further background on the colonial histories that converged on the ancestral lands of central California and northeastern Indians during the early nineteenth century, see Kent G. Lightfoot, *Indians, Missionaries, and Merchants: The Legacy of Colonial Encounters on the California Frontiers* (Berkeley: University of California Press, 2005); Stephen W. Silliman, *Lost Laborers in Colonial California: Native Americans and the Archaeology of Rancho Petaluma* (Tucson: University of Arizona Press, 2004); and Hurtado, *Indian Survival on the California Frontier*. Regarding anthropological designations of Indigenous cultural areas and their connections to Round Valley, see Bauer, *We Were All like Migrant Workers Here*, 18. Regarding the interactions of Yuki Indians, Round Valley's original inhabitants, with Spanish settlers and Russian, Mexican, and Anglo fur trappers and traders, see Bauer, *We Were All like Migrant Workers Here*, 31–32.

21. For seminal works on this broader context, see Walter Rodney, *How Europe Underdeveloped Africa* (London: Bogle-L'Ouverture, 1972); Eric R. Wolf, *Europe and the People without History* (Berkeley: University of California Press, 1982); Cedric J. Robinson, *Black Marxism: The Making of the Black Radical Tradition* (Chapel Hill: University of North Carolina Press, 2000); and Mike Davis, *Late Victorian Holocausts: El Niño Famines and the Making of the Third World* (New York: Verso, 2001).

22. Lightfoot, *Indians, Missionaries, and Merchants*, 5–6; and Silliman, *Lost Laborers in Colonial California*, 8–9, 12–13, 16, 54–55, 62–63. Also see Margaret A. Ramsland, "The Forgotten Californians," Chico, CA, 1974, BANC MSS 75/8 c, Bancroft Library, University of California, Berkeley.

23. Cheryl I. Harris, "Whiteness as Property," *Harvard Law Review* 106, no. 8 (June 1993): 1721–24. See also Almaguer, *Racial Fault Lines*, esp. chaps. 4 and 5; and Brendan C. Lindsay, *Murder State: California's Native American Genocide, 1846–1873* (Lincoln: University of Nebraska Press, 2012).

24. Almaguer, *Racial Fault Lines*, esp. chaps. 4 and 5.

25. As historian Richard White has noted, a central and consistent theme in the histories of Native American peoples broadly speaking has been the effort by White Americans "to bring Indian resources, land, and labor into the market." White, *The Roots of Dependency: Subsistence, Environment, and Social Change among the Choctaw, Pawnees, and Navajos* (Lincoln: University of Nebraska Press, 1983), xv. Regarding the particular histories of labor, land, and resource commodification in Northern California and the genocidal implications of regional development in Round Valley, see Lindsay, *Murder State*; Frank H. Baumgardner, *Killing for Land in Early California: Indian Blood at Round Valley* (New York: Algora, 2005); and Benjamin Madley, *An American Genocide: The United States and the California Indian Catastrophe* (New Haven, CT: Yale University Press, 2016).

26. Bauer, *We Were All like Migrant Workers Here*, 8; Hurtado, *Indian Survival on the California Frontier*, 1; Lindsay, *Murder State*; and Madley, *American Genocide*.

27. The foundational work on this subject is Sherburne Cook, *The Conflict between the California Indian and White Civilization* (Berkeley: University of California Press, 1976). Also see George Foster, "Summary of Yuki Culture," *University of California Publications in Anthropological Records* 5 (1900–1947): 155–244; Frank Essene, "Cultural Elements Distribution: XXI Round Valley," *Anthropological Records* 8 (1945): 1–144;

Amelia Susman, "The Round Valley Indians of California: An Unpublished Chapter in Acculturation of Seven [or Eight] Indian Tribes," *Contributions to the University of California Archaeological Research Facility* 31 (1976); Virginia Miller, *Ukomno'm: The Yuki Indians of Northern California* (Socorro, NM: Ballena, 1979); Lynwood Carranco and Estle Beard, *Genocide and Vendetta: The Round Valley Wars of Northern California* (Norman: University of Oklahoma Press, 1981); William Secrest, *When the Great Spirit Died: The Destruction of the California Indians, 1850–1860* (Sanger, CA: Word Dancer, 2002); Benjamin Madley, "California's Yuki Indians: Defining Genocide in Native American History," *Western Historical Quarterly* 39 (Autumn 2008): 303–32; Baumgardner, *Killing for Land in Early California*; and Madley, *American Genocide*.

28. Hurtado, *Indian Survival on the California Frontier*, 1; see also Bauer, *We Were All like Migrant Workers Here*, 9.

29. Bauer, *We Were All like Migrant Workers Here*; Hurtado, *Indian Survival on the California Frontier*; and Nicolas G. Rosenthal, *Reimagining Indian Country: Native American Migration and Identity in Twentieth-Century Los Angeles* (Chapel Hill: University of North Carolina Press, 2012). For works that address Native accommodations to modernization and racial capitalism beyond California, see Richard White, *Middle Ground: Indians, Empires, and Republics in the Great Lakes Region, 1650–1815* (Cambridge: Cambridge University Press, 1991); and Claudio Saunt, Barbara Krauthamar, Tiya Miles, Celia E. Naylor, and Circe Sturm, "Rethinking Race and Culture in the Early South," *Ethnohistory* 53, no. 2 (Spring 2006): 399–405. My framing here is also informed by David Graeber, "The New Anarchists," *New Left Review* 13 (January–February 2002): 61–73.

30. Rosenthal, *Reimagining Indian Country*, 31–32.

31. The quotation "a real old-fashioned wild-west celebration" is from "Frontier Days Show Will Be Ready Soon," *Willits News*, June 24, 1932, 1. Also see "Frontier Days Show Is Real Drawing Card," *Willits News*, July 8, 1932, 1 "Round Valley Items of General Interest," *Willits News*, April 21, 1933, 3; "Now Listen!," *Willits News*, November 3, 1933, 1–2; "Songs and Dress of All Nations on the Program," *Redwood Journal*, February 9, 1934, 4; "Pocahontas and Redmen Prepare for Big Event," *Redwood Journal*, February 20, 1934, 6; "Pocahontas and Redmen Unite in Annual Event," *Redwood Journal*, March 2, 1934, 4; "Frontier Days Plans Indicate Best Show Ever Held in Willits," *Willits News*, May 10, 1935, 1; "Frontier Days Notes," *Willits News*, May 24, 1935, 1; "Frontier Days Notes," *Willits News*, June 21, 1935, 1; "Frontier Days Notes," *Willits News*, June 28, 1935, 1; "Willits Invites the World to Ninth Annual Frontier Days," *Willits News*, June 28, 1935, 4; "Great Crowd Here for Frontier Days," *Willits News*, July 5, 1935, 1; "Attendance at Frontier Days Best in Years," *Willits News*, July 12, 1935, 1; and "Record Tourist Year Predicted for California," *Willits News*, July 12, 1935, 8.

32. Bauer, *We Were All like Migrant Workers Here*, 2–3, 37–39, 52–53.

33. Ramsland, *Forgotten Californians*; and William Poole, "Retracing the Trail of Tears," *San Francisco Chronicle: This World*, August 7, 1988, 8–9.

34. Ramsland, *Forgotten Californians*, 3–5, 20; and William Poole, "Retracing the Trail of Tears," *San Francisco Chronicle: This World*, August 7, 1988, 8–9.

35. Agnes Duncan and Joe Happy, oral history, interview by Les Lincoln, June 22, 1990, transcript, 8, box 1, folder: "Agnes Duncan and Joe Happy," Round Valley Oral History Project; and Adaline Figueroa, oral history, interview by Les Lincoln, April 18, 1990, transcript, 6–7, box 1, folder: "Adaline Figueroa," Round Valley Oral History Project. For an in-depth exploration of the telling of history by California Indians, see Bauer, *California through Native Eyes*.

36. Figueroa, oral history, 3.

37. Bauer, *We Were All like Migrant Workers Here*, 121–22.

38. Bauer, *We Were All like Migrant Workers Here*, 122.

39. Bauer, *We Were All like Migrant Workers Here*, 84.

40. Bauer, *We Were All like Migrant Workers Here*, 83–84.

41. Bauer, *We Were All like Migrant Workers Here*, 83.

42. Bauer, *We Were All like Migrant Workers Here*, 6.

43. Rosenthal, *Reimagining Indian Country*, 2; and Susan Lobo, ed., *Urban Voices: The Bay Area American Indian Community* (Tucson: University of Arizona Press, 2002), 3–17.

44. Bauer, *We Were All like Migrant Workers Here*, 94, 100, 102, 104.

45. June Britton, quoted in Bauer, *We Were All like Migrant Workers Here*, 92. Also see Bauer, *We Were All like Migrant Workers Here*, 94, 100, 102, 104.

46. John Cook, quoted in Bauer, *We Were All like Migrant Workers Here*, 179.

47. Meeting minutes, meeting held April 3, 1937, in Berkeley, California, convening representatives of the BIA, Resettlement Administration, Indian Service, Heller Foundation, and Indian Defense Association, 23, box 1, folder: "National Archives and Records Administration—Archives I, RG 75, Central Classified Files, 1907–1939, Sacramento Area Office, Box 89: 41441-1937," William J. Bauer Jr. Research Files, Round Valley Public Library, Covelo, CA (hereafter cited as Bauer Research Files). Also see Bauer, *We Were All like Migrant Workers Here*, 94.

48. Stephen Knight, quoted in report by Senate Committee on Indian Affairs, San Francisco, November 28, 1928, 18, box 1, folder: "National Archives and Records Administration—San Bruno, CA, RG 75, Sacramento Area Office, Coded Records, 1910–1958, Box 5: Senate Committee, Nov. 19–20, 1928," Bauer Research Files; and Bauer, *We Were All like Migrant Workers Here*, 71, 104.

49. Leland Fulwider Jr., oral history, interview by Acklan Willits, April 23, 1990, transcript, 1–2, 6, 7–8, 16, box 1, folder: "Leland Fulwider Junior," Round Valley Oral History Project; Armstead Want, oral history, interview by Acklan Willits, May 5, 1990, transcript, 12, 14, box 1, folder: "Armstead Want," Round Valley Oral History Project; Duncan and Happy, oral history interview transcript, 5, 9; Doran Lincoln, oral history, interview by Acklan Willits, April 25, 1990, transcript, 2, box 1, folder: "Doran Lincoln," Round Valley Oral History Project; and Bauer, *We Were All like Migrant Workers Here*, 92–93, 102–4.

50. Bauer, *We Were All like Migrant Workers Here*, 178–79.

51. Meeting minutes, April 3, 1937, Berkeley, Calif., 15.

52. Meeting minutes, August 27, 1936, San Francisco, 3, box 1, folder: "National Archives and Records Administration—Archives I, RG 75, Central Classified Files, 1907–1939, Sacramento Area Office, Box 80: 30358-1933," Bauer Research Files.

53. "A Birdseye View of Indian Policy, Historic and Contemporary," Subcommittee of the Appropriation Committee, House of Representatives, December 30, 1935, 2, folder: "Round Valley Indians," Mendocino County Historical Society, Ukiah, CA.

54. Meeting minutes, April 3, 1937, Berkeley, Calif., 16.

55. O. H. Lipps to Lynn J. Frazier, October 17, 1932, box 1, folder: "National Archives and Records Administration—San Bruno, RG 75, California, Sacramento Area Office, Coded Records, 1910–1958, Box 45, Folder: Senatorial Investigation Committee, 1932" (hereafter cited as "NARA, Box 45: SIC 1932"), Bauer Research Files.

56. Bauer, *We Were All like Migrant Workers Here*, 199; and Thomas Biolsi, "'Indian Self-Government' as a Technique of Domination," *American Indian Quarterly* 15, no. 1 (Winter 1991): 23–28; Vine Deloria, Jr. and Clifford Lytle, *The Nations Within: The Past and Future of American Indian Sovereignty* (New York: Pantheon Books, 1984), 140–53; Graham Taylor, *The New Deal and American Indian Tribalism: The Administration of the Indian Reorganization Act, 1934–1945* (Lincoln: University of Nebraska Press, 1980); Lawrence C. Kelly, "The Indian Reorganization Act: The Dream and the Reality," *Pacific Historical Review* 44, no. 3 (Aug. 1975): 291–312.

57. Biolsi, "'Indian Self-Government' as a Technique of Domination," 27.

58. Ida Mary Willits Soares, oral history, interview by Acklan Willits, April 10, 1990, transcript, 10, box 1, folder: "Ida Mary Willits Soares," Round Valley Oral History Project.

59. Ivye Ortinier to O. H. Lipps, July 1, 1934, box 1, folder: "National Archives and Records Administration—San Bruno, CA, RG 75, Sacramento Area Office, Coded Records, 1910–1958, Box 4: Wheeler-Howard Act, #3" (hereafter cited as "NARA, Box 4: WHA #3"), Bauer Research Files; Ivye Ortinier to Roy Nash, August 13, 1935, box 1, folder: "NARA, Box 4: WHA #3," Bauer Research Files; Mary Duncan to Roy Nash, November 7, 1935, box 1, folder: (hereafter cited as "NARA, Box 262: Native Arts"), Bauer Research Files; Georgia Campbell to Roy Nash, November 7, 1935, box 1, folder: "NARA, Box 262: Native Arts," Bauer Research Files; R. Belden to O. H. Lipps, September 3, 1934, box 1, folder: "NARA, Box 4: WHA #3," Bauer Research Files; R. Belden to "Sir," July 31, 1935, box 1, folder: "NARA, Box 4: WHA #3," Bauer Research Files; Georgia O'Connell to O. H. Lipps, July 17, 1935, box 1, folder: "NARA, Box 4: WHA #3," Bauer Research Files; and William Stillwell to O. H. Lipps, August 8, 1934, box 1, folder: "NARA, Box 4: WHA #3," Bauer Research Files.

60. Bauer, *We Were All like Migrant Workers Here*, 200–202.

61. Luis Alvarez, "Reggae Rhythms in Dignity's Diaspora: Globalization, Indigenous Identity, and the Circulation of Cultural Struggle," *Popular Music and Society* 31, no. 5 (December 2008): 575–97.

62. Stuart Hall, "Notes on Deconstructing 'the Popular,'" in *Cultural Resistance Reader*, ed. Stephen Duncombe (New York: Verso, 2002), 187, 192.

63. This description of the necessity and limitations of formal political channels draws on Paul Gilroy's notion of the "politics of fulfilment," that is, "the notion that a future society will be able to realize the social and political promise that present society has left unaccomplished." Gilroy, *Small Acts: Thoughts on the Politics of Black Cultures* (New York: Serpent's Tail, 1993), 133–34. To regard culture as a wider arena of

political possibility is not to suggest that it is not also (like formal politics) an uneven terrain that is shaped and impacted by dominant forces. As Stuart Hall notes, "there is a continuous and necessarily uneven and unequal struggle, by the dominant culture, constantly to disorganize and reorganize popular culture; to enclose and confine its definitions and forms within a more inclusive range of dominant forms." Hall, "Notes on Deconstructing 'the Popular,'" 187.

64. C. L. R. James, quoted in Barbara Ransby, *Ella Baker and the Black Freedom Movement: A Radical Democratic Vision* (Chapel Hill: University of North Carolina Press, 2003), 374. The quote from Gilroy comes from his definitions of what he calls "the politics of transfiguration." See Gilroy, *Small Acts*, 133–34.

65. For seminal examples, see LeRoi Jones, *Blues People: Negro Music in White America* (1963; reprint, New York: Harper Perennial, 1999); Clyde Woods, *Development Arrested: The Blues and Plantation Power in the Mississippi Delta* (New York: Verso, 1998); and Américo Paredes, *With a Pistol in His Hand: A Border Ballad and Its Hero* (Austin: University of Texas Press, 1958).

66. William Oandasan, "The Poet Is a Voice: Interview with William Oandasan 2/12/85," *Wicazo Sa Review* 2, no. 1 (Spring 1986): 4–5.

67. Wendy Rose, introduction to William Oandasan, *Round Valley Songs* (Minneapolis: West End, 1984), iv–v.

68. Kun, *Audiotopia*, 23. Also see Lipsitz, *Dangerous Crossroads*; and Alvarez, "Reggae Rhythms in Dignity's Diaspora."

69. Alvarez, "Reggae Rhythms in Dignity's Diaspora," 576.

70. Fulwider, oral history, 7; Want, oral history, 19, 31, 50; and Willits, oral history, 7, 10–11.

71. Duncan and Happy, oral history, 11.

72. Willits, oral history, 7–8.

73. Fulwider, oral history, 7.

74. Lipsitz, *Footsteps in the Dark*, 84–85.

75. Regarding oppositional and anti-essentialist epistemologies in jazz, see Kevin Fellezs, "Silenced but Not Silent: Asian Americans and Jazz," in *Alien Encounters: Popular Culture in Asian America*, ed. Mimi Thi Nguyen and Thuy Linh Nguyen Tu (Durham, NC: Duke University Press, 2007), 69–110. Also regarding the politics of difference and racial anti-essentialism in music, see George Lipsitz, "Cruising around the Historical Bloc: Postmodern and Popular Music in East Los Angeles," in *The Subcultures Reader*, ed. Ken Gelder and Sarah Thornton (New York: Routledge, 1997), 350–59. Regarding the commodification of jazz and uses of minstrelsy in mass culture, see Michael Rogin, *Blackface, White Noise: Jewish Immigrants in the Hollywood Melting Pot* (Berkeley: University of California Press, 1996); and Graham Cassano, "Working Class Self Fashioning in *Swing Time* (1936)," *Critical Sociology* 40, no. 3 (May 2014): 329–47.

76. Want, oral history, 31, 50.

77. Fulwider, oral history, 7.

78. Willits, oral history, 10–11.

79. Willits, oral history, 8.

80. Willits, oral history, 7–8.

81. Willits, oral history, 7.

82. Bauer, *We Were All like Migrant Workers Here*, 71–72, 93–94.

83. Allan H. Anderson, *To the Ends of the Earth: Pentecostalism and the Transformation of World Christianity* (Oxford: Oxford University Press, 2013).

84. L. A. Dorrington to the Commissioner of Indian Affairs, November 18, 1929, box 1, folder: "National Archives and Records Administration—San Bruno, CA, RG 75, Sacramento Area Office, Coded Records, 1910–1958, Box 173: Churches" (hereafter cited as "NARA, Box 173: Churches"), Bauer Research Files; and Bauer, *We Were All like Migrant Workers Here*, 194.

85. L. A. Dorrington to the Commissioner of Indian Affairs, August 6, 1928, 3, box 1, folder: "National Archives and Records Administration—Archives I, RG 75, Central Classified Files, 1907–1939, Sacramento Area Office, Box 79: 17518-1928" (hereafter cited as "NARA, Box 79: 17518-1928"), Bauer Research Files. For an example of Schillinger's advocacy, see Rev. Schillinger to Commissioner of Indian Affairs, April 6, 1928, box 1, folder: "NARA, Box 79: 17518-1928," Bauer Research Files.

86. Foster, "Summary of Yuki Culture," 219; L. A. Dorrington to the Commissioner of Indian Affairs, November 18, 1929; and Assistant Commissioner to O. H. Lipps, October 2, 1931, box 1, folder: "NARA, Box 173: Churches," Bauer Research Files.

87. "Petition: We the undersigned are very much interested in the Penticostal movement [sic] . . . ," n.d., box 1, folder: "NARA, Box 173: Churches," Bauer Research Files.

88. Foster, "Summary of Yuki Culture," 219; and Bauer, *We Were All like Migrant Workers Here*, 198.

89. Foster, "Summary of Yuki Culture," 219–20.

90. "Prayer of Petition," February 25, 1930, box 1, folder: "NARA, Box 173: Churches," Bauer Research Files.

91. "Prayer of Petition," February 25, 1930.

92. Regarding those who celebrated the apparent social conservatism that Pentecostalism brought, see L. A. Dorrington to the Commissioner of Indian Affairs, November 18, 1929; Foster, "Summary of Yuki Culture," 221; and Bauer, *We Were All like Migrant Workers Here*, 196, 198. Regarding the destabilizing effect of Pentecostalism for social relations in the region, see B. Clark to Commissioner of Indian Affairs, February 6, 1930, box 1, folder: "NARA, Box 173: Churches," Bauer Research Files.

93. Regarding the global dimensions of Pentecostalism, see Anderson, *To the Ends of the Earth*.

94. The aspects of the religion that made it distinctly appealing to multiethnic working-class people were precisely the features that elites tended to fear most.

95. I credit Michael Widener for his insight into the resonance of Pentecostalism among working-class communities during the early twentieth century. Conversation with Michael Widener, June 19, 2013.

96. Gordon MacGregor, "Report of the Pit River Indians of California," Office on Indian Affairs, Applied Anthropology Unit, 1936, http://faculty.humanities.uci.edu/tcthorne/Historyskills/Dr_%20Gordon%20Macgregor%20Pit%20River.htm.

97. MacGregor, "Report of the Pit River Indians of California."

98. Foster, "Summary of Yuki Culture," 219.

99. As Kent G. Lightfoot has underscored, this was an old practice that dated back to earlier stages of Spanish missionary colonialism. Lightfoot, *Indians, Missionaries, and Merchants*, 183.

100. Foster, "Summary of Yuki Culture," 219–220; and L. L. Loofbouroe to the Commissioner of Indian Affairs, February 20, 1930, box 1, folder: "NARA, Box 173: Churches," Bauer Research Files.

101. Foster, "Summary of Yuki Culture," 219.

102. Conversation with Michael Widener, June 19, 2013.

103. Foster, "Summary of Yuki Culture," 220.

104. Foster, "Summary of Yuki Culture," 220.

105. Foster, "Summary of Yuki Culture," 221.

106. Foster, "Summary of Yuki Culture," 220.

107. Foster, "Summary of Yuki Culture," 222.

108. Foster, "Summary of Yuki Culture," 221.

109. Maggie Dorman, quoted in Foster, "Summary of Yuki Culture," 221.

110. Willits, oral history, 8–10.

111. Pomo Mother's Club [elsewhere also called Pomo Women's Club] Constitution and By-Laws, n.d., box 1, folder: "National Archives and Records Administration—San Bruno, CA, RG 75, Sacramento Area Office, Coded Records, 1910–1958, Box 25: Pomo Women's Club, 1943," Bauer Research Files.

112. Willits, oral history, 10.

113. Willits, oral history, 10.

114. Regarding the rethinking of revolution, freedom, and democracy articulated here, see John Holloway, *Change the World without Taking Power* (New York: Pluto, 2010), 218–19, 224–25.

CONCLUSION

1. Carlos Bulosan, "My California," n.d., vertical file, 1534, Carlos Bulosan Papers, Accession No. 0581-010, Special Collections, University of Washington Libraries.

2. Lorena Hickok to Harry Hopkins, July 1, 1934, 1, box 11, folder: "Lorena Hickok reports to Harry Hopkins, May through August 1934," Lorena Hickok Papers, Accession No. MS 59-2, Franklin D. Roosevelt Library Archives, Hyde Park, NY.

3. Lorena Hickok to Aubrey Williams, August 15, 1934, 2, 5, box 11, folder: "Lorena Hickok reports to Harry Hopkins, May through August 1934," Lorena Hickok Papers.

4. Lorena Hickok to Harry Hopkins, July 1, 1934, 9. Also regarding California's resistance to New Deal order, see Richard Lowitt, *The New Deal and the West* (Bloomington: Indiana University Press, 1984).

5. Murray Reed Benedict, "The Problem of Balance between Agriculture and Industry," presentation at Social Science Research Conference, San Francisco, CA, June 15–17, 1932, transcription in "Notes Social Science Research Conference," carton 7, folder 11, Murray Reed Benedict Papers, BANC MSS 2009/109, Bancroft Library, University of California, Berkeley; Carl F. Kraenzel, "Sociological Phases of the Farm Labor Problem," *Proceedings of the Annual Meeting (Western Farm Economics Association)* 10 (June 24, 25, and 26, 1937): 100; George B. Herington, "Discussion of Dr. Paul

S. Taylor's Paper Entitled 'The Place of Farm Labor in Society,'" *Proceedings of the Annual Meeting (Western Farm Economics Association)* 12 (June 14, 15, and 16, 1939): 95. See also, for example, Walter U. Furhiman, "Discussion: Farm Labor," *Proceedings of the Annual Meeting (Western Farm Economics Association)* 10 (June 24, 25, and 26, 1937): 90–92; Paul S. Taylor, "Migratory Farm Labor in the United States," *Monthly Labor Review* 44, no. 3 (March 1937): 537–54; Maynard C. Krueger, "Economic and Political Radicalism," *American Journal of Sociology* 40, no. 6 (May 1935): 764–71; Ella Winter, "What Next in California?" *Pacific Affairs* 8, no. 1 (March 1935): 86–89; Paul S. Taylor, "Putting the Unemployed at Productive Labor," *The Annals of the American Academy of Political and Social Science* 176 (November 1934): 104–10.

6. Herington, "Discussion of Dr. Paul S. Taylor's Paper," 95; Kraenzel, "Sociological Phases of the Farm Labor Problem," 101.

7. Carole Shammas, "A New Look at Long-Term Trends in Wealth Inequality in the United States," *American Historical Review* 98, no. 2 (April 1993): 412–31.

8. Ira Katznelson, *When Affirmative Action Was White: An Untold History of Racial Inequality in Twentieth-Century America* (New York: W. W. Norton, 2005), chap. 2; George Lipsitz, *The Possessive Investment in Whiteness: How White People Profit from Identity Politics* (Philadelphia: Temple University Press, 2006); George Lipsitz, *American Studies in a Moment of Danger* (Minneapolis: University of Minnesota Press, 2001), 49; and Michael Brown, *Race, Money, and the American Welfare State* (Ithaca, NY: Cornell University Press, 1999).

9. Stan Weir, *Singlejack Solidarity* (Minneapolis: University of Minnesota Press, 2004), 285–86. Also see Nelson Lichtenstein, *Labor's War at Home: The CIO in World War II* (Philadelphia: Temple University Press, 2003).

10. George Lipsitz, "The Struggle for Hegemony," *Journal of American History* 75, no. 1 (June 1988): 148–49.

11. Larry Isaac, "Movement of Movements: Culture Moves in the Long Civil Rights Struggle," *Social Forces* 87, no. 1 (September 2008): 36, 47.

12. These epistemologies would play a significant role in animating multiracialist and internationalist movements in general and the initiatives of Third World studies in particular during the 1960s, which Gary Y. Okihiro chronicles in *Third World Studies: Theorizing Liberation* (Durham, NC: Duke University Press, 2016). Also regarding relational and multiracial movements, see Luis Alvarez, "From Zoot Suits to Hip Hop: Towards a Relational Chicana/o Studies," *Latino Studies* 5 (2007): 53–75; Luis Alvarez, *The Power of the Zoot: Youth Culture and Resistance during World War II* (Berkeley: University of California Press, 2008); Daniel Widener, "Another City Is Possible: Interethnic Organizing in Contemporary Los Angeles," *Race/Ethnicity: Multidisciplinary Global Contexts* 1, no. 2 (Spring 2008): 189–219; Daniel Widener, *Black Arts West: Culture and Struggle in Postwar Los Angeles* (Durham, NC: Duke University Press, 2010); Daniel Widener, "'Perhaps the Japanese Are to Be Thanked?' Asia, Asian Americans, and the Construction of Black California," *Positions: East Asia Cultures Critique* 11, no. 1 (2003): 135–81; Gaye Theresa Johnson, *Spaces of Conflict, Sounds of Solidarity: Music, Race, and Spatial Entitlement in Los Angeles* (Berkeley: University of California Press, 2013); Dayo F. Gore, *Radicalism at the Crossroads: African American Women*

Activists in the Cold War (New York: New York University Press, 2011); Cynthia A. Young, *Soul Power: Culture, Radicalism, and the Making of a U.S. Third World Left* (Durham, NC: Duke University Press, 2006); Laura Pulido, *Black, Brown, Yellow, and Left: Radical Activism in Los Angeles* (Berkeley: University of California Press, 2006); and Rachel Ida Buff, *Against the Deportation Terror: Organizing for Immigrant Rights in the Twentieth Century* (Philadelphia: Temple University Press, 2018).

ARCHIVAL AND MANUSCRIPT COLLECTIONS

Bass, Charlotta. Collection. MSS 002. Southern California Library for Social Studies and Research, Los Angeles.

Bauer, William J., Jr. Research Files. Round Valley Public Library, Covelo, CA.

Benedict, Murray Reed. Papers. BANC MSS 2009/109. Bancroft Library, University of California, Berkeley.

Biographical Document File Collection. Manuscript Collection M024/1. Corona Public Library, Corona, CA.

Borough, Reuben. Papers. Collection 927. Special Collections, Charles E. Young Research Library, University of California, Los Angeles.

Brown, Archie. Collection larc.ms.0087. Accession No. 1992/005. Labor Archives and Research Center, San Francisco State University.

Bulosan, Carlos. Papers. Accession No. 0581-010 and 0581-011. Special Collections, University of Washington Libraries.

California Ephemera Collection. Collection 200. Special Collections, Charles E. Young Research Library, University of California, Los Angeles.

Coast Committee. Case-1934 Records. International Longshoremen's and Warehousemen's Union Archives, San Francisco.

Darcy, Sam. Papers. TAM 124. Tamiment Library and Robert F. Wagner Labor Archives, New York University.

Department of Corrections Records. F3717. California State Archives, Sacramento.

Galarza, Ernesto. Papers. Collection M0224. Department of Special Collections, Stanford University Libraries, Stanford, CA.

Hickok, Lorena. Papers. Accession No. MS 59-2. Franklin D. Roosevelt Library Archives, Hyde Park, NY.

Labor Research Association Records. TAM 129. Tamiment Library and Robert F. Wagner Labor Archives, New York University.

Lewis, William J. Collection. Accession No. 1997/021. Labor Archives and Research Center, San Francisco State University.

Library of Social History Collection. Collection 91004. Hoover Institution Archives, Stanford University.

McWilliams, Carey. Papers, 1894–1982. Collection 1319. Special Collections, Charles E. Young Research Library, University of California, Los Angeles.

McWilliams, Carey. Papers, Card Files, 1930–1940. Collection 1243. Special Collections, Charles E. Young Research Library, University of California, Los Angeles.

Miller, Loren. Papers. mssMiller Papers. Huntington Library, San Marino, CA.

Monographs Prepared for a Documentary History of Migratory Farm Labor, 1938, Federal Writers' Project. BANC MSS 72/187c. Bancroft Library, University of California, Berkeley.

Mosk, Ed. Papers. Collection MS 049. Southern California Library for Social Studies and Research, Los Angeles.

Park, Marlene, and Gerald Markowitz New Deal Art Research Collection. Accession No. 00-11. Franklin D. Roosevelt Library Archives, Hyde Park, NY.

Pittman, John. Papers. TAM 188. Tamiment Library and Robert F. Wagner Labor Archives, New York University.

Ramsland, Margaret A. "The Forgotten Californians," Chico, CA, 1974. Bancroft Library, University of California, Berkeley.

"Round Valley Indians" folder. Mendocino County Historical Society, Ukiah, CA.

San Francisco Waterfront Strikes Scrapbooks, 1934–1948. Vols. 1–3. BANC MSS 2004/187c. Bancroft Library, University of California, Berkeley.

Taylor, Paul Schuster. Papers. BANC MSS 84/38c. Bancroft Library, University of California, Berkeley.

Weintraub, Hyman, and William Goldberg Papers. Collection 831. Special Collections, Charles E. Young Research Library, University of California, Los Angeles.

Works Progress Administration (WPA) Folk Music Project. Music Library, University of California, Berkeley.

Yoneda, Elaine Black. Collection. Accession Nos. 1992/033 and 1992/055. Labor Archives and Research Center, San Francisco State University.

Yoneda, Karl G. Papers. Collection 1592. Special Collections, Charles E. Young Research Library, University of California, Los Angeles.

ORAL HISTORY INTERVIEWS

Bridges, Harry. "Harry Bridges: An Oral History about Longshoring." Edited by Harvey Schwartz. July 27, 2004. International Longshoremen's and Warehousemen's Union (ILWU) Oral History Collection. ILWU Archives, San Francisco. http://www.ilwu.org/?page_id=2616.

Cayton, Revels. Oral history. BBC interview, July 1975. Richard S. Hobbs Oral History Interviews with Revels Cayton. Accession No. 5483-001. University of Washington Libraries.

Central Avenue Sounds, Oral History Program, Special Collections, Charles E. Young
Research Library, University of California, Los Angeles.
Bryant, Clora. Interview by Steven L. Isoardi, March–April 1990.
Collette, Buddy. Interview by Steven L. Isoardi, August 1989–January 1990.
Douglass, William. Interview by Steven L. Isoardi, February–March 1990.
Hurte, Leroy. Interview by Steven L. Isoardi, July 1995.
Kelso, Jackie. Interview by Steven L. Isoardi, March–May 1990.
Ortega, Anthony. Interview by Steven L. Isoardi, September–November 1994.
Clifton, Florence McChesney. "California Democrats, 1934–1950." Oral history. Inter-
view by Amelia R. Fry, August 9, 1972. California Democrats in the Earl Warren Era,
Earl Warren Oral History Project. Regional Oral History Office, Bancroft Library,
University of California, Berkeley.
Clifton, Robert. "The Democratic Party, Culbert L. Olson, and the Legislature." Oral
history. Interview by Amelia R. Fry, October 6, 1972. California Democrats in the
Earl Warren Era, Earl Warren Oral History Project. Regional Oral History Office,
Bancroft Library, University of California, Berkeley.
Combined Asian American Resources Project Interviews. BANC MSS 80/31c. Bancroft
Library, University of California, Berkeley.
Lee, Jane.
Loo, Chalsa.
Low, Frances and Howard.
Low, May and Edwin.
Hawkins, Augustus F. Oral history. Interview by Carlos Vásquez, January 15, Decem-
ber 10 and 12, 1988. UCLA Oral History Program, for the California State Archives
State Government Oral History Program. Special Collections, Charles E. Young
Research Library, University of California, Los Angeles.
Lehman, Harry. Oral history. March 28, 1997. Archives of American Art, Smithson-
ian Institution, Washington, DC. http://www.aaa.si.edu/collections/interviews/oral
-history-interview-harold-lehman-12894.
McWilliams, Carey. "Honorable in All Things Oral History Transcript: The Memoirs
of Carey McWilliams." Interview by Joel R. Gardner, July 10–19, 1978. Collection
300/195. Special Collections, Charles E. Young Research Library, University of
California, Los Angeles.
"Oral Histories of Workers in California Agriculture: The 1930s." Labor Archives and
Research Center, San Francisco State University.
Luz, Manuel. Interview by Joan L. Zoloth, November 1976.
Maneze, Frank. Interview by Joan L. Zoloth, November 1976.
"Oral History Project: African Americans in San Francisco Prior to 1945." San Fran-
cisco Public Library.
Alley, Edward. Interview by Jesse J. Warr, September 19, 1978.
Finis, Kenneth. Interview by Jesse J. Warr, June 7, 1978.
Scott, Lora Toombs. Interview by Jesse J. Warr, August–November 1978.
Round Valley Oral History Project. Round Valley Public Library, Covelo, CA.
Duncan, Agnes, and Joe Happy. Interview by Les Lincoln, June 22, 1990.

Figueroa, Adaline. Interview by Les Lincoln, April 18, 1990.

Fulwider, Leland, Jr. Interview by Acklan Willits, April 23, 1990.

Lincoln, Doran. Interview by Acklan Willits, April 25, 1990.

Soares, Ida Mary Willits. Interview by Acklan Willits, April 10, 1990.

Want, Armstead. Interview by Acklan Willits, May 5, 1990.

Willits, Elizabeth Lenore. Interview by Acklan Willits, November 11, 1990.

Sánchez, John. Oral history. Interview by Harvey Schwartz, March 31, 1998. Labor Archives and Research Center, San Francisco State University.

Tosti, Don. Oral history. Interview by Anthony Macias, August 20, 1998. Don Tosti Papers. California Ethnic and Multicultural Archives (CEMA) 88. Department of Special Collections, University Libraries, University of California, Santa Barbara.

Watkins, Earl T. Oral history: "Earl T. Watkins: Jazz Drummer and Union Official." Interview by Caroline Crawford, 2003. Regional Oral History Office, Bancroft Library, University of California, Berkeley.

PERIODICALS

American Democracy of California

California Eagle

Chicago Tribune

Collier's

Corona Courier

Daily Worker

EPIC News

Hispano América (San Francisco)

Illustrated Daily News

El Imparcial (San Francisco)

Independent Review

Los Angeles Evening Herald Express

Los Angeles Sentinel

Los Angeles Times

New York Times

La Opinión

Redwood Journal

Rodo Shimbun-Labor News

Sacramento Bee

San Bernardino County Sun

San Francisco Business

San Francisco Chronicle

San Francisco Spokesman

San Francisco Sun-Reporter

Waterfront Striker

Waterfront Worker

Western Worker

Willits News

PUBLISHED MATERIALS

Acuña, Rodolfo. *Occupied America: The Chicano's Struggle toward Liberation*. 1st ed. San Francisco: Canfield, 1972.

Allen, Theodore W. *The Invention of the White Race*. Vol. 1, *Racial Oppression and Social Control*. New York: Verso, 2012.

Allen, Theodore W. *The Invention of the White Race*. Vol. 2, *The Origin of Racial Oppression in Anglo-America*. New York: Verso, 2012.

Almaguer, Tomás. *Racial Fault Lines: The Historical Origins of White Supremacy in California*. Berkeley: University of California Press, 1994.

Alvarez, Luis. "From Zoot Suits to Hip Hop: Towards a Relational Chicana/o Studies." *Latino Studies* 5 (2007): 53–75.

Alvarez, Luis. *The Power of the Zoot: Youth Culture and Resistance during World War II*. Berkeley: University of California Press, 2008.

Alvarez, Luis. "Reggae Rhythms in Dignity's Diaspora: Globalization, Indigenous Identity, and the Circulation of Cultural Struggle." *Popular Music and Society* 31, no. 5 (December 2008): 575–97.

Anderson, Allan H. *To the Ends of the Earth: Pentecostalism and the Transformation of World Christianity*. Oxford: Oxford University Press, 2013.

Andrés, Benny J., Jr. "Invisible Borders: Repatriation and Colonization of Mexican Migrant Workers along the California Borderlands during the 1930s." *California History* 88, no. 4 (2011): 5–21.

Andrés, Benny J., Jr. *Power and Control in the Imperial Valley: Nature, Agribusiness, and Workers on the California Borderland, 1900–1940*. College Station: Texas A&M University Press, 2015.

Back, Les. "X Amount of Sat Siri Akal! Apache Indian, Reggae Music, and Intermezzo Culture." In *Negotiating Identities: Essays on Immigration and Culture in Present-Day Europe*, edited by Aleksandra Alund and Raoul Granqvist, 139–66. Amsterdam: Rodopi, 1995.

Balderrama, Francisco E., and Raymond Rodríguez. *Decade of Betrayal: Mexican Repatriation in the 1930s*. Rev. ed. Albuquerque: University of New Mexico Press, 2006.

Baldoz, Rick. *The Third Asiatic Invasion: Migration and Empire in Filipino America, 1898–1946*. New York: New York University Press, 2011.

Balthasar, Benjamin. *Anti-imperialist Modernism: Race and Transnational Radical Culture from the Great Depression to the Cold War*. Ann Arbor: University of Michigan Press, 2016.

Barrera, Mario. *Race and Class in the Southwest: A Theory of Racial Inequality*. Notre Dame, IN: University of Notre Dame Press, 1979.

Barrett, James R. *History from the Bottom Up and the Inside Out: Ethnicity, Race, and Identity in Working-Class History*. Durham, NC: Duke University Press, 2017.

Barron, Stephanie, Ilene Fort, and Sheri Bernstein. *Made in California: Art, Image, and Identity, 1900–2000*. Berkeley: University of California Press, 2000.

Bauer, William J., Jr. *California through Native Eyes: Reclaiming History*. Seattle: University of Washington Press, 2016.

Bauer, William J., Jr. *We Were All like Migrant Workers Here: Work, Community, and Memory on California's Round Valley Reservation, 1850–1941*. Chapel Hill: University of North Carolina Press, 2009.

Baumgardner, Frank H. *Killing for Land in Early California: Indian Blood at Round Valley*. New York: Algora, 2005.

Benton-Cohen, Katherine. *Borderline Americans: Racial Division and Labor War in the Arizona Borderlands*. Cambridge, MA: Harvard University Press, 2009.

Benton-Cohen, Katherine. *Inventing the Immigration Problem: The Dillingham Commission and Its Legacy*. Cambridge, MA: Harvard University Press, 2018.

Bernstein, Irving. *The Turbulent Years: A History of the American Worker, 1933–1941*. Chicago: Haymarket Books, 1969.

Bernstein, Shana. *Bridges of Reform: Interracial Civil Rights Activism in Twentieth-Century Los Angeles*. New York: Oxford University Press, 2010.

Biolsi, Thomas. "'Indian Self-Government' as a Technique of Domination." *American Indian Quarterly* 15, no. 1 (Winter 1991): 23–28.

Blake, Fay M., and H. Morton Newman. "Upton Sinclair's Epic Campaign." *California History* 63, no. 4 (Fall 1984): 305–12.

Bloch, Louis. "Report on the Strike of the Imperial Valley Cantaloupe Pickers." In *Mexicans in California: Report of Governor C. C. Young's Mexican Fact-Finding Committee*, directed by Will J. French, G. H. Hecke, and Anna L. Saylor, 135–47. San Francisco: California State Printing Office, 1930.

Bredrenner, Candice Lewis. *A Nationality of Her Own: Women, Marriage, and the Law of Citizenship*. Berkeley: University of California Press, 1998.

Broussard, Albert S. *Black San Francisco: The Struggle for Racial Equality in the West, 1900–1954*. Lawrence: University of Kansas Press, 1993.

Brown, Elsa Barkley. "Negotiating and Transforming the Public Sphere: African American Political Life in the Transition from Slavery to Freedom." *Public Culture* 7 (1994): 107–46.

Brown, Michael. *Race, Money, and the American Welfare State*. Ithaca, NY: Cornell University Press, 1999.

Buff, Rachel Ida. *Against the Deportation Terror: Organizing for Immigrant Rights in the Twentieth Century*. Philadelphia: Temple University Press, 2018.

Buhle, Paul. *Marxism in the United States: A History of the American Left*. New York: Verso, 2013.

Bulosan, Carlos. *America Is in the Heart*. Seattle: University of Washington Press, 2014.

Burke, Robert E. *Olson's New Deal in California*. Berkeley: University of California Press, 1953.

California Secretary of State. *Statement of Vote in General Election on November 6, 1934*. Sacramento: State Printing Office, 1934.

Camacho, Alicia Schmidt. *Migrant Imaginaries: Latino Cultural Politics in the U.S.-Mexico Borderlands*. New York: New York University Press, 2008.

Carranco, Lynwood, and Estle Beard. *Genocide and Vendetta: The Round Valley Wars of Northern California*. Norman: University of Oklahoma Press, 1981.

Cassano, Graham. "Working Class Self Fashioning in *Swing Time* (1936)." *Critical Sociology* 40, no. 3 (May 2014): 329–47.

Chan, Loren B. "California during the Early 1930s: The Administration of James Rolph, Jr., 1931–1934." *Southern California Quarterly* 63, no. 3 (1981): 262–82.

Chen, Yong. *Chinese San Francisco, 1850–1943: A Trans-Pacific Community*. Stanford, CA: Stanford University Press, 2000.

Cherny, Robert W. "Prelude to the Popular Front: The Communist Party in California, 1931–35." *American Communist History* 1, no. 1 (2002): 5–42.

Cherny, Robert W., Gretchen Lemke-Santangelo, and Richard Griswold del Castillo. *Competing Visions: A History of California*. Boston: Houghton Mifflin, 2005.

Clark, Clinton. *Remember My Sacrifice: The Autobiography of Clinton Clark, Tenant Farm Organizer and Early Civil Rights Activist*. Baton Rouge: Louisiana State University Press, 2007.

Cohen, Lizabeth. *Making a New Deal: Industrial Workers in Chicago, 1919–1939*. Cambridge: Cambridge University Press, 1991.

Cook, Sherburne. *The Conflict between the California Indian and White Civilization*. Berkeley: University of California Press, 1976.

Cowie, Jefferson. *The Great Exception: The New Deal and the Limits of American Politics*. Princeton, NJ: Princeton University Press, 2016.

Cowie, Jefferson, and Nick Salvatore. "The Long Exception: Rethinking the Place of the New Deal in American History." *International Labor and Working-Class History* 74 (Fall 2008): 3–32.

Creel, George. *Rebel at Large: Recollections of Fifty Crowded Years*. New York: Putnam, 1947.

Daniel, Cletus E. *Bitter Harvest: A History of California Farmworkers, 1870–1941*. Berkeley: University of California Press, 1982.

Daniels, Douglas Henry. *Pioneer Urbanites: A Social and Cultural History of Black San Francisco*. Berkeley: University of California Press, 1991.

David, Paul A., and Gavin Wright. "Increasing Returns and the Genesis of American Resource Abundance." *Industrial and Corporate Change* 6, no. 2 (1997): 203–45.

Davis, Mike. *City of Quartz: Excavating the Future in Los Angeles*. New York: Vintage Books, 1992.

Davis, Mike. *Late Victorian Holocausts: El Niño Famines and the Making of the Third World*. New York: Verso, 2001.

Davis, Mike. "Sunshine and the Open Shop: Ford and Darwin in 1920s Los Angeles." In *Metropolis in the Making: Los Angeles in the 1920s*, edited by Tom Sitton and William Deverell, 96–122. Berkeley: University of California Press, 2001.

Deloria, Vine, Jr. and Clifford Lytle. *The Nations Within: The Past and Future of American Indian Sovereignty*. New York: Pantheon Books, 1984.

Denning, Michael. *The Cultural Front: The Laboring of American Culture in the Twentieth Century*. New York: Verso, 1996.

Deverell, William. *Whitewashed Adobe: The Rise of Los Angeles and the Remaking of Its Mexican Past*. Berkeley: University of California Press, 2004.

Draper, Theodore. *The Roots of American Communism*. New York: Viking, 1957.

Du Bois, W. E. B. *Black Reconstruction in America, 1860–1880*. 1935. New York: Free Press, 1992.

Du Bois, W. E. B. "The Color Line Belts the World." In *W. E. B. Du Bois: A Reader*, edited by David Levering Lewis, 42–43. New York: Henry Holt, 1995. Originally published in *Collier's Weekly*, October 20, 1906.

Edwards, Brent Hayes. *The Practice of Diaspora: Literature, Translation, and the Rise of Black Internationalism*. Cambridge, MA: Harvard University Press, 2003.

Edwards, Brent Hayes. "Shadow of Shadows." *Positions: East Asia Cultures Critique* 11, no. 1 (2003): 11–49.

Eley, Geoff. *Forging Democracy: The History of the Left in Europe, 1850–2000*. Oxford: Oxford University Press, 2000.

Ellison, Ralph. "Harlem Is Nowhere." *Harper's Magazine*, August 1964, 53–57.

Enciso, Fernando Saúl Alanís. *They Should Stay There: The Story of Mexican Migration and Repatriation during the Great Depression*. Translated by Russ Davidson. Chapel Hill: University of North Carolina Press, 2017.

Enstad, Nan. *Ladies of Labor, Girls of Adventure: Working Women, Popular Culture, and Labor Politics at the Turn of the Twentieth Century*. New York: Columbia University Press, 1999.

Espiritu, Yen Le. *Home Bound: Filipino American Lives across Cultures, Communities, and Countries*. Berkeley: University of California Press, 2003.

Essene, Frank. "Cultural Elements Distribution: XXI Round Valley." *Anthropological Records* 8 (1945): 1–144.

Faue, Elizabeth. *Community of Suffering and Struggle: Women, Men, and the Labor Movement in Minneapolis, 1915–1945*. Chapel Hill: University of North Carolina Press, 1991.

Federal Writers' Project of the Works Progress Administration. *Los Angeles in the 1930s: The WPA Guide to the City of Angels*. Berkeley: University of California Press, 2011.

Fekete, Liz. "The Emergence of Xeno-Racism." *Race and Class* 43, no. 2 (2001): 23–40.

Fellezs, Kevin. "Silenced but Not Silent: Asian Americans and Jazz." In *Alien Encounters: Popular Culture in Asian America*, edited by Mimi Thi Nguyen and Thuy Linh Nguyen Tu, 69–110. Durham, NC: Duke University Press, 2007.

Fischlin, Daniel, Ajay Heble, and George Lipsitz. *The Fierce Urgency of Now: Improvisation, Rights, and the Ethics of Cocreation*. Durham, NC: Duke University Press, 2013.

Flamming, Douglas. *Bound for Freedom: Black Los Angeles in Jim Crow America*. Berkeley: University of California Press, 2005.

Flores, Juan. "Reclaiming Left Baggage: Some Early Sources for Minority Studies." *Cultural Critique* 59 (Winter 2005): 187–206.

Foster, George. "Summary of Yuki Culture." *University of California Publications in Anthropological Records* 5 (1900–1947): 155–244.

Foucault, Michel. *"Society Must Be Defended": Lectures at the Collège de France, 1975–76*. Translated by David Macey. New York: Picador, 2003.

Fowler, Josephine. *Japanese and Chinese Immigrant Activists: Organizing in American and International Communist Movements, 1919–1933*. New Brunswick, NJ: Rutgers University Press, 2007.

Fraser, Steve, and Gary Gerstle, eds. *The Rise and Fall of the New Deal Order, 1930–1980*. Princeton, NJ: Princeton University Press, 1989.

French, Will J., G. H. Hecke, and Anna L. Saylor, dirs. *Mexicans in California: Report of Governor C. C. Young's Mexican Fact-Finding Committee*. San Francisco: California State Printing Office, 1930.

Furhiman, Walter U. "Discussion: Farm Labor." *Proceedings of the Annual Meeting (Western Farm Economics Association)* 10 (June 24, 25, and 26, 1937): 90–92.

Garza, Melita M. *They Came to Toil: Newspaper Representations of Mexicans and Immigrants in the Great Depression*. Austin: University of Texas Press, 2018.

Gascoyne, David. *A Short Survey of Surrealism*. San Francisco: City Lights, 1982.

Gerstle, Gary. *Working-Class Americanism: The Politics of Labor in a Textile City, 1914–1960*. New York: Cambridge University Press, 1989.

Gilroy, Paul. *Small Acts: Thoughts on the Politics of Black Cultures*. New York: Serpent's Tail, 1993.

Godfrey, Brian J. *Neighborhoods in Transition: The Making of San Francisco's Ethnic and Nonconformist Communities*. Berkeley: University of California Press, 1988.

Godfrey, Brian J. "Urban Development and Redevelopment in San Francisco." *Geographical Review* 87, no. 3 (July 1997): 310–33.

González, Gilbert G. "Company Unions, the Mexican Consulate, and the Imperial Valley Agricultural Strikes, 1928–1934." *Western Historical Quarterly* 27, no. 1 (Spring 1996): 53–73.

González, Gilbert, and Raúl Fernández. *A Century in Chicano History: Empire, Nations, and Migration*. New York: Routledge, 2003.

Gonzales-Day, Ken. *Lynching in the West, 1850–1935*. Durham, NC: Duke University Press, 2006.

Gore, Dayo F. *Radicalism at the Crossroads: African American Women Activists in the Cold War*. New York: New York University Press, 2011.

Graeber, David. "The New Anarchists." *New Left Review* 13 (January–February 2002): 61–73.

Gramsci, Antonio. *Selections from the Prison Notebooks*. Edited by Quintin Hoare and Geoffrey Nowell Smith. New York: International Publishers, 1971.

Gregory, James N. *American Exodus: The Dust Bowl Migration and Okie Culture in California*. New York: Oxford University Press, 1989.

Gregory, James N. "Upton Sinclair's 1934 EPIC Campaign: Anatomy of a Political Movement." *Labor: Studies in Working-Class History of the Americas* 12, no. 4 (December 2015): 51–81.

Gregory, James N. "The West and Workers, 1870–1930." In *A Companion to the American West*, edited by William Deverell, 240–55. Malden, MA: Blackwell, 2004.

Grieve, Victoria. *The Federal Art Project and the Creation of Middlebrow Culture*. Urbana: University of Illinois Press, 2009.

Grindon, Gavin. "Surrealism, Dada, and the Refusal of Work: Autonomy, Activism, and Social Participation in the Radical Avant-Garde." *Oxford Art Journal*, 34, no. 1 (2011): 79–96.

Guevarra, Rudy P., Jr. *Becoming Mexipino: Multiethnic Identities and Communities in San Diego*. New Brunswick, NJ: Rutgers University Press, 2012.

Guevarra, Rudy P., Jr. "Mabuhay Compañero: Filipinos, Mexicans, and Labor Organizing in Hawai'i and California, 1920s–1940s." In *Transnational Crossroads: Remapping the Americas and the Pacific*, edited by Camilla Fojas and Rudy P. Guevarra Jr., 171–97. Lincoln: University of Nebraska Press, 2012.

Guglielmo, Jennifer. *Living the Revolution: Italian Women's Resistance and Revolution in New York City*. Chapel Hill: University of North Carolina Press, 2012.

Gutiérrez, David G. *Walls and Mirrors: Mexican Americans, Mexican Immigrants, and the Politics of Ethnicity*. Berkeley: University of California Press, 1995.

Guzmán, Romeo. "'My Dear Sir Mr. President': Repatriates, the Great Depression, and the Right to Return." Unpublished manuscript, June 2020.

Guzmán, Romeo. "The Transnational Life and Letters of the Venegas Family, 1920s to 1950s." *History of the Family* 21, no. 3 (June 2016): 457–82.

Haas, Lizbeth. *Conquests and Historical Identities in California, 1769–1936*. Berkeley: University of California Press, 1996.

Hahn, Steven. *A Nation under Our Feet: Black Political Struggles in the Rural South from Slavery to the Great Migration*. Cambridge, MA: Belknap Press of Harvard University Press, 2003.

Hairston, Monica. "Gender, Jazz, and the Popular Front." In *Big Ears: Listening for Gender in Jazz Studies*, edited by Nicole Rustin and Sherrie Tucker, 64–89. Durham, NC: Duke University Press, 2008.

Halberstam, Judith. *In a Queer Time and Place: Transgender Bodies, Subcultural Lives*. New York: New York University Press, 2005.

Hall, Linda B., and Don M. Coerver. *Revolution on the Border: The United States and Mexico, 1910–1920*. Albuquerque: University of New Mexico Press, 1988.

Hall, Stuart. "Notes on Deconstructing 'the Popular.'" In *Cultural Resistance Reader*, edited by Stephen Duncombe, 185–92. New York: Verso, 2002.

Hall, Stuart, and Tony Jefferson, eds. *Resistance through Rituals: Youth Sub-cultures in Post-war Britain*. London: Hutchinson, 1976.

Hall, Wilbur J. "Just like Dixie Land." *Sunset* 24, no. 2 (1910): 173–75.

Harris, Cheryl I. "Whiteness as Property." *Harvard Law Review* 106, no. 8 (June 1993): 1709–91.

Heatherton, Christina. "The Color Line and the Class Struggle: The Mexican Revolution and Convergences of Radical Internationalism, 1910–1946." PhD diss., University of Southern California, 2012.

Heatherton, Christina. "Relief and Revolution: Southern California Struggles against Unemployment in the 1930s." In *The Rising Tide of Color: Race, State Violence, and Radical Movements across the Pacific*, edited by Moon Ho Jung, 159–87. Seattle: University of Washington Press, 2014.

Heatherton, Christina. "The University of Radicalism: Ricardo Flores Magón and Leavenworth Penitentiary." *American Quarterly* 66, no. 3 (September 2014): 557–81.

Hebdige, Dick. *Subculture: The Meaning of Style*. New York: Routledge, 1994.

Hemingway, Andrew. *Artists on the Left: American Artists and the Communist Movement, 1926–1956.* New Haven, CT: Yale University Press, 2002.

Herington, George B. "Discussion of Dr. Paul S. Taylor's Paper Entitled 'The Place of Farm Labor in Society.'" *Proceedings of the Annual Meeting (Western Farm Economics Association)* 12 (June 14, 15, and 16, 1939): 91–95.

Hernández, Kelly Lytle. *Migra! A History of the U.S. Border Patrol.* Berkeley: University of California Press, 2010.

Hoffman, Abraham. *Unwanted Mexican Americans in the Great Depression: Repatriation Pressures, 1929–1939.* Tucson: University of Arizona Press, 1974.

Holloway, John. *Change the World without Taking Power.* New York: Pluto, 2010.

Holloway, John. *Crack Capitalism.* London: Pluto, 2010.

Holloway, John, and Eloína Peláez, eds. *Zapatista! Reinventing Revolution in Mexico.* London: Pluto, 1998.

Honey, Michael K. *Southern Labor and Black Civil Rights: Organizing Memphis Workers, Working Class in American History.* Urbana: University of Illinois Press, 1993.

Horne, Gerald. *Communist Front? The Civil Rights Congress, 1946–1956.* Rutherford, NJ: Fairleigh Dickinson University Press, 1988.

Horsman, Reginald. *Race and Manifest Destiny: The Origins of American Racial Anglo-Saxonism.* Cambridge, MA: Harvard University Press, 1981.

Hurewitz, Daniel. *Bohemian Los Angeles and the Making of Modern Politics.* Berkeley: University of California Press, 2007.

Hurlburt, Laurance P. *The Mexican Muralists in the United States.* Albuquerque: University of New Mexico Press, 1989.

Hurtado, Albert L. *Indian Survival on the California Frontier.* New Haven, CT: Yale University Press, 1988.

Isaac, Larry. "Movement of Movements: Culture Moves in the Long Civil Rights Struggle." *Social Forces* 87, no. 1 (September 2008): 33–63.

Issel, William. "'Citizens outside Government': Business and Urban Policy in San Francisco and Los Angeles, 1890–1932." *Pacific Historical Review* 57, no. 2 (May 1988): 117–45.

Issel, William, and Robert W. Cherny. *San Francisco, 1865–1932: Politics, Power, and Urban Development.* Berkeley: University of California Press, 1986.

Isserman, Maurice. "Notes from Underground." *Nation* 260, no. 23 (June 12, 1995): 846–56.

Jacobson, Matthew Frye. *Whiteness of a Different Color: European Immigrants and the Alchemy of Race.* Cambridge, MA: Harvard University Press, 1999.

James, C. L. R. "Walter Rodney and the Question of Power." Lecture originally presented at "Walter Rodney, Revolutionary and Scholar" memorial symposium, University of California, January 30, 1981. Published by Race Today Collective. Montreal: Blackrose, 1982.

Jamieson, Stuart. *Labor Unionism in California Agriculture.* Washington, DC: U.S. Government Printing Office, 1945.

Johnson, Gaye Theresa. *Spaces of Conflict, Sounds of Solidarity: Music, Race, and Spatial Entitlement in Los Angeles.* Berkeley: University of California Press, 2013.

Jones, LeRoi. *Blues People: Negro Music in White America*. 1963. Reprint, New York: Harper Perennial, 1999.

Jung, Moon-Kie. *Reworking Race: The Making of Hawaii's Interracial Labor Movement*. New York: Columbia University Press, 2010.

Kahn, Judd. *Imperial San Francisco: Politics and Planning in an American City, 1897–1906*. Lincoln: University of Nebraska Press, 1979.

Karlstron, Paul, ed. *On the Edge of America: California Modernist Art, 1900–1950*. Berkeley: University of California Press, 1996.

Katznelson, Ira. *Fear Itself: The New Deal and the Origins of Our Time*. New York: W. W. Norton, 2013.

Katznelson, Ira. *When Affirmative Action Was White: An Untold History of Racial Inequality in Twentieth-Century America*. New York: W. W. Norton, 2005.

Kay, Lily. *The Molecular Vision of Life: Caltech, the Rockefeller Foundation, and the Rise of the New Biology*. Oxford: Oxford University Press, 1993.

Kazin, Michael. "The Great Exception Revisited: Organizer Labor and Politics in San Francisco and Los Angeles, 1870–1940." *Pacific Historical Review* 55, no. 3 (August 1986): 371–402.

Kelley, Robin D. G. *Freedom Dreams: The Black Radical Imagination*. Boston: Beacon, 2002.

Kelley, Robin D. G. *Hammer and Hoe: Alabama Communists during the Great Depression*. Chapel Hill: University of North Carolina Press, 1990.

Kelley, Robin D. G. *Race Rebels: Culture, Politics, and the Black Working Class*. New York: Free Press, 1996.

Kelley, Robin D. G. *Yo Mama's Dysfunktional! Fighting the Culture Wars in Urban America*. Boston: Beacon, 2008.

Kelly, Lawrence C. "The Indian Reorganization Act: The Dream and the Reality." *Pacific Historical Review* 44, no. 3 (August 1975): 291–312.

Kimeldorf, Howard. *Reds or Rackets? The Making of Radical and Conservative Unions on the Waterfront*. Berkeley: University of California Press, 1988.

Kimmel, Michael. *Manhood in America: A Cultural History*. 3rd ed. Oxford: Oxford University Press, 2011.

Klehr, Harvey. *The Heyday of American Communism: The Depression Decade*. New York: Basic, 1984.

Klehr, Harvey, and John Earl Haynes. *The American Communist Movement: Storming Heaven Itself*. New York: Twayne, 1992.

Kraenzel, Carl F. "Sociological Phases of the Farm Labor Problem." *Proceedings of the Annual Meeting (Western Farm Economics Association)* 10 (June 24, 25, and 26, 1937): 98–101.

Krueger, Maynard C. "Economic and Political Radicalism." *American Journal of Sociology* 40, no. 6 (May 1935): 764–71.

Kun, Josh. *Audiotopia: Music, Race, and America*. Berkeley: University of California Press, 2005.

Kurashige, Lon. *Japanese American Celebration and Conflict: A History of Ethnic Identity and Festival, 1934–1990*. Berkeley: University of California Press, 2002.

Kurashige, Scott. "The Many Facets of Brown: Integration in a Multiracial Society." *Journal of American History* 91, no. 1 (June 2004): 56–68.

Kurashige, Scott. "Organizing from the Margins: Japanese American Communists in Los Angeles during the Great Depression." In *Race Struggles*, edited by Theodore Koditschek, Sundiata Keita Cha-Jua, and Helen A. Neville, 211–30. Urbana: University of Illinois Press, 2009.

LaPier, Rosalyn, and David R. M. Beck. "A 'One Man Relocation Team': Scott Henry Peters and American Indian Urban Migration in the 1930s." *Western Historical Quarterly* 45, no. 1 (Spring 2014): 17–36.

Larrowe, Charles P. *Harry Bridges: The Rise and Fall of Radical Labor in the United States*. New York: Lawrence Hill, 1972.

Lee, Anthony. *Painting on the Left: Diego Rivera, Radical Politics, and San Francisco's Public Murals*. Berkeley: University of California Press, 1999.

Lenin, Vladimir Ilyich. *"Left-Wing" Communism and Infantile Disorder: A Popular Essay in Marxian Strategy and Tactics*. Honolulu: University Press of the Pacific, 2001.

Lenin, Vladimir Ilyich. "What Is to Be Done?" In *Essential Works of Lenin: "What Is to Be Done?" and Other Writings*, edited by Henry Christman, 53–176. New York: Dover, 1987.

Leonard, Karen. *Making Ethnic Choices: California's Punjabi Mexican Americans*. Philadelphia: Temple University Press, 2010.

Lewis, Earl. "To Turn as on a Pivot: Writing African Americans into a History of Overlapping Diasporas." *American Historical Review* 100 (June 1995): 765–87.

Lew-Williams, Beth. "Before Restriction Became Exclusion: America's Experiment in Diplomatic Immigration Control." *Pacific Historical Review* 83, no. 1 (2014): 24–56.

Lichtenstein, Nelson. *Labor's War at Home: The CIO in World War II*. Philadelphia: Temple University Press, 2003.

Lightfoot, Kent G. *Indians, Missionaries, and Merchants: The Legacy of Colonial Encounters on the California Frontiers*. Berkeley: University of California Press, 2005.

Limerick, Patricia. *The Legacy of Conquest: The Unbroken Past of the American West*. New York: W. W. Norton, 1987.

Limón, José. *Mexican Ballads, Chicano Poems: History and Influence in Mexican-American Social Poetry*. Berkeley: University of California Press, 1992.

Lindsay, Brendan C. *Murder State: California's Native American Genocide, 1846–1873*. Lincoln: University of Nebraska Press, 2012.

Lipsitz, George. "Abolition Democracy and Global Justice." *Comparative American Studies* 2, no. 3 (2004): 271–86.

Lipsitz, George. *American Studies in a Moment of Danger*. Minneapolis: University of Minnesota Press, 2001.

Lipsitz, George. "Cruising around the Historical Bloc: Postmodern and Popular Music in East Los Angeles." In *The Subcultures Reader*, edited by Ken Gelder and Sarah Thornton, 350–59. New York: Routledge, 1997.

Lipsitz, George. *Dangerous Crossroads: Popular Music, Postmodernism, and the Poetics of Place*. London: Verso, 1994.

Lipsitz, George. *Footsteps in the Dark: The Hidden Histories of Popular Music*. Minneapolis: University of Minnesota Press, 2007.

Lipsitz, George. *The Possessive Investment in Whiteness: How White People Profit from Identity Politics*. Philadelphia: Temple University Press, 2006.

Lipsitz, George. *Rainbow at Midnight: Labor and Culture in the 1940s*. Urbana: University of Illinois Press, 1994.

Lipsitz, George. "Stan Weir: Working Class Visionary." Afterword to *Singlejack Solidarity*, by Stan Weir. Minneapolis: University of Minnesota Press, 2004.

Lipsitz, George. "The Struggle for Hegemony." *Journal of American History* 75, no. 1 (June 1988): 146–50.

Lipsitz, George. *Time Passages: Collective Memory and American Popular Culture*. Minneapolis: University of Minnesota Press, 1990.

Lobo, Susan, ed. *Urban Voices: The Bay Area American Indian Community*. Tucson: University of Arizona Press, 2002.

Lotchin, Roger W. *The Bad City in the Good War: San Francisco, Los Angeles, Oakland, and San Diego*. Bloomington: Indiana University Press, 2003.

Lotchin, Roger W. "The Darwinian City: The Politics of Urbanization in San Francisco between the World Wars." *Pacific Historical Review* 48, no. 3 (August 1979): 357–81.

Lotchin, Roger W. *Fortress California, 1910–1961*. New York: Oxford University Press, 1992.

Lowe, Lisa. *Immigrant Acts: On Asian American Cultural Politics*. Durham, NC: Duke University Press, 1996.

Lowitt, Richard. *The New Deal and the West*. Bloomington: Indiana University Press, 1984.

Mabalon, Dawn Bohulano. *Little Manila Is in the Heart: The Making of the Filipina/o American Community in Stockton, California*. Durham, NC: Duke University Press, 2013.

MacGregor, Gordon. "Report of the Pit River Indians of California." Office on Indian Affairs, Applied Anthropology Unit, 1936. http://faculty.humanities.uci.edu/tcthorne/Historyskills/Dr_%20Gordon%20Macgregor%20Pit%20River.htm.

Macias, Anthony. *Mexican American Mojo: Popular Music, Dance, and Urban Culture in Los Angeles, 1935–1968*. Durham, NC: Duke University Press, 2008.

MacLean, Nancy. "Getting New Deal History Wrong." *International Labor and Working-Class History* 74 (Fall 2008): 49–55.

Madley, Benjamin. *An American Genocide: The United States and the California Indian Catastrophe*. New Haven, CT: Yale University Press, 2016.

Madley, Benjamin. "California's Yuki Indians: Defining Genocide in Native American History." *Western Historical Quarterly* 39 (Autumn 2008): 303–32.

Martin, Laura Renata. "'California's Unemployed Feed Themselves': Conservative Intervention in the Los Angeles Cooperative Movement, 1931–1934." *Pacific Historical Review* 81, no. 1 (February 2013): 33–62.

Marx, Karl, and Fredrich Engels. "Feuerbach: Opposition of the Materialist and Idealist Outlook." In *The German Ideology: Part I and Selections from Parts II and III*, edited by C. J. Arthur, 39–91. New York: International Publishers, 1970.

Marx, Karl, and Friedrich Engels. *Karl Marx and Frederick Engels: Letters to Americans, 1848–1895.* Translated and edited by Leonard E. Mins. New York: International Publishers, 1953.

May, Lary. *The Big Tomorrow: Hollywood and the Politics of the American Way.* Chicago: University of Chicago Press, 2000.

May, Lary. *Screening Out the Past: The Birth of Mass Culture and the Motion Picture Industry.* Chicago: University of Chicago Press, 1983.

McBroome, Delores Nason. "Harvests of Gold: African American Boosterism, Agriculture and Investment in Allensworth and Little Liberia." In *Seeking El Dorado: African Americans in California,* edited by Lawrence B. de Graaf, Mevin Mulroy, and Quintard Taylor, 149–80. Seattle: University of Washington Press, 2001.

McKeown, Adam. "Global Migration, 1846–1940." *Journal of World History* 15, no. 2 (June 2004): 155–89.

McWilliams, Carey. *California: The Great Exception.* 1949. Westport, CT: Greenwood, 1971.

McWilliams, Carey. *Factories in the Field: The Story of Migratory Farm Labor in California.* 1935. Berkeley: University of California Press, 2000.

McWilliams, Carey. *Southern California: An Island on the Land.* 1946; Salt Lake City: Gibbs Smith, 1973.

Mei, June. "Economic Origins of Emigration: Guangdong to California, 1850–1882." *Modern China* 5, no. 4 (October 1979): 463–501.

Mertes, Tom, ed. *A Movement of Movements: Is Another World Really Possible?* New York: Verso, 2004.

Miller, Virginia. *Ukomno'm: The Yuki Indians of Northern California.* Socorro, NM: Ballena, 1979.

Mitchell, Greg. *The Campaign of the Century: Upton Sinclair's Race for Governor of California and the Birth of Media Politics.* New York: Random House, 1992.

Molina, Natalia. *Fit to Be Citizens? Public Health and Race in Los Angeles, 1879–1939.* Berkeley: University of California Press, 2006.

Molina, Natalia. *How Race Is Made in America: Immigration, Citizenship, and the Historical Power of Racial Scripts.* Berkeley: University of California Press, 2014.

Monroy, Douglas. "Fence Cutters, *Sedicioso,* and First-Class Citizens: Mexican Radicalism in America." In *The Immigrant Left in the United States,* edited by Paul Buhle and Dan Georgakas, 11–44. Albany: State University of New York Press, 1996.

Monroy, Douglas. *Rebirth: Mexican Los Angeles from the Great Migration to the Great Depression.* Berkeley: University of California Press, 1999.

Moreno, Luisa. "Caravans of Sorrow: Noncitizen Americans of the Southwest." In *Between Two Worlds: Mexican Immigrants in the United States,* edited by David G. Gutiérrez, 119–24. Wilmington, DE: Scholarly Resources, 1996.

Moss, Rick. "Not Quite Paradise: The Development of the African American Community in Los Angeles through 1950." *California History* 75, no. 3 (Fall 1996): 222–35.

Murphey, Edith V. A., and Lucy Young. "Out of the Past: A True Indian Story, Told by Lucy Young of Round Valley Reservation, to Edith V. A. Murphey." *California Historical Society Quarterly* 20, no. 4 (December 1941): 349–64.

Naison, Mark. *Communists in Harlem during the Depression*. Urbana: University of Illinois Press, 1983.

Nelson, Bruce. "The 'Lords of the Docks' Reconsidered: Race Relations among West Coast Longshoremen, 1933–61." In *Waterfront Workers: New Perspectives on Race and Class*, edited by Calvin Winslow, 155–92. Urbana: University of Illinois Press, 1998.

Nelson, Bruce. "Unions and the Popular Front: The West Coast Waterfront in the 1930s." *International Labor and Working-Class History* 30 (Fall 1986): 59–78.

Nelson, Bruce. *Workers on the Waterfront: Seamen, Longshoremen, and Unionism in the 1930s*. Urbana: University of Illinois Press, 1988.

Ngai, Mae M. *Impossible Subjects: Illegal Aliens and the Making of Modern America*. Princeton, NJ: Princeton University Press, 2004.

Nicolaides, Becky M. *My Blue Heaven: Life and Politics in the Working-Class Suburbs of Los Angeles, 1920–1965*. Chicago: University of Chicago Press, 2002.

Oandasan, William. "The Poet Is a Voice: Interview with William Oandasan 2/12/85." *Wicazo Sa Review* 2, no. 1 (Spring 1986): 2–9.

Oandasan, William. *Round Valley Songs*. Minneapolis: West End, 1984.

Okihiro, Gary Y. *Third World Studies: Theorizing Liberation*. Durham, NC: Duke University Press, 2016.

Olmstead, Alan L., and Paul W. Rhode. "The Evolution of California Agriculture, 1850–2000." In *California Agriculture: Dimensions and Issues*, edited by Jerome B. Siebert, 1–28. Berkeley: University of California Press, 2004.

Paredes, Américo. *With a Pistol in His Hand: A Border Ballad and Its Hero*. Austin: University of Texas Press, 1958.

Parker, Kunal. *Making Foreigners: Immigration and Citizenship Law in America, 1600–2000*. New York: Cambridge University Press, 2015.

Pascoe, Peggy. *What Comes Naturally: Miscegenation Law and the Making of Race in America*. London: Oxford University Press, 2010.

Patel, Kiran Klaus. *The New Deal: A Global History*. Princeton, NJ: Princeton University Press, 2016.

Pearson, Chad. *Reform or Repression: Organizing America's Anti-union Movement*. Philadelphia: University of Pennsylvania Press, 2015.

Peiss, Kathy. *Cheap Amusements: Working Women and Leisure in Turn-of-the-Century New York*. Philadelphia: Temple University Press, 1985.

Perales, Monica. *Smeltertown: Making and Remembering a Southwest Border Community*. Chapel Hill: University of North Carolina Press, 2010.

Perry, Louis B., and Richard S. Perry. *A History of the Los Angeles Labor Movement, 1911–1941*. Berkeley: University of California Press, 1963.

Peters, Paul, and George Sklar. *Stevedore: A Play in Three Acts*. London: Jonathan Cape, 1935.

Plagens, Peter. *Sunshine Muse: Art on the West Coast, 1945–1970*. Berkeley: University of California Press, 1999.

Polanyi, Karl. *The Great Transformation: The Political Origins of Our Time*. 1944. Boston: Beacon, 2001.

Prashad, Vijay. "Bruce Lee and the Anti-imperialism of Kung-Fu: A Polycultural Adventure." *Positions: East Asia Cultures Critique* 11, no. 1 (2003): 59–90.

Pulido, Laura. *Black, Brown, Yellow, and Left: Radical Activism in Los Angeles*. Berkeley: University of California Press, 2006.

Quam-Wickham, Nancy. "Who Controls the Hiring Hall? The Struggle for Job Control in the ILWU during World War II." In *The CIO's Left-Led Unions*, edited by Steven Rosswurm, 41–68. New Brunswick, NJ: Rutgers University Press, 1991.

Quin, Mike. *The Big Strike*. Olema, CA: Olema, 1949.

Ramírez, Marla Andrea. "The Making of Mexican Illegality: Immigration Exclusions Based on Race, Class Status, and Gender." *New Political Science* 40, no. 2 (2018): 317–35.

Ransby, Barbara. *Ella Baker and the Black Freedom Movement: A Radical Democratic Vision*. Chapel Hill: University of North Carolina Press, 2003.

Reisler, Mark. "Always the Laborer, Never the Citizen: Anglo Perceptions of the Mexican Immigrant during the 1920s." *Pacific Historical Review* 45, no. 2 (May 1976): 231–54.

Reisler, Mark. *By the Sweat of Their Brow: Mexican Immigrant Labor in the United States, 1900–1941*. Westport, CT: Greenwood, 1976.

Robinson, Cedric J. *Black Marxism: The Making of the Black Radical Tradition*. Chapel Hill: University of North Carolina Press, 2000.

Robinson, Cedric J. *Terms of Order: Political Science and the Myth of Leadership*. Chapel Hill: University of North Carolina Press, 2016.

Rodney, Walter. *How Europe Underdeveloped Africa*. London: Bogle-L'Ouverture, 1972.

Roediger, David R. *History against Misery*. Chicago: Charles H. Kerr, 2006.

Roediger, David R. *Seizing Freedom: Slave Emancipation and Liberty for All*. New York: Verso, 2014.

Roediger, David R. *The Wages of Whiteness: Race and the Making of the American Working Class*. London: Verso, 1991.

Roediger, David R. *Working toward Whiteness: How America's Immigrants Became White; The Strange Journey from Ellis Island to the Suburbs*. New York: Basic Books, 2006.

Roediger, David R., and Elizabeth D. Esch. *The Production of Difference: Race and the Management of Labor in U.S. History*. New York: Oxford University Press, 2012.

Rogin, Michael. *Blackface, White Noise: Jewish Immigrants in the Hollywood Melting Pot*. Berkeley: University of California Press, 1996.

Rose, Wendy. Introduction to *Round Valley Songs*, by William Oandasan, iv–x. Minneapolis: West End, 1984.

Rosemont, Franklin. "Notes on Surrealism as a Revolution against Whiteness." In "Surrealism: Revolution against Whiteness." Special issue, *Race Traitor*, no. 9 (Summer 1998): 19–29.

Rosemont, Franklin, and Robin D. G. Kelley, eds. *Black, Brown, and Beige: Surrealist Writings from Africa and the Diaspora*. Austin: University of Texas Press, 2009.

Rosemont, Penelope, ed. *Surrealist Women: An International Anthology*. Austin: University of Texas Press, 1998.

Rosenberg, Daniel. "The IWW and Organization of Asian Workers in Early 20th Century America." *Labor History* 36, no. 1 (1995): 77–87.

Rosenthal, Nicolas G. *Reimagining Indian Country: Native American Migration and Identity in Twentieth-Century Los Angeles*. Chapel Hill: University of North Carolina Press, 2012.

Ruiz, Vicki L. *Cannery Women, Cannery Lives: Mexican Women, Unionization, and the California Food Processing Industry, 1930–1950*. Albuquerque: University of New Mexico Press, 1987.

Ruiz, Vicki L. "Una Mujer sin Frontiers: Luisa Moreno and Latina Labor Activism." *Pacific Historical Review* 73, no. 1 (February 2004): 1–20.

Ryan, Mary P. *Women in Public: Between Banners and Ballots, 1825–1880*. Baltimore: Johns Hopkins University Press, 1992.

Sánchez, George J. *Becoming Mexican American: Ethnicity, Culture, and Identity in Chicano Los Angeles, 1900–1945*. Oxford: Oxford University Press, 1993.

Sandos, James A. *Rebellion in the Borderlands: Anarchism and the Plan of San Diego, 1904–1923*. Norman: University of Oklahoma Press, 1992.

Sandoval, Tomás F. Summers, Jr. *Latinos at the Golden Gate: Creating Community and Identity in San Francisco*. Chapel Hill: University of North Carolina Press, 2013.

Sandoval, Tomás F. Summers, Jr. "Mission Stories, Latino Lives: The Making of San Francisco's Latino Identity, 1945–1970." PhD diss., University of California, Berkeley, 2002.

Saunt, Claudio, Barbara Krauthamar, Tiya Miles, Celia E. Naylor, and Circe Sturm. "Rethinking Race and Culture in the Early South." *Ethnohistory* 53, no. 2 (Spring 2006): 399–405.

Saxton, Alexander. *The Indispensable Enemy: Labor and the Anti-Chinese Movement in California*. Berkeley: University of California Press, 1971.

Saxton, Alexander. *The Rise and Fall of the White Republic: Class Politics and Mass Culture in Nineteenth-Century America*. New York: Verso, 1990.

Schrank, Sarah. *Art and the City: Civic Imagination and Cultural Authority in Los Angeles*. Philadelphia: University of Pennsylvania Press, 2009.

Scott, Allen John, and Edward W. Soja. *The City: Los Angeles and Urban Theory at the End of the Twentieth Century*. Berkeley: University of California Press, 1996.

Scott, James C. *Domination and the Arts of Resistance: Hidden Transcripts*. New Haven, CT: Yale University Press, 1990.

Scott, James C. *Weapons of the Weak: Everyday Forms of Peasant Resistance*. New Haven, CT: Yale University Press, 1985.

Secrest, William. *When the Great Spirit Died: The Destruction of the California Indians, 1850–1860*. Sanger, CA: Word Dancer, 2002.

Selvin, David F. *A Terrible Anger: The 1934 Waterfront and General Strikes in San Francisco*. Detroit: Wayne State University Press, 1996.

Shah, Nayan. *Contagious Divides: Epidemics and Race in San Francisco's Chinatown*. Berkeley: University of California Press, 2001.

Shammas, Carole. "A New Look at Long-Term Trends in Wealth Inequality in the United States." *American Historical Review* 98, no. 2 (April 1993): 412–31.

Sides, Josh. *L.A. City Limits: African American Los Angeles from the Great Depression to the Present*. Berkeley: University of California Press, 2003.

Silliman, Stephen W. *Lost Laborers in Colonial California: Native Americans and the Archaeology of Rancho Petaluma.* Tucson: University of Arizona Press, 2004.

Sine, Elizabeth E. "Grassroots Multiracialism: Imperial Valley Farm Labor and the Making of Popular Front California from Below." *Pacific Historical Review* 85, no. 2 (May 2016): 227–54.

Singh, Nikhil Pal. *Black Is a Country: Race and the Unfinished Struggle for Democracy.* Cambridge, MA: Harvard University Press, 2004.

Smith, Richard Cándida. *Utopia and Dissent: Art, Poetry, and Politics in California.* Berkeley: University of California Press, 1995.

Soja, Edward W. *My Los Angeles: From Urban Restructuring to Regional Urbanization.* Berkeley: University of California Press, 2014.

Soja, Edward W. *Postmodern Geographies: The Reassertion of Space in Critical Social Theory.* New York: Verso, 1989.

Spector, Frank. *Story of the Imperial Valley.* New York: International Labor Defense, n.d.

Starr, Kevin. *Endangered Dreams: The Great Depression in California.* Oxford: Oxford University Press, 1996.

Starr, Kevin. *Inventing the Dream: California through the Progressive Era.* Oxford: Oxford University Press, 1985.

Starr, Kevin. *Material Dreams: Southern California through the 1920s.* Oxford: Oxford University Press, 1990.

Streeby, Shelley. *Radical Sensations: World Movements, Violence, and Visual Culture.* Durham, NC: Duke University Press, 2013.

Susman, Amelia. "The Round Valley Indians of California: An Unpublished Chapter in Acculturation of Seven (or Eight) Indian Tribes." *Contributions to the University of California Archaeological Research Facility* 31 (1976).

Takaki, Ronald T. *Iron Cages: Race and Culture in Nineteenth-Century America.* New York: Knopf, 1979.

Taylor, Graham. *The New Deal and American Indian Tribalism: The Administration of the Indian Reorganization Act, 1934–1945.* Lincoln: University of Nebraska Press, 1980.

Taylor, Paul S. *Mexican Labor in the United States: Imperial Valley.* Berkeley: University of California Press, 1928.

Taylor, Paul S. "Migratory Farm Labor in the United States." *Monthly Labor Review* 44, no. 3 (March 1937): 537–54.

Taylor, Paul S. "Putting the Unemployed at Productive Labor." *The Annals of the American Academy of Political and Social Science* 176 (November 1934): 104–10.

Taylor, Quintard. *In Search of the Racial Frontier: African Americans in the American West, 1528–1990.* New York: W. W. Norton, 1998.

Thompson, E. P. "Time, Work-Discipline, and Industrial Capitalism." *Past and Present* 38 (December 1967): 56–97.

U.S. Census Bureau. *Fifteenth Census of the United States, 1930: Population.* Washington, DC: National Archives and Records Administration, 1931–33.

U.S. Senate Committee on Education and Labor. *Violations of Free Speech and Rights of Labor, Report No. 1150, Part 1.* Washington, DC: U.S. Government Printing Office, 1942.

van den Berghe, Pierre L. *Race and Racism: A Comparative Perspective*. New York: Wiley, 1978.

Varzally, Allison. *Making a Non-white America: Californians Coloring outside Ethnic Lines, 1925–1955*. Berkeley: University of California Press, 2008.

Virdee, Satnam. *Racism, Class, and the Racialized Outsider*. London: Palgrave Macmillan, 2014.

Walker, Richard A. "California's Golden Road to Riches: Natural Resources and Regional Capitalism." *Annals of the Association of American Geographers* 91, no. 1 (2001): 167–99.

Walker, Richard A. "Industry Builds the City: The Suburbanization of Manufacturing in the San Francisco Bay Area, 1850–1940." *Journal of Historical Geography* 27, no. 1 (2001): 36–57.

Wall, Wendy. "Gender and the 'Citizen Indian.'" In *Writing the Range: Race, Class, and Culture in the Women's West*, edited by Elizabeth Jameson and Susan Armitage, 202–29. Norman: University of Oklahoma Press, 1997.

Weber, Devra Anne. *Dark Sweat, White Gold: California Farm Workers, Cotton, and the New Deal*. Berkeley: University of California Press, 1996.

Weber, Devra Anne. "The Organizing of Mexicano Agricultural Workers: Imperial Valley and Los Angeles, 1928–1934, an Oral History Approach." *Aztlán* 3, no. 2 (1973): 307–50.

Weber, Devra Anne. "Raiz Fuerte: Oral History and Mexicana Farmworkers." *Oral History Review* 17, no. 2 (Autumn 1989): 47–62.

Weir, Stan. *Singlejack Solidarity*. Minneapolis: University of Minnesota Press, 2004.

White, Richard. *Middle Ground: Indians, Empires, and Republics in the Great Lakes Region, 1650–1815*. Cambridge: Cambridge University Press, 1991.

White, Richard. "Race Relations in the American West." *American Quarterly* 38, no. 3 (1986): 396–416.

White, Richard. *The Roots of Dependency: Subsistence, Environment, and Social Change among the Choctaw, Pawnees, and Navajos*. Lincoln: University of Nebraska Press, 1983.

Widener, Daniel. "Another City Is Possible: Interethnic Organizing in Contemporary Los Angeles." *Race/Ethnicity: Multidisciplinary Global Contexts* 1, no. 2 (Spring 2008): 189–219.

Widener, Daniel. *Black Arts West: Culture and Struggle in Postwar Los Angeles*. Durham, NC: Duke University Press, 2010.

Widener, Daniel. "'Perhaps the Japanese Are to Be Thanked?' Asia, Asian Americans, and the Construction of Black California." *Positions: East Asia Cultures Critique* 11, no. 1 (2003): 135–81.

Wild, Mark. *Street Meeting: Multiethnic Neighborhoods in Early Twentieth-Century Los Angeles*. Berkeley: University of California Press, 2005.

Winter, Ella. "What Next in California?" *Pacific Affairs* 8, no. 1 (March 1935): 86–89.

Wolf, Eric R. *Europe and the People without History*. Berkeley: University of California Press, 1982.

Wollenberg, Charles. "Huelga, 1928 Style: The Imperial Valley Cantaloupe Workers' Strike." *Pacific Historical Review* 38, no. 1 (February 1969): 45–58.

Woods, Clyde. *Development Arrested: The Blues and Plantation Power in the Mississippi Delta*. New York: Verso, 1998.

Young, Cynthia A. *Soul Power: Culture, Radicalism, and the Making of a U.S. Third World Left*. Durham, NC: Duke University Press, 2006.

Yung, Judy. *Unbound Feet: A Social History of Chinese Women in San Francisco*. Berkeley: University of California Press, 1995.

Zecker, Robert. *"A Road to Peace and Freedom": The International Workers Order and the Struggle for Economic Justice and Civil Rights, 1930–1954*. Philadelphia: Temple University Press, 2018.

Zimmer, Kenyon. *Immigrants against the State: Yiddish and Italian Anarchism in America*. Urbana: University of Illinois Press, 2015.

Page numbers in italics refer to figures.

Jefferson High School, 168, 169, 171
Jewish populations, 100, 115, 145, 149, 152
Johnson-Reed Act (Immigration Act of 1924), xiv, 50, 237n44
Johnson, Hiram, 53
Jones, H. E. (Reverend), 119
Jordan High School, 168, 169
Jung, Moon-Kie, 35

Kadish, Reuben, 149, 152
Kelley, Robin D. G., 8, 15, 163, 216n32, 217n34
Kelso, Jackie (Jack Kelson), 165–66, *169*, 172
Keyser, Edith, 103
Koreans, 30
Kraenzel, Carl, 205
Kun, Josh, 176, 189

labor: as a site of grassroots political activity, 16, 19, 20; as a site of social management, 29–30, 51–52, 81–82, 205; base in California, xiii–xiv, 6; relationship to art, 17–18; working-class culture and, 13–14, 78–79. *See also* strikes; unions
Labor Research Association, 83
La Follette Civil Liberties Committee, xiii
La Opinión, 86, 92, 121; "Respuestas desde México" ("Answers from Mexico"), 94–95
Latinx populations, 19, 48; civil rights organizing and, 98–99; immigrant expulsion and, 83; in Imperial Valley, 38; in Los Angeles, 138; in San Francisco, 51, 53, 54, 64. *See also* Mexican Americans; Mexican nationals
League of United Latin American Citizens, 87, 96
Lehman, Harold, 149, 152, 153–54
Lewis, Crosby, 170
Lewis, William J., 62
Lipsitz, George, 18, 163, 176, 206, 245n9, 254n13
Los Angeles: anti-unionism within, 20, 138–39, 142–44, 146; cultural construction as a "city of the future," 139–40, 141–42, 146–47; demographics of, 144–45; deportation raids within, 82; economic modernization within, xi, xiii, 141, 143–44, 146–47; as open shop city, 142–44; South, 145–46, 158, 164–68; as a stronghold of white supremacy, 144–46. *See also* Central Avenue (Los Angeles); Watts (Los Angeles)

Los Angeles Police Department (LAPD), 138, 146, 154, 157. *See also* Red Squads (Los Angeles Police Department)
Los Angeles Sentinel, 116–17, 119–20, 161
Low, Edwin, 55
Lowitt, Richard, xvi
Luz, Manuel, 33

MacGregor, Gordon, 185, 195
Macias, Anthony, 172
Magonism/Magonistas, 8, 26, 36, 213n9
management. *See* social management
Maneze, Frank, 36
Marine Workers Industrial Union (MWIU), 60, 64, 66, 68, 71; Filipino-American Alliance, 67–68, 69
Martin, Charlie, 170
Marx, Karl, xii
masculinity, 38, 59, 206, 211n23; alternative expressions of, Black, racialization of, 138; California demographics and, xiv; EPIC and, 114, 117; in organized labor, 48, 53, 72; jazz and, 170–71; New Deal and, 5, 206; oppositional expressions of, 73; White working-class manhood and, 53
mass culture, xi, 147–48, 150, 163, 191
Mayo, Morrow, 142
Mayorga, Aristrides, 121–22
McDonald, Frank C., 78–79
McFarland, Eleanor Banning, 116
McGrady, Edward, 69
McLane, Albert, 176, 253n4
McLane, Everett, 176, 253n4
McWilliams, Carey, xiv, xv, 36, 86, 110, 112, 131
Mendocino County, 177, 186; economic development in, 181, 183
Merchants and Manufacturers Association (M&M), 143, 146, 256n18, 247n32
Merriam, Frank, 69, 115, 117, 122, 123, 129
Mexican Americans, ix, xii, 2, 7, 100–101, 211n21; in agricultural strikes, 10, 19, 25–26, 42–43, 78, 223n54; California demographics and, xiii; civil rights organizing among 87, 98–99; EPIC and, 120–21; in Imperial Valley, 30–32, 34–37, 39, 40, 41; in Los Angeles, 144, 145, 164, 168, 173; in Mendocino County, 179, 183, 184; Mexican immigrants, relationship with, 87; revolutionary traditions and, 35, 213n9; in San Francisco, 51;

Royal, Marshall, 164
Rubio, Pascual Ortiz, 92
Ryan, Joseph, 62, 70

Samish, Artie, 112
Sample, Paul, 152
Sánchez, George, 139
Sánchez, John, 34, 39
San Francisco, 43; anti-immigrant attitudes
    within, 52–53; business leadership power
    within, 52; economic development in,
    xi, 49–50; ethnic enclaves in, 54–55;
    interethnic community formation, 55–57;
    as port of entry for immigrants, 47, 52;
    racial/ethnic composition of, 50–52;
    racism in organized labor within, 53, 62;
    radical political traditions within, 53–54;
    urban cosmopolitanism, 47–48, 49; water-
    front workforce in, 51–52. See also Great
    Depression: in San Francisco; West Coast
    waterfront strike (1934)
Saxton, Alexander, 53
Schillinger, Leon, 193
Schrank, Sarah, 149
Scott, James C., 17
Scott, Lora Toombs, 55
Scottsboro Nine, x, 64, 138; artistic rendering
    of, 154
Scully, Frank, 115
shape up, 60; replacement by low-man-out
    (rotation) system, 72, 233n116
Sherman Institute, 182
shoeshining, 165–66
Sinclair, Upton, 8; gubernatorial campaign
    of (1934), 20, 105, 109, 112, 113–22, 129,
    131; I, Governor of California, and How
    I Ended Poverty, 110, 125; New Deal and,
    124–27, 243n92; on race, 117–18; Roosevelt
    and, 125; smear campaign against, 123–24.
    See also End Poverty in California (EPIC)
    campaign
Siqueiros, David Alfaro, 149, 150–51;
    América Tropical, 152–3, 153; Workers'
    Meeting, 151
Sixty-Second District (Los Angeles), African
    Americans in, 119–20; election of 1934 and,
    104, 112, 122, 129
Slater, Vernon, 165

social management, xii; in agricultural labor,
    29–31, 32–33; immigrant expulsion as, 83,
    86; Indian policy and, 186–87; national
    membership as a mechanism of, 73, 82; po-
    litical repression as, 154–55; racial division as
    an instrument of, xiv; in the search for order
    in 1930s California, xi, 2, 7, 73, 204; U.S. west
    as a model for the nation, xiv, 211n15; in
    waterfront labor market, 47–48, 52;
Social Security Act, 5, 97, 105, 131–32, 205
social warrant, 17, 100, 131
Soja, Edward W., xii
Sorge, Friedrich, xii
Soromengo, Blackie, 70
South Asians-30
Sperry, Howard, 71
Spokesman (San Francisco), 63, 64, 66–67
Stevedore (Peters and Sklar), 137–39, 161–62,
    244–45n2
strikes, 8, 11; in California agriculture during
    the 1930s, 26–27, 42; cantaloupe strike in
    Imperial Valley (1928), 25, 28, 35, 37–38;
    connections between rural and urban,
    43–45, 57; cotton strike in San Joaquin
    Valley (1933), 26, 77–79, 81, 97; expulsion
    drives and, 86–87; lettuce strike in Impe-
    rial Valley (January 1930), 10, 19, 25–26,
    35; Mexicali-Imperial Valley agricultural
    strike (1922), 26, 36; pea strike in Imperial
    Valley (1934), 42; as "a small revolution,"
    72; waterfront strike in San Francisco
    (1936–37), 56. See also West Coast water-
    front strike (1934)
surrealism, 107, 152, 215n21; as framework for
    studying social movements, 11, 12, 14–15,
    215n21, 216n32; working class culture and,
    3, 11, 19, 20, 141, 173–174, 200, 202–3

theater. See community theater
Torrence, Floyd, 58
transnationalism: in California workforce,
    xii; in grassroots belonging, 10–11, 81,
    94–95, 101; in cultural expressions, 178,
    189–90, 192, 196; "overlapping diasporas"
    in California and, 18, 202
Truich, Louis, 59
Turnham, Floyd, 164
Tydings-McDuffie Act (1934), 83